ABOUT THE AUTHOR

JOHN TIPPLE is Professor of History at California State College at Los Angeles. He previously taught at Stanford where he received his Ph.D. degree. He is the author of THE NEW ORDER: ALEXANDER HAMILTON AND THOMAS JEFFERSON and THE PROBLEMS OF PROGRESS: ANDREW CARNEGIE AND HENRY GEORGE.

Professor Tipple is writing a four-volume work, THE PRAGMATIC NATION: A HISTORY OF AMERICAN SOCIAL THOUGHT SINCE 1865, of which CRISIS OF THE AMERICAN DREAM is the first published volume.

JOHN TIPPLE

Crisis of the American Dream

A History of American Social Thought
1920 – 1940

PEGASUS/NEW YORK

Foreword

Within the compass of four volumes, *The Pragmatic Nation: A History of American Social Thought Since 1865,* I have attempted to give an account of the important ideas which have influenced the political, economic, and social development of modern America. In choosing the readings in these volumes I have not been greatly concerned with literary values but have tried to treat of ideas in their meaningful social context, making my selections solely on the basis of their intrinsic worth as clear and valid expressions of the dominant ideas of the time. The main divisions of the study reflect major changes in the outlook and material framework of American society. Volume I, *The Great Money Machine,* begins after the Civil War and follows the evolution of the United States from a simple agricultural and commercial society to an industrial economy created by and ideologically dependent upon the findings of nineteenth-century science. Volume II, *The Capitalist Revolution,* is concerned with the overthrow of the established system and practices of individualistic capitalism by the organized power of corporate capitalism and with the pragmatic revolt against traditionalism that followed in its wake. The present volume, *Crisis of the American Dream,* third in historical sequence, carries the account through the boom days of the twenties and the depression-ridden thirties, marking the collapse of the business order

and the faltering emergence of the welfare state. Volume
IV, *The Paradox of Power,* considers the contemporary conflict between the individual and the organization and the
search for assurance in a technological society.

The task of measuring the historical significance of ideas
is an extremely difficult one. Perhaps the most vexing question for the historian to answer is: What portion of the public was moved by and won for a particular idea? Yet ideas
have consequences, and this pragmatic consideration has
been my chief criterion. As Justice Holmes observed, "Every
idea is an incitement. It offers itself for belief and if believed it is acted upon." Important ideas are consequential
ideas, whether they come from politicians or professors,
businessmen or philosophers. The active American mind
has never been confined to the genteel tradition of acade-
mies but has taken ideas wherever it found them, from the
market place as well as the lecture hall. The historian,
being a product of his time, faces the additional danger of
reading into history the ideas and opinions of a later day.
In this sense, there is considerable truth in Voltaire's wit-
ticism: "History is only a pack of tricks we play on the
dead." The best defense against playing such tricks on the
dead is to let the living speak for themselves, as I have
tried to do by introducing contemporary writing within
the historical context of the time.

Essentially history is concerned with the dialectical struggle between persistence and change, between the old and
the new. For every accepted idea there are always a host
of challengers or rival "truths" competing for acceptance
at any given time in history. Therefore, to bring into this
study a genuine sense of historical dynamism, I have en-
deavored to follow the example of history itself by presenting with every dominant idea a counter-idea which,
if not its direct antithesis, offers another point of view. To
capture the authentic flavor of the times, the major issues
are documented by excerpts from contemporary writings
which follow each section and which are indicated by an

asterisk at the appropriate point in the text. By giving the losing as well as the winning side and by allowing the proponents to speak for themselves, I have sought to avoid the dishonest practice of presenting the regnant American ideology as a homogeneous body of unchallengeable "truths" resting upon the nearly unanimous consent of history.

I am, of course, heavily indebted to the critical historians and the many students of American society who have enabled me to build upon their careful research. Especially am I indebted to my wife, Edith, for practical and spiritual aid and to John Jensen of Pegasus for invaluable editorial advice.

J.T.

Santa Barbara, June 4, 1967

Table of Contents

Introduction

Since colonial days, Americans had boasted that man would find, and in this country had largely found, the good life that was denied to the antiquated and corrupt nations of the old world. Although poverty had proved to be the all-pervasive fact of history, its reality never had been truly accepted by good Americans who, as the fortunate possessors of a new land with unlimited natural wealth, held to the stubborn belief that the right of all Americans to share, and to share increasingly, in the gains of industry and progress was sanctioned by higher law.

This vision of America as a materialistic heaven on earth where man could realize his highest aspirations amid abundance had become, by the 1920's, an indispensable part of the American dream. A kind of "virtuous materialism," the American dream envisaged the establishment of a new order of universal prosperity which would not corrupt but would energize the soul, freeing man for higher and finer things. That was why, as Tocqueville remarked, every new method that led by a shorter road to wealth, every machine that spared labor, every invention that diminished the cost of production, every discovery that facilitated pleasures or added to comforts, seemed to Americans to be the grandest effort of the human intellect. That was why, also, wide-awake Americans in the twenties with their automobiles, radios, vacuum cleaners, telephones, bathtubs, subways, steam shovels, tractors, and automatic lathes believed universal prosperity was an accomplished fact. For ten thousand years mankind had been struggling toward this materialistic Eden, and only in the United States did the goal appear in sight.

The American outlook was dominated by the youthful dream that anybody could become a millionaire. Widespread stories of fabulous fortunes made overnight in stocks or real estate so excited the normal desire to get rich quick that most Americans, along with President Hoover, were convinced the end of the rainbow was just around the corner. At the height of prosperity, the *Ladies Home Journal* ran an article by John J. Raskob, a General Motors executive, entitled "Everybody Ought to Be Rich," and nearly everyone tried. Money-mad Americans feverishly chased the elusive dollar from Wall Street to the Florida swamplands, trying everything from advertising to bootlegging, selling anything from "The Skin You Love to Touch" to a happy life in Christ, always hoping in the end to "put it over" by promising much and giving little.

Then, with terrible suddenness, the Wall Street crash of 1929 and the ensuing depression turned the dream of universal prosperity into a horrible nightmare. Americans woke from their patriotic slumbers to find themselves in a stricken land of empty factories and idle machines where fear vanquished hope, and hunger and poverty stalked the streets. The national quest no longer was the high-flown pursuit of millions but the down-to-earth demand for a job and enough to eat. The temper of the disillusioned thirties was no less materialistic, perhaps more so, but it was more realistic. Where the American of the 1920's innocently pursued a private materialistic heaven, trusting his extravagant hopes to the unfailing beneficence of providence, his more worldly counterpart ten years later faced the cold-hearted reality of depression and tried by rational means to achieve collective security here and now.

Essentially the conflict of these years was over the nature of the good society. In the twenties the contest was between the victorious supporters of "normalcy" and social reformers fighting for equal rights. In the thirties, with positions now reversed, the debate was between the triumphant political activists of the New Deal and disinherited individualists united in bitter resistance to the general welfare state. These conflicting points of view ran like contrapuntal themes through both decades and were a distinctly American version of the eternal struggle between those who accept and support the status quo and those who are critical of the existing order and advocate change.

Yet, though the specific problems were new, the issues were, for the most part, old. The battle cries had been sounded half a century before, and the battle lines drawn during the Progressive era. The individualistic rhetoric of the defenders of the economic system and the critics of the New Deal was drawn from the doctrines of nineteenth-century liberalism. Though almost totally irrelevant to the modern technological economy, the habits of mind and action of the earlier period still persisted and operated to retard social change in the interests of a narrowly construed economic liberty. Not that those who accepted the existing state of things in the twenties were completely opposed to progress, rather they envisaged progress as continuous technological change taking place in an immutable social order. Similarly, the fighting faith of their opponents—the parlor liberals of the twenties and the militant New-Dealers of the thirties—could be traced to late nineteenth- and early twentieth-century critics of laissez-faire who believed human advancement demanded social change to meet the unforeseen exigencies of technical progress. Their belief that liberal democratic values could be achieved in a complex industrial society only by practical state action had been advanced earlier by Henry George, Lester Ward, Simon Patten, Herbert Croly, and Walter Weyl.

Although the New Deal was collectivist rather than individualistic in temper and national instead of local in terms of action, its programs and theories had been largely worked out in the past. The acceptance and regulation of big business called for by Theodore Roosevelt's New Nationalism reappeared in the National Industrial Recovery Act, while the antitrust point of view of Woodrow Wilson's New Freedom emerged once again in the Public Utilities Holding Company Act and the Temporary National Economic Committee. But, though borrowing from the two major strains of Progressivism, the interventionist program of the New Deal owed much more to Hamiltonian mercantilism and to its modern manifestation during World War I. The wartime experience of economic mobilization provided not only the example for many of the emergency agencies but also the democratic rationale for fighting the depression. Hoover's Reconstruction Finance Corporation, for example, was frankly modeled after the War Finance Corporation, just as Roosevelt's National Recovery Administration rested squarely on the example of the War Industries Board. Both Presidents, moreover, employed the metaphor of war to mobilize public opinion for government intervention in the economy. In short, the New Deal like its more modest predecessor was in its methods and aims a traditional answer to a radical dilemma.

As long as Americans had believed they were able to fulfill their ideal of the good life merely by keeping intact their political institutions and by the selfish pursuit of private ends, their allegiance to the achievement of a better American future had been, as Herbert Croly once suggested, more a matter of words than deeds. But Americans of the twenties who had looked upon democracy merely as the end product of mass production and had confidently expected ethical rejuvenation as a by-product of prosperity found themselves in the thirties confronted by an overproduction of things and a shortage of values. With a deep sense of national failure, they discovered they must, as a nation, redefine their faith and give it democratic shape and intelligent direction. The American dream was no longer to be propagated merely by words—it was to be fulfilled not by more economic freedom but by a measure of social discipline, not by greater trust in immutable laws but by more confidence in the ability of Americans to control what they had created.

The Businessman
and the Politician

I

America in the 1920's belonged to the businessman. Literally and spiritually, the businessman owned the country. "There is no doubt," rejoiced *Nation's Business*, the organ of the United States Chamber of Commerce, "that the American business man is the foremost hero of the American people today." Amid booming prosperity, the head of the Chamber's civic development department proudly proclaimed the American businessman to be "the most influential person in the nation . . . perhaps the most influential figure in the world." From across the ocean the London *Times* and other European journals confirmed the claim, applauding American industry for raising up "a race of supermen."[1]

If the businessman had "made good," the politician was in disgrace. After all of President Wilson's lofty moralizing, the results had been profoundly disappointing to the American people. The "peace," even more than the war, had been a disillusionment. Even those who had believed in the war were appalled by a peace which promised merely a lull of temporary exhaustion and of preparation for more destructive and futile wars to come. The League of Nations, at best, seemed to offer only mocking hopes of avoiding new wars, and after endless wrangling between the President and Congress, it had become a pumped-up issue the people were tired of hearing about. As a consequence, those Americans who had entrusted their dreams of a better world to soldiers and politicians felt hopelessly betrayed and deluded. Their disenchantment with the politician was cruelly manifested by "poor Woodrow's astounding unpopularity," a dramatic reversal of public opinion which startled even the cynical Henry L. Mencken, the popular wit of the day. The President, Mencken observed, had come from Paris in 1919 "ranking with the master-minds of the ages" and then, less than a year later, was regarded by everyone save a few fanatics as "a devious and foolish fellow, whom the nation will be well rid of on March 4."[2]

The default of political leadership was declared by *American Industries*, speaking for the National Association of Manufacturers, to be "the one conspicuous failure of American life." As *Nation's Business* reminded its readers, it was because of the inability of the politician to meet the needs of society that the businessman now occupied "a position of leadership which the business man had never held before." The coming age was his, but the businessman was warned that "he was on trial" and, like his political predecessor in leadership, must expect to answer for his stewardship.[3]

While politics had seemingly degenerated, American business had made conspicuous progress. For about two years before the United States declared war against Germany, American industry had begun to prosper by the sale of goods to the European belligerents. Profits were enormous, for the hard-pressed Allies were ready to pay virtually whatever the producers asked. As sole purchasing agent for Great Britain and France, J. P. Morgan & Company ladled out billions of dollars in war orders to great American manufacturing corporations. Within three months, for instance, Bethlehem Steel received two huge orders, one for $83 million and another for $63 million, and the profits of United States Steel jumped from $76 million in 1912–1914 to $478 million in 1917.[4] Because of such tremendous profits, American capitalism, which had always been Europe's debtor, emerged from the war as the world's greatest creditor.

The twenties likewise proved to be very good years for business. After a short postwar depression, production, profits, and consumption rose spectacularly. Although there was a virtually permanent depression in agriculture and considerable unemployment in some distressed mining and manufacturing areas, dividends and real wages were high and rising. True, the richer were getting richer much faster than the poor were getting less poor, but the *average* level of living in the United States was undoubtedly the highest in the world. The federal budget showed a surplus year after year, and the federal debt was steadily reduced. As stock prices rocketed skyward in 1929, it appeared to the casual observer that America was on the way to becoming the richest nation in history, and credit for this booming prosperity went to the businessman.

Powerful and unashamed, the American businessman acknowledged the tribute and, basking in popular adulation, forgot that not many years before he had been held up to public scorn as a capitalist villain and robber baron. Good times brought forgiveness. Business was entering a new era, said the Chicago *Daily News*: "the period of prosecution and restriction is over."[5] Business was taking charge of the country, business was running the world, but, as a writer in *Harper's* observed, business had changed; it was not the same as thirty, twenty, or even ten years ago. "The world is becoming spiritualized. Business shows it." As faith in business as a way of life spread throughout the country, the belief flourished that the businessman "can do what governments cannot." Business was exalted as the

chief instrument of society, and government was relegated
to an inferior role. "Who are the managers of the United
States in these days?" asked *Life* magazine. "Who take care
of undertakings that they think are necessary and put them
through? Who but the managers of the industrial enterprises of the country?" On the basis of actual performance—
its contribution to the well-being of society—business was
adjudged the most important institution of America.[6]

Among Americans the feeling grew that the central institutions of society were economic rather than political.
Unlike government, it was argued, economic institutions
wielded power primarily over things rather than people;
therefore, economic power was less oppressive and more
democratic than political power ever could be. True democracy, the readers of *Nation's Business* were told, was thus
economic rather than political: "The 'voters' are the people
who spend money for goods. Their dollars are their votes.
By the aid of prices the people 'elect' the producers who
will serve them; they also 'elect' the kinds of goods to be
made and the amount of employment for the wage earners.
By the aid of prices the people decide what industries shall
have capital; they determine who will make profits and
who shall go 'broke.'" Since suffrage was universal under
economic democracy—insofar as the individual's dollars
were his votes—the power of business was not to be feared
because in actuality "the people organize and direct the
whole business and industrial system." From this argument
it followed logically that government was not even a "necessary evil" but an unnecessary extravagance. So appealing
was this point of view to the editors of *American Industries*
that they quoted the praiseful article from *Life* with added
emphasis, answering affirmatively the question: *"Are we
approaching a millennium in which visible government
will not be necessary and in which the job of running the
world will slip away from obstructive politicians and be
taken over by men trained in the shop?"* Thus, it would

appear, American businessmen shared with Karl Marx the hopeful expectation that government would eventually wither away.[7]

If, as the businessman insisted, the main institutions of society were economic rather than political, then there was little or no room for either the politician or the political party. "The professional agitator or politician can hardly be expected to know where business is striving to get as well as business itself." Not only did the direction of business affairs require an expertise that no politician could be expected to have, but there was also a marked disparity in the comparative capacities of the businessman and the politician. Put bluntly, businessmen had "better ability and philosophy" and were "more useful than writers, soap box orators, politicians and statesmen." Since the beginning of the industrial period, about 1870—it was explained in *American Industries*—"the men of real ability in the United States have devoted their time, their energy, and their money to the pursuit of wealth." Business experience itself, as James Prothro has pointed out, was thought also to exert an elevating influence which enhanced this original superiority: first, by bringing out "the best side of a man"; second, by implanting a tolerance toward "the weaknesses of their fellow men"; third, by developing a realistic outlook free from sentimentality.[8]

II

By comparison, politicians as a class were deemed an unsavory lot. As most businessmen saw it, politics was the sort of occupation that appealed to "men who would rather agitate than work" and so attracted "a distinctly cheap and parasitic class." Consequently, though success was the only criterion of ability in business, the opposite was true in politics. Unlike business, the political experience was regarded as essentially degrading. Instead of bringing out the best side of a man, it brought out the worst, for suc-

cess in politics meant demagoguery, the unprincipled court-
ing of popular favor; instead of cultivating a tolerance of
the weaknesses of men, politics preyed upon them; instead
of inculcating a realistic outlook, it encouraged a maudlin
sentimentality which distorted "the simple facts of life"
and subverted whatever habits of thrift, common sense,
and economy the people naturally had.[9] Apparently the
businessman's low estimate of the politician was shared
by most Americans in the 1920's. When a reporter asked
students, "How many of you are going into politics?" the
question brought instantly the most derisive of laughs.
Though there might be excuses for the bootlegger and gang-
ster, the politician seemed to be the only man in America
for whom no legitimate defense could be made.[10]

If the politician was scorned, the political party was
dreaded. To businessmen, the political party, being nothing
more than a gang of self-seeking incompetents, displayed
all the vices of the individual politician writ large, plus
an infinitely greater capacity to inflict damage. As for the
business and financial world, said the *Wall Street Journal,*
"The less it has to do with politics, the better it is pleased."
With the common run of politicians, the president of the
National Association of Manufacturers told fellow industrialists, "it has ceased to be a question of what is good for
the country, what is American, or what is constitutional.
It is rather what is best for the party and for his own political self-perpetuation."[11] If government dominated by
political groups was incapable of "broad, sound national
policies," no group was more obviously dedicated to the
public interest than American business. Said the president
of the Chamber of Commerce, "The individual welfare of
all the people is wrapped up today as never before in a
proper understanding· and proper relationship between
government and business."[12]

To business leaders, the "proper relationship" between
business and government meant simply that the direction
of America should be in the hands of its most successful

institution. Organized business should replace the political party as the force directing the machinery of government. For the maximum benefit of all of the people, government need only respond to business views expressed "without color or self-interest," and the proper relationship would be automatically established. As announced at the National Association of Manufacturers' convention of 1920, "The crying need of the hour" was "a business government for a business people."[13]

And then, almost magically, out of the darkness and chaos of politics came Warren G. Harding with the right answer. "This is essentially a business country," said the Republican presidential candidate. "That is why we need business sense in charge of American administration." Instead of concerning himself with the "impossible democracy" of Wilson, President Harding declared the aim of his administration was to "get back to the methods of business." Harding's willingness to accept business ideas as his own was matched and even exceeded by his successor in the White House, Calvin Coolidge. Where the more loquacious Harding had said, "The business of America is the business of everybody in America," Coolidge with typical Yankee bluntness went straight to the point, saying, "The business of America is business."[14] The perfect coincidence of Coolidge's views with those of business led the *Wall Street Journal* to comment: "Never before, here or anywhere else, has a government been so completely fused with business."[15]

Although Coolidge was rightly regarded as "the businessman's president," he was still a politician by trade, and not until the election of Herbert Hoover in 1928 did the old dream of "a businessman in the White House" approach complete realization. As *Nation's Business* noted with enthusiasm, "Mr. Hoover, the engineer in politics, is a business man—plus." Like Harding and Coolidge, Hoover showed during the campaign that he had a "proper understanding" of the "proper relationship" between government and business by lauding "the wise policies" of his Republican predecessors which had "introduced a new basis in government." His election, both the *Nation* and the *New Republic* grudgingly conceded, marked the conversion of the vast majority of Americans to the political creed of the businessman. "The historical role of Mr. Hoover is apparently to try the experiment of seeing what business can do when given the steering wheel. Mr. Hoover insists that there should be a steering wheel, but he will also let business do the driving." With Hoover politics was an adjunct of business, and he was thoroughly convinced there were virtually no limits to the progress that could be obtained through the understanding cooperation of government in business.[16]

"We in America today," Herbert Hoover said confidently on the eve of his election in 1928, "are nearer to the final triumph over poverty than ever before in the history of any land. The poorhouse is vanishing from among us. We have not yet reached the goal, but, given a chance to go forward with the policies of the last eight years, we shall soon with the help of God be in sight of the day when poverty will be banished from this nation."[17]

III

President Hoover had been in the White House only seven months when the business and financial world was shaken by the greatest stock-market crash in history. In a few devastating weeks thirty billion dollars disappeared in thin air, and with it vanished the American dream of unending prosperity. Not only did millions of investors lose their lifetime savings overnight, but thousands of banks and corporations, which only weeks before had seemed as sound as bedrock, were forced into bankruptcy and crashed like a great avalanche down the Main Street of every city and town in America sweeping smaller businesses before them. Debts mounted, purchases dropped, factories shut down, workers lost their jobs, wages and prices were slashed. Farmers, already hard hit, were unable to meet their debts and faced mortgage foreclosures. As the depression deepened, national income fell to almost half the level of 1929, unemployment climbed steadily upward, and across the nation tattered breadlines became a permanent feature in city streets.

For the average American the widespread loss of employment was beyond doubt the most conspicuous disaster of the Great Depression. As ex-President Coolidge sagely remarked at the time, "When more and more people are thrown out of work, unemployment results."[18] Immediately after the stock-market crash in the fall of 1929 unemployment was said to have jumped in two weeks from 700,000 to 3,100,000. By 1933, when Hoover left the presidency, the mounting flood of joblessness had reached fifteen million, and one out of every three wage or salary earners in the United States was totally without work. Of course, this proportion was not evenly distributed throughout the country. Some areas were much harder hit than others. For example, in 1932 it was reported that in a small town in southern Illinois only two persons of the population of 1350 had jobs. Nor did unemployment figures account for those working only part time or those who were self-employed but without any income.

Statistics, however, are bloodless and unable to convey the incalculable human cost of unemployment. Enforced idleness not only destroyed purchasing power, but broke the spirits of once industrious and resourceful Americans, undermined their health, and robbed them of self-respect. Once meager savings were depleted, debts piled up, rents or mortgages went unpaid, and families were turned into the streets. The situation of millions of jobless Americans was summed up by the report of the California Unemployment Commission:

Many households have been dissolved; little children parceled out to friends, relatives, or charitable homes; husbands and wives, parents and children separated, temporarily or permanently. Homes in which life savings were invested and hopes bound up have been lost never to be recovered. Men, young and old, have taken to the road. They sleep each night in a new flophouse. Day after day the country over, they stand in the breadlines for food which carries with it the suggestion "move on, we don't want you." In spite of the unpalatable stew and the comfortless flop-houses, the army of homeless grows alarmingly. Existing accommodations fail to shelter the homeless; jails must be opened to lodge honest job-hunters. Destitution reaches the women and children. New itinerant types develop: "women vagrants" and "juvenile transients." There are no satisfactory methods of dealing with these thousands adrift. Precarious ways of existing, questionable methods of "getting by" rapidly develop. The law must step in and brand as criminals those who have neither desire nor inclination to violate accepted standards of society.[19]

Even for those who had not joined the "migration of despair" and were listed as "employed" there was little security or hope for the future. To a fortunate few one manufacturing company in Detroit paid men ten cents and women four cents an hour; while others not so lucky stood on street corners shining shoes or peddling apples in the shivering cold.

For these millions of bewildered and disillusioned Americans there was little hope of relief. After several months of depression neither private charity nor local government could begin to cope with the widespread poverty and hunger. Washington offered no help, for President Hoover firmly believed that relief was the responsibility of state and local government only. Federal relief, he told distressed Americans, would destroy "character" and strike at "the roots of self-government." Not until the summer of 1932, after three bitter winters of depression, did Hoover consent to any federal relief action. In the meantime, bleak settlements known ironically as "Hoovervilles" sprang up all across the country in vacant lots and on the outskirts of cities. "Anyone who wants actually to see civilization creaking," the *New Yorker* reported in the spring of 1932, "will do well to visit the corner of West and Spring Streets. . . . There is a whole village of shacks and huts there, made of packing boxes, barrel staves, pieces of corrugated iron, and whatever else the junkman doesn't want, and the people who live there do so because the New York Central hasn't gotten around to driving them off." [20]

Without adequate clothing, shelter, or food, human suffering reached tragic proportions. In the rural communities of West Virginia, where distress was intense, Quakers providing relief weighed undernourished children and fed only those who were more than ten percent underweight; in New York City in 1931 there were ninety-five deaths from starvation. While one family lived for weeks on flour and water paste, others hunted the garbage cans of their more affluent neighbors. "One vivid, gruesome moment of those dark days we shall never forget," wrote a shocked reporter, describing conditions in Chicago in the late spring of 1932. "We saw a crowd of some fifty men fighting over a barrel of garbage which had been set outside the back door of a restaurant. American citizens fighting for scraps of food like animals!" In other parts of the country there were "hunger riots" in which several hundred unemployed men and women raided grocery stores, smashing plate glass windows and helping themselves to meat and canned goods.[21]

Despair reached a peak in the summer of 1932 when some twenty thousand homeless, penniless veterans descended on Washington, D.C. Gathering spontaneously from all over the nation, jobless ex-soldiers hitch-hiked, "road the rods," or came in old jalopies to lobby for passage of a veterans' bonus bill. At first Washington tolerated the Bonus Army, allowing them to set up a makeshift community or "Hooverville" within sight of the White House; but after the bill failed in the Senate and many veterans stayed

The crisis of one American's dream—no money, no work, no hope. For millions like him the great depression was a personal tragedy. With no way out, job gone or business bankrupt, the once industrious and resourceful citizen who had always earned his own way lost faith in himself and society.

---

on—having no place to go—President Hoover called out the U.S. Army to disperse them. Under command of General Douglas MacArthur and his aide, Major Dwight D. Eisenhower, the troops attacked with tanks and tear gas, driving thousands of unarmed veterans and their wives and children before them and setting fire to the ramshackle huts. There was virtually no resistance, but two veterans were shot to death, two policemen received fractured skulls, a bystander was shot in the shoulder, a veteran's ear was severed by a cavalry saber and another veteran was bayoneted in the hip, a dozen persons were injured by bricks and clubs, and more than a thousand gassed. On the next day reporters were told that "the President was pleased," but public reaction was shock and dismay.[22]

IV

Something was gravely wrong in America. There was poverty amid plenty, hunger in the midst of abundance, and hopelessness in a land of boundless opportunity. Homeless people slept in doorways or on park benches while houses and warm apartments sat empty. In the cities people starved in the shadow of bulging warehouses; in the country farmers burned great piles of wheat and slaughtered surplus cows, hogs, sheep, leaving the carcasses for the buzzards. Broken, spiritless men, jobless for two or three years, huddled in dreary lines before soup kitchens and stared mutely at the ghostly factories whose dusty, unmanned machines were capable of producing shoes, clothes, all the countless things they needed so desperately. "Society," Alfred Kazin remarked, "was no longer a comfortable abstraction, but a series of afflictions." America in depression presented such a melancholy spectacle to the world that, in 1931, natives of the Cameroons in West Africa sent over $3.77 for the relief of "the starving." Yet, by all counts, the United States was still the richest nation in the world—possessing abundant resources, unexcelled "know-how," a plentitude of skilled labor, and an unlimited capacity to produce.[23]

The devastating contrast between Hoover's promise in 1928 of two chickens in every pot and two cars in every garage and the hard actualities of unemployment, breadlines, and bankruptcies in 1932 forced Americans to take a new look at their economic system. Now for the first time they clearly saw serious flaws in the economy which hitherto had been overlooked or concealed by the brilliant razzle-dazzle of the stock market. The crash had not only exposed a heavily overloaded corporate structure capitalized on future prosperity a generation in advance, but also disclosed the fact that American business in the twenties had sheltered an exceptional number of promoters, grafters, swindlers, impostors, and frauds—an ethical phenomenon characterized by John Kenneth Galbraith as "a kind of flood tide of corporate larceny." Testimony before the U.S. Senate Committee on Banking and Currency brought to light "a shocking corruption in our banking system, a widespread repudiation of old-fashioned standards of honesty and fair-dealing in the creation and sale of securities, and a merciless exploitation of the vicious possibilities of intricate corporate chicanery." Samuel Insull, who had been celebrated as a "financial miracle-maker" and nationally respected as suzerain of a vast and labyrinthine utilities empire, had taken flight to escape criminal trial and left behind bewildered investors holding billions in worthless securities; and not long afterward, the president of the New York Stock Exchange, Richard Whitney, was convicted and sent to Sing Sing Prison for appropriating his clients' funds.[24]

Businessmen generally, however, refused to accept responsibility for the depression. While they had eagerly and proudly taken credit for prosperity, they blamed the depression upon impersonal forces beyond their control. In fact, business leaders tended to disclaim that there were any economic problems at all. In the face of widespread suffering, Andrew Mellon, one of the "biggest" of big businessmen, said, "I do not believe . . . there is anything fundamentally wrong with the social system." With the nation plunging into the worst depression in its history, the president of the National Association of Manufacturers assured hungry and jobless Americans that he saw nothing "to weaken the confidence of understanding minds in the essential parts of our American economic system." So-called "economic" problems, it was suggested, were "fundamentally moral problems," and could be more easily solved if approached with that understanding. Rather than engaging in misguided schemes of unemployment relief, the government was urged to address itself to the problem of crime. Obviously, as James Prothro remarked, the business community—

in alarm for its prestige and profits—had to a considerable extent lost contact with reality.[25]

Under these damaging circumstances, the stock of the American businessman fell to an all-time low. If in 1929 he had been at the pinnacle of popularity, by 1932 he was almost completely discredited. Distrusted, his prestige gone, the businessman sought a comfortless anonymity. "It is almost literally true," said *Christian Century*, "that, in the realm of industry and finance, there are no more big names." The general public no longer believed business leadership had any necessary relation to the general welfare. Where once the leader in corporate finance and industry had been superstitiously regarded as a kind of superman endowed with super-intelligence and preternatural shrewdness, now the businessman was described as "abysmally ignorant" and charged with seldom having troubled himself to understand the economic system under which he operated. How far down the road of disillusionment the American people had traveled since October, 1929, was unexpectedly revealed by the investment analyst and respected business authority, John Moody, who announced in 1932: "Today the superman superstition is a wreck; things have gone so far that even the supermen themselves have lost faith in their own wisdom and judgment; blunder after blunder has been their portion since 1927, and most of them have recently been throwing up their arms in despair. They are now admitting that they are just ordinary 'damned fools,' after all. And they are largely right, perhaps for the first time in their lives."[26]

Plainly the businessman's complacency had been shattered, and the "big men" of Wall Street and industry seemed as bewildered as anyone else. Most business leaders, Dun & Bradstreet found, were without plans and slow in discussing termination of the depression. Richard Whitney, head of the New York Stock Exchange, proposed leaving it to the law of supply and demand to right things, while the industrialist Harvey S. Firestone said that the application of the Golden Rule would bring revival. Walter P. Chrysler, auto magnate, urged American consumers—at least half of whom were broke, on relief, and unemployed—to "buy now," and Henry Ford offered tenuous consolation by declaring the slump to be "more wholesome" than false prosperity. Andrew Mellon, multimillionaire head of the Treasury under Coolidge and a business leader celebrated for his financial acumen, candidly admitted: "None of us has any means of knowing when and how we shall emerge from the valley of the depression." And Charles M. Schwab of Bethlehem Steel, who had been one of the clarion voices of prosperity, frankly confessed: "I'm afraid, every man is afraid."[27]

With business leadership bankrupt, the country turned again to the politician and government for a way out. The people seemed to have lost interest in business goals, but were showing a new interest in national economic planning. As some conservatives noted with alarm, there appeared to be a growing tendency to exalt the power of political action over economic conditions. Instead of an economic policy of no "dictation or interference by the Government with business" which Hoover had proudly announced to the Chamber of Commerce after the 1929 crash, the public and, astoundingly enough, the Chamber itself now favored cooperation under government control. Although the professional politician was still depreciated, the incoming Roosevelt administration brought a new group to Washington in 1933. The new politician, as W. M. Kiplinger of the well-known letter bureau noted, was a different breed. There was no average type; there were professors, lawyers, economists, an endless stream of "bright young men." Most had become politicians only recently, and the majority were amateurs at the business of governing. They were a new set of officials with a new set of ideas. Although the "brain trust," as the group of young intellectuals around the President were known, was composed of men with all sorts of theories, the

Back to Normalcy

I

After the Armistice of November, 1918, the earnest desire of millions of Americans was to pick up life where they had left off, to resume the old familiar pattern of living with as little interruption as possible. But, to their frustration, they found the way to the past blocked. War unsettles all things, and though the United States had escaped physical devastation, two years of contrived hate, calculated destruction, and mass murder had left the country in a state of emotional shell shock. The forces of war, world events, and new developments at home had all conspired to change America.

War, "the devil's answer to human progress," wrote William Allen White, had left America disorganized and demoralized. After the Armistice, war contracts had been abruptly canceled, production dropped precipitately, and thousands of workers in war industries were suddenly jobless. Reconversion of the country's vast industrial system to peacetime uses was left to chance, and the resulting economic instability and hardship was further complicated by the ill-timed dumping of some 4,000,000 ex-soldiers into the already burdened labor market. Abandoned by an ungrateful nation and turned out of the army to shift for themselves, embittered jobless veterans swelled the ranks of discontented Americans who stood helplessly by while wartime prosperity vanished in a cloud of upward spiraling prices. By late 1919 the purchasing power of the prewar dollar had shrunk from 100 to 45. Food costs had jumped 84 percent, clothing 114.5 percent, and furniture 125 percent. For the average American family the cost of living was 99 percent higher than it had been before the beginning of the war in 1914. Hardest hit were salaried people who were worse off than at any time since the Civil War. While the white-collar class struggled gamely, if vainly, against the rising cost of living, organized labor, which had made great gains during the war, fought to hold its position, demanding higher wages and going out on strike to get them. In 1919 alone there were 3600 strikes involving more than 4,000,000 workers. There seems little doubt that rampant inflation was behind much of the industrial unrest, and had the government made any attempt or shown any inclination to deal realistically with the economic instability caused by reconversion, demobilization, and inflation, widespread discontent might have been avoided. As it was, however, the Wilson administration—obsessed with the troubles of Europe—ignored social and economic difficulties at home. The result was that the social pressures building up finally erupted in an explosive series of bombings, riots, and lynchings which, along with strikes, convinced many frightened Americans that revolution was here. Bewildered and frustrated, the American people looked angrily for the devil and, not finding him, invented one—the Bolshevik.[1]

So began the great witch-hunt of 1919–1920. In part an escape from personal tensions, the Red Scare was chiefly a crowd manifestation, a carry-over of war-bred fears and passions into the problems of peace. As Wilson had predicted, war would brutalize America. "Once lead this people into war," he told the editor of the New York *World*, "and they'll forget there ever was such a thing as tolerance." Certainly, under leadership of the President, the government by rigid suppression of dissident opinion and by organized propaganda had done everything it could to inculcate hate, prejudice, and 100% Americanism on a massive scale. In the patriotic vocabulary of hatred the villain had been the German Kaiser; in the hysterical liturgy of 1919 it was the Russian Bolshevik. "Reds" replaced "Huns" as the target of patriotic bigotry, and almost overnight "Bolshevik" became the epithet for all that was evil and wrong in America. Liberals and radicals, progressives and revolutionaries, reformers and crackpots—all those who did not particularly agree with the way things were going—were tagged "Bolsheviki" and subjected to persecution. Instead of making scapegoats of pacifists, slackers, and draft-dodgers, self-styled super-patriots and former spy-chasers turned on persons and groups whose opinions they hated and feared, demanding with vehement intolerance their absolute loyalty to the status quo.[2]

Although the menace of Bolshevism was greatly exaggerated, popular fears were not entirely groundless. Behind the smoldering threat of revolution there were real live Bolsheviks who, in the first vainglorious hours of success, had boasted that the Russian Revolution of 1917 was but the first step in the world-wide overthrow of capitalism. Under the slogan "Workers of the World unite, you have nothing to lose but your chains," the Bolsheviks launched a propaganda offensive calculated to strike terror into the hearts of uneasy capitalists everywhere. By words, and not by deeds—for the Russian revolutionaries had not yet gained complete control at home—the Third International challenged world capitalism and urged the proletariat to seize power, arm the workers, and abolish private property. Concerned over the aggressive program of Bolshevism, alarmed capitalists prevailed upon President Wilson to send small forces of American troops to both northern Russia and Siberia in 1918, and though this "limited intervention" was largely a sop to conservative fears and was short-lived, it served nonetheless to dramatize the issue in the United States, and to heighten tensions between American radicals and conservatives. Sensational horror stories in the conservative press claiming the Bolsheviki had an electric guillotine that lopped off five hundred heads an hour and portraying Bolshevik rule as a "compound of slaughter, confiscation, anarchy, and universal disorder" were countered in left-wing journals by fulsome praise for the Bolshevik revolution and charges that capitalistic imperialism was seeking to destroy the only true "people's government" that existed.[3]

Fear of subversion led to a mounting clamor for government action. Under normal conditions, the existence in the United States of a radical minority of some 70,000 hard-core Communists probably would not have caused much alarm, but a succession of unusual and spectacular events beginning with the Seattle general strike of 1919 and followed by a rash of bombing incidents and May Day riots in various cities across the nation brought Attorney General A. Mitchell Palmer into the crusade against the Reds in the fall of 1919. Under his direction and using the specially created Federal Bureau of Investigation as an anti-radical task force, the federal government launched a nationwide purge of radicals which was conducted in such an aggressive, lawless fashion that it was labeled "Palmer's Reign of Terror." Early in January, 1920, the Department of Justice rounded up more than four thousand suspected radicals, holding them incommunicado and treating many with extreme brutality. Attorney General Palmer justified his actions on the basis of imminent revolution, maintaining that only by such militant tactics could the advance of "red radicalism" be halted in the United States.[*]

In such an atmosphere of intolerance, "Americanism" was perversely applied to anything representing the status quo, while patriotism became an excuse for any illiberal action by economic and political conservatives. Vigilante groups of super-patriots from the newly formed American Legion or the recently resurrected Ku Klux Klan often

[*] A. Mitchell Palmer, *The Case Against the "Reds."* See page 55.

took matters into their own hands, beating, torturing, and, in a few instances, lynching persons suspected of being less than 100% Americans. As the hysteria grew, school teachers, college professors, clergymen, public officials, and other prominent citizens were bullied, smeared, and subjected to outrageous restrictions. Yale, Radcliffe, and Vassar were condemned as hotbeds of Bolshevism, and the American Civil Liberties Union was disparaged as a "Bolshevik front." Middle-class intellectuals who read Karl Marx or liberal reformers who objected to vigilante injustices were branded "Parlor Reds" and proclaimed to be more dangerous than the "nut" who throws a bomb. Despite warnings from the newspapers that the government might be carrying this "anti-red business" too far, Attorney General Palmer exploited the issue of radicalism for all it was worth, partly out of genuine fear of Communist subversion but also to advance his political ambitions. Palmer finally overreached himself, however, by direly predicting an impending "Red" revolution on May 1, 1920. There were sensational headlines and feverish precautions, but not a single disturbance took place in the entire nation. After the May Day fiasco, which was denounced in newspapers as a "mare's nest hatched in the Attorney General's brain," there was growing criticism of the government's anti-red activities. Twelve of the nation's most prominent lawyers issued a report condemning the "utterly illegal acts" of the Department of Justice and charging that it had violated the Constitution by inflicting cruel and unusual punishments, making arrests without warrant, engaging in unreasonable searches and seizures, compelling persons to be witnesses against themselves, and misusing the office of Attorney General by issuing anti-radical propaganda patently designed to affect public opinion in advance of court decisions.[4] Among these outspoken critics was Professor Zechariah Chafee, Jr., of Harvard, who also published independently a vigorous defense of free speech in which he argued that there

McCall in *The Portland Telegram*, Portland, Oregon

In the national hysteria following the war America became obsessed by the specter of "Bolshevism." Haunted by fear of revolution, vigilante bands of super-patriots from the newly formed American Legion beat, bullied, and in some cases lynched persons suspected of being less than 100% Americans.

was both an individual interest and a social interest in the attainment of truth.*

II

Though the Red Scare collapsed, the crusade for 100% Americanism continued through most of the decade. The herd demand for conformity, the marked dislike of any variation in thought or action, and the "joyful willingness to use force to eradicate such differences" were all, as George Mowry observed, part of the end product of mass mental conscription during the war.[5] In such an intellectual environment persecution was bound to flourish. Wartime intolerance was kept alive by organized hate-groups, the most vicious and insidious of which was the Ku Klux Klan. Dedicated to the ideal of "pure Americanism," the Klan fed upon the pet hatreds and fears of white Anglo-Saxon Protestants—against Catholics, "niggers," Jews, and foreigners. Reactivated in Georgia in 1915, the Klan limped along until 1919–1920, when, nourished by the hysteria and violence of those postwar years, it grew to gigantic proportions. By 1924 its membership reached the staggering total of four and a half million, and its political influence was a force to be reckoned with in the South, the Midwest, and on the Pacific Coast. Not only did the Klan's gospel of hate and bigotry succeed by inflaming white against black and yellow, gentile against Jew, Protestant against Catholic, but its preposterous mummery—the secret ritual, the flaming cross, the white robe and hood, the Grand Goblins, King Kleagles, and Imperial Wizards—had great sales appeal for simple-minded adults who for ten dollars could find adventure and excitement by becoming a Knight of the Invisible Empire. Retailing

*Zechariah Chafee, Jr., *The Case for Free Speech*. See page 62.

hate, it turned out, was a profitable business, reportedly netting more than twenty million dollars to the original promoters.

The Klan, as the Imperial Wizard Hiram Wesley Evans made embarrassingly clear, was pledged to preserve the white race and Anglo-Saxon culture from mongrelization and contamination, and was prepared, if necessary, to take direct action.* In Alabama, for instance, the Klan's fight for "Americanism" led to: "A lad whipped with branches until his back was ribboned flesh; a Negress beaten and left helpless to contract pneumonia from exposure and die; a white girl, divorcée, beaten into unconsciousness in her own home; a naturalized foreigner flogged until his back was a pulp because he married an American woman; a Negro lashed until he sold his land to a white man for a fraction of its value." From all over the country came similar reports of Klan beatings and atrocities, while the forces of law and order, in most instances, scrupulously observed a strict neutrality.[6]

As always, the chief victim of intolerance was the Negro. Although Henry Ford—the American Janus whose rural bigotry was financed by the proceeds of mass-production—purveyed fantastic lies about the intrigues of "international Jewry" in his Dearborn *Independent*, going so far in anti-Semitism as to declare Einstein a "colossal humbug," the Jew in the United States was never subjected to the widespread persecution that dogged the Negro. During the war Negroes had been accepted in the military services, and there had been a great northward migration of Negroes in search of high wages in the war industries. As more and more Negroes invaded the factories and slums of northern cities, racial tensions built up. White workers, jealous of their status, resented the competition of black laborers and excluded them from unions. After the Armistice Negroes were pushed out of the more desirable jobs they had held during the manpower shortage of the war years, but

*Hiram Wesley Evans, *The Klan's Fight for Americanism*. See page 68.

the taste of temporary prosperity and partial acceptance as workers and soldiers which had given the Negroes new hope had also inspired a new disposition to fight against racial discrimination. The result was an explosion of interracial strife, the worst the nation had ever seen. During the first year following the war, more than seventy Negroes were lynched in the South, some of them veterans still in uniform; and in the "Red Summer" of 1919 race riots broke out in twenty-five American cities. In Washington, D.C., and Chicago, mobs took over the cities for days—whites and Negroes beating, stabbing, shooting one another in the streets. For nearly a week, Chicago was in a virtual state of civil war, and when order was finally restored, it was found that fifteen whites and twenty-three Negroes had been killed, five hundred thirty-seven people injured, and a thousand left homeless and destitute.

Tragically futile, roughly suppressed, these postwar protests by an urban Negro minority marked a new disposition to revolt against the philosophy of accommodation that had dominated Negro thought since the beginning of the twentieth century. To black slum-dwellers confronted with the hopeless prospect of a lifetime of poor housing, mass unemployment, and racial persecution, the only way out seemed to be offered by Marcus Garvey, an ambitious West Indian Negro who came to the United States in 1916. Appealing to the growing despair among black Americans, Garvey renounced all hope of any assistance or understanding from the whites: "For over three hundred years the white man had been our oppressor, and he naturally is not going to liberate us to the higher freedom—the truer liberty—the truer Democracy. We have to liberate ourselves."

Not only did Garvey repudiate Booker T. Washington's policy of conciliation and gradualism, he denounced practically the entire Negro leadership, rejecting the militant elitism of W. E. B. DuBois along with the more moderate black-and-white alliance of the N.A.A.C.P. Both were spurious because, said Garvey, the Negro could never ex-

Negro World

ONE GOD, ONE AIM, ONE DESTINY

A Newspaper Devoted Solely to the Interests of the Negro Race

VOL. VIII. No. 24   NEW YORK, SATURDAY, JULY 31, 1920   PRICE: THREE CENTS IN GREATER NEW YORK, FIVE CENTS ELSEWHERE IN THE U. S. A., TEN CENTS IN FOREIGN COUNTRIES

GREAT WORLD CONVENTION OF NEGROES

Members of the Race From All Parts of the World to Assemble at Liberty Hall, New York, Sunday, August 1, at 10 A. M.—Biggest and Most Representative Assemblage in History of the Race

CONSTITUTION OF NEGRO LIBERTY IS TO BE WRITTEN

The Negro World, July 31, 1920. from *World's Work*, XLI, December 1920, p. 161

pect to gain social equality in this country by political agitation of any kind. Garvey taught that Negroes, instead of trying to be "white folks' niggers," should take pride in purity of race, exalting black over white and even deprecating the light-brown skins of people like DuBois, who was of mixed ancestry. The prejudice of the white race against the black race, he insisted, was due not so much to color as to condition—"because as a race, to them, we have accomplished nothing; we have built no nation, no government; because we are dependent on them for our economic and political existence." The only thing left for the Negroes to do, therefore, was to organize the world over and to build up a mighty nation of their own in Africa. Until the black man reached that point of independence, Garvey declared, he would count for nothing.° As World War I had freed many subject peoples, so he prophesied the next war would bring a changed world politically in which "Africa for the Africans" was no longer a dream but a progressive reality. Despite strong opposi-

°Marcus Garvey, *The Negro's Struggle for Survival*. See page 75.

"Black ideals, black industry, black United States (of Africa), and black religion," Marcus Garvey told his followers, was the only solution to the Negro problem. So marchers in the great parade which opened the annual fifth convention of the Provisional Republic of Africa carried this painting of the Ethiopian Christ.

---

tion from middle-class Negroes and intellectuals, Garvey was able to attract a larger following than any Negro leader in America. Membership in his Universal Negro Improvement Association reputedly ran as high as several million. With amazing drive Garvey organized cooperative enterprises—grocery stores, laundries, restaurants, hotels, a steamship line—and printed his own newspaper, which had wide circulation among Negroes. Although after a few years his grandiose schemes collapsed due to poor judgment and possible fraudulent practices, Garvey's success, as Gunnar Myrdal pointed out, not only proved it was possible to activate the Negro masses but testified to the great unrest in the American Negro community which, DeBois predicted, would some day "burst in fire and blood."[7]

III

Behind the floggings, church burnings, and lynchings were the fears of poorer and less educated white folk who were attempting desperately to stem the tide of change that threatened the mores and beliefs of small-town America. The Ku Klux Klan, prohibition, fundamentalism, and xenophobia were, as Walter Lippmann perceived, "an extreme but authentic expression of the politics, the social outlook, and the religion of the older American village civilization making its last stand against what looks to it like an alien invasion." This alien invasion was in fact the new urban civilization with its radical ideas, cosmopolitan ways, and its irresistible economic and technical power. Beer and Bolshevism, Darwinism and the Bible, the Pope and Nordic supremacy were all part of a mythology which expressed symbolically the impact of a vast and dreaded social change.[8]

Just as the Klan's intimidation of the Negro in the South was an attempt to use terror to preserve an archaic social system, so the campaign in certain rural localities to prevent the teaching of Darwinism was an effort to resist urban forces of change, to erect legal barriers against a scientific rationalism that threatened to undermine the spiritual foundations of the village civilization. Since most of the nation thought the question of evolution had been settled some fifty years before, the country was startled, and completely fascinated, by the breaking out in 1925 of the old controversy between science and Christian fundamentalism. In the little mountain town of Dayton, John T. Scopes, a high school biology teacher, was brought to trial for violating a Tennessee statute which forbade the teaching in public schools of any theory that denied "the conception of the divine creation of man as put in the Bible" and held in its stead that man was "descended from a lower order of animal."

Immediately dubbed the "Monkey Trial" by an opportunistic press, the case attracted international attention. To Scopes' defense came Clarence Darrow, nationally renowned defense lawyer and an admitted agnostic, while William Jennings Bryan, the folk-hero of rural America since 1896 and more recently named the "Fundamentalist Pope" by H. L. Mencken, was retained to assist the prosecution. In a bitter cross-examination, Bryan, who had denounced evolution as "a bloody, brutal doctrine" and vowed a "duel to the death," attacked the defense for trying "to

---

In the bizarre "Monkey Trial" at Dayton, Tennessee, in 1925, Clarence Darrow (in galluses), representing the A.C.L.U., defended John T. Scopes (seated behind Darrow in shirtsleeves, with folded arms) against the charge of teaching evolution. More than a skirmish between religious Fundamentalists and Modernists, it was the last stand of the older rural civilization against the radical ideas and alien ways of the new urban civilization.

cast ridicule on everybody who believes in the Bible."* In retaliation, Darrow, after lashing out against "this foolish, mischievous, and wicked act," proclaimed that his only purpose was to prevent "bigots and ignoramuses from controlling the education of the United States."†

Yet the trial was not simply a contest between the forces of religious bigotry and intellectual freedom, though this was an important issue. In this bizarre war between country and city, the quixotic provincialism of Bryan was pitted against the urbane sarcasm of Darrow, a truly mundane belief in religion against an almost superstitious faith in science. Although the anti-evolutionists won the Scopes case, they were defeated in the long run, for the worldwide derision aroused by the trial destroyed evolution as a valid intellectual issue. Science had become the chief power in modern civilization, and, said the *New Republic*, "Theoretically it is possible for a man or a state to prefer the civilization of bygone days to his own. But practically, no one does and no one can. . . ." Bryan, having become a pathetic figure of fun, died soon afterward. But his last battle was more than a mere exercise in fanaticism. He had at any rate, remarked Lippmann, fought "for the memory of a civilization which in its own heyday, and by its own criteria, was as valid as any other."9

The crusade to preserve America as it was found political expression in the presidential election of 1920. The people—after eight years of Wilson and fighting for principles, first at home and then abroad—were "tired of issues, sick at heart of ideals, and weary of being noble." We Americans, said Alvin Johnson, "thought we were settling the world, but straightway it became more unsettled than ever. We thought we were winning undying gratitude from mankind, but returned travelers keep telling us that America is unpopular everywhere. . . . We thought we were attaining a new national unity, but sectionalism and

*William Jennings Bryan, *Faith of Our Fathers*. See page 80.
†Clarence Darrow, *In Defense of Reason*. See page 88.

class feeling are more rampant than ever before. We have our inflated cost of living, our crushing taxation, our discount on government bonds to remind us of our participation in great events. But we'd like to forget it all." Things had gone amiss; and the American people, afraid of the future and plagued by unfamiliar problems, sought to escape their troubles by turning back the hands of time.[10]

IV

Rightly sensing the underlying temper of the country, the Republicans nominated Senator Warren G. Harding for the Presidency. An almost perfect specimen of the average 100% American, Harding personified himself as "Main Street come to Washington." Main Street was for him "the epitome of success, soundness, enterprise, orthodoxy, every worthy quality which he had in mind when he rolled out his unctuous encomiums of Americanism." Harding, wrote Lippmann, was distinguished by the fact that nothing distinguished him. "Put him into the White House," declared Mencken, "and you will put every president of every Chamber of Commerce into the White House, and every chairman of every Y.M.C.A. boob-squeezing drive, and every sales manager of every shoe factory, and every reader of the *Saturday Evening Post* and every abhorrer of the Bolsheviki." As befitted a modest, home-loving, small-town American, Harding conducted an informal campaign from his front porch where he smiled at visitors and shook hands with a firm grip.[11]

In politics and economics Harding stood just about where McKinley did in 1900. "Harding stands for a kind of candid and unpretentious reaction that everyone can respect, and that a great many people desire," said the *New Republic*. He was, the *Nation* grumbled, "McKinley come to life again," and the Washington *Post* concurred, finding the comparison "excellent." "Harding is of the McKinley type—safe, sound, courageous, and always ready to listen

Harding and Coolidge

Two Earnest Americans

soon to be President and Vice-President

and what they represent

Harding and Coolidge, your next President and Vice-President, stand for these things:

Absolute control of the United States by the United States. No foreign dictation. No foreign control expressed or implied.

Americans can govern their country without Europe's assistance.

Administrative economy and efficiency—an end to the scandalous squandering of national resources, reckless taxation and reckless spending.

Protection and encouragement for American workers and business men.

Prosperity restored and permanent.

Respect for American traditions and for American Independence, which are the foundations of this government.

On the fourth of July, in future as in the past, one flag will be seen. One is enough.

Independence means *independence*, now as in 1776.

This country will remain American. Its next President will remain in our own country. American affairs will be discussed by American public servants in the City of Washington, not in some foreign capital.

We decided long ago that we objected to foreign government of our people.

If four million Americans could take care of themselves and their own affairs one hundred and forty years ago, one hundred million Americans—25 times as many—can do the same now.

Harding and Coolidge will prove all this to the whole of Europe, Asia and Africa, when you send them to Washington.

Republican National Committee

Let's be done with wiggle and wobble

The Republican National Committee, Washington, D.C.

Disillusioned by the failure of Wilson's crusade to make the world safe for democracy and fearing foreign control by the League of Nations, Americans in the presidential election of 1920 voted for a return to "normalcy" and isolationism.

to counsel." Acting as if nothing had occurred in the past two decades, Republican leaders had turned to Ohio for another negative statesman to be the safe and sound apostle of business as usual. In economics, Harding was regarded as having "reached the benevolent capitalist stage"; in politics, the candidate proclaimed his sincere devotion to an "idealism of a simple and old-fashioned kind" which sought "a new freedom from too much government in business and not enough business in government."* Turning his back upon the "folly, waste, grotesque experimentation" of the Wilson administration, Senator Harding plumped resolutely for the *status quo pro ante:* "America's present need is not heroics, but healing; not nostrums but normalcy; not revolution, but restoration; not agitation, but adjustment; not surgery, but serenity; not the dramatic, but the dispassionate; not experiment, but equipoise; not submergence in internationality, but sustainment in triumphant nationality." No one need fear the ultimate outcome, promised Harding, because "immutable laws have challenged the madness of all experiment."[12]

The only significant alternative in 1920 to Harding's banal appeal for "normalcy" came from Eugene V. Debs. Regarded as the "leading presidential impossibility," Debs was in the Atlanta federal prison when he was selected to run for the fifth time as the Socialist candidate for President. Along with a handful of prominent Americans—William Jennings Bryan, Jane Addams, Senators La Follette and Norris—Debs had opposed the preparedness drive and battled for true neutrality. When the United States joined the Allies, Debs refused to go along, and after a speech at Canton, Ohio, in 1918 in which he contended it was not a war for national defense but a war for capitalist profits, he was arrested, convicted, and sentenced to ten years imprisonment for treason. Ironically, barely a year later, President Wilson publicly expressed the same point of view: "Is there any man here or woman—let me say is there any child—who does not know that the seed of war in the modern world is industrial and commercial rivalry? . . . This

---

*Warren G. Harding, *Back to Normalcy.* See page 94.

was a commercial war." Yet, despite recommendation from Attorney General Palmer, Wilson adamantly refused to pardon Debs.[13]

Popularly regarded as a senseless martyr to his convictions rather than a criminal, Debs was described by the *New York Times* as a "man of great kindliness and of excellent private character, qualities which have caused a degree of love for him almost amounting to worship among his followers." But for all his good qualities, Debs was still an untamed revolutionist. From his jail cell he stubbornly declared for Lenin's Third International, telling a reporter from the New York *World,* "I am heart and soul with the Russian revolution." As a "catastrophic revolutionary," Debs was committed to the dictatorship of the proletariat but believed it possible that by peaceful revolution—ballots not bullets—American workers could take over the industrial system and run it for use and not for profit. There seems little doubt that the choice of Debs as a presidential candidate was a personal tribute rather than an acceptance of his ideas of social revolution, for American Socialists were basically conservative, and the convention which chose Debs and drew up the platform was dominated by the moderate wing of the party. Though more radical than his supporters, Debs endorsed the platform which, Socialist dogma aside, offered a provocative program for social democracy, proposing among other things full civil, political, and educational rights for Negroes.*

But, infected with anti-radical hysteria, the American people were in no mood for change. Psychopathic fears of radicalism reached such a fever-pitch in 1920 that during a trial of some Communists at Boston the government expert unwittingly branded a section read from President Woodrow Wilson's *The New Freedom* as good Communist doctrine and pronounced it just cause for the deportation of the author. In New York five duly elected Socialist

---

*Eugene V. Debs, A *Last Call for Revolution.* See page 98.

representatives were unlawfully denied seats in the state assembly, and shortly afterward the Socialist party was declared illegal and its candidates barred from the state ballot. Perhaps the most graphic indication of the prevailing state of mind was the controversial trial of two Italian-born anarchists, Sacco and Vanzetti, who though allegedly sentenced to death for robbery and murder were seemingly convicted by a Massachusetts jury for the dual crime of being pacifists and radicals. With nonconformity a political and social crime, Debs had no expectation of being elected. Election results confirmed the observation of Paris *Le Matin* that Socialism in the United States was "exotic and alien," for Debs polled less than a million votes as compared to the twenty-five million votes cast for his more conventional Republican and Democratic opponents.[14]

With President Harding in the White House the people could once more relax, secure in the belief they were back on the American way. Although less than one-half of the electorate bothered to vote, they decisively chose restoration over revolution. In every previous election since 1896, at least one of the major parties had offered a candidate who believed that the public welfare demanded more or less drastic changes in national organization and policy. In 1920, however, neither the Republicans nor the Democrats made an honest bid for progressive support, a fact which, for Herbert Croly, was a sign of political bankruptcy and meant the eclipse of liberalism and progressivism as an effective force in American politics. Harding's frank resurrection of McKinley Republicanism was, under these conditions, an honest avowal of political neutrality. "We must strive for normalcy to reach stability" was meaningless rhetoric, and his clarion cry to "Stabilize America first, prosper American first, think of America first, exalt America first!" was comfortingly non-controversial. A vote for Harding was an empty hurrah for McKinley—a postponement of issues, not an evasion.[15]

As a formula for the good society, normalcy equated

national happiness with business prosperity and, in its more obvious sense, was a condition which could be expressed in concrete facts and figures; but, in a subtle and perhaps more important sense, it was a psychological condition, a national state of mind. As a member of the cabinet suggested, the "curing and restorative qualities of President Harding's personality" had affected the spiritual temper of the country. Certainly it seemed that the nation, like the President, proposed to cure excitement with serenity, to meet injustice with platitudes, to overcome greed with innocence, and in childlike faith to conquer change with nostalgia.[16]

Readings:

Back to Normalcy

A. Mitchell Palmer (1872–1936)

*Ambitious, dogmatic, and combative, he was
known as the "Fighting Quaker." From 1919 to
1921, as Attorney-General in Wilson's cabinet,
he achieved great notoriety fighting labor
unions and chasing suspected radicals. Bitterly
denounced in liberal circles for his unconstitutional actions at the time of the Red Scare
and charged with mishandling some $600 mil-
lions in alien property, he spent his last months
in office facing congressional investigating committees. Cleared of all charges of dishonesty
and malfeasance, he retired in 1921 from public
life but not from politics. In 1932 he supported Franklin D. Roosevelt and was credited
with writing most of the campaign platform.*

THE CASE AGAINST THE "REDS"

In this brief review of the work which the Department of
Justice has undertaken, to tear out the radical seeds that

From *Forum*, LXIII (Feb., 1920), 173–5, 181–5.

have entangled American ideas in their poisonous theories, I desire not merely to explain what the real menace of communism is, but also to tell how we have been compelled to clean up the country almost unaided by any virile legislation. Though I have not been embarrassed by political opposition, I have been materially delayed because the present sweeping processes of arrests and deportation of seditious aliens should have been vigorously pushed by Congress last spring. The failure of this is a matter of record in the Congressional files.

The anxiety of that period in our responsibility when Congress, ignoring the seriousness of these vast organizations that were plotting to overthrow the Government, failed to act, has passed. The time came when it was obviously hopeless to expect the hearty co-operation of Congress, in the only way to stamp out these seditious societies in their open defiance of law by various forms of propaganda.

Like a prairie-fire, the blaze of revolution was sweeping over every American institution of law and order a year ago. It was eating its way into the homes of the American workman, its sharp tongues of revolutionary heat were licking the altars of the churches, leaping into the belfry of the school bell, crawling into the sacred corners of American homes, seeking to replace marriage vows with libertine laws, burning up the foundations of society.

Robbery, not war, is the ideal of communism. This has been demonstrated in Russia, Germany, and in America. As a foe, the anarchist is fearless of his own life, for his creed is a fanaticism that admits no respect of any other creed. Obviously it is the creed of any criminal mind, which reasons always from motives impossible to clean thought. Crime is the degenerate factor in society.

Upon these two basic certainties, first that the "Reds" were criminal aliens, and secondly that the American Government must prevent crime, it was decided that there could be no nice distinctions drawn between the theoretical ideals of the radicals and their actual violations of our national laws. An assassin may have brilliant intellectuality, he may be able to excuse his murder or robbery with fine oratory, but any theory which excuses crime is not wanted in America. This is no place for the criminal to flourish, nor will he do so, so long as the rights of common citizenship can be exerted to prevent him.

Our Government in Jeopardy

It has always been plain to me that when American citizens unite upon any national issue, they are generally right, but it is sometimes difficult to make the issue clear to them. If the Department of Justice could succeed in attracting the attention of our optimistic citizens to the issue of internal revolution in this country, we felt sure there would be no revolution. The Government was in jeopardy. My private information of what was being done by the organization known as the Communist Party of America, with headquarters in Chicago, of what was being done by the Communist Internationale under their manifesto planned at Moscow last March by Trotzky, Lenine and others, addressed "To the Proletariats of All Countries," of what strides the Communist Labor Party was making, removed all doubt. In this conclusion we did not ignore the definite standards of personal liberty, of free speech, which is the very temperament and heart of the people. The evidence was examined with the utmost care, with a personal leaning toward freedom of thought and word on all questions.

The whole mass of evidence, accumulated from all parts of the country, was scrupulously scanned, not merely for the written or spoken differences of viewpoint as to the Government of the United States, but, in spite of these things, to see if the hostile declarations might not be sincere in their announced motive to improve our social order. There was no hope of such a thing.

By stealing, murder and lies, Bolshevism has looted Russia not only of its material strength, but of its moral force. A small clique of outcasts from the East Side of New York has attempted this, with what success we all know. Because a disreputable alien—Leon Bronstein, the man who now calls himself Trotzky—can inaugurate a reign of terror from his throne room in the Kremlin; because this lowest of all types known to New York can sleep in the Czar's bed, while hundreds of thousands in Russia are without food or shelter, should Americans be swayed by such doctrines?

Such a question, it would seem, should receive but one answer from America. . . .

Will Deportations Check Bolshevism?

Behind, and underneath, my own determination to drive from our midst the agents of Bolshevism with increasing vigor and with greater speed, until there are no more of them left among us, so long as I have the responsible duty of that task, I have discovered the hysterical methods of these revolutionary humans with increasing amazement and suspicion. In the confused information that sometimes reaches the people, they are compelled to ask questions which involve the reasons for my acts against the "Reds." I have been asked, for instance, to what extent deportation will check radicalism in this country. Why not ask what will become of the United States Government if these alien radicals are permitted to carry out the principles of the Communist Party as embodied in its so-called laws, aims and regulations?

There wouldn't be any such thing left. In place of the United States Government we should have the horror and terrorism of bolsheviki tyranny such as is destroying Russia now. Every scrap of radical literature demands the overthrow of our existing government. All of it demands obedience to the instincts of criminal minds, that is, to the lower appetites, material and moral. The whole purpose of communism appears to be a mass formation of the criminals of the world to overthrow the decencies of private life, to usurp property that they have not earned, to disrupt the present order of life regardless of health, sex or religious rights. By a literature that promises the wildest dreams of such low aspirations, that can occur to only the criminal minds, communism distorts our social law.

The chief appeal communism makes is to "The Worker." If they can lure the wage-earner to join their own gang of thieves, if they can show him that he will be rich if he steals, so far they have succeeded in betraying him to their own criminal course.

Read this manifesto issued in Chicago:

THE COMMUNIST PARTY MANIFESTO

The world is on the verge of a new era. Europe is in revolt. The masses of Asia are stirring uneasily. Capitalism is in collapse. The workers of the world are seeing a new light and securing new courage. Out of the night of war is coming a new day.

The spectre of communism haunts the world of capitalism. Communism, the hope of the workers to end misery and oppression.

The workers of Russia smashed the front of international Capitalism and Imperialism. They broke the chains of the terrible war; and in the midst of agony, starvation and the attacks of the Capitalists of the world, they are creating a new social order.

The class war rages fiercely in all nations. Everywhere the workers are in a desperate struggle against their capitalist masters. The call to action has come. The workers must answer the call!

The Communist Party of America is the party of the working class. The Communist Party proposes to end Capitalism and organize a workers' industrial republic. The workers must control industry and dispose of the product of industry. The Communist Party is a party realizing the limitation of all existing workers' organizations and proposes to develop the revolutionary movement necessary to free the workers from the oppression of Capitalism. The Communist Party insists that the problems of the American worker are identical with the problems of the workers of the world.

These are the revolutionary tenets of Trotzky and the

Communist Internationale. Their manifesto further embraces the various organizations in this country of men and women obsessed with discontent, having disorganized relations to American society. These include the I.W.W.'s, the most radical socialists, the misguided anarchists, the agitators who oppose the limitations of unionism, the moral perverts and the hysterical neurasthenic women who abound in communism. The phraseology of their manifesto is practically the same wording as was used by the Bolsheviks for their International Communist Congress.

Naturally the Communist Party has bored its revolutionary points into the Socialist Party. They managed to split the Socialists, for the so-called Left Wing of the Socialist Party is now the Communist Party, which specifically states that it does not intend to capture the bourgeoisie parliamentary state, but to conquer and destroy, and that the final objective, mass action, is the medium intended to be used in the conquest and destruction of the bourgeoisie state to annihilate the parliamentary state, and introduce a revolutionary dictatorship of the Proletariat. . . .

There is no legislation at present which can reach an American citizen who is discontented with our system of American Government, nor is it necessary. The dangerous fact to us is that the Communist Party of America is actually affiliated and adheres to the teaching program and tactics of the 3d Internationale. Consider what this means.

The first congress of the Communist Nationale held March 6, 1919, in Moscow, subscribed to by Trotzky and Lenine, adopted the following:

This makes necessary the disarming of the bourgeoisie at the proper time, the arming of the laborer, and the formation of a communist army as the protectors of the rules of the proletariat and the inviolability of the social structure.

When we realize that each member of the Communist Party of America pledges himself to the principles above set forth, deportation of men and women bound to such a theory is a very mild reformatory sentence.

Have the "Reds" Betrayed Labor?

If I were asked whether the American Federation of Labor had been betrayed by the "Reds," I should refer the inquiry to the manifesto and constitution of the Communist Party of America, in which, under the heading, "Revolutionary Construction," the following paragraph appears:

But the American Federation of Labor, as a whole, is hopelessly reactionary. At its recent convention the A. F. of L. approved the Versailles Peace Treaty and the League of Nations, and refused to declare its solidarity with Soviet Russia. It did not even protest the blockade of Russia and Hungary! This convention, moreover, did all in its power to break radical unions. The A. F. of L. is united with the Government, securing a privileged status in the governing system of State Capitalism. A Labor Party is being organized—much more conservative than the British Labor Party.

It has been inferred by the "Reds" that the United States Government, by arresting and deporting them, is returning to the autocracy of Czardom, adopting the system that created the severity of Siberian banishment. My reply to such charges is, that in our determination to maintain our government we are treating our alien enemies with extreme consideration. To deny them the privilege of remaining in a country which they have openly deplored as an unenlightened community, unfit for those who prefer the privileges of Bolshevism, should be no hardship. It strikes me as an odd form of reasoning that these Russian Bolsheviks who extol the Bolshevik rule, should be so unwilling to return to Russia. The nationality of most of the alien "Reds" is Russian and German. There is almost no other nationality represented among them. . . .

It is my belief that while they have stirred discontent in

our midst, while they have caused irritating strikes, and while they have infected our social ideas with the disease of their own minds and their unclean morals, we can get rid of them! and not until we have done so shall we have removed the menace of Bolshevism for good.

Zechariah Chafee, Jr. (1885–1957)

Appointed to the law faculty of Harvard University in 1916, he wrote his well-known defense of free speech largely by accident. As a young assistant professor hard up for money, he warmly welcomed an offer by the **New Republic** *in 1918 to write an article on the Espionage Act cases. Later, because of the interest it aroused, it was expanded into a book. His argument was not chiefly a legal one, nor did he place his confidence in the courts alone. In his opinion, the protection of freedom of speech rested primarily with people of sound minds rather than with sound laws.*

THE CASE FOR FREE SPEECH

And though all the winds of doctrine were let loose to play upon the earth, so Truth be in the field, we do injuriously by licensing and prohibiting to misdoubt her strength. Let her and Falsehood grapple; who ever knew Truth put to the worse, in a free and open encounter?—MILTON, *Areopagitica.*

Never in the history of our country, since the Alien and Sedition Laws of 1798, has the meaning of free speech been

Reprinted by permission of the publishers from Zechariah Chafee, Jr., *Free Speech in the United States* (Cambridge, Mass.: Harvard University Press), pp. 3, 30–5. Copyright, 1941, by the President and Fellows of Harvard College. First published in 1920.

the subject of such sharp controversy as to-day. Over nineteen hundred prosecutions and other judicial proceedings during the war, involving speeches, newspaper articles, pamphlets, and books, have been followed since the armistice by a widespread legislative consideration of bills punishing the advocacy of extreme radicalism. It is becoming increasingly important to determine the true limits of freedom of expression, so that speakers and writers may know how much they can properly say, and governments may be sure how much they can lawfully and wisely suppress. . . .

It is now clear that the First Amendment fixes limits upon the power of Congress to restrict speech either by a censorship or by a criminal statute, and if the Espionage Act exceeds those limits it is unconstitutional. It is sometimes argued that the Constitution gives Congress the power to declare war, raise armies, and support a navy, that one provision of the Constitution cannot be used to break down another provision, and consequently freedom of speech cannot be invoked to break down the war power. I would reply that the First Amendment is just as much a part of the Constitution as the war clauses, and that it is equally accurate to say that the war clauses cannot be invoked to break down freedom of speech. The truth is that all provisions of the Constitution must be construed together so as to limit each other. In a war as in peace, this process of mutual adjustment must include the Bill of Rights. There are those who believe that the Bill of Rights can be set aside in war time at the uncontrolled will of the government. The first ten amendments were drafted by men who had just been through a war. The Third and Fifth Amendments expressly apply in war. A majority of the Supreme Court declared the war power of Congress to be restricted by the Bill of Rights in *Ex Parte* Milligan, which cannot be lightly brushed aside, whether or not the majority went too far in thinking that the Fifth Amendment would have prevented Congress from exercising the war power under the particular circumstances of that case. If the First Amendment is to mean anything, it must restrict powers which are expressly granted by the Constitution to Congress, since Congress has no other powers.° It must apply to those activities of government which are most liable to interfere with free discussion, namely, the postal service and the conduct of war.

The true meaning of freedom of speech seems to be this. One of the most important purposes of society and government is the discovery and spread of truth on subjects of general concern. This is possible only through absolutely unlimited discussion, for, as Bagehot points out, once force is thrown into the argument, it becomes a matter of chance whether it is thrown on the false side or the true, and truth loses all its natural advantage in the contest. Nevertheless, there are other purposes of government, such as order, the training of the young, protection against external aggression. Unlimited discussion sometimes interferes with these purposes, which must then be balanced against freedom of speech, but freedom of speech ought to weigh very heavily in the scale. The First Amendment gives binding force to this principle of political wisdom.

Or to put the matter another way, it is useless to define free speech by talk about rights. The agitator asserts his constitutional right to speak, the government asserts its constitutional right to wage war. The result is a deadlock. Each side takes the position of the man who was arrested for swinging his arms and hitting another in the nose, and asked the judge if he did not have a right to swing his arms in a

---

°United States Constitution, Art. I, § 1: "All legislative powers herein granted shall be vested in a Congress." Amendment X: "The powers not delegated to the United States by the Constitution, nor prohibited by it to the States, are reserved to the States respectively or to the people."

"This government is acknowledged by all to be one of enumerated powers. The principle that it can exercise only the powers granted to it, would seem too apparent."—Marshall, C.J., in McCulloch v. Maryland, 4 Wheat. (U.S.) 316, 405 (1819). See also Taney, C.J., in Ex parte Merryman, Taney, 236, 260 (1861), and Brewer, Jr., in Kansas v. Colorado, 206 U.S. 46, 81 (1907).

free country. "Your right to swing your arms ends just where the other man's nose begins." To find the boundary line of any right, we must get behind rules of law to human facts. In our problem, we must regard the desires and needs of the individual human being who wants to speak and those of the great group of human beings among whom he speaks. That is, in technical language, there are individual interests and social interests, which must be balanced against each other, if they conflict, in order to determine which interest shall be sacrificed under the circumstances and which shall be protected and become the foundation of a legal right. It must never be forgotten that the balancing cannot be properly done unless all the interests involved are adequately ascertained, and the great evil of all this talk about rights is that each side is so busy denying the other's claim to rights that it entirely overlooks the human desires and needs behind that claim.

The rights and powers of the Constitution, aside from the portions which create the machinery of the federal system, are largely means of protecting important individual and social interests, and because of this necessity of balancing such interests the clauses cannot be construed with absolute literalness. The Fourteenth Amendment and the obligation of contracts clause, maintaining important individual interests, are modified by the police power of the states, which protects health and other social interests. The Thirteenth Amendment is subject to many implied exceptions, so that temporary involuntary servitude is permitted to secure social interests in the construction of roads, the prevention of vagrancy, the training of the militia or national army. It is common to rest these implied exceptions to the Bill of Rights upon the ground that they existed in 1791 and long before, but a less arbitrary explanation is desirable. Not everything old is good. Thus the antiquity of peonage does not constitute it an exception to the Thirteenth Amendment; it is not now demanded by any strong social interest. . . . The Bill of Rights does not crystallize antiquity. It seems better to say that long usage does not create an exception to the absolute language of the Constitution, but demonstrates the importance of the social interest behind the exception.

The First Amendment protects two kinds of interests in free speech. There is an individual interest, the need of many men to express their opinions on matters vital to them if life is to be worth living, and a social interest in the attainment of truth, so that the country may not only adopt the wisest course of action but carry it out in the wisest way. This social interest is especially important in war time. Even after war has been declared there is bound to be a confused mixture of good and bad arguments in its support, and a wide difference of opinion as to its objects. Truth can be sifted out from falsehood only if the government is vigorously and constantly cross-examined, so that the fundamental issues of the struggle may be clearly defined, and the war may not be diverted to improper ends, or conducted with an undue sacrifice of life and liberty, or prolonged after its just purposes are accomplished. Legal proceedings prove that an opponent makes the best cross-examiner. Consequently it is a disastrous mistake to limit criticism to those who favor the war. Men bitterly hostile to it may point out evils in its management like the secret treaties, which its supporters have been too busy to unearth. If a free canvassing of the aims of the war by its opponents is crushed by the menace of long imprisonment, such evils, even though made public in one or two newspapers, may not come to the attention of those who had power to counteract them until too late.

The history of the last five years shows how the objects of a war may change completely during its progress, and it is well that those objects should be steadily reformulated under the influence of open discussion not only by those who demand a military victory, but by pacifists who take a different view of the national welfare. Further argument for the existence of this social interest becomes unnecessary if we recall the national value of the opposition in former wars.

The great trouble with most judicial construction of the Espionage Act is that this social interest has been ignored and free speech has been regarded as merely an individual interest, which must readily give way like other personal desires the moment it interferes with the social interest in national safety. . . . The failure of the courts in the past to formulate any principle for drawing a boundary line around the right of free speech has not only thrown the judges into the difficult questions of the Espionage Act without any well-considered standard of criminality, but has allowed some of them to impose standards of their own and fix the line at a point which makes all opposition to this or any future war impossible. For example:

> No man should be permitted, by deliberate act, or even unthinkingly, to do that which will in any way detract from the efforts which the United States is putting forth or serve to postpone for a single moment the early coming of the day when the success of our arms shall be a fact.[*]

The true boundary line of the First Amendment can be fixed only when Congress and the courts realize that the principle on which speech is classified as lawful or unlawful involves the balancing against each other of two very important social interests, in public safety and in the search for truth. Every reasonable attempt should be made to maintain both interests unimpaired, and the great interest in free speech should be sacrificed only when the interest in public safety is really imperiled, and not, as most men believe, when it is barely conceivable that it may be slightly affected. In war time, therefore, speech should be unrestricted by the censorship or by punishment, unless it is clearly liable to cause direct and dangerous interference with the conduct of the war.

---

[*]United States *v.* "The Spirit of '76," 252 Fed. 946. Another good example is United States *v.* Schoberg, Bull. Dept. Just., No. 149.

Hiram Wesley Evans (1879–   )

*A Texan born, a dentist by profession, and a
thirty-second degree Mason, he supposedly represented the reform leadership in the Klan.
Taking over in the early twenties after a congressional investigation had revealed wholesale
corruption and graft, he cleaned up finances
and tried to create a new image of the Klan as
a law-abiding, peace-loving organization. Although as Imperial Wizard he officially disa-
vowed violence, his directives apparently were
not always heeded by local Klansmen. Deeply
suspicious of liberals and intellectuals, he
identified with the common people, appealing to
their ignorance and prejudices, and at times
displayed a remarkable intellecutal naiveté. For
instance, when asked why the Klansmen did
not parade with their hoods raised, he replied,
"The morale of the Klan would kill itself."*

THE KLAN'S
FIGHT FOR AMERICANISM

The Ku Klux Klan is an organization which gives expression, direction and purpose to the most vital instincts,
hopes and resentments of the old stock Americans, provides
them with leadership, and is enlisting and preparing them
for militant, constructive action toward fulfilling their racial
and national destiny. . . . The Klan literally is once more
the embattled American farmer and artisan, coordinated into
a disciplined and growing army, and launched upon a definite
crusade for Americanism! . . .

From *North American Review*, CCXXIII (Mar., 1926), 49–56, 60–1.

We are a movement of the plain people, very weak in the matter of culture, intellectual support, and trained leadership. We are demanding, and we expect to win, a return of power into the hands of the everyday, not highly cultured, not overly intellectualized, but entirely unspoiled and not de-Americanized, average citizen of the old stock. Our members and leaders are all of this class—the opposition of the intellectuals and liberals who held the leadership, betrayed Americanism, and from whom we expect to wrest control, is almost automatic.

This is undoubtedly a weakness. It lays us open to the charge of being "hicks" and "rubes" and "drivers of second hand Fords." We admit it. Far worse, it makes it hard for us to state our case and advocate our crusade in the most effective way, for most of us lack skill in language. Worst of all, the need of trained leaders constantly hampers our progress and leads to serious blunders and internal troubles. If the Klan ever should fail it would be from this cause. All this we on the inside know far better than our critics, and regret more. Our leadership is improving, but for many years the Klan will be seeking better leaders, and the leaders praying for greater wisdom. . . .

But we have no fear of the outcome. Since we indulge ourselves in convictions, we are not frightened by our weaknesses. We hold the conviction that right will win if backed with vigor and consecration. We are increasing our consecration and learning to make better use of our vigor. We are sure of the fundamental rightness of our cause, as it concerns both ourselves and the progress of the world. We believe that there can be no question of the right of the children of the men who made America to own and control America. We believe that when we allowed others to share our heritage, it was by our own generosity and by no right of theirs. We believe that therefore we have every right to protect ourselves when we find that they are betraying our trust and endangering us. We believe, in short, that we have the right to make America *American* and for Americans. . . .

Our critics have accused us of being merely a "protest movement," of being frightened; they say we fear alien competition, are in a panic because we cannot hold our own against the foreigners. That is partly true. We are a protest movement—protesting against being robbed. We are afraid of competition with peoples who would destroy our standard of living. We are suffering in many ways, we have been betrayed by our trusted leaders, we are half beaten already. But we are not frightened nor in a panic. We have merely awakened to the fact that we must fight for our own. We are going to fight—and win!

The Klan does not believe that the fact that it is emotional and instinctive, rather than coldly intellectual, is a weakness. All action comes from emotion, rather than from ratiocination. Our emotions and the instincts on which they are based have been bred into us for thousands of years; far longer than reason has had a place in the human brain. They are the many-times distilled product of experience; they still operate much more surely and promptly than reason can. For centuries those who obeyed them have lived and carried on the race; those in whom they were weak, or who failed to obey, have died. They are the foundations of our American civilization, even more than our great historic documents; they can be trusted where the fine-haired reasoning of the denatured intellectuals cannot.

Thus the Klan goes back to the American racial instincts, and to the common sense which is their first product, as the basis of its beliefs and methods. The fundamentals of our thought are convictions, not mere opinions. We are pleased that modern research is finding scientific backing for these convictions. We do not need them ourselves; we know that we are right in the same sense that a good Christian knows that he has been saved and that Christ lives—a thing which the intellectual can never understand. These convictions are no more to be argued about than is our love for our children; we are merely willing to state them for the enlightenment and conversion of others.

There are three of these great racial instincts, vital elements in both the historic and the present attempts to build an America which shall fulfill the aspirations and justify the heroism of the men who made the nation. These are the instincts of loyalty to the white race, to the traditions of America, and to the spirit of Protestantism, which has been an essential part of Americanism ever since the days of Roanoke and Plymouth Rock. They are condensed into the Klan slogan: "Native, white, Protestant supremacy."

First in the Klansman's mind is patriotism—America for Americans. He believes religiously that a betrayal of Americanism or the American race is treason to the most sacred of trusts, a trust from his fathers and a trust from God. He believes, too, that Americanism can only be achieved if the pioneer stock is kept pure. There is more than race pride in this. Mongrelization has been proven bad. It is only between closely related stocks of the same race that interbreeding has improved men; the kind of interbreeding that went on in the early days of America between English, Dutch, German, Huguenot, Irish and Scotch.

Racial integrity is a very definite thing to the Klansman. It means even more than good citizenship, for a man may be in all ways a good citizen and yet a poor American, unless he has racial understanding of Americanism, and instinctive loyalty to it. It is in no way a reflection on any man to say that he is un-American; it is merely a statement that he is not one of us. It is often not even wise to try to make an American of the best of aliens. What he is may be spoiled without his becoming American. The races and stocks of men are as distinct as breeds of animals, and every boy knows that if one tries to train a bulldog to herd sheep, he has in the end neither a good bulldog nor a good collie.

Americanism, to the Klansman, is a thing of the spirit,

a purpose and a point of view, that can only come through instinctive racial understanding. It has, to be sure, certain defined principles, but he does not believe that many aliens understand those principles, even when they use our words in talking about them. Democracy is one, fairdealing, impartial justice, equal opportunity, religious liberty, independence, self-reliance, courage, endurance, acceptance of individual responsibility as well as individual rewards for effort, willingness to sacrifice for the good of his family, his nation and his race before anything else but God, dependence on enlightened conscience for guidance, the right to unhampered development—these are fundamental. But within the bounds they fix there must be the utmost freedom, tolerance, liberalism. In short, the Klansman believes in the greatest possible diversity and individualism within the limits of the American spirit. But he believes also that few aliens can understand that spirit, that fewer try to, and that there must be resistance, intolerance even, toward anything that threatens it, or the fundamental national unity based upon it.

The second word in the Klansman's trilogy is "white." The white race must be supreme, not only in America but in the world. This is equally undebatable, except on the ground that the races might live together, each with full regard for the rights and interests of others, and that those rights and interests would never conflict. Such an idea, of course, is absurd; the colored races today, such as Japan, are clamoring not for equality but for their supremacy. The whole history of the world, on its broader lines, has been one of race conflicts, wars, subjugation or extinction. This is not pretty, and certainly disagrees with the maudlin theories of cosmopolitanism, but it is truth. The world has been so made that each race must fight for its life, must conquer, accept slavery or die. The Klansman believes that the whites will not become slaves, and he does not intend to die before his time.

Moreover, the future of progress and civilization depends on the continued supremacy of the white race. The forward movement of the world for centuries has come entirely from it. Other races each had its chance and either failed or stuck fast, while white civilization shows no sign of having reached its limit. Until the whites falter, or some colored civilization has a miracle of awakening, there is not a single colored stock that can claim even equality with the white; much less supremacy.

The third of the Klan principles is that Protestantism must be supreme; that Rome shall not rule America. The Klansman believes this not merely because he is a Protestant, nor even because the Colonies that are now our nation were settled for the purpose of wresting America from the control of Rome and establishing a land of free conscience. He believes it also because Protestantism is an essential part of Americanism; without it America could never have been created and without it she cannot go forward. Roman rule would kill it. . . .

Let it be clear what is meant by "supremacy." It is nothing more than power of control, under just laws. It is not imperialism, far less is it autocracy or even aristocracy of a race or stock of men. What it does mean is that we insist on our inherited right to insure our own safety, individually and as a race, to secure the future of our children, to maintain and develop our racial heritage in our own, white, Protestant, American way, without interference. . . .

In the National Government our interest is along the same lines, with special emphasis on anti-alien and pro-American legislation. Also, far more than in local affairs, we take pains to support men who understand and are loyal to the best American traditions. Apart from that the Klan takes no interest in any government matters except those having a direct bearing on decency and honesty. . . .

The Negro, the Klan considers a special duty and problem of the white American. He is among us through no wish of his; we owe it to him and to ourselves to give him full protection and opportunity. But his limitations are evident; we will not permit him to gain sufficient power to control our civilization. Neither will we delude him with promises of social equality which we know can never be realized. The Klan looks forward to the day when the Negro problem will have been solved on some much saner basis than miscegenation, and when every State will enforce laws making any sex relations between a white and a colored person a crime. . . .

The most menacing and most difficult problem facing America today is this of the permanently unassimilable alien. The only solution so far offered is that of Dr. Eliot, president emeritus of Harvard. After admitting that the melting pot has failed—thus supporting the primary position of the Klan!—he adds that there is no hope of creating here a single, homogeneous race-stock of the kind necessary for national unity. He then suggests that, instead, there shall be a congeries of diverse peoples, living together in sweet harmony, and all working for the good of all and of the nation! This solution is on a par with the optimism which foisted the melting pot on us. Diverse races never have lived together in such harmony; race antipathies are too deep and strong. If such a state were possible, the nation would be too disunited for progress. One race always ruled, one always must, and there will be struggle and reprisals till the mastery is established—and bitterness afterwards. And, speaking for us Americans, we have come to realize that if all this could possibly be done, still within a few years we should be supplanted by the "mere force of breeding" of the low standard peoples. We intend to see that the American stock remains supreme.

Marcus M. Garvey (1887-1940)

A Jamaican Negro, he became convinced that he had a mission as leader of the black race when he read Up from Slavery, *the autobiography of Booker T. Washington. In 1916 he moved to New York where in a few years he had gathered a mass following of several million Negroes. The climax of his astonishing American career occurred in 1920 when he presided over a mammoth international convention in New York, representing Negroes from all parts of the world. His triumph, however, was short-lived. Though personally honest and sincere, he was inexperienced in business matters and unwise in the choice of some of his subordinates. As a result, in 1923 he was tried and sentenced for mail fraud. Although his sentence was commuted by President Coolidge, he was deported in 1927 and never regained his popular following.*

THE NEGRO'S
STRUGGLE FOR SURVIVAL

Surely the soul of liberal, philanthropic, liberty-loving, white America is not dead.

It is true that the glamor of materialism has, to a great degree, destroyed the innocence and purity of the national conscience, but still, beyond our politics, beyond our soulless industrialism, there is a deep feeling of human sympathy that touches the soul of white America, upon which the un-

From *The Philosophy and Opinions of Marcus Garvey* (New York: The Universal Publishing House, 1923), pp. 1–6.

fortunate and sorrowful can always depend for sympathy, help and action.

It is to that feeling that I appeal for four hundred million Negroes of the world, and fifteen millions of America in particular.

There is no real white man in America, who does not desire a solution of the Negro problem. Each thoughtful citizen has probably his own idea of how the vexed question of races should be settled. To some the Negro could be gotten rid of by wholesale butchery, by lynching, by economic starvation, by a return to slavery, and legalized oppression, while others would have the problem solved by seeing the race all herded together and kept somewhere among themselves; but a few—those in whom they have an interest—should be allowed to live around as the wards of a mistaken philanthropy; yet, none so generous as to desire to see the Negro elevated to a standard of real progress and prosperity, welded into a homogeneous whole, creating of themselves a mighty nation, with proper systems of government, civilization and culture, to mark them admissible to the fraternities of nations and races without any disadvantage. . . .

Negroes are human beings—the peculiar and strange opinions of writers, ethnologists, philosophers, scientists and anthropologists notwithstanding. They have feelings, souls, passions, ambitions, desires, just as other men, hence they must be considered.

Has white America really considered the Negro in the light of permanent human progress? The answer is NO.

Men and women of the white race, do you know what is going to happen if you do not think and act now? One of two things. You are either going to deceive and keep the Negro in your midst until you have perfectly completed your wonderful American civilization with its progress of art, science, industry and politics, and then, jealous of your own success and achievements in those directions, and with the greater jealousy of seeing your race pure and unmixed, cast him off to die in the whirlpool of economic starvation, thus getting rid of another race that was not intelligent enough to live, or, you simply mean by the largeness of your hearts to assimilate fifteen million Negroes into the social fraternity of an American race, that will neither be white nor black! Don't be alarmed! We must prevent both consequences. No real race loving white man wants to destroy the purity of his race, and no real Negro conscious of himself, wants to die, hence there is room for an understanding, and an adjustment. And that is just what we seek.

Let white and black stop deceiving themselves. Let the white race stop thinking that all black men are dogs and not to be considered as human beings. Let foolish Negro agitators and so-called reformers, encouraged by deceptive or unthinking white associates, stop preaching and advocating the doctrine of "social equality," meaning thereby the social intermingling of both races, intermarriages, and general social co-relationship. The two extremes will get us nowhere, other than breeding hate, and encouraging discord, which will eventually end disastrously to the weaker race.

Some Negroes, in the quest of position and honor, have been admitted to the full enjoyment of their constitutional rights. Thus we have some of our men filling high and responsible government positions, others, on their own account, have established themselves in the professions, commerce and industry. This, the casual onlooker, and even the men themselves, will say carries a guarantee and hope of social equality, and permanent racial progress. But this is the mistake. There is no progress of the Negro in America that is permanent, so long as we have with us the monster evil—prejudice.

Prejudice we shall always have between black and white, so long as the latter believes that the former is intruding upon their rights. So long as white laborers believe that black laborers are taking and holding their jobs, so long as white artisans believe that black artisans are performing the work that they should do; so long as white men and women believe that black men and women are filling the positions

that they covet; so long as white political leaders and statesmen believe that black politicians and statesmen are seeking
the same positions in the nation's government; so long as
white men believe that black men want to associate with,
and marry white women, then we will ever have prejudice,
and not only prejudice, but riots, lynchings, burnings, and
God to tell what next will follow! . . .

In another one hundred years white America will have
doubled its population; in another two hundred years it will
have trebled itself. The keen student must realize that the
centuries ahead will bring us an over-crowded country; opportunities, as the population grows larger, will be fewer;
the competition for bread between the people of their own
class will become keener, and so much more so will there be
no room for two competitive races, the one strong, and the
other weak. To imagine Negroes as district attorneys, judges,
senators, congressmen, assemblymen, aldermen, government
clerks and officials, artisans and laborers at work, while
millions of white men starve, is to have before you the bloody
picture of wholesale mob violence that I fear, and against
which I am working.

No preaching, no praying, no presidential edict will control the passion of hungry unreasoning men of prejudice
when the hour comes. It will not come, I pray, in our
generation, but it is of the future that I think and for which
I work.

A generation of ambitious Negro men and women, out from
the best colleges, universities and institutions, capable of
filling the highest and best positions in the nation, in industry,
commerce, society and politics! Can you keep them back?
If you do so they will agitate and throw your constitution in
your faces. Can you stand before civilization and deny the
truth of your constitution? What are you going to do then?
You who are just will open the door of opportunity and say
to all and sundry, "Enter in." But, ladies and gentlemen,
what about the mob, that starving crowd of your own race?
Will they stand by, suffer and starve, and allow an opposite,

competitive race to prosper in the midst of their distress? If you can conjure these things up in your mind, then you have the vision of the race problem of the future in America.

There is but one solution, and that is to provide an outlet for Negro energy, ambition, and passion, away from the attractions of white opportunity and surround the race with opportunities of its own. If this is not done, and if the foundation for same is not laid now, then the consequence will be sorrowful for the weaker race, and disgraceful to our ideals of justice, and shocking to our civilization.

The Negro must have a country and a nation of his own. If you laugh at the idea, then you are selfish and wicked, for you and your children do not intend that the Negro shall discommode you in yours. If you do not want him to have a country and a nation of his own; if you do not intend to give him equal opportunities in yours, then it is plain to see that you mean that he must die, even as the Indian, to make room for your generations.

Why should the Negro die? Has he not served America and the world? Has he not borne the burden of civilization in this Western world for three hundred years? Has he not contributed of his best to America? Surely all this stands to his credit. But there will not be enough room and the one answer is "find a place." We have found a place; it is Africa, and as black men for three centuries have helped white men build America, surely generous and grateful white men will help black men build Africa.

And why shouldn't Africa and America travel down the ages as protectors of human rights and guardians of democracy? Why shouldn't black men help white men secure and establish universal peace? We can only have peace when we are just to all mankind; and for that peace, and for the reign of universal love, I now appeal to the soul of white America. Let the Negroes have a government of their own. Don't encourage them to believe that they will become social equals and leaders of the whites in America, without first on their own account proving to the world that they are capable of evolving a civilization of their own. The white race can best help the Negro by telling him the truth and not by flattering him into believing that he is as good as any white man without first proving the racial, national, constructive metal of which he is made.

Stop flattering the Negro about social equality, and tell him to go to work and build for himself. Help him in the direction of doing for himself, and let him know that self-progress brings its own reward.

William Jennings Bryan (1860-1925)

At the time of the Scopes trial, the once prodigious "Boy Orator of the Platte" was definitely an old man, and his great days were behind him. Having early demonstrated his superior powers as an orator on Chautauqua platforms, he won the Democratic Presidential nomination in 1896 with his famous "Cross of Gold" speech. From 1896 until 1912 he was the virtually undisputed leader of the Democratic party, running three times as its unsuccessful Presidential candidate. His last public office before slipping into near oblivion was Secretary of State in Wilson's cabinet, from which he resigned because of differences over his stand for strict neutrality. Perhaps, as Mencken said, Bryan lived too long. "He came into life a hero, a Galahad, in bright and shining armor. He was passing out a poor mountebank."

From a proposed address in defense of Tennessee's law against the teaching of evolution in the public schools which was never given because arguments to the jury by counsel on both sides were dispensed with by agreement. Reprinted in *World's Most Famous Court Trial* (Cincinnati: National Book Co., 1925), pp. 321–5, 337–8.

FAITH OF OUR FATHERS

Demosthenes, the greatest of ancient orators, in his "Oration on the Crown," the most famous of his speeches, began by supplicating the favor of all gods and goddesses of Greece. If, in a case which involved only his own fame and fate, he felt justified in petitioning the heathen gods of his country, surely we, who deal with the momentous issues involved in this case, may well pray to the Ruler of the universe for wisdom to guide us in the performance of our several parts in this historic trial.

Let me, in the first place, congratulate our cause that circumstances have committed the trial to a community like this and entrusted the decision to a jury made up largely of the yeomanry of the state. The book in issue in this trial contains on its first page two pictures contrasting the disturbing noises of a great city with the calm serenity of the country. It is a tribute that rural life has fully earned.

I appreciate the sturdy honesty and independence of those who come into daily contact with the earth, who, living near to nature, worship nature's God, and who, dealing with the myriad mysteries of earth and air, seek to learn from revelation about the Bible's wonder-working God. I admire the stern virtues, the vigilance and the patriotism of the class from which the jury is drawn, and am reminded of the lines of Scotland's immortal bard, which, when changed but slightly, describe your country's confidence in you:

> "O Scotia, my dear, my native soil!
>   For whom my warmest wish to Heaven is sent,
> Long may thy hardy sons of rustic toil
>   Be blest with health, and peace, and sweet content!
> "And, oh, may Heav'n their simple lives prevent
>   From luxury's contagion, weak and vile!
> Then, howe'er crowns and coronets be rent,

A virtuous populace may rise the while,
And stand, a wall of fire, around their much-loved isle."

Let us now separate the issues from the misrepresentations, intentional or unintentional, that have obscured both the letter and the purpose of the law. This is not an interference with freedom of conscience. A teacher can think as he pleases and worship God as he likes, or refuse to worship God at all. He can believe in the Bible or discard it; he can accept Christ or reject Him. This law places no obligations or restraints upon him. And so with freedom of speech; he can, so long as he acts as an individual, say anything he likes on any subject. This law does not violate any right guaranteed by any constitution to any individual. It deals with the defendant, not as an individual, but as an employee, an official or public servant, paid by the state, and therefore under instructions from the state.

Right of the State to Control Public Schools

The right of the state to control the public schools is affirmed in the recent decision in the Oregon case, which declares that the state can direct what shall be taught and also forbid the teaching of anything "manifestly inimical to the public welfare." The above decision goes even farther and declares that the parent not only has the right to guard the religious welfare of the child, but is in duty bound to guard it. That decision fits this case exactly. The state had a right to pass this law, and the law represents the determination of the parents to guard the religious welfare of their children.

It need hardly be added that this law did not have its origin in bigotry. It is not trying to force any form of religion on anybody. The majority is not trying to establish a religion or to teach it—it is trying to protect itself from the effort of an insolent minority to force irreligion upon the children under the guise of teaching science. . . .

Religion is not hostile to learning, Christianity has been the greatest patron learning has ever had. But Christians know that "the fear of the Lord is the beginning of wisdom" now just as it has been in the past, and they therefore oppose the teaching of guesses that encourage godlessness among the students.

Neither does Tennessee undervalue the service rendered by science. The Christian men and women of Tennessee know how deeply mankind is indebted to science for benefits conferred by the discovery of the laws of nature and by the designing of machinery for the utilization of these laws. Give science a fact and it is not only invincible, but it is of incalculable service to man. If one is entitled to draw from society in proportion to the service that he renders to society, who is able to estimate the reward earned by those who have given to us the use of steam, the use of electricity, and enabled us to utilize the weight of water that flows down the mountainside? Who will estimate the value of the service rendered by those who invented the phonograph, the telephone and the radio? Or, to come more closely to our home life, how shall we recompense those who gave us the sewing machine, the harvester, the threshing machine, the tractor, the automobile and the method now employed in making artificial ice? The department of medicine also opens an unlimited field for invaluable service. Typhoid and yellow fever are not feared as they once were. Diphtheria and pneumonia have been robbed of some of their terrors, and a high place on the scroll of fame still awaits the discoverer of remedies for arthritis, cancer, tuberculosis and other dread diseases to which mankind is heir.

Christianity welcomes truth from whatever source it comes, and is not afraid that any real truth from any source can interfere with the divine truth that comes by inspiration from God Himself. It is not scientific truth to which Christians object, for true science is classified knowledge, and nothing therefore can be scientific unless it is true.

Evolution Not Truth; Merely an Hypothesis

Evolution is not truth; it is merely an hypothesis—it is millions of guesses strung together. It had not been proven in the days of Darwin; he expressed astonishment that with two or three million species it had been impossible to trace any species to any other species. It had not been proven in the days of Huxley, and it has not been proven up to today. It is less than four years ago that Prof. Bateson came all the way from London to Canada to tell the American scientists that every effort to trace one species to another had failed—every one. He said he still had faith in evolution, but had doubts about the origin of species. But of what value is evolution if it cannot explain the origin of species? While many scientists accept evolution as if it were a fact, they all admit, when questioned, that no explanation has been found as to how one species developed into another. . . .

But while the wisest scientists cannot prove a pushing power, such as evolution is supposed to be, there is a lifting power that any child can understand. The plant lifts the mineral up into a higher world, and the animal lifts the plant up into a world still higher. So, it has been reasoned by analogy, man rises, not by a power within him, but only when drawn upward by a higher power. There is a spiritual gravitation that draws all souls toward heaven, just as surely as there is a physical force that draws all matter on the surface of the earth towards the earth's center. Christ is our drawing power; He said, "I, if I be lifted up from the earth, will draw all men unto Me," and His promise is being fulfilled daily all over the world.

It must be remembered that the law under consideration in this case does not prohibit the teaching of evolution up to the line that separates man from the lower forms of animal life. The law might well have gone farther than it does and prohibit the teaching of evolution in lower forms of life; the law is a very conservative statement of the people's opposition to an anti-Biblical hypothesis. The defendant was not content to teach what the law permitted; he, for reasons of his own, persisted in teaching that which was forbidden for reasons entirely satisfactory to the law-makers. . . .

Does it not seem a little unfair not to distinguish between man and lower forms of life? What shall we say of the intelligence, not to say religion, of those who are so particular to distinguish between fishes and reptiles and birds, but put a man with an immortal soul in the same circle with the wolf, the hyena and the skunk? What must be the impression made upon children by such a degradation of man? . . .

But it is not a laughing matter when one considers that evolution not only offers no suggestions as to a Creator but tends to put the creative act so far away as to cast doubt upon creation itself. And while it is shaking faith in God as a beginning, it is also creating doubt as to a heaven at the end of life. Evolutionists do not feel that it is incumbent upon them to show how life began or at what point in their long-drawn-out scheme of changing species man became endowed with hope and promise of immortal life. God may be a matter of indifference to the evolutionists and a life beyond may have no charm for them, but the mass of mankind will continue to worship their Creator and continue to find comfort in the promise of their Savior that He has gone to prepare a place for them. Christ has made of death a narrow, star-lit strip between the companionship of yesterday and the reunion of tomorrow; evolution strikes out the stars and deepens the gloom that enshrouds the tomb.

If the results of evolution were unimportant, one might require less proof in support of the hypothesis, but before accepting a new philosophy of life, built upon a materialistic foundation, we have reason to demand something more than guesses; "we may well suppose" is not a sufficient substitute for "Thus saith the Lord." . . .

In 1900—twenty-five years ago—while an international peace congress was in session in Paris, the following editorial appeared in *L'Univers:*

"The spirit of peace has fled the earth because evolution has taken possession of it. The plea for peace in past years has been inspired by faith in the divine nature and the divine origin of man; men were then looked upon as children of one Father, and war, therefore, was fratricide. But now that men are looked upon as children of apes, what matters it whether they are slaughtered or not? . . ."

Let us, then, hear the conclusion of the whole matter. Science is a magnificent material force, but it is not a teacher of morals. It can perfect machinery, but it adds no moral restraints to protect society from the misuse of the machine. It can also build gigantic intellectual ships, but it constructs no moral rudders for the control of storm-tossed human vessels. It not only fails to supply the spiritual element needed but some of its unproven hypotheses rob the ship of its compass and thus endangers its cargo.

In war, science has proven itself an evil genius; it has made war more terrible than it ever was before. Man used to be content to slaughter his fellowmen on a single plane —the earth's surface. Science has taught him to go down into the water and shoot up from below and to go up into the clouds and shoot down from above, thus making the battlefield three times as bloody as it was before; but science does not teach brotherly love. Science has made war so hellish that civilization was about to commit suicide; and not we are told that newly discovered instruments of destruction will make the cruelties of the late war seem trivial in comparison with the cruelties of wars that may come in the future. If civilization is to be saved from the wreckage threatened by intelligence not consecrated by love, it must be saved by the moral code of the meek and lowly Nazarene. His teachings, and His teachings alone, can solve the problems that vex the heart and perplex the world.

The world needs a Savior more than it ever did before, and there is only one Name under heaven given among men whereby we must be saved. It is this Name that evolution degrades, for, carried to its logical conclusion, it robs Christ of the glory of a virgin birth, of the majesty of His deity and mission and of the triumph of His resurrection. It also disputes the doctrine of the atonement.

It is for the jury to determine whether this attack upon the Christian religion shall be permitted in the public schools of Tennessee by teachers employed by the state and paid out of the public treasury. This case is no longer local, the defendant ceases to play an important part. The case has assumed the proportions of a battle-royal between unbelief that attempts to speak through so-called science and the defenders of the Christian faith, speaking through the legislators of Tennessee. It is again a choice between God and Baal; it is also a renewal of the issue in Pilate's court. . . .

Again force and love meet face to face, and the question, "What shall I do with Jesus?" must be answered. A bloody, brutal doctrine—Evolution—demands, as the rabble did nineteen hundred years ago, that He be crucified. That cannot be the answer of this jury representing a Christian state and sworn to uphold the laws of Tennessee. Your answer will be heard throughout the world; it is eagerly awaited by a praying multitude. If the law is nullified, there will be rejoicing wherever God is repudiated, the Savior scoffed at and the Bible ridiculed. Every unbeliever of every kind and degree will be happy. If, on the other hand, the law is upheld and the religion of the school children protected, millions of Christians will call you blessed and, with hearts full of gratitude to God, will sing again that grand old song of triumph:

> "Faith of our fathers, living still,
> In spite of dungeon, fire and sword;
> O how our hearts beat high with joy

> Whene'er we hear that glorious word—
> Faith of our fathers—holy faith;
> We will be true to thee till death!"

Clarence Darrow (1857–1938)

A famous criminal lawyer, he was started on his career in the 1890's by the liberal governor of Illinois, John Peter Altgeld. Noted for his defense of unpopular causes, he defended, at one time or another, the eight anarchists in the Haymarket case, Eugene Debs and the American Railway Union, Big Bill Haywood of the Western Federation of Miners, the McNamara brothers who bombed the anti-union Los Angeles Times, and the "thrill-murderers" Loeb and Leopold before he confronted the aging Bryan in 1925. A defense lawyer by conviction, his trial arguments were based on his philosophic view that men acted in response to social and physiological forces which they could not control and usually did not recognize.

IN DEFENSE OF REASON

I remember, long ago, Mr. Bancroft wrote this sentence, which is true: "That it is all right to preserve freedom in constitutions, but when the spirit of freedom has fled from the hearts of the people, then its matter is easily sacrificed under law." And so it is, unless there is left enough of the spirit of freedom in the state of Tennessee, and in the United States, there is not a single line of any constitution that can withstand bigotry and ignorance when it

From the second day's proceedings as recorded in the *World's Most Famous Trial* (Cincinnati: National Book Co., 1925), pp. 75, 77–8, 82–4, 87.

seeks to destroy the rights of the individual; and bigotry and ignorance are ever active. Here, we find today as brazen and as bold an attempt to destroy learning as was ever made in the middle ages, and the only difference is we have not provided that they shall be burned at the stake, but there is time for that, Your Honor, we have to approach these things gradually. . . .

What is the Bible? . . . It is a book primarily of religion and morals. It is not a book of science. Never was and was never meant to be. Under it there is nothing prescribed that would tell you how to build a railroad or a steamboat or to make anything that would advance civilization. It is not a textbook or a text on chemistry. It is not big enough to be. It is not a book on geology; they knew nothing about geology. It is not a book on biology; they knew nothing about it. It is not a work on evolution; that is a mystery. It is not a work on astronomy. The man who looked out at the universe and studied the heavens had no thought but that the earth was the center of the universe. But we know better than that. We know that the sun is the center of the solar system. And that there are an infinity of other systems around about us. They thought the sun went around the earth and gave us light and gave us night. We know better. We know the earth turns on its axis to produce days and nights. They thought the earth was 4,004 years before the Christian Era. We know better. I doubt if there is a person in Tennessee who does not know better. They told it the best they knew. And while suns may change all you may learn of chemistry, geometry and mathematics, there are no doubt certain primitive, elemental instincts in the organs of man that remain the same, he finds out what he can and yearns to know more and supplements his knowledge with hope and faith.

That is the province of religion and I haven't the slightest fault to find with it. . . .

The state by constitution is committed to the doctrine of education, committed to schools. It is committed to teaching and I assume when it is committed to teaching it is committed to teaching the truth—ought to be anyhow—plenty of people to do the other. It is committed to teaching literature and science. My friend has suggested that literature and science might conflict. I cannot quite see how, but that is another question. But that indicates the policy of the state of Tennessee and wherever it is used in construing the unconstitutionality of this act it can only be used as an indication of what the state meant and you could not pronounce a statute void on it, but we insist that this statute is absolutely void because it contravenes Section 3, which is headed "the right of worship free." . . . If this section of the constitution which guarantees religious liberty in Tennessee cannot be sustained in the spirit it cannot be sustained in the letter. What does it mean? What does it mean? I know two intelligent people can agree only for a little distance, like a company walking along in a road. They may go together a few blocks and then one branches off. The remainder go together a few more blocks and another branches off and still further some one else branches off and the human minds are just that way, provided they are free, of course; the fundamentalists may be put in a trap so they cannot think differently if at all, probably not at all, but leave two free minds and they may go together a certain distance, but not all the way together. There are no two human machines alike and no two human beings have the same experiences and their ideas of life and philosophy grow out of their construction of the experiences that we meet on our journey through life. It is impossible, if you leave freedom in the world, to mold the opinions of one man upon the opinions of another—only tyranny can do it—and your constitutional provision, providing a freedom of religion, was meant to meet that emergency. I will go further—there is nothing else—since man—I don't know whether I dare say evolved—still, this isn't a school—since man was created out of the dust of the earth—out of hand—there is nothing else,

Your Honor, that has caused the difference of opinion, of bitterness, of hatred, of war, of cruelty, that religion has caused. With that, of course, it has given consolation to millions.

But it is one of those particular things that should be left solely between the individual and his Maker, or his God, or whatever takes expression with him, and it is no one else's concern.

How many creeds and cults are there this whole world over? No man could enumerate them. At least as I have said, 500 different Christian creeds, all made up of differences, Your Honor, every one of them, and these subdivided into small differences, until they reach every member of every congregation. Because to think is to differ, and then there are any number of creeds older and any number of creeds younger, than the Christian creed, any number of them, the world has had them forever. They have come and they have gone, they have abided their time and have passed away, some of them are here still, some may be here forever, but there has been a multitude, due to the multitude and manifold differences in human beings, and it was meant by the constitutional convention of Tennessee to leave these questions of religion between man and whatever he worshiped, to leave him free. Has the Mohammedan any right to stay here and cherish his creed? Has the Buddhist a right to live here and cherish his creed? Can the Chinaman who comes here to wash our clothes, can he bring his joss and worship it? Is there any man that holds a religious creed, no matter where he came from, or how old it is or how false it is, is there any man that can be prohibited by any act of the legislature of Tennessee? Impossible? The constitution of Tennessee, as I understand, was copied from the one that Jefferson wrote, so clear, simple, direct, to encourage the freedom of religious opinion, said in substance, that no act shall ever be passed to interfere with complete religious liberty. Now is this it or is not this it? What do you say? What does it do? . . . Can a legislative body say, "You cannot read a book or take a lesson, or make a talk on science until you first find out whether you are saying against Genesis." It can unless that constitutional provision protects me. It can. Can it say to the astronomer, you cannot turn your telescope upon the infinite planets and suns and stars that fill space, lest you find that the earth is not the center of the universe and there is not any firmament between us and the heaven. Can it? It could—except for the work of Thomas Jefferson, which has been woven into every state constitution of the Union, and has stayed there like the flaming sword to protect the rights of man against ignorance and bigotry, and when it is permitted to overwhelm them, then we are taken in a sea of blood and ruin that all the miseries and tortures and carrion of the middle ages would be as nothing. They would need to call back these men once more. But are the provisions of the constitutions that they left, are they enough to protect you and me, and everyone else in a land which we thought was free? Now, let us see what it says: "All men have a natural and indefeasible right to worship Almighty God according to the dictates of their own conscience."

That takes care, even of the despised modernist, who dares to be intelligent. "That no man can of right be compelled to attend, erect or support any place of worship, or to maintain any minister against his consent; that no human authority can in any case whatever control or interfere with the rights of conscience in any case whatever"—that does not mean whatever, that means, "barring fundamentalist propaganda." It does not mean whatever at all times, sometimes maybe—and that "no preference shall be given by law to any religious establishment or mode of worship." . . .

And along comes somebody who says we have got to believe it as I believe it. It is a crime to know more than I know. And they publish a law to inhibit learning. Now, what is in the way of it? First, what does the law say? This law says that it shall be a criminal offense to teach in the public schools any account of the origin of man that is in conflict with the divine account in the Bible. It makes the Bible the yard stick to measure every man's intellect, to measure every man's intelligence and to measure every man's learning. Are your mathematics good? Turn to I Elijah ii, is your philosophy good? See II Samuel iii, is your astronomy good? See Genesis, Chapter 2, Verse 7, is your chemistry good? See—well, chemistry, see Deuteronomy iii-6, or anything that tells about brimstone. Every bit of knowledge that the mind has, must be submitted to a religious test. Now, let us see, it is a travesty upon language, it is a travesty upon justice, it is a travesty upon the constitution to say that any citizen of Tennessee can be deprived of his rights by a legislative body in the face of the constitution. . . .

If today you can take a thing like evolution and make it a crime to teach it in the public school, tomorrow you can make it a crime to teach it in the private schools, and the next year you can make it a crime to teach it to the hustings or in the church. At the next session you may ban books and the newspapers. Soon you may set Catholic against Protestant and Protestant against Protestant, and try to foist your own religion upon the minds of men. If you can do one you can do the other. Ignorance and fanaticism is ever busy and needs feeding. Always it is feeding and gloating for more. Today it is the public school teachers, tomorrow the private. The next day the preachers and the lecturers, the magazines, the books, the newspapers. After while, Your Honor, it is the setting of man against man and creed against creed until with flying banners and beating drums we are marching backward to the glorious ages of the sixteenth century when bigots lighted fagots to burn the men who dared to bring any intelligence and enlightment and culture to the human mind.

Warren G. Harding (1865-1923)

*Twenty-ninth President of the United States, he
was a genial, handsome, densely ignorant man
whose life seemed to be directed by expediency
rather than conviction. As William Allen
White observed, "At best he was a dub who had
made his reputation running with the [Republi-
can] political machine in Ohio, making Memorial Day addresses for the Elks, addressing
service clubs—the Rotarians, Kiwanians, or
the Lions—uttering resounding platitudes, and
saying nothing because he knew nothing."
The major achievement of his administration,
the Washington Naval Conference for naval
limitation, was largely forgotten in the
scandalous exposures after his death of corruption in the major departments of government,
which stamped his administration as both corrupt and incompetent.*

BACK TO NORMALCY

My Countrymen: When one surveys the world about him
after the great storm, noting the marks of destruction
and yet rejoicing in the ruggedness of the things which
withstood it, if he is an American he breathes the clarified
atmosphere with a strange mingling of regret and new
hope. We have seen a world passion spend its fury, but
we contemplate our Republic unshaken, and hold our civilization secure. Liberty—liberty within the law—and civilization are inseparable, and though both were threatened we
find them now secure; and there comes to Americans the

From Inaugural Address of President Warren G. Harding, *Congressional Record*, 67th Cong., Spec. sess., Mar. 4, 1921, LXI, pt. 1, 4–6.

profound assurance that our representative government is the highest expression and surest guaranty of both. . . .

The recorded progress of our Republic, materially and spiritually, in itself proves the wisdom of the inherited policy of noninvolvement in Old World affairs. Confident of our ability to work out our own destiny, and jealously guarding our right to do so, we seek no part in directing the destinies of the Old World. We do not mean to be entangled. We will accept no responsibility except as our own conscience and judgment, in each instance, may determine.

Our eyes never will be blind to a developing menace, our ears never deaf to the call of civilization. We recognize the new order in the world, with the closer contacts which progress has wrought. We sense the call of the human heart for fellowship, fraternity, and cooperation. We crave friendship and harbor no hate. But America, our America, the America builded on the foundation laid by the inspired fathers, can be a party to no permanent military alliance. It can enter into no political commitments, nor assume any economic obligations which will subject our decisions to any other than our own authority. . . .

Since freedom impelled, and independence inspired, and nationality exalted, a world supergovernment is contrary to everything we cherish and can have no sanction by our Republic. This is not selfishness; it is sanctity. It is not aloofness; it is security. It is not suspicion of others; it is patriotic adherence to the things which made us what we are. . . .

Our supreme task is the resumption of our onward, normal way. Reconstruction, readjustment, restoration—all these must follow. I would like to hasten them. . . .

We contemplate the immediate task of putting our public household in order. We need a rigid and yet sane economy, combined with fiscal justice, and it must be attended by individual prudence and thrift, which are so essential to this trying hour and reassuring for the future.

The business world reflects the disturbance of war's re-action. Herein flows the lifeblood of material existence. The economic mechanism is intricate and its parts interdependent, and has suffered the shocks and jars incident to abnormal demands, credit inflations, and price upheavals. The normal balances have been impaired, the channels of distribution have been clogged, the relations of labor and management have been strained. We must seek the readjustment with care and courage. Our people must give and take. Prices must reflect the receding fever of war activities. Perhaps we never shall know the old levels of wage again, because war invariably readjusts compensations, and the necessaries of life will show their inseparable relationship, but we must strive for normalcy to reach stability. All the penalties will not be light nor evenly distributed. There is no way of making them so. There is no instant step from disorder to order. We must face a condition of grim reality, charge off our losses, and start afresh. It is the oldest lesson of civilization. I would like Government to do all it can to mitigate; then, in understanding, in mutuality of interest, in concern for the common good, our tasks will be solved. No altered system will work a miracle. Any wild experiment will only add to the confusion. Our best assurance lies in efficient administration of our proven system.

The forward course of the business cycle is unmistakable. Peoples are turning from destruction to production. Industry has sensed the changed order and our own people are turning to resume their normal, onward way. The call is for productive America to go on. I know that Congress and the administration will favor every wise Government policy to aid the resumption and encourage continued progress.

I speak for administrative efficiency, for lightened tax burdens, for sound commercial practices, for adequate credit facilities, for sympathetic concern for all agricultural problems, for the omission of unnecessary interference of Government with business, for an end to Government's experiment in business, and for more efficient business in government administration. With all of this must attend a mindfulness of the human side of all activities, so that social, industrial, and economic justice will be squared with the purposes of a righteous people. . . .

If revolution insists upon overturning established order, let other peoples make the tragic experiment. There is no place for it in America. When world war threatened civilization we pledged our resources and our lives to its preservation, and when revolution threatens we unfurl the flag of law and order and renew our consecration. Ours is a constitutional freedom where the popular will is the law supreme and minorities are sacredly protected. Our revisions, reformations, and evolutions reflect a deliberate judgment and an orderly progress, and we mean to cure our ills, but never destroy or permit destruction by force. . . .

We would not have an America living within and for herself alone, but we would have her self-reliant, independent, and ever nobler, stronger, and richer. Believing in our higher standards, reared through constitutional liberty and maintained opportunity, we invite the world to the same heights. But pride in things wrought is no reflex of a completed task. Common welfare is the goal of our national endeavor. Wealth is not inimical to welfare; it ought to be its friendliest agency. There never can be equality of rewards or possessions so long as the human plan contains varied talents and differing degrees of industry and thrift, but ours ought to be a country free from great blotches of distressed poverty. We ought to find a way to guard against the perils and penalties of unemployment. We want an America of homes, illumined with hope and happiness, where mothers, freed from the necessity for long hours of toil beyond their own doors, may preside as befits the hearthstone of American citizenship. We want the cradle of American childhood rocked under conditions so wholesome and so hopeful that no blight may touch it in its development, and we want to provide that no selfish interest, no material necessity, no lack of opportunity, shall prevent the gaining of that education so essential to best citizenship.

There is no short cut to the making of these ideals into glad realities. The world has witnessed, again and again, the futility and the mischief of ill-considered remedies for social and economic disorders. But we are mindful today, as never before, of the friction of modern industrialism, and we must learn its causes and reduce its evil consequences by sober and tested methods. Where genius has made for great possibilities, justice and happiness must be reflected in a greater common welfare.

Eugene V. Debs (1855-1926)

A perennial rebel and martyr, he began his career as a locomotive fireman and, in 1893, was made president of the American Railway Union. After the union was broken in the Pullman Strike of 1894, he was convicted and imprisoned on a juridical sophism. When released, he helped organize the Socialist party and was five times its candidate for President. As Ray Ginger has pointed out, he never doubted his moral responsibility for the welfare of his brothers and was convinced the common people were being crucified by an outmoded economic system. Though an advocate of class-conscious industrial unionism and a founder of the International Workers of the World, he broke with the revolutionary union when it resorted to force and violence. A sincere, perhaps naïve reformer, he always spoke his mind, regardless of consequences. Because in 1918 he had frankly told Americans: "Quit going to war. Stop murdering one another for the profit and glory of the

ruling classes. Cultivate the arts of peace.
Humanize humanity. Civilize civilization," he
was sent to jail for obstructing the conscription
act.

A LAST CALL
FOR REVOLUTION

In the national campaign of 1920 the Socialist Party calls upon all American workers of hand and brain, and upon all citizens who believe in political liberty and social justice, to free the country from the oppressive misrule of the old political parties, and to take the government into their own hands under the banner and upon the program of the Socialist Party.

The outgoing administration, like Democratic and Republican administrations of the past, leaves behind it a disgraceful record of solemn pledges unscrupulously broken and public confidence ruthlessly betrayed.

It obtained the suffrage of the people on a platform of peace, liberalism and social betterment, but drew the country into a devastating war, and inaugurated a régime of despotism, reaction and oppression unsurpassed in the annals of the republic.

It promised to the American people a treaty which would assure to the world a reign of international right and true democracy. It gave its sanction and support to an infamous pact formulated behind closed doors by predatory elder statesmen of European and Asiatic imperialism. Under this pact territories have been annexed against the will of their populations and cut off from their sources of sustenance; nations seeking their freedom in the exercise of much heralded right of self-determination have been

From the Socialist Party Platform of 1920 in Kirk H. Porter and Donald B. Johnson, eds. *National Party Platforms* (Urbana: University of Illinois Press, 1961), pp. 238–41. Reprinted by permission of the publisher.

brutally fought with armed force, intrigue and starvation blockades.

To the millions of young men, who staked their lives on the field of battle, to the people of the country who gave unstintingly of their toil and property to support the war, the Democratic administration held out the sublime ideal of a union of the peoples of the world organized to maintain perpetual peace among nations on the basis of justice and freedom. It helped create a reactionary alliance of imperialistic governments, banded together to bully weak nations, crush working-class governments and perpetuate strife and warfare.

While thus furthering the ends of reaction, violence and oppression abroad, our administration suppressed the cherished and fundamental rights and civil liberties at home.

Upon the pretext of war-time necessity, the Chief Executive of the republic and the appointed heads of his administration were clothed with dictatorial powers (which were often exercised arbitrarily), and Congress enacted laws in open and direct violation of the constitutional safeguards of freedom of expression.

Hundreds of citizens who raised their voices for the maintenance of political and industrial rights during the war were indicted under the Espionage Law, tried in an atmosphere of prejudice and hysteria and are now serving inhumanly long jail sentences for daring to uphold the traditions of liberty which once were sacred in this country.

Agents of the Federal government unlawfully raided homes and meeting places and prevented or broke up peaceable gatherings of citizens.

The postmaster-general established a censorship of the press more autocratic than that ever tolerated in a régime of absolutism, and has harassed and destroyed publications on account of their advanced political and economic views, by excluding them from the mails.

And after the war was in fact long over, the administration has not scrupled to continue a policy of repression and terrorism under the shadow and hypocritical guise of war-time measures.

It has practically imposed involuntary servitude and peonage on a large class of American workers by denying them the right to quit work and coercing them into acceptance of inadequate wages and onerous conditions of labor. It has dealt a foul blow to the traditional American right of asylum by deporting hundreds of foreign-born workers by administrative order, on the mere suspicion of harboring radical views, and often for the sinister purpose of breaking labor strikes.

In the short span of three years our self-styled liberal administration has succeeded in undermining the very foundation of political liberty and economic rights which this republic has built up in more than a century of struggle and progress.

Under the cloak of a false and hypocritical patriotism and under the protection of governmental terror the Democratic administration has given the ruling classes unrestrained license to plunder the people by intensive exploitation of labor, by the extortion of enormous profits and by increasing the cost of all necessities of life. Profiteering has become reckless and rampant, billions have been coined by the capitalists out of the suffering and misery of their fellow men. The American financial oligarchy has become a dominant factor in the world, while the condition of the American workers has grown more precarious.

The responsibility does not rest upon the Democratic party alone. The Republican party, through its representatives in Congress and otherwise, has not only openly condoned the political misdeeds of the last three years, but has sought to outdo its Democratic rival in the orgy of political reaction and repression. Its criticism of the Democratic administrative policy is that it is not reactionary and drastic enough.

America is now at the parting of the roads. If the outraging of political liberty and concentration of economic power into the hands of the few is permitted to go on, it can have only one consequence, the reduction of the country to a state of absolute capitalist despotism.

We particularly denounce the militaristic policy of both old parties, of investing countless hundreds of millions of dollars in armaments after the victorious completion of what was to have been the "last war." We call attention to the fatal results of such a program in Europe, carried on prior to 1914, and culminating in the Great War; we declare that such a policy, adding unbearable burdens to the working class and to all the people, can lead only to the complete Prussianization of the nation, and ultimately to war; and we demand immediate and complete abandonment of this fatal program.

The Socialist Party sounds the warning. It calls upon the people to defeat both parties at the polls, and to elect the candidates of the Socialist Party to the end of restoring political democracy and bringing about complete industrial freedom. . . .

To achieve this end the Socialist Party pledges itself to the following program:

1. Social

1. All business vitally essential for the existence and welfare of the people, such as railroads, express service, steamship lines, telegraphs, mines, oil wells, power plants, elevators, packing houses, cold storage plants and all industries operating on a national scale, should be taken over by the nation.

2. All publicly owned industries should be administered jointly by the government and representatives of the workers, not for revenue or profit, but with the sole object of securing just compensation and humane conditions of employment to the workers and efficient and reasonable service to the public.

3. All banks should be acquired by the government, and incorporated in a unified public banking system.

4. The business of insurance should be taken over by the government, and should be extended to include insurance against accident, sickness, invalidity, old age and unemployment, without contribution on the part of the worker.

5. Congress should enforce the provisions of the Thirteenth, Fourteenth and Fifteenth Amendments with reference to the Negroes, and effective federal legislation should be enacted to secure to the Negroes full civil, political, industrial and educational rights.

2. *Industrial*

1. Congress should enact effective laws to abolish child labor, to fix minimum wages, based on an ascertained cost of a decent standard of life, to protect migratory and unemployed workers from oppression, to abolish detective and strike-breaking agencies and to establish a shorter work-day in keeping with increased industrial productivity.

3. *Political*

1. The constitutional freedom of speech, press and assembly should be restored by repealing the Espionage Law and all other repressive legislation, and by prohibiting the executive usurpation of authority.

2. All prosecutions under the Espionage Law should be discontinued, and all persons serving prison sentences for alleged offenses growing out of religious beliefs, political views or industrial activities should be fully pardoned and immediately released.

3. No alien should be deported from the United States on account of his political views or participation in labor struggles, nor in any event without proper trial on specific charges. The arbitrary power to deport aliens by administrative order should be repealed.

4. The power of the courts to restrain workers in their struggles against employers by the Writ of Injunction or otherwise, and their power to nullify congressional legislation, should be abrogated.

5. Federal judges should be elected by the people and be subject to recall.

6. The President and the Vice-President of the United States should be elected by direct popular election, and be subject to recall. All members of the Cabinet should be elected by Congress and be responsible at all times to the vote thereof.

7. Suffrage should be equal and unrestricted in fact as well as in law for all men and women throughout the nation.

8. Because of the strict residential qualification of suffrage in this country, millions of citizens are disfranchised in every election; adequate provision should be made for the registration and voting of migratory workers.

9. The Constitution of the United States should be amended to strengthen the safeguards of civil and political liberty, and to remove all obstacles to industrial and social reform and reconstruction, including the changes enumerated in this program, in keeping with the will and interest of the people. It should be made amendable by a majority of the voters of the nation upon their own initiative, or upon the initiative of Congress.

Dollar Democracy

I

The American people had traveled along the road to normalcy slightly more than two years when, in 1923, President Harding unexpectedly died and was succeeded by Vice President Calvin Coolidge. Considered "a pre-eminently safe man," Coolidge had certified his orthodoxy by his candid veneration of the dollar and proved his patriotism by publishing an anti-radical tract entitled "Are the 'Reds' Stalking Our College Women?" He had been catapulted into the headlines by his resolutely unsympathetic attitude toward the Boston police strike of 1919, when as Governor of Massachusetts he dispatched a telegram to Samuel Gompers, head of the American Federation of Labor, refusing arbitration and maintaining, "There is no right to strike against the public safety by anybody, anywhere, anytime." The country's newspapers applauded, and overnight Coolidge became a national hero. On the strength of this opportune slogan Coolidge was started on his way to the White House.[1]

Unlike the jovial Harding, who had wallowed in "equivocal verbosity," Coolidge was publicly taciturn and sourly Puritanical, but like his predecessor Coolidge displayed an almost mystical devotion to the status quo. Change, he firmly believed, resulted in more harm than good. "Four-

fifths of all our troubles in this life would disappear," he
once remarked, "if we would only sit down and keep
still." With Coolidge, commented Lippmann, inactivity
was a political philosophy and a party program. Not merely a soft and easy desire to let things slide, it was "a grim,
determined, alert inactivity" which kept the President occupied constantly at the task of neutralizing and thwarting
political activity wherever it showed signs of life. This
policy of "active inactivity" suited the mood and certain
needs of the country admirably. Everybody who was making money wanted to let well enough alone. Prosperous
America, it was said, "wanted above everything the status
quo," and "was worshiping on padded knee the God of
things as they were."[2]

But while a national policy of political inactivity suited
the business interests, it did not suit organized labor, which
was kept at a disadvantage under the status quo. Partly
as a result of the Red Scare, labor had been driven into a
hopeless position in the twenties. Not only had the labor
movement been badly mauled in 1919–1920, losing more
than a million members in two years, but lingering public
suspicion of labor radicalism after the bitterly controversial
Steel Strike of 1919 was used by employer groups to frus-
trate unionism. Though Scare-inspired prejudice against
aliens had led to restrictive immigration laws in 1924, any
potential benefits as far as labor was concerned were wasted
in a hostile social climate which stressed individualism and
had no use for collective action.

By launching a nationwide propaganda drive identifying
organized labor's insistence upon the closed shop as "un-
American," employer organizations—notably the National
Association of Manufacturers with assistance from the Bankers Association and the United States Chamber of Commerce—were able to severely cripple labor unionism. In
a flood of anti-labor literature distributed to the press,
churches, banks, schools, colleges, businesses, and to local
chambers of commerce, unionism and un-Americanism were

made to appear synonymous, while at the same time business was apotheosized as the champion of the open shop or the "American Plan," as it was now popularly labeled, which was skillfully presented as the major bulwark against the "Soviet methods" and the "subversive foreign concept" of unionism.[3]

Though the public was led to believe that anything less than the open shop was "un-American" and "un-patriotic," the real issue was not radicalism, but the much more basic question of union versus no union. Allegedly the open shop was one "with equal opportunity for all and special privileges for none," where non-union and union men received the same treatment, but actually in most cases so-called "open" shops were normally non-union shops. Anti-union employers were not only relieved of the obligation to hire only union members, but, more important from management's point of view, they were in the very advantageous position of being able to bargain on an individual rather than a collective basis. Behind the "patriotic" propaganda of the open shop was the employer's knowledge that without the closed or union shop it was impossible for labor to organize American industry. As open-shop sentiment gained wide support among the public and the press, business leaders pressed their advantage:[4] E. H. Gary, chairman of United States Steel, was reported in the *New York Times* as saying he saw no necessity for labor unions at present; and Charles N. Fay, prominent utilities executive and former vice-president of the N.A.M., told businessmen the time was now ripe for strict government control of labor.°

If America in the twenties was an employer's paradise, a major reason was the hostile attitude of the courts and the law toward labor. From the viewpoint of the law organized labor, unlike organized business, was not accepted as a legitimate institution of American society. Though in

°Charles N. Fay, *No Right to Strike.* See page 122.

theory the law treated both sides equally, in reality the law and the existing economic situation favored the employer: "The law recognized the equal freedom of the employers to destroy labor organizations and to deny the right of employees to join trade unions. An employer could coerce or threaten his employees to keep them from organizing. He could discharge them if they joined a union, and he could refuse to hire anyone who was a member. He could decline to deal with any union of his employees or to recognize the organization or any of its officers or agents as representatives of the employees. He was free to organize a company union of his own and force his employees to join it." Labor's actions, on the other hand, were severely limited. For instance, labor's chief weapon, the strike, was illegal if the court did not approve its purpose—and usually the courts did not approve of strikes for union recognition or for the closed shop. Equally crippling were the restrictions fixed by the courts upon the conduct of strikers: threats, coercion, intimidation (including psychic intimidation) were unlawful but so were boycotts and most picketing. Chief Justice Taft declared even peaceful picketing illegal on grounds that the word "picket" was "sinister" and suggested "a militant purpose."[5]

Beyond doubt, the two most powerful weapons used by the courts were the injunction and the Sherman Act. Usually invoked under the anti-trust provisions of the Sherman Act (which originally had been intended to apply only to the monopolistic practices of big business), the injunction commonly prohibited the employment of force, coercion, and intimidation; prevented or regulated picketing; barred boycotts, trespass, use of the epithet "scab," and payment of strike benefits. Sometimes the court order went so far as to forbid workers to strike or the union to hold meetings. The height of absurdity was reached in Iowa in 1930 when an injunction, in effect, prohibited a striker from telling his wife there was a controversy over wages and put him into contempt of court if he did so. Even though the Clayton

Act passed in 1914 during the first Wilson administration—and rashly hailed as labor's Magna Carta—had specifically forbidden application of anti-trust laws to labor organizations and prohibited use of injunctions in labor disputes, the courts by various legal evasions nevertheless issued more injunctions and applied the anti-trust laws against labor in more cases in the 1920's than in any similar period of American history. In short, under these adverse circumstances, all that American laborers had was a right to try to organize if they could get away with it; and whether they could or not depended in last measure upon the courts.[6]

Without public confidence and unable to gain any sympathy from either government or the courts, the position of organized labor steadily deteriorated in the twenties. Magazines and newspapers were full of articles and editorials with such titles as "The Collapse of Organized Labor," "Decline of Organized Labor in America," and "The Twilight of the A. F. of L." By 1930 union membership amounted to barely 10 percent of the labor force, about half that of 1920, and great segments of American industry were completely unorganized, including such important industries as steel, automobiles, rubber, textiles, and electrical equipment. With real wages and salaries rising 20.6 percent between 1923 and 1929, there was little incentive to organize among skilled workers, and under mounting pressure from business and the press the attitude of organized labor shifted from militancy to respectability. Labor leadership pursued a gentle policy of "concord rather than conflict" so successfully that thousands of abandoned American workers would have readily agreed with Mencken that the A. F. of L. was not a labor organization at all but "simply a balloon mattress interposed between capital and labor to protect the former from the latter."[7]

The most graphic portrayal of the plight of unionism in the twenties was the fate of the United Mine Workers. In 1920 the union was the largest and most powerful in

America; at the end of the decade, it lay in ruins. The initial cause of its extraordinary decline was a falling market brought about by an overproduction of coal. As coal prices plunged downward, mine operators sought to cut the wages of miners, two-thirds of whom according to the U.S. Coal Commission were already earning less than a living wage. The union under John L. Lewis balked, vowing "No Backward Step!" In insisting on the maintenance of an American wage standard in the coal fields, Lewis argued, the UMW was only acting according to the theory of the free-enterprise system—"that the ultimate prosperity of all is best assured by the utmost endeavor of each to better his own condition."*

Certainly living conditions of the miners were far below the American standard. After visiting 800 mining communities in 1923, of which 713 were company-owned, representatives of the U.S. Coal Commission found housing generally poor: "In the worst of the company-controlled communities the state of disrepair at times runs beyond the power of verbal description or even of photographic illustration, since neither words nor pictures can portray the atmosphere of abandoned dejection or reproduce the smells. Old, unpainted board and batten houses—batten going or gone, and boards fast following, roofs broken, porches staggering, steps sagging, a riot of rubbish, and a medley of odors— such are features of the worst camps." In company-owned dwellings less than three percent had bathtubs or toilets, fewer than fourteen percent running water. But far worse than living in squalor and filth, the miner living in a company town usually forfeited his right to citizenship, lost the rights of free speech and free assemblage, and if he complained of any grievance, he was liable to be summarily dismissed and blacklisted, and his family turned out into the street.[8]

When Lewis refused to agree to a wage reduction, the

---

*John L. Lewis, *The Miners' Fight for American Standards*. See page 127.

operators set about the systematic destruction of the union. Although John D. Rockefeller, Jr., publicly denounced the labor policy of the operators as "both unwise and unjust," his was a lone voice among mine owners. Like the Railroad Labor Board, most of them were inclined to regard the theory of "the living wage" as "a bit of mellifluous phraseology" and no doubt felt that its application would bring the nation's industry to "communistic ruin." The offensive was taken by the Pittsburgh Coal Company, the largest producer in the country, which had recently passed into the hands of the Mellon banking interests (Treasury Secretary Andrew Mellon and his brother owned 25 percent of the stock). After having had a contract with the miners for thirty-five years, the company closed down in 1924 and then a year later, in violation of its agreement, reopened on a non-union basis. When the UMW struck to enforce the contract, Pittsburgh Coal evicted the miners and their families from company houses and brought in Negro and white strikebreakers, employing armed guards for their protection—many of whom were thoughtfully provided by the Governor of Pennsylvania. War broke out in the coal fields, and how many lives were lost from starvation and violence will never be known. But, as a reporter from the New York *Daily News* discovered, conditions were almost beyond belief:

I have just returned from a visit to "Hell-in-Pennsylvania." I have seen horrible things there; things which I almost hesitate to enumerate and describe. I can scarcely expect my story to be believed. I did not believe it myself when the situation was first outlined to me. Then I went into the coal camps of western and central Pennsylvania and saw for myself.

. . . Many times it seemed impossible to think that we were in modern, civilized America.

We saw thousands of women and children, literally starving to death. We found hundreds of destitute families living in crudely constructed bare-board shacks. They had been evicted from their homes by the coal companies. We unearthed a system of despotic tyranny reminiscent of Czar-ridden Siberia at its worst. We found police brutality and industrial slavery. We discovered the weirdest flock of injunctions that ever emanated from American temples of justice.

We unearthed evidence of terrorism and counterterrorism; of mob beatings and near lynchings; of dishonesty, graft, and heartlessness. . . .

The mine fields are a bubbling cauldron of trouble. If it boils over—and it threatens to do so—blood must flow freely and many lives pay the forfeit.

When the United Mine Workers tried to organize West Virginia in 1924, they ran into determined resistance from mine operators. Union miners attempting to march into non-union areas were met by a force of 2,000 men, including state troopers with machine-guns and tanks.

United Press International, Inc.

As Irving Bernstein has noted, the combination of armed power and starvation virtually destroyed the union. By 1928 the UMW bargained for only twenty percent of the nation's bituminous miners, and wages had dropped from $7.50 to as little as $1.50 a day.[9]

II

The miners were not the only group outside the orbit of the business boom. Nearly eleven million Americans engaged in farming were left behind when the Harding-Coolidge prosperity bandwagon started rolling. Like labor, the farmers as a class had prospered during the war; like labor, they had suffered badly in the postwar depression. But while the skilled laborer made a recovery—real wages rose and employment in manufacturing industries declined only slightly—for most of the decade the farmer knew only distress. Between 1920 and 1932, total farm income dropped 66⅔ percent. Although President Coolidge piously maintained that the government was devoted to the promotion of "business" in the all-inclusive sense of employer and employee, industry and agriculture, facts proved otherwise.* As farm leaders complained, the interests of the farmers were either ignored or evaded by those responsible for the direction of national policies. While endorsing positive aid to business and industry, President Coolidge opposed bills intended to help distressed farmers, taking the position that the farmer should not depend upon governmental price-fixing (as industry did upon the protective tariff) but that simple and direct methods put into operation by the farmer himself were the only real sources of restoration. Such obvious discrimination by government produced a political insurrection.[10]

Charging as had William Jennings Bryan in 1896 that the definition of the businessman had been made too limited,

---

*Calvin Coolidge, *Government and Business*. See page 133.

Senator Robert M. La Follette of Wisconsin emerged in 1924 as the national champion of the forgotten farmer and the downtrodden laborer. In the complacent twenties Senator La Follette was still a fighting liberal, and as presidential candidate of the Progressive party, he demanded in a platform which he himself wrote a drastic redistribution of economic power and opportunity.° His program, the *New Republic* reported, was "a frank demand for a better recognition of the economic interests of two large classes which are considered to have been the victims of economic discrimination from the government as conducted both by the Democratic and Republican parties—the farmers and wage-earners." Like the Populists of an earlier day, La Follette found the existing economy was too largely a one-class economy and the existing state too largely a one-class state, and so he declared "the one paramount issue of the 1924 campaign" was to "break the combined power of the private monopoly system over the political and economic life of the American people."[11]

Though the cry of "monopoly" had an old familiar ring, this was a different brand of Progressivism. Where the Progressivism of twelve years before had been a spontaneous, idealistic program of political action based upon the assumption that the American commonwealth was a complete and essentially classless democracy, the Progressivism of 1924, by contrast, was "a calculated, determined experiment in group resistance to the economic and social classes in control of political authority." Rather than mere political revivalism, it was a kind of economic *macht-politik*, a frank acceptance of power politics. The machinery of the federal government had been used for the benefit of industry, finance, and commerce, and it was only just— the new Progressives argued—that it be used for labor and agriculture. When their argument was hypocritically denounced as "un-American" and "a vicious European prac-

°Robert M. La Follette, *Government and the People.* See page 139.

tice," especially by those who had been in the habit of receiving such legislative favors, La Follette countered by pointing out that similar invasions of economic law were committed daily by other private groups: "We have built up in this country an artificial business structure which throttles the natural law of supply and demand. The price of steel is fixed by private interests. The price of cloth is fixed by private interests. In virtually every line of manufactured commodities a few interests fix the prices. The conservatives, so-called, have nothing to say about that. They support it. But when it is proposed that the government fix prices to save from destruction the great agricultural industry, upon which the country is absolutely dependent, these conservatives throw up their hands in terror."

These Progressive demands of the mid-twenties marked the recasting of the old Wilsonian formulas and the creation of new ones patterned after the Populist program of the nineties. Instead of putting their faith in trust-busting with the hope that this would either preserve or restore a healthy state of competition, the farmers "tossed such thoughts out of the window" and called for restrictive devices patterned after those which had proved so beneficial to big business—tariff, restricted production, price control, cooperative marketing. If big business by its own efforts and those of government could be insured against the hazards of competition, then conceivably agriculture and labor, both perilously exposed to the risks of the market, could also be protected. The farm Progressives, like their Populist forebears, openly identified the state as the primary economic force in American society, clearly perceiving it to be the arbiter of advantage or the instrument of exploitation.[12]

While prospects for third parties in the United States have never been very promising, in 1924 there were at least some grounds for hope. The Harding ideal of normalcy—that government existed primarily to bring prosperity to business—had been notoriously successful. When elected,

Harding had promised to take the government out of business, but what he really meant, said the *Nation*, was that he would "put the government *into* business; that it would become the ally and partner of the get-rich-quick men, the speculators, and the promoters." In its short life of two years and five months, the Harding administration was responsible "for more concentrated robbery and rascality than any other in the whole history of the Federal Government." Early in 1924 Congressional committees brought to light scandals in the departments of Justice, Navy, and the Interior, in the Veterans Bureau, and in the Office of the Alien Property Custodian. The major scandal involved the secret leasing of naval oil reserve lands to private interests led by Harry F. Sinclair and Edward L. Doheny. Senate investigation disclosed that Secretary of the Interior Albert B. Fall had received a $25,000 "loan" from Sinclair and $100,000 from Doheny. Though Fall, the politician, was convicted of bribery, sentenced to one year in prison, and fined $100,000, the two businessmen were acquitted, which would seem to confirm the old Biblical adage that it is "more blessed to give than to receive."[13]

Adopting a policy of silence concerning the scandals, President Coolidge and the Republican party couched their election appeal in terms of prosperity, tax reduction, and freedom of business enterprise. The issue in 1924, Coolidge declared, was "whether America will allow itself to be degraded into a communistic or socialistic state or whether it will remain American." But, from his point of view, Providence had already decreed the outcome. American institutions compelled the loyalty and support of the people because they were founded on righteousness and because they were profitable. "You believe in [America]," the President told his countrymen, because "it is right" and because "it has paid." Under the slogan "Coolidge or Chaos" the Republicans scared millions of timid, ignorant, and uneasy voters into agreeing with them. The business-oriented press branded La Follette "an enemy to the country" be-

GONE DRY

—Sykes in the Philadelphia *Evening Public Ledger.*

Sykes in the Philadelphia *Evening Public Ledger,*
from *Literary Digest,* November 15, 1924, p. 10

In the presidential election of 1924, Senator Robert M. La Follette ran as the champion of the forgotten farmer and down-trodden worker, but despite lurid scandals and opposition from organized labor, the meretricious combination of Coolidge and prosperity proved invincible.

cause of his opposition to American participation in the war, successfully misrepresented his program as "half-baked" Communism, and slurringly insinuated that Soviet Russia was financing his campaign. In spite of the wholesale scandals under the Republican regime and though the A. F. of L. timidly endorsed the Progressives, the meretricious combination of Coolidge and prosperity proved invincible. La Follette lost to the business candidate by more than ten million votes.[14]

III

No doubt Republican smears cost La Follette many votes, but millions of Americans preferred to play safe with Coolidge because they were politically indifferent. They did not look to the Progressives for relief from poverty and economic servitude because, remarked Lippmann, most of them were finding it by themselves. With prosperity still fairly widely diffused, there was no pressing reason for an alignment of "haves" and "have nots." The system was not yet bankrupt—even though its liabilities already threatened to exceed its assets. It was still a going concern, enormously serviceable and with many valuable unexhausted reserves.[15]

Although the Chamber of Commerce advertised the ideal of "Service" and the National Association of Manufacturers made much of the "spirit of human brotherhood" in industry, the business politics of the twenties placed stubborn limitations on social and economic progress. In Mr. Coolidge's utopia, the rich businessman was not so much an oppressor of the poor as an instrument of divine Providence. As the President explained it, "More and more men are seeking to live in obedience to the law of service under which those of larger possessions confer larger benefits upon their fellow men. The greater their power the greater their service."[16] Under this conception there was to be, on the part of government, the least possible interference with private affairs. Self-reliance and private initiative could be safely stimulated because the social system carried within itself the remedy for its own disorders. These hoary concepts of laissez-faire capitalism were redefined in the twenties by Julius H. Barnes, president of the U.S. Chamber of Commerce, as the "Philosophy of Fair Play."*

As promulgated, the ideal of fair play assumed that all members of society were playing the same game under the same rules with government acting as an impartial umpire; in play, however, the game was usually "fixed." Team play between government and business to bridge the obstacles of trade was allowed, but for non-business classes to seek favors from government was to break the rules of the game. The equivocal nature of the business commitment to "fair play" was clearly revealed in a statement of principles adopted by the Chamber of Commerce in 1921. Although the first article of faith affirmed that "individual initiative, . . . stimulated by active and free competition,

*Julius H. Barnes, *The Philosophy of Fair Play*. See page 146.

is the guarantee of sound national progress," the tenth confirmed with equal conviction that a "proper function of government is to render service to business where such service cannot adequately be provided by individual initiative." The way it worked out, the faithful public stood complacently by while their business rulers self-righteously availed themselves of the services of government. Under the prevailing interpretation of the rules of the game, the Harding and Coolidge administrations raised the tariff rates thirty-two times for favored industries, and in line with the Mellon plan of shifting taxes from the rich to the poor, the government repealed the excess-profits tax, cut inheritance taxes, and reduced the maximum income tax on big taxpayers from 65 to 20 percent.[17]

The outcome, after nearly ten years of such "fair play," was an economy in which the share of the income of the top 10 percent had been increasing until it reached nearly 48 percent of the national total by 1929, while that of the lowest 10 percent had been steadily falling. That same upper 10 percent had amassed 86 percent of the total savings as compared to the 2 percent put aside by 80 percent of the nation. In the golden year of prosperity 1929, the Brookings Institution disclosed that only 2.3 percent of American families had annual incomes of over $10,000, 71 percent less than $2500, and 60 percent less than $2000. At 1929 prices, economists estimated that $2000 a year was sufficient to supply only basic necessities—any income below that represented poverty. Hence, in 1929, approximately 60 percent of American families were estimated to be living in or on the edge of poverty.[18]

Although heralded as a New Era in business, the twenties revealed that American business in general was not yet aware of its social responsibilities. There was never a lack of sporadic examples of business benevolence—cafeterias, swimming pools, glee clubs, baseball teams, group-insurance plans, and even profit-sharing schemes for employees—but such programs were never widely realized, being usually confined to a few large corporations. Though, on the one hand, *Fortune* might exalt "the new capitalism" as "a social conception as radical as Stalinism in its ultimate purpose," on the other, the spectacle of U.S. Steel working its employees an average of 54.6 hours a week in 1929 and denying them an equitable share in prosperity (between 1923 and 1929 weekly earnings fell while profits almost doubled) belied serious recognition of the wage-earner as "a purchaser, a partner, and the key to production." While the new emphasis upon human relations in industry reflected, in part, a growing awareness of the relationship between the morale of the work force and its productive efficiency, its central purpose was, as always, the avoidance of trade unionism. Further, the highly publicized paternalism which surrounded such activities tended to obscure rather than to define the interest of the workers in the improvement of their own status. To a good many employers it was merely a shrewd method of flattering employees into believing they had something to do with the determination of industrial conditions without according them any real power. Yet it cannot be denied that where programs of welfare capitalism were seriously undertaken working conditions improved, employment was steadier, and workers developed a closer attachment to the employer. But, as *Fortune* emphasized, it was still paternalism, and paternalism "fails more often than it succeeds," because it refuses to come to grips with the main issue.[19]

The main issue, R. H. Tawney pointed out, was not merely that a large number of workers derived a meager and precarious livelihood from industries which yielded a small minority of persons considerable affluence, but that it involved "a position of privilege among the latter, and subordination among the former." "Kiss Me Clubs," the workers' derogatory term for company unions, and all the other trappings of benevolent autocracy were no substitute for industrial democracy. Wages, hours, the day-to-day problems of the worker, it was argued, involved "political" considerations—"self-determination, the consent of the governed, and a voice for the wage earner."[20]

While industry since the Industrial Revolution had been developing in the direction of autocracy, politics had been developing in the direction of democracy. Industrial democracy, therefore, was regarded as inevitable because political power had been given to the workers. Once given a consciousness of their power and a solidarity of purpose, the workers could get by political means most of these things they were now unable to obtain by industrial means. If business leaders did not adapt themselves, did not follow political democracy with industrial democracy—warned Edward A. Filene, a liberal businessman of Boston—then the workers would use their political power as a means of getting industrial democracy.*

---

* Edward A. Filene, *Business and Social Progress.* See page 150.

Readings:

Dollar Democracy

Charles Norman Fay (1848-1944)

A Phi Beta Kappa from Harvard, he achieved some prominence writing on public affairs from the elitist viewpoint of a former public utilities executive, a vice-president of the National Association of Manufacturers, and as a member of the Chamber of Commerce. His views were strongly anti-labor and anti-government, and his constant theme was that American businessmen should take over the direction of the country because the workers and voters did not have the ability to think for themselves.

NO RIGHT TO STRIKE

Our existing labor situation demands a change. There are, according to the census, some 42 million "gainfully employed" workers of both sexes, over 10 years of age, in the United States. About 24 million of them (viz., in agriculture, trade, the professions, civil and domestic service) are and

From *Business in Politics, Suggestions for Leaders in American Business* (Cambridge: Cosmos Press, Inc., 1926), pp. 34–5, 37, 39–42, 44–5.

probably will remain practically out of reach of labor organization. Of the 18 million in employments that *can* be "organized," about 3½ million actually are enrolled in some thousands of unions, mainly affiliated with one or other of the American Federation of Labor, the Railway Brotherhoods, the Amalgamated Clothing Workers and the I. W. W. That is, about one in every five of the organizable workers are actually organized—about one in twelve of all workers—and not far from one in twenty-four of the whole population (83 million) over 10 years of age. The locomotive engineers are said to head the list, 96 percent organized. The percentage in other skilled trades is not nearly so great, and averages apparently about 40 percent in most crafts.

Nevertheless, *by the simple device of nation-wide craft organization,* enough of the members of any single skilled craft (such as the Railway Workers or the United Mine Workers) can conspire to quit work simultaneously, seriously to cripple production or transportation, for instance, of coal, food, etc.; and in a very few days or weeks can freeze or starve many millions of helpless and unoffending people throughout the regions "struck."

In most crafts, however, the *majority* of workers are *unorganized;* and, if left free to take the jobs abandoned by the conspirators, and accept the wages refused by them, they sooner or later are very sure to do so—that is, when wages and conditions offered are those current in the neighborhood—and the strike fails.

It is, indeed, so essential to the success of a strike to prevent the free flow of free labor to the jobs vacated, that the whole policy and practice of trades unionism is built upon three main principles: (1) the solidarity of, and the monopoly of work by, union labor; (2) the denial of the right to work of nonunion men; and (3) the physical, social and political *coercion* of workers, employers and public outside of the unions, by absolute prevention of nonunion work.

The union man is taught to believe that the job he quits while on strike *nevertheless remains his job,* which no other worker has any right to take. He is taught to call the nonunion worker by the vile name of "scab"; and to consider it no crime to kill or maim the man who would take *his* place, or to dynamite the plant of the employer who would offer it to any one but himself, and on his own terms, or to terrorize all who would deal with that employer. "The right to *organize,*" and to *strike,* and thus to *coerce,* by stopping work, and preventing its performance by other hands, *"come what may in industry,"* is guaranteed, so runs the Gompers gospel, by the Constitution of the United States to every working man; while any limitation thereof, by the law or the courts, is "wage slavery," industrial serfdom! But that gospel is false! . . .

Now, Mr. Gompers and his lieutenants in the American "labor movement" have strenuously stretched this right, as recognized by the courts—of a group of employees to quit *their particular employer collectively*—into the so-called "right to organize"; that is, the right to *combine any or all of the employees of any or all employers in any or all crafts* into *nation-wide* unions and federations, prepared and financed, far in advance, to strike and hold up *entire* trades or industries, whole cities, whole regions, even the entire country, *for wages or conditions better than those obtainable without coercion in the open labor market.* This they have done, well knowing that the cost incurred must be passed along to and borne by the whole public, *and they openly say so!* . . .

You [the members of the Chambers of Commerce and the great Business Associations throughout the United States] are not only able, but are deeply interested, it seems to me, to stir up a public demand both on Congress and the state legislatures for laws declaring, as Governor Coolidge declared during the Boston police strike, *that there is no right to strike against the public safety.* You might well go still farther, in this land of free government, and teach the voters that *there is no right to strike against the public pocket.* The great American people is surely not so feeble as to let itself forever be "held up" at will by this or that minute but "organized" minority.

There seems to me a clear moral as well as legal distinction to be drawn between what might be called the *retail* and the *wholesale* organization of labor. Let us grant, for the sake of argument (though it is usually untrue), that the poor workingman is at such a practical disadvantage in dealing with his rich employer, that it is natural and fair to let him combine with fellow workmen *in the same shop* to "bargain collectively" for them all; and thus throw their collective need of many jobs into the scale, against his collective need of many workers. Also, let us grant that an isolated combination of workers, against an isolated employer here and there, is a matter of comparative indifference to the public; a local effort, in which most of us have no great concern. Then let us grant that under such conditions the public, the law and the courts are apt to deal kindly with the workman on strike, and to ignore the oldtime law forbidding combination in restraint of trade. The thing might be called "retail" organization of labor and be winked at as fairly legitimate.

But, suppose such an organization to be *expanded, to cover a whole industry*—is not then the single employer, are not all employers, and the public, put at unfair disadvantage? Take the case of the United Mine Workers; which is a vast army of occupation of all the great coal mines of the country, except a few in West Virginia and Kentucky, which thus far refuse to unionize. Suppose (as has often occurred, both in anthracite and bituminous coal) that it is the open purpose of this half-million army *to hold up coal supply* now and again, until its demands are enforced by reason of coal famine, *and at public expense!* . . . *Do you think 110 million Americans will always sit still, while half a million coal miners or railway workers freeze or starve the crowd into paying hold-up wages far above what the open market pays the rest of us?*

It is my own conviction that public opinion is ripe for lawful control of organized labor. The right to "organize" and to "strike" against an individual employer may as heretofore be conceded as a reasonable makeweight in "collective bargaining"—*to those who desire to bargain in that way,* without limiting the freedom of those who prefer to bargain individually. *But the time has come for the law to put an end to organization of whole crafts against the whole public!* . . .

But, gentlemen, *the mass of the people will never, or else but slowly, learn that fact from the politicians,* who naturally cater to the organized labor vote. Nor will they learn it from the press (which echoes talk, but seldom starts it), *until some conspicuous personage or organization first proclaims it.* I submit once more that *you* are the national leaders, conspicuous individually and by your great associations, who best understand the economic and constitutional rights both of the workers you employ and the customers you serve—that is, those of the whole people. It is my conviction that you ought, for the common good as well as your own peace and profit, to take the initiative in this important matter. The time has fully come to *suppress by law all wholesale organization of labor,* for the purpose of fixing wages, or controlling, limiting or preventing work, production or transportation; *that is, organization involving the employees of more than one and the same employer.*

And for consistency it is time, too, to repeal the provisions of the Clayton Act exempting farmer and labor organizations from the penalties of the laws against combination in restraint of trade. . . .

It is the psychological moment—with coal and building and garment workers' strikes impending upon an unoffending people, whose declared intent it is to starve or freeze the public into submission *not only by stopping work* of production and transportation by the strikers themselves, but by *preventing, no matter how,* the willing work of others—it is, I repeat, the perfect moment to rouse that public in its own defense. I urge you, gentlemen of the great associations, to go to the press, to Congress and the legislatures, for the embodiment in law of Calvin Coolidge's celebrated dictum—perhaps omitting the word "safety"— that *there is no right to strike against the public, by anybody, anywhere, anytime.* For, I think, the day of reckoning has fully come, when the American people, having learned not to confuse conspiracy against the community with mutual benefit work, will clearly distinguish between selfishness and liberty, between class and democracy; and will serve notice on organized labor that no fraction of the public is strong enough to plunder the whole. Especially is it your duty and privilege, as broadly educated men, to teach your less informed fellow citizens the needed lesson in morals, economics and politics—that no man or group of men ought to or can get more out of the community by doing less for the community.

John L. Lewis (1880-   )

A fearless, aggressive labor leader, he was born into a poor Welsh mining family in Iowa. At fifteen, he went down into the mines, digging coal in Colorado, Wyoming, and Montana, copper in Arizona, and silver in Utah. After helping to drag the mutilated bodies of 236 miners from the hazardous Union Pacific Mine at Hannah, Wyoming, in 1905, he turned his efforts to unionism, becoming president in 1920 of the United Mine Workers, the then largest and most powerful union in America. Following Samuel Gompers' doctrine that tactics, not ideals, made

a labor movement, he operated opportunistically,
as Irving Bernstein said, "compromising only
with reality." Since he believed the world was
not amenable to persuasion, he had no faith in
arbitration and placed his reliance on power
alone. This ruthless faith eventually made him
the most powerful labor leader in America.

THE MINERS' FIGHT FOR AMERICAN STANDARDS

Primarily the United Mine Workers of America insists upon the maintenance of the wage standards, guaranteed by the existing contractual relations in the industry, in the interests of its own membership. It is acting in that respect exactly as any other individual, organization, or corporation would do under like circumstances. The theory of our system of free enterprise is that the ultimate prosperity of all is best assured by the utmost endeavor of each to better his own condition. Trade unionism is an integral part of the existing system of industry first called by its critics capitalism. The word once used in reproach has in these times been adopted with pride by the advocates and defenders of the system, as was the case in regard to great religious sects and political parties, which adopted as badges of honor the names first hurled at them as epithets.

Distrust and hostility toward the business system wane as it is becoming better understood how the general prosperity and individual and family welfare of modern peoples has been increased by the use of capital in production to multiply the productive power of man's labor, whether of hand or brain. Trade unionism is a phenomenon of capitalism quite similar to the corporation. One is essentially a pooling of labor for purposes of common action in production

From *The Miners' Fight for American Standards* (Indianapolis: Bell Publishing Co., 1925), pp. 40–1, 43–9, 51–2.

and in sales. The other is a pooling of capital for exactly the same purposes. The economic aims of both are identical —gain.

The strange survival of pre-capitalist mentality that makes so many persons subconsciously resent high wages for workingmen, or action by workingmen, to better their condition, while lauding exactly similar efforts by capital to get more profits and avoid losses, is back of these demands that labor act upon other motives than are expected of capital and voluntarily sacrifice its wages to increase the profits of others. It is the feudal mind speaking in a capitalist age.

But in insisting on the maintenance of an American wage standard in the coal fields the United Mine Workers is also doing its part, probably more than its part, to force a reorganization of the basic industry of the country upon scientific and efficient lines. The maintenance of these rates will accelerate the operation of natural economic laws, which will in time eliminate uneconomic mines, obsolete equipment and incompetent management.

Any concession of wage reductions will serve to delay this process of reorganization, by enabling the unfit to hold out a little longer. . . .

Finally in its refusal to countenance any backward step on the wage question the United Mine Workers of America is doing its part to maintain the general prosperity of the United States and all the people in it.

Nothing is more significant of the revolution in economic thinking and methods of study, that has followed the swing of economic thought toward the study of the science from the consumption standpoint, and from the accumulation of accurate statistical measurements of the national income and consumption of goods, than the change in attitude on the wage question.

That the purchasing power of the American masses is the pivot upon which our whole economic system turns, and that a reduction in that purchasing power is instantly registered, not only in the distress of the masses but the shrinkage of profits and the destruction of capital values, has become so evident in the post-war period that it is becoming quite difficult to find advocates of the low wage theories, formerly so popular among financiers and industrial management. . . .

In every discussion of business prospects now, the rate of employment is featured and every gain in employment is noted as an augury of better business, because of the increased purchasing power that it implies.

If a wage cut is noted, the attempt is always made to minimize its effect upon the prospects of business by arguments to show that this particular class of wages is higher than the general level. Seldom is it argued now that a reduction of the general level would be beneficial.

In defense of any cut, it is argued that by a balancing process, not only the labor affected, but all labor, may expect a renewed advance toward higher levels yet.

The professional enemies of organized labor, the open shop organizations, say next to nothing now about lower wages. Only a few years ago it was their great selling argument. Cities which have been long noted for the open shop proclivities of their chambers of commerce, among them Los Angeles, no longer advertise to the world that they have low wage rates. Capital it seems can no longer be lured to low wage communities, because capital is becoming ever more concerned with selling what it produces, and it knows that its sales will be restricted in low wage markets.

Perhaps it is in the advertising field that this revolution in economic thought can be seen best.

Advertising under modern conditions has become almost the life of great new industries, that have sprung up as a result of recent advances of science. Advertising is no longer a mere mode of selling. It has become an instrument for the education of the people into new desires and demands. In seeking customers, the newspapers and advertising agencies themselves have become great advertisers of their market areas. What do they feature most—the pay-rolls and high wages of the industries in their cities and states.

Not only has American economic thought and business practice swung around to the high wage theory, but American domestic and foreign governmental policies are more and more in tune with it.

The working people are admonished almost daily by statesmen and the newspapers of the high wage rates here, as compared to those abroad. We have been shown in tables and diagrams how the higher wage rate of the American worker is accounted for by the greater amount of power per man employed in moving the machinery with which he works, and how the wage rates of the various countries compare to the amount of capital per worker invested.

In all these studies it is assumed as a matter of course, that the worker not only is entitled to share in this greater production, but it is also admitted that if he did not share in such a manner that he could as a consumer help to adequately dispose of the product, the whole system would crash to pieces.

Almost unanimous recognition of these facts, which a generation ago were pooh-poohed by Gradgrind economists and scouted as trade union heresies, has so colored our political activities that Congress passed the recent immigration restriction law by an overwhelming majority. Fifty years ago business interests almost succeeded in defeating labor's demand for the exclusion of Chinese coolie labor and the economists of that day denounced the effort to maintain a high wage standard as economic suicide.

In the matter of wages, the prosperity of the United States today in contrast to the crippled industries of the nations which cling to the low wage fallacies is the crag of fact against which all the theories of a contrary nature have been broken to bits.

High paid American skilled labor can sell its machine-made wares in China and Japan. Our exports of manufactures have been steadily increasing in competition with the cheapest labor in the world.

Our foreign trade experts tell us that the cheap labor countries will never catch us, as long as we keep our lead in the method we have inaugurated—mass production. Mass production can only be maintained by a purchasing power in the home market sufficient to make it possible.

Yet in the face of this almost universal recognition of the vital importance of maintaining American purchasing power in order to keep up our productive pace, it is proposed to inaugurate a cheap labor system in the industry upon which all the others depend—the mining of coal. The absurdity, nay the effrontery of the demand is staggering—when it is examined in the light of what is happening in every other department of industry and in home and foreign trade. . . .

The United Mine Workers would be false not only to itself, but a traitor to the future of America, if it allowed this great industry to fade out of the American picture and, by its maladjustment to the rest of the industrial machine, halt the progress now being made toward a substantial degree of industrial democracy.

For rest assured that if the mining industry be long kept out of pace with the rest of America, out of gear with the big machine, it will slow up the whole works. The industrial system is too closely interdependent to admit of such incongruities being long maintained. . . .

When the United Mine Workers of America declares that it will take no backward step, this great Union speaks in unison with the heart beats of America, and puts into economic language the very essence of the American spirit.

Calvin Coolidge (1872-1933)

The thirtieth President of the United States, he was a dull, taciturn, Puritanical Yankee who had no noticeable bad habits except an addiction to long afternoon naps in the White House. After becoming President on Harding's death, he was elected again in 1924 as the businessman's choice. Declaring he did not "choose to run" in 1928, he told Congress on Dec. 4 of the same year, "The country . . . can anticipate the future with optimism." Then, opportunely, he slipped out of Washington before the 1929 crash.

GOVERNMENT AND BUSINESS

This time and place naturally suggest some consideration of commerce in its relation to Government and society. We are finishing a year which can justly be said to surpass all others in the overwhelming success of general business. We are met not only in the greatest American metropolis, but in the greatest center of population and business that the world has ever known. If any one wishes to gauge the power which is represented by the genius of the American spirit, let him contemplate the wonders which have been wrought in this region in the short space of 200 years. Not only does it stand unequaled by any other place on earth, but it is impossible to conceive of any other place where it could be equaled.

The foundation of this enormous development rests upon commerce. New York is an imperial city, but it is not a seat of government. The empire over which it rules is not

Address before the Chamber of Commerce of the State of New York, New York City, November 10, 1925, from *Foundations of the Republic: Speeches and Addresses of Calvin Coolidge* (New York: Charles Scribner's Sons, 1926), pp. 317–22. Reprinted by permission of the publishers.

political, but commercial. The great cities of the ancient world were the seats of both government and industrial power. The Middle Ages furnished a few exceptions. The great capitals of former times were not only seats of government but they actually governed. In the modern world government is inclined to be merely a tenant of the city. Political life and industrial life flow on side by side, but practically separated from each other. When we contemplate the enormous power, autocratic and uncontrolled, which would have been created by joining the authority of government with the influence of business, we can better appreciate the wisdom of the fathers in their wise dispensation which made Washington the political center of the country and left New York to develop into its business center. They wrought mightily for freedom.

The great advantages of this arrangement seem to me to be obvious. The only disadvantages which appear lie in the possibility that otherwise business and government might have had a better understanding of each other and been less likely to develop mutual misapprehensions and suspicions. If a contest could be held to determine how much those who are really prominent in our government life know about business, and how much those who are really prominent in our business life know about government, it is my firm conviction that the prize would be awarded to those who are in government life. This is as it ought to be, for those who have the greater authority ought to have the greater knowledge. But it is my even firmer conviction that the general welfare of our country could be very much advanced through a better knowledge by both of those parties of the multifold problems with which each has to deal. . . .

While I have spoken of what I believed would be the advantages of a more sympathetic understanding, I should put an even stronger emphasis on the desirability of the largest possible independence between government and business. Each ought to be sovereign in its own sphere. When government comes unduly under the influence of business, the tendency is to develop an administration which closes the door of opportunity; becomes narrow and selfish in its outlook, and results in an oligarchy. When government enters the field of business with its great resources, it has a tendency to extravagance and inefficiency, but, having the power to crush all competitors, likewise closes the door of opportunity and results in monopoly. . . .

While there has been in the past and will be in the future a considerable effort in this country of different business interests to attempt to run the Government in such a way as to set up a system of privilege, and while there have been and will be those who are constantly seeking to commit the Government to a policy of infringing upon the domain of private business, both of these efforts have been very largely discredited, and with reasonable vigilance on the part of the people to preserve their freedom do not now appear to be dangerous.

When I have been referring to business, I have used the word in its all-inclusive sense to denote alike the employer and employee, the production of agriculture and industry, the distribution of transportation and commerce, and the service of finance and banking. It is the work of the world. In modern life, with all its intricacies, business has come to hold a very dominant position in the thoughts of all enlightened peoples. Rightly understood, this is not a criticism, but a compliment. In its great economic organization it does not represent, as some have hastily concluded, a mere desire to minister to selfishness. . . . It is something far more important than a sordid desire for gain. It could not successively succeed on that basis. It is dominated by a more worthy impulse; it rests on a higher law. True business represents the mutual organized effort of society to minister to the economic requirements of civilization. It is an effort by which men provide for the material needs of each other. While it is not an end in itself, it is the important means for the attainment of a supreme end. It rests squarely on the law of service. It has for its main reliance truth and faith and justice. In its larger sense it is one of the greatest contributing forces to the moral and spiritual advancement of the race.

It is the important and righteous position that business holds in relation to life which gives warrant to the great interest which the National Government constantly exercises for the promotion of its success. This is not exercised as has been the autocratic practice abroad of directly supporting and financing different business projects, except in case of great emergency; but we have rather held to a democratic policy of cherishing the general structure of business while holding its avenues open to the widest competition, in order that its opportunities and its benefits might be given the broadest possible participation. While it is true that the Government ought not to be and is not committed to certain methods of acquisition which, while partaking of the nature of unfair practices, try to masquerade under the guise of business, the Government is and ought to be thoroughly committed to every endeavor of production and distribution which is entitled to be designated as true business. Those who are so engaged, instead of regarding the Government as their opponent and enemy, ought to regard it as their vigilant supporter and friend. . . .

It is my belief that the whole material development of our country has been enormously stimulated by reason of the general insistence on the part of the public authorities that economic effort ought not to partake of privilege, and that business should be unhampered and free. This could never have been done under a system of freight-rate discriminations or monopolistic trade associations. These might have enriched a few for a limited period, but they never would have enriched the country, while on the firmer foundation of justice we have achieved even more ample individual fortunes and a perfectly unprecedented era of general prosperity. This has resulted in no small part from the general acceptance on the part of those who own and control the wealth of the Nation, that it is to be used not to oppress but to serve. It is that policy, sometimes perhaps imperfectly expressed and clumsily administered, that has animated the National Government. In its observance there is unlimited opportunity for progress and prosperity.

It would be difficult, if not impossible, to estimate the contribution which government makes to business. It is notorious that where the government is bad, business is bad. The mere fundamental precepts of the administration of justice, the providing of order and security, are priceless. The prime element in the value of all property is the knowledge that its peaceful enjoyment will be publicly defended. If disorder should break out in your city, if there should be a conviction extending over any length of time that the rights of persons and property could no longer be protected by law, the value of your tall buildings would shrink to about the price of what are now water fronts of old Carthage or what are now corner lots in ancient Babylon. It is really the extension of these fundamental rights that the Government is constantly attempting to apply to modern business. It wants its rightful possessors to rest in security, it wants any wrongs that they may suffer to have a legal remedy, and it is all the time striving through administrative machinery to prevent in advance the infliction of injustice.

These undoubtedly represent policies which are wise and sound and necessary. That they have often been misapplied and many times run into excesses, nobody can deny. Regulation has often become restriction, and inspection has too frequently been little less than obstruction. This was the natural result of those times in the past when there were practices in business which warranted severe disapprobation. It was only natural that when these abuses were reformed by an aroused public opinion a great deal of prejudice which ought to have been discriminating and directed only at certain evil practices came to include almost the whole domain of business, especially where it had been gathered into large units. After the abuses had been discontinued the prejudice remained to produce a large amount of legislation, which, however well meant in its application to trade, undoubtedly hampered but did not improve. It is this misconception and misapplication, disturbing and wasteful in their result, which the National Government is attempting to avoid. Proper regulation and control are disagreeable and expensive. They represent the suffering that the just must endure because of the unjust. They are a part of the price which must be paid to promote the cause of economic justice.

Undoubtedly if public vigilance were relaxed, the generation to come might suffer a relapse. But the present generation of business almost universally throughout its responsible organization and management has shown every disposition to correct its own abuses with as little intervention of the Government as possible. This position is recognized by the public, and due to the appreciation of the needs which the country has for great units of production in time of war, and to the better understanding of the service which they perform in time of peace, . . . a new attitude of the public mind is distinctly discernible toward great aggregations of capital. Their prosperity goes very far to insure the prosperity of all the country. The contending elements have each learned a most profitable lesson.

This development has left the Government free to advance from the problems of reform and repression to those of economy and construction. A very large progress is being made in these directions. [As a result] our country is in a state of unexampled and apparently sound and well distributed prosperity.

Robert M. La Follette (1856-1925)

Liberal statesman and a leading Progressive, he fought against entrenched political groups to become governor of Wisconsin in 1901 and was twice reelected. His program, based upon direct appeal to the people, was known as the "Wisconsin idea" and served as a model of progressive government. In 1906 he took a seat in the U.S. Senate to which he was reelected three times. He drafted the program for the National Progressive Republican League, campaigned for the Progressive nomination in 1912, but lost to Theodore Roosevelt, partly as a result of a physical breakdown. He opposed the declaration of war with Germany, but supported most of the war measures. As a liberal leader in postwar years, he proposed the resolution for a Senate inquiry into Teapot Dome and other oil leases made during the Harding administration.

GOVERNMENT AND THE PEOPLE

The great issue before the American people today is the control of government and industry by private monopoly.

For a generation the people have struggled patiently, in the face of repeated betrayals by successive administrations, to free themselves from this intolerable power which has been undermining representative government.

Through control of government, monopoly has steadily extended its absolute dominion to every basic industry.

In violation of law, monopoly has crushed competition, stifled private initiative and independent enterprise, and

From the Progressive Party Platform of 1924, Kirk H. Porter and Donald B. Johnson, eds., *National Party Platforms, 1840–1956* (Urbana: University of Illinois Press, 1956), pp. 252–5. Reprinted by permission of the publisher.

without fear of punishment now exacts extortionate profits upon every necessity of life consumed by the public.

The equality of opportunity proclaimed by the Declaration of Independence and asserted and defended by Jefferson and Lincoln as the heritage of every American citizen has been displaced by special privilege for the few, wrested from the government of the many.

That tyrannical power which the American people denied to a king, they will no longer endure from the monopoly system. The people know they cannot yield to any group the control of the economic life of the nation and preserve their political liberties. They know monopoly has its representatives in the halls of Congress, on the Federal bench, and in the executive departments; that these servile agents barter away the nation's natural resources, nullify acts of Congress by judicial veto and administrative favor, invade the people's rights by unlawful arrests and unconstitutional searches and seizures, direct our foreign policy in the interests of predatory wealth, and make wars and conscript the sons of the common people to fight them.

The usurpation in recent years by the federal courts of the power to nullify laws duly enacted by the legislative branch of the government is a plain violation of the Constitution. Abraham Lincoln, in his first inaugural address, said: "The candid citizen must confess that if the policy of the government, upon vital questions affecting the whole people, is to be irrevocably fixed by decisions of the Supreme Court, the people will have ceased to be their own rulers, having to that extent practically resigned their government into the hands of their eminent tribunal." The Constitution specifically vests all legislative power in the Congress, giving that body power and authority to override the veto of the president. The federal courts are given no authority under the Constitution to veto acts of Congress. Since the federal courts have assumed to exercise such veto power, it is essential that the Constitution shall give the Congress the right to override such judicial veto, otherwise the Court will make itself master over the other coordinate branches of the government. The people themselves must approve or disapprove the present exercise of legislative power by the federal courts.

The present condition of American agriculture constitutes an emergency of the gravest character. The Department of Commerce report shows that during 1923 there was a steady and marked increase in dividends paid by the great industrial corporations. The same is true of the steam and electric railways and practically all other large corporations. On the other hand, the Secretary of Agriculture reports that in the fifteen principal wheat growing states more than 108,000 farmers since 1920 have lost their farms through foreclosure or bankruptcy; that more than 122,000 have surrendered their property without legal proceedings, and that nearly 375,000 have retained possession of their property only through the leniency of their creditors, making a total of more than 600,000 or 26 percent of all farmers who have virtually been bankrupted since 1920 in these fifteen states alone.

Almost unlimited prosperity for the great corporations and ruin and bankruptcy for agriculture is the direct and logical result of the policies and legislation which deflated the farmer while extending almost unlimited credit to the great corporations; which protected with exorbitant tariffs the industrial magnates, but depressed the prices of the farmers' products by financial juggling while greatly increasing the cost of what he must buy; which guaranteed excessive freight rates to the railroads and put a premium on wasteful management while saddling an unwarranted burden on to the backs of the American farmer; which permitted gambling in the products of the farm by grain speculators to the great detriment of the farmer and to the great profit of the grain gambler.

Awakened by the dangers which menace their freedom

and prosperity the American people still retain the right and courage to exercise their sovereign control over their government. In order to destroy the economic and political power of monopoly, which has come between the people and their government, we pledge ourselves to the following principles and policies:

The House Cleaning

We pledge a complete housecleaning in the Department of Justice, the Department of the Interior, and the other executive departments. We demand that the power of the Federal Government be used to crush private monopoly, not to foster it.

Natural Resources

We pledge recovery of the navy's oil reserves and all other parts of the public domain which have been fraudulently or illegally leased, or otherwise wrongfully transferred, to the control of private interests; vigorous prosecution of all public officials, private citizens and corporations that participated in these transactions; complete revision of the water-power act, the general leasing act, and all other legislation relating to the public domain. We favor public ownership of the nation's water power and the creation and development of a national super-water-power system, including Muscle Shoals, to supply at actual cost light and power for the people and nitrate for the farmers, and strict public control and permanent conservation of all the nation's resources, including coal, iron and other ores, oil and timber lands, in the interest of the people.

Railroads

. . . We declare for public ownership of railroads with definite safeguards against bureaucratic control, as the only final solution of the transportation problem.

Tax Reduction

We favor reduction of Federal taxes upon individual incomes and legitimate business, limiting tax exactions strictly to the requirements of the government administered with rigid economy, particularly by curtailment of the eight hundred million dollars now annually expended for the army and navy in preparation for future wars; by the recovery of the hundreds of millions of dollars stolen from the Treasury through fraudulent war contracts and the corrupt leasing of the public resources; and by diligent action to collect the accumulated interest upon the eleven billion dollars owing us by foreign governments.

We denounce the Mellon tax plan as a device to relieve multi-millionaires at the expense of other tax payers, and favor a taxation policy providing for immediate reductions upon moderate incomes, large increases in the inheritance tax rates upon large estates to prevent the indefinite accumulation by inheritance of great fortunes in a few hands; taxes upon excess profits to penalize profiteering, and complete publicity, under proper safeguards, of all Federal tax returns.

The Courts

We favor submitting to the people, for their considerate judgment, a constitutional amendment providing that Congress may by enacting a statute make it effective over a judicial veto.

We favor such amendment to the constitution as may be necessary to provide for the election of all Federal Judges, without party designation, for fixed terms not exceeding ten years, by direct vote of the people.

The Farmers

We favor drastic reduction of the exorbitant duties on manufactures provided in the Fordney-McCumber tariff legislation, the prohibiting of gambling by speculators and profiteers in agricultural products; the reconstruction of the Federal Reserve and Federal Farm Loan Systems, so as to eliminate control by usurers, speculators and international financiers, and to make the credit of the nation available upon fair terms to all and without discrimination to business men, farmers and home-builders. We advocate the calling of a special session of Congress to pass legislation for the relief of American agriculture. We favor such further legislation as may be needful or helpful in promoting and protecting cooperative enterprises. We demand that the Interstate Commerce Commission proceed forthwith to reduce by an approximation to pre-war levels the present freight rates on agricultural products, including live stock, and upon the materials required upon American farms for agricultural purposes.

Labor

We favor abolition of the use of injunctions in labor disputes and declare for complete protection of the right of farmers and industrial workers to organize, bargain collectively through representatives of their own choosing, and conduct without hindrance cooperative enterprises.

We favor prompt ratification of the Child Labor amendment, and subsequent enactment of a Federal law to protect children in industry. . . .

War Veterans

We favor adjusted compensation for the veterans of the late war, not as charity, but as a matter of right, and we demand that the money necessary to meet this obligation of the government be raised by taxes laid upon wealth in proportion to the ability to pay, and declare our opposition to the sales tax or any other device to shift this obligation onto the backs of the poor in higher prices and increased cost of living. We do not regard the payment at the end of a long period of a small insurance as provided by the law recently passed as in any just sense a discharge of the nation's obligations to the veterans of the late war. . . .

Popular Sovereignty

Over and above constitutions and statutes and greater than all, is the supreme sovereignty of the people, and with them should rest the final decision of all great questions of national policy. We favor such amendments to the Federal Constitution as may be necessary to provide for the direct nomination and election of the President, to extend the initiative and referendum to the federal government, and to insure a popular referendum for or against war except in cases of actual invasion.

Peace on Earth

We denounce the mercenary system of foreign policy under recent administrations in the interests of financial imperialists, oil monopolists and international bankers, which has at times degraded our State Department from its high service as a strong and kindly intermediary of defenseless governments to a trading outpost for those interests and concession-seekers engaged in the exploitations of weaker nations, as contrary to the will of the American people, destructive of domestic development and provocative of war. We favor an active foreign policy to bring about a revision of the Versailles treaty in accordance with the terms of the armistice, and to promote firm treaty agreements with all nations to outlaw wars, abolish conscription, drastically reduce land, air and naval armaments, and guarantee public referendum on peace and war.

Julius H. Barnes (1873-1959)

A close friend of Herbert Hoover and one of the nation's leading industrialists, he became best known to the public as president of the United States Chamber of Commerce, a post that he held from 1921 to 1924. In his statements and speeches he revealed himself as a staunch supporter of rugged individualism, attributing the advance of American industry to a general adherence to the theory of private ownership rather than government control.

THE PHILOSOPHY OF FAIR PLAY

If one should attempt to define the American social and political philosophy in a single phrase it might be described as the PHILOSOPHY OF FAIR PLAY.

In America the various sports of our youth teach the principles of team play and of fair play. On every baseball diamond and football field the qualities of fortitude and courage and fair play, inspired by loyalty to club or town or college, are instilled in our young men.

Americans, therefore, clearly recognize that it is a violation of this fair play when combinations of wealth and power are made to the detriment of the public. And it was to preserve the national policy of fair play that the theory of government regulation was evolved.

This regulation, however, which controls practices and affects earnings, must, in the national interest, be restrained and wise and generous. It must attract the enlistment of capital and the service of superior individual ability in

From Julius H. Barnes, *The Genius of American Business* (New York: Doubleday, Page & Co., 1924), pp. 6–13.

order that regulated industry may march in step with non-regulated industry in the development of economies and of service.

It is not fair play for the necessary power of regulating those public services which inevitably possess the character of monopoly—such as railroad, traction services, or other public utilities—to be administered with such a narrow view of selfish interest and in such total disregard of solemn responsibility that the investments which created these public services will be undermined or destroyed. There is every evidence, however, that we have passed the era of unfair and short-sighted, over-rigid regulation, and that we are dealing with regulated public services with a more enlightened vision of fair play.

It is not fair play for the State to overman public-service corporations for political support, provide service below the actual cost of operation, and make up the resultant deficit from the assessment of public moneys raised through taxation.

It is not fair play for special sections of our people, numerically strong, to levy, through unequal and unwise taxation, and in a spirit of envy and resentment, an unfair burden, against those other groups more fortunate than themselves.

The range of employment opportunity is constantly widened with the establishment of new enterprises; and taxation which destroys the human incentive of prospective earnings against the unusual hazards of new ventures, and which stifles the willingness to take the risks of new business ventures, is unwise as well as a violation of fundamental fair play.

It is not fair play for a group of men temporarily in a position of authority in national legislation to vote, for any purpose, gigantic appropriations from the national treasury and then seek to avoid the responsibility of providing the revenues from which those appropriations can be paid. In fact, to leave to their successors the perplexing problem of providing the means of payment, while they short-sightedly seek the present approval of those who benefit by their reckless draft upon the public funds, is a distressing violation of the principles of fair play.

It is not fair play for a government exercising exclusive authority to issue currency denominations in which are recorded the savings of thrift and self-denial—the provision of life insurance protection for survivors—and on the stability of which depends the healthy functioning of trade and commerce, on which in turn rest employment and opportunity, and, therefore, the happiness and content of its peoples deliberately to inflate or deflate the value of that traditional measure of value with its resultant distress and disaster.

It should be America's chief pride, in these recent years of reckless currency inflation in other lands, that its record has been one of intelligent effort to keep stable its currency; and this has been the greatest contribution on the part of the Government to the preservation of fair play. . . .

It is not fair play to-day for organizations of men, associated for lawful activities and rightful ends, to stand unequal before the law. No exceptions should be made for organizations of labour or organizations of growers. The time will come, and soon, when these inequalities will be removed because they violate the fundamental human sense of fair play.

It is not fair play for organizations of men to deny the right to work to men who hold views different from theirs. It is increasingly clear that public opinion condemns organizations that, by force and violence, offend thus the public sense of fair play.

It is not fair play for organizations, with whatever claim of proper purpose, to avoid their own responsibility by shrouding their identity behind the mask and hood. Organizations of that character can maintain their existence only if the community departs entirely from the ideals which preserve fair play.

It is not fair play that either from human laws or from social customs, a system should be evolved which would encase a man in the social stratum in which he has been placed by the accident of birth.

In the Old World this rigid caste system freezes into social strata and strifles individual talent and ambition. It is, in fact, the cause of and the excuse for the injection into government of organizations frankly devoted to the interest of a single section of their people. But where no doors are closed by accident of birth or station against those possessed of superior ability or devoted to superior effort there is no excuse for the formation of political influence on the basis of trade or social position.

Labour parties or farm blocs have no lasting place under the American conditions of fair play. . . .

Organized business does not arrogate to itself a superiority of understanding of the ethics of fair play, nor does it plume itself as expressly the champion of that cause which carries a deep appeal to men of every station. Organized business, however, responsible not only for its own well-being, but because of its position as largely the director of industry, and, therefore, responsible for the opportunities and employment of many times its number, has an especially keen appreciation of the atmosphere in which human activities may prosper.

Organized business has keenly appreciated that the incentive to all effort rests on the confidence that superior service, in any form, will be rewarded, and those rewards secured and protected.

Under conditions of absolute fair play between individuals, society apportions through the processes of trade a sure and fair reward to those individuals who serve it best by new inventions, or superior ability in production, or superior methods of distribution.

In our short national history, under the stimulus of this individualistic fair play, we have led the world in applying science and invention through the service of industry to the enlargement of human comfort and contentment.

Edward A. Filene (1860–1937)

As head of a prominent Boston department store, he introduced a series of innovations in merchandising and personnel management which brought him a fortune and proved to him that the efficient performance of a needed social service would bring the best long-run business profit. Always receptive to new ideas, he encouraged profit-sharing, unemployment and medical insurance, and credit-unions for workers. Although he was one of the founders of the United States Chamber of Commerce, he broke openly with the organization in 1936 when he became impatient with what seemed to him to be the unenlightened and self-destructive opinions expressed by its business leadership.

BUSINESS AND SOCIAL PROGRESS

I believe that the modern business system, despised and derided by innumerable reformers, will be both the inspiration and the instrument of the social progress of the future. Such a statement cannot go far without encountering vigorous dispute. The air is filled with voices asserting that the modern business system stands squarely across the path that leads to a decent social order. On all hands there are men

From *The Way Out* (Garden City: Doubleday, Page & Co., 1926), pp. 29–32, 34–6, 39–40, 43–7.

who contend that we can assure social progress only by destroying the business system and reorganizing our life upon a communistic or near communistic basis. And multiplied thousands of men and women who are far from being communists indict the modern business system as the tyrant rather than the tool of mankind.

Now, I am under no delusion about the social efficiency of our industrial civilization. Despite the fact that science is daily making life more livable and interesting, daily devising ways and means for shifting burdens from the backs of men to the backs of machines, daily widening the range of men's interests by rapid transportation and communication, and broadening the scope of existence generally, the time of the majority of mankind is still occupied almost entirely in the business of providing food, clothing, and shelter, with little time or training for lifting life to a higher level—even if the means were at hand. This is plainly indefensible, if it is to be accepted as the inevitable result of the business system; . . . yet I am convinced that the social progress of the future will be achieved not by the destruction of the business system but by its further and finer development. The modern business system is at present more or less lawless, but the pressure of necessity during the next ten or twenty years will enforce its reform. Unless I wholly misinterpret the signs of the time, we are now in the morning hours of a period in which business men, in order to survive and succeed, will be compelled to adopt the sort of policies that will give us an increasingly better social order. During the next ten or twenty years we shall come to see from practical experience that there is nothing necessarily contradictory between successful business and social progress. Success in both will demand the same principles and the same practices. Commercial success and social welfare, in the days ahead, will stem from the same root.

The average man and the average student of social con-

ditions too often start with the premise that business by
its very nature is anti-social. Certainly conspicuous business
success has been so regarded. And we are obliged to admit
that much of it in the past has been. But the point I want
to make is that business must henceforth function in a
changed world—a world in which good business policies
will be found to be good social policies.

What I mean concretely is this: Social progress demands
coöperation, the modification or—to borrow a word from
the psychoanalyst—the sublimation of the class struggle, the
access of every man, woman, and child to a decently adequate supply of the necessities of life, and the release of
the individual from the things that prevent his living a
creative and contented life. In the past, successful business has often blocked the way to a realization of these
socially necessary ends. But coming conditions are going
to compel business men to make changes in policy and in
action that will result in just these things. The business
policies that will enable men to make the big business
successes of the next ten or twenty years will produce
these things as by-products. . . .

In times past, business could be successful despite many
anti-social policies and practices, because society was not
in the tight corner it is in today. The business man of the
past was in very much the same position as the pioneer
who could afford to be recklessly wasteful in a virgin land.
Business, until now, has been on what might be called a
pioneering spree. Only lately have economy and the wisest
possible handling of men and material become absolute
essentials to business success.

As H. G. Wells makes a character in one of his later
novels say, "In the days before the war it was different.
A little grabbing or cornering was all to the good. All to
the good. It prevented things being used up too fast. And
the world was running by habit; the inertia was tremendous. You could take all sorts of liberties. But all this is
altered. We're living in a different world."

We are, indeed, living in a different world. In place of abundance we have shortage in most nations. Instead of a simple world with lots of elbow room we have a world complicated and crowded. In place of dominant captains of industry and docile labourers we have captains of industry in insecure seats and a labour mass become articulate and conscious of its political and economic power. In short, we are now living in a world in which the reckless and wasteful methods of the exploiter are a social menace and the creative methods of the scientific, socially minded business man a social necessity. . . .

The wise business man, seeing that we have passed the time when reckless, wasteful, exploitative, and anti-social methods could be made profitable, will, as I have suggested, turn to the scientific development of business. He will do this not merely because a new social conscience constrains him but primarily because sound business intelligence and competition force him to do it. When the character in Mr. Wells's novel said that we were living in a new world, he went on to say, "It's a new public. It's—wild. It'll smash up the show if we go too far." Now, I am not suggesting that the business man will or should base all his policies upon the fear of social revolution. I am saying only that the new economic and social conditions that have come as a result of the increasing industrialism, the increasing complexity, and the increasing interdependence of society, that the particular economic muddle of transition into which the war plunged the world, and especially the newly awakened mind of labour, all mean that the business of the future cannot be commercially successful unless it is socially sound. . . .

But the one thing that makes business predominantly the instrument for social progress—if we only use it wisely— is the fact that business men control the progress of this country. They control the progress of the country not because they are either geniuses or pirates or because they have joined in any dark plot to capture and loot the com-

mon people. They are neither more grasping nor more public spirited than other men. They control the progress of
the country simply because this is an industrial nation and
their hands happen to be on the levers of power.

Whether they are blundering or brilliant, whether they
are actuated by sinister motives or by social vision, they
still control the processes of production, distribution, and
consumption. And these three processes touch our lives at
more points and oftener than all the torch-light processions,
congressional debates, and reform movements that have
taken place since the first politician mounted the stump
and the first reformer challenged the status quo. What
business men think and do about production, distribution,
and consumption is therefore the most important single
factor to be considered in any study of the possible arrest
or advancement of social progress. It is not so much the
attitude of business men toward "public questions" as it
is their attitude toward "business questions" that counts in
the history of social advance. . . .

The successful businesses of the future will be the businesses that improve the processes and reduce the costs of
production, rid distribution of its present indefensible wastes,
bring the price of the necessities of life lower and lower,
shorten the hours of labour and enlarge the margin of
leisure, eliminate periodic depressions and recurrent unemployment, limit the area of the industrial battlefield and
enlarge the floor space of the council chamber, create
better and better working conditions, pay higher real wages,
and increase the comfort and prosperity of both their employees and their customers.

These are the things that the facts prove will be not op-
tional but obligatory upon the business man who wants to
succeed in a big way during the next ten or twenty years.
And these are the things that will give us decent social
progress.

CHAPTER THREE

Collapse of the
Old Order

I

Prosperity in the twenties had come to mean a rate of
advance rather than an actual state of affairs. A progressive concept, the more abundant life in America was regarded as a constantly accelerating process measured in
gross output of goods. Rising statistics, like new skyscrapers,
proclaimed American technology the wonder of the world.
Between 1919 and 1929, horsepower per worker in manufacturing shot up 50 percent and output per man hour 72
percent; and in the short seven years before 1929, production expanded 34 percent, and national income nearly
doubled. Equally impressive was the upward climb of security prices and the fantastic activity in Wall Street. Sales
on the New York Stock Exchange leaped from 236 million
shares in 1923 to 1,125 million in 1928, an amazing phenomenon hailed by an astonished financial expert as "an
economic revolution of the profoundest character." With
"a new age" in the offing, political problems were forgotten, and more and more Americans were inclined to
explain their society in terms of productivity, profits, and
stock-market quotations.[1]

This economic revolution, New Era publicists argued, was bringing an equality of prosperity to the American people which few reformers had ever believed possible. Not only was wealth increasing at a rapid rate, but, they claimed, never before had so much purchasing power been put into the hands of the masses. By 1928, even former critics of the business system were lulled into conceding that the prospects were pleasing. "Big business in America," granted Lincoln Steffens, once a hard-hitting opponent of plutocracy, "is producing what the Socialists held up as their goal: food, shelter, and clothing for all." Practice had moved faster than theory, wrote Walter Lippmann. "The more or less unconscious and unplanned activities of businessmen are for once more novel, more daring, and in general more revolutionary than the theories of the progressives."[2] According to the optimistic views of Harvard economist Thomas Nixon Carver, who equated capitalism with the security of private property, we were in way of establishing a kind of economic democracy in the United States without resorting to the "socialistic" intervention of government in the economy.*

Then came the crash of 1929, and the vaunted "economic revolution" turned overnight into an economic debacle. Americans made the sudden shocking discovery that not only had "equal prosperity" been an illusion but the "New Era" had turned out to be the same old story of "boom and bust" that had dogged the American economy since 1819. Yet, though historically the pattern was familiar—business failure, unemployment, social dislocation, and widespread human suffering—the American dilemma at the beginning of the thirties, as Adolf Berle pointed out, was unique in the economic history of the world: "We had warehouses bursting with foodstuffs of all kinds. We had a manufacturing plant second to none, with a more than ample supply of trained workmen, a technical staff of unchallenged

*Thomas Nixon Carver, *What Capitalism Is and What It Does*. See page 177.

efficiency. Every desire for goods or gadgets, for services or scenery, could be satisfied. And yet the great machine was slowly coming to a dead center. In the face of supply, men went hungry; in the face of unexampled possibilities for luxury, life was rapidly slipping toward squalor. The law of supply and demand, which theoretically means that when there is a want business promptly supplies it, had been hit below the belt by the more accurate law that business will supply only an effective demand. In business language, it doesn't matter what the customer wants, but what he can pay for." Since men were hungry in the presence of unsalable surpluses, it was clear that the country had not suffered a calamity of nature but a breakdown in the management of its wealth. Candid observers, who only a few years before had praised businessmen for their daring, were now forced to revise their opinions and to conclude with Lippmann that the development of the American economy had been "gravely perverted."[3]

Since the beginning of the twentieth century, the material welfare of the country had come to depend more and more upon the full use and free run of technique. Any defect or hindrance in technical management, any intrusion of non-technical considerations, any failure or obstruction at any point unavoidably resulted, as Veblen forecast in 1921, in "a disproportionate set-back to the balanced whole" and brought "a disproportionate burden of privation" on all those people whose fortunes were in any way linked to the technological economy. As later economic research confirmed, Veblen's analysis of the origins of depression in a technological society was largely borne out by events.[4]

By the 1920's, the phenomenal gain in technological efficiency made it theoretically possible for industry to turn out more and more goods, cheaper and faster, for more people. But actually, instead of passing on these savings to workers in the form of higher wages (factory productivity rose 55%, hourly wages 2%) or to consumers in the form of lower prices (consumer prices declined only 3%),

During the depression when bleak villages of shacks and packing-boxes known ironically as "Hoovervilles" sprang up on vacant lots and on the outskirts of cities, troubled America began to question an economic system which provided fortunes for a few and left millions without the basic comforts of life.

business kept the profits or expended them in a way which tended to enlarge savings and productive capacity without increasing or spreading purchasing power. The immediate effect of such business practices was to aggravate the unequal distribution of income, already accentuated by the drastic drop in farm income, by concentrating income in the upper groups—in 1929 the top 5 percent claimed 33.5 percent of the national income. Dividends went up 64 percent, and profits, interest, and rent, which went largely to upper-income groups, increased 45 percent; whereas the real annual wages of workers in industry and agriculture—

upon whom national purchasing power chiefly depended—
rose a mere 10.9 percent. In relation to increased productivity, this was too low to buy the goods and services
industry was able to produce at the prices business demanded. The end result of the prevailing business policy
of taking the last cent of profit was a chronic maladjustment between production and consumption which so un-
balanced the economy in favor of the businessman as to
destroy his own market and bring on a national economic
catastrophe.[5]

With business leadership apparently indifferent to the
urgent needs of the country, Americans now asked whether
it was any longer practicable to leave control of the economic system solely in the hands of businessmen. If the
businessmen who ruled America in the twenties were responsible for the biggest boom in history, said the *New
Republic*, "then it follows that they are also personally
responsible for the world's biggest depression." Techno-
logically, the nation had already solved the problem of
production—the industrial system was able to produce more
than enough to go around—but businessmen striving for their
own personal gain had erected a dam between production
and distribution with the paradoxical result, as Elmer
Davis noted in *Harper's*, that people were "starving to
death because there is too much food and freezing to death
because there is too much coal." Those who did not view
the depression as an inevitable, inherent aspect of the economy traced the cause of failure to the traditional attitude
of the businessman who looked upon the economic system
as a glorified gaming table whereby the American people
were—if lucky—fed, sheltered, and clothed. Business, John
Dewey pointed out, was essentially irrational, "a gamble
in uncertainties," but the production and distribution of
goods were not themselves business. "In business they
became cards in a game in which all trumps are in possession of capital." After all, asked Stuart Chase, a popular
writer on economic problems, what was an economic

cial interpretation of liberty was historically conditioned and was a product of the attack against economic monopolies created and sanctioned by the mercantilist policies of eighteenth-century monarchies, Hoover put forward his ideas as immutable truths good at all times and places. Though aware that liberty was a result of the "unending battle against economic domination," he looked at the twentieth century from the viewpoint of the eighteenth, narrowly conceiving government as the only serious enemy of liberty, and more or less overlooked the growing threat of economic domination by large corporations. While he called for regulation to prevent legal monopoly, he believed government should aim chiefly at stimulating and liberating economic forces, not at restraining or diverting them. Ironically Hoover, the staunch individualist, as Secretary of Commerce under Harding and Coolidge and later as President, encouraged the concentration of economic power by pushing trade associations in industry and advocating government sanction of business combination. Thus, wittingly or unwittingly, he reintroduced into government the mercantilist policy of favoritism and support to certain vested interests, against which early nineteenth-century liberals had so strenuously fought.[7]

Hoover's economic philosophy, however, proved to be a more accurate reflection of faith than of fact. His absolute belief obscured the fact that, whatever merits the creed may have had in the past, individualism was no longer applicable in the twenties to an economy in which the most powerful individuals were huge corporations, not persons at all (except by legal courtesy). At the end of the decade, Professors Adolf A. Berle and Gardiner C. Means of Columbia disclosed that nearly two-thirds of the industrial wealth of the country had changed from individual to corporate ownership. Not only had the continuing tendency of business to combine into large corporations significantly altered the picture of economic life as painted by Adam Smith, but Professors Berle and Means found that most of the accepted

concepts of individualism—private property, private enterprise, individual initiative, competition—were no longer
valid in a predominantly corporate economy.*

Their research further revealed that the dominant creed
of individualism had played into the hands of privileged
groups by serving as a kind of apologetics for the existing
economic regime. While touting the virtues of individualism,
business-minded Republican administrations had followed a
neomercantilist policy of non-regulation and cooperation
which had permitted big business to merge and combine
without hindrance from government. Investigation by Professor Means showed that by 1930 the combined assets of the
200 largest non-banking corporations (.07 percent of American corporations) amounted to nearly half of all corporate
wealth in the United States. The dominant position of the
large corporation was further emphasized by the fact that
these same 200 giants received at least 43.2 percent of all
corporate income (corporations with profits of more than
$1 million accounted for 80% of all corporate profits in
1929) and controlled roughly 22 percent of the total wealth
of the nation. These huge corporations, which were growing
much faster than the smaller companies, had come to
dominate most major industries—if not all industry in the
United States. Whether or not economic control was actually
vested in the 64 big businessmen who were picked out in
1930 as the real "rulers" of the country, there was little
doubt that the basic premise of individualism—equal
opportunity—was, in the economic realm, only a polite
fiction.[8]

If, as Hoover asserted, a social system could only be
judged by its results—whether it brought permanent and
continuous progress—then clearly events of 1929 and after
decreed that individualism was no longer a practicable
system of social management. Despite good intentions and

*Adolf A. Berle, Jr., and Gardiner C. Means, *Economic Organization.* See page
193.

valiant effort, President Hoover was never able to reconcile his brand of individualism with the social responsibility demanded of him. Part of his difficulty was due to the assumption that the economic crisis was temporary and would work itself out, but the chief obstacle was his firm belief that government intervention was a denial of American principles, a lack of confidence in the self-reliant individual. In 1930 he told Congress: "Economic depression can not be cured by legislative action or executive pronouncement. Economic wounds must be healed by the action of the cells of the economic body—the producers and consumers themselves." Accordingly the President resorted to moral suasion to prevent unemployment and loss of wages, which proved ineffective because business disregarded its pledge to maintain wages and jobs, desperately trying to cut them faster than prices fell. With the problem of relief, it was a similar story. Federal relief, Hoover informed broke and jobless Americans, would destroy "character" and strike at "the roots of self-government." Instead, amid growing destitution, he called upon local government and private charity to relieve the distress of millions of citizens, but the program broke down before it got underway because the states did almost nothing, and local governments soon ran out of money. By 1932, 100 cities had no relief appropriations at all. New Orleans refused new applicants; Dallas and Houston gave no relief to Mexican and Negro families. In face of mass unemployment and widespread hunger, President Hoover held doggedly to his faith, blocking a Congressional bill which would have provided direct relief and vast public works.

Finally, after private actions and individual decisions had failed to cure the depression, the President decided reluctantly upon direct intervention in the economic system, making federal funds available for public works, industry, and agriculture. A major fault of the Hoover program, however, was that his remedies applied largely to the top of the economy—financial institutions and business corporations—rather than the bottom where the need was most desperate. For example, Hoover approved loans to private capitalists for purposes of profit but, at the same time, forbade the federal government either to give or lend a dollar to an unemployed man so that he might keep himself and his family alive. Yet, in proposing the federal government interfere with economic forces and take measures to counter the depression, President Hoover by his standards acted boldly, and he went as far as his faith would allow. [9]

III

In last analysis Hoover's failure to come to grips with the problems of depression was due to his inability to invoke the collective powers of government on behalf of the masses. This diffidence on his part stemmed from an elitist distrust of democracy and a genuine fear of the state. His view was that "the mass does not think but only feels." Acts and ideas that led to progress came from the individual, not from the crowd which had no mind of its own. "The crowd is credulous, it destroys, it consumes, it hates, and it dreams—but it never builds." It followed, then, that "popular desires are no criteria to the real need," and the task of constructive leadership was to firmly resist the clamor of the mob. Civilizations fell, Hoover believed, because great masses of men became impregnated with wrong ideas and wrong social philosophies—the most dangerous of which, in his opinion, was the Socialist delusion that government could produce economic equality by political action. Though troubled by the great abuses the depression had exposed in the economic system, the President, like his conservative business supporters, had an even more acute dread of "a regimented economy dictated by government through bureaucracy." He therefore determinedly opposed the centralization of relief in the federal government on grounds that it would concentrate power in the federal government by the erection of a huge political bureaucracy and that relief would itself become an instrument of patronage and the means for creation of a totalitarian state.[10]

While national planning, to an assertive individualist such as President Hoover, was "national regimentation," to socially minded thinkers such as Lewis Mumford and John Dewey it was more than an emergency measure, it was an inevitable consequence of the advance of technology. Invincible technological trends, declared Dewey, made the social control of economic forces necessary if the goals of democracy were to be realized. Those who shouted "regi-

---

In summer of 1932, some 20,000 homeless, penniless veterans descended upon Washington to lobby for passage of a veteran's bonus bill. After the bill failed in the Senate, President Hoover called out the U.S. Army to drive them from the capital at bayonet point.

Wide World Photos

mentation" had failed to see that effective liberty was a function of the social conditions existing at any time. As favored beneficiaries of the economic regime, they were blind to the fact that private control of the new forces of production operated in the same way as unchecked political power, imposing harsh regimentation upon millions of their fellow Americans. "Brain-truster" Rexford Tugwell also believed the role of the New Deal was to free the country from private economic regimentation. Big business had created a "supertrust" outside our political forms which threatened to swamp the state in the backwash of its progress. Hence the choice facing the American people in the thirties, as Tugwell saw it, was that either the government would supervise the businessmen, or the businessmen would supervise the government as they had done in the 1920's.[11]

If the state could organize for war, why—asked the theorists—could it not organize for peace and plenty? If it could mobilize against a foreign enemy, why not against enemies close at hand—hunger, poverty, and unemployment? If planning was necessary for the nation to exert its maximum military power, then, it was argued, national planning was necessary for maximum social power. Wars, in the past, had frequently helped to break the economic deadlock of depression because people gladly gave to government in wartime power and money for military purposes that they would not allow it to use or spend in peacetime for constructive aid to themselves. But, as the economist Paul H. Douglas put it, since going to war to get out of depression was like burning one's house down to roast pigs, there was a strong argument for national planning as an economic equivalent for war.[12]

Such "collectivist measures" were repudiated by Walter Lippmann, who saw them as an American manifestation of the worldwide trend toward totalitarianism. While admitting that planning was necessary and feasible under war conditions, he argued that peacetime planning was in-

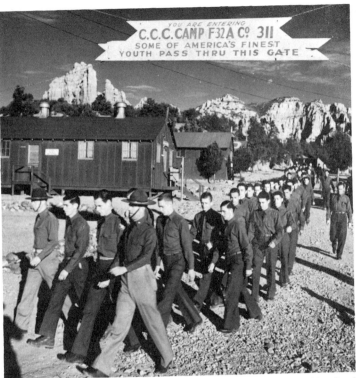

While New Deal measures against the depression were decried as "national regimentation," the Civilian Conservation Corps rescued many young Americans from meaningless lives of poverty and despair and made them useful citizens.

compatible with democracy.° Although twenty-five years before in his *Preface to Politics* Lippmann had held that disorder and misery could be overcome only by the organized forces of government, he reversed his position in the thirties. Everywhere he observed men who called themselves Communists, Socialists, Fascists, Nazis, and even "liberals" unanimously holding that only through the power

°Walter Lippmann, *The Servile State.* See page 203.

of the state could men be made happy. Instead, Lippmann now believed that, by a kind of tragic irony, all attempts to rationalize society under the auspices of the state must lead inevitably to an intolerable choice between liberty and security.[13]

However, as breadlines lengthened and Hoovervilles proliferated, the mood of the country became more rebellious. Rumors of revolution were widespread during the last months of the Hoover administration, and many feared the muttering retreat of the Bonus Army might be the spark to set off a bloody conflagration. *Harper's*, a normally unexcitable magazine, played up the possibilities of revolution at great length, asking on one occasion: "What is the American with the revolutionary birthright thinking about these days? His own country and the world are now in the midst of a vast economic upheaval. The system of production and distribution have been badly jammed, and some of the parts will never again be of any use. . . . The word revolution is heard at every hand; we seem to face revolutions of all sorts and kinds." In 1931, the Secret Service had attracted front-page attention by "uncovering" an alleged Communist plot to seize Washington, and the dean of the Harvard School of Business warned that capitalism was skirting a revolution that might change the whole future of Western civilization. These and other scare stories prompted the *Nation* to note forebodingly that the apprehensions of those in charge showed businessmen clearly realized the justifiable threat to their control of social arrangements. Yet, despite all the talk of revolution, except for a few riots, there was never any concerted attempt to overthrow the established order. Those who suffered most—the masses of jobless and hungry Americans—were curiously inert, "awaiting nothing more drastic than the return of prosperity."[14]

In the end, as Thurman Arnold observed, there was no uprising of the downtrodden, only panic on the part of the well-to-do. After the industrial situation had gotten beyond their control, the business leadership simply fled from responsibility. By their timorous abdication, which had been predicted by Veblen in 1921, the businessmen confessed their inability any longer to take care of the country's material welfare. Trapped in its own dogma, the business community was unable to propose or even to reconcile itself to bold and drastic remedies. Businessmen, *Harper's* observed, were too frightened: "frightened at what the present situation might lead to and frightened still more at the thought of trying any different policies than those which have prevailed in the past." Instead of defending capitalism by a positive leadership which accepted social responsibility and met the real needs of the majority of people, the laggard business directorate fought a series of rearguard engagements to maintain its privileges. Faced with new problems for which their methods and ways of thinking were completely inadequate, business leaders found that they were unable to exorcise the specter of depression by invoking the old catchwords, and they retreated in disorder and terror. "Business, which nobody dared to frighten," marveled the radio commentator Elmer Davis, "is afraid at last of its own shadow."[15]

When business failed as a governing force, a government based upon a tradition of inaction and non-interference was compelled to rush in and fill the vacuum. By popular mandate the incoming Roosevelt administration was called upon to rescue the ailing economy and to correct by governmental action the shortcomings of the old economic order. Since the chief fault of the old order had been a failure in technical management—"private planning" wholly out of social control had brought national economic ruin—the problems business passed to government were ultimately to be resolved only by technical means. As President Franklin D. Roosevelt told American voters, in order to achieve the full employment of industry and manpower and to bring about an equitable and sufficient supply of goods and services to the people at large, it was necessary to add to the traditional political role of government a new economic role and to extend the positive powers of government into economic affairs.* "We see things now that we could not see along the way. The tools of government which we had in 1933 are outmoded. We have had to forge new tools for a new role of government operating in a democracy—a role of new responsibility for new needs and increased responsibility for old needs long neglected." The new role of "progressive government" was to create and maintain a balance between the various elements within the economy: "What we seek is balance in our economic system—balance between agriculture and industry, and balance between the wage earner, the employer, and the consumer." To carry out this interventionist role, the positive program of government under the New Deal involved the regulation of private enterprise, economic planning, governmental ownership and operation of commercial and industrial enterprises, and the extension of economic aid and services to individuals and private groups.[16]

The revolutionary expansion of the powers of government under the New Deal provoked resistance and criticism from Right and Left—from those who had wealth and power and those who had neither but claimed possession of the formula for the future. The movement of the Right was composed of prosperous businessmen and lawyers, was elitist and capitalistic in outlook, favored monopolistic business, and inclined toward state capitalism or Fascism. The movement of the Left was made up of Marxist writers and intellectuals, was studiously proletarian in view, attacked capitalistic institutions, and tended logically toward state socialism or Communism. Though at opposite ends of the political spectrum, these two rival minority groups had common origins and ends. Both were radical collectivist movements born in rebellion against the free market; both in extreme and desperate form ended in totalitarianism;

*Franklin D. Roosevelt, *The Welfare State.* See page 210.

both distrusted democratic liberalism and bitterly assailed the New Deal, each purportedly seeing behind it the deceitful machinations of the other. On the Right, the American Liberty League, speaking for corporate wealth and all those fearful of encroachment on vested rights, protested unbridled government and denounced the New Deal as "socialistic"; on the Left, dogmatic Marxists of the Socialist and Communist parties rejected the "Roosevelt Revolution" as a capitalist counter-revolution exploiting democracy for the purposes of "social Fascism."[17]

IV

As things turned out, however, the New Deal yielded neither to socialism nor totalitarianism, but evolved what Robert Heilbroner has called "a new form of *guided* capitalism." Rather than a radical revision of capitalism, the New Deal followed a policy of economic interventionism based upon government responsibility for the economic security and prosperity of the whole society. Despite business protests of "regimentation," the New Deal never moved as far toward collectivism as its critics feared. President Roosevelt, said Secretary of Labor Frances Perkins, "always resisted the frequent suggestion of the Government's taking over railroads, mines, etc., on the ground that it was unnecessary and would be a clumsy way to get the service needed." While recognizing that the economy had slowed down and the forces within it were no longer in equilibrium, Roosevelt refused to concede to the Marxists that the mechanism had permanently broken down. Instead of taking over and running everything, he proposed only to repair it and make it run again. "We took the middle road," said the President in 1936. "We used the facilities and resources available only to Government, to permit individual enterprise to resume its normal functions in a socially sound competitive order." Though condemned by men of wealth as a traitor to his class, Roosevelt through the New Deal may have checked the power of capitalism, but as Socialists bitterly complained, he did not kill capitalism.[18]

Innovation, not revolution, was the trade-mark of the New Deal. A politics of expediency in the sense that it sought pragmatic, not ideological answers, the New Deal searched for acceptable solutions to problems rather than imposing preconceived solutions. As Tugwell stressed at the time, its method was democratic experimentalism. It looked forward to "no antiseptic utopia and no socialistic paradise," but to "a changing system in which free American human beings can live their changing lives." Rarely did New Deal measures or New Dealers as a group represent a clear-cut ideological preference. "Total planners and piecemeal planners, budget-balancers and deficit spenders, trust-regulators and trust-busters, protectionists and free-traders, 'sound money' proponents and inflationists," wrote Heinz Eulau, "all vied with each other under the hospitable tent that was the New Deal." Yet, despite its ideological elusiveness, nearly all measures sponsored by Roosevelt—emergency relief, farm aid, social security, conservation, banking and securities reform, fair labor standards—were in the mainstream of American democratic tradition and involved strengthening the state not at the expense of society but for the benefit of society. It is noteworthy, for example, that the most "socialistic" undertaking of the New Deal, the Tennessee Valley Authority, caused private enterprise to flourish in an area where previously it had barely existed—after 1933 the rate of growth of private industry was greater in the Tennessee Valley than in the rest of the nation.[19]

At bottom the chief difference and underlying conflict between the New Deal and its Republican predecessors was not, as Hoover insisted, between two philosophies of government—for, after all, Hoover and Roosevelt were both capitalists rather than socialists, both democrats rather than totalitarians—but, as more accurately described by Roosevelt, between two theories of prosperity. Where Hoover associated the good of all with the prosperity of a chosen group—the businessmen of the country—and directed national policy primarily for their benefit, Roosevelt regarded public power as an instrument for the benefit of all the nation. While Hoover provided aid at the top of the economy calculated to "trickle down" from the producers to the mass of people, Roosevelt gave help at both top and bottom, and widened the scope of government to include direct aid to farmers being starved off their lands and to workers shut out of idle factories. For the first time, under the New Deal, the federal government underwrote the economic security of the farmer, as had been done for the businessman and industrialist since the 1860's, and offered organized labor the kind of governmental encouragement and cooperation that in the past had been the exclusive prerogative of organized business.

As a consequence, under New Deal auspices, not only was there a marked rise in farm income and prices, but organized labor made phenomenal gains. With government and the courts now guaranteeing the right of labor "to organize and bargain collectively," there was a rush to join unions. In 1935, John L. Lewis formed the Committee for Industrial Organization which, on being expelled from the A. F. of L., became a rival specializing in industrial unions. Hundreds of thousands of unskilled workers for whom there had been no place in old-fashioned craft unions flocked to join the C.I.O., whose membership in two years jumped to four million. Under the ruthless, dynamic leadership of the beetle-browed Lewis, the C.I.O. moved into industries which hitherto had successfully resisted unionization, especially steel and autos. Faced with widespread "sit down" strikes, United States Steel capitulated. General Motors resisted, only to surrender after a terrific struggle. Although subsequent strikes against "Little Steel" failed, there was no doubt that organized labor under the New Deal won a legitimate position in the economy as a "countervailing force" to the organized power of big business.[20]

In recognizing the interdependence of agriculture, industry, business and labor, and of the welfare of all, the New Deal employed mercantilist principles and methods advocated by Alexander Hamilton in 1791. By its bold approach to the problems of depression, Eugene Golob suggested, it "revived the mercantilist's willingness to experiment and his lack of fear of innovation" and, at the same time, directed to popular ends the Hamiltonian concept that government was to interest itself directly in the welfare of the citizenry. Under the New Deal, the narrow neomercantilist policy of the Hoover administration was democratized and greatly broadened in scope, and the eighteenth-century concern with money and fiscal management applied with renewed vigor. But private property was never seriously threatened, and private enterprise, though regulated more carefully, remained still the basic characteristic of the economy. So one may conclude with Golob: "If there was a 'Roosevelt revolution,' with the one possible exception of its hastening of the inevitable recognition of labor's place in society, it was only in the minds of those who had lost touch with the past. If the New Deal was 'radical,' it was so only in the sense that it constituted a radical return to the conservative tradition of the mercantilists." Historic confirmation of the triumph of neomercantilism was the moving of the economic capital of the United States from New York City to Washington, D.C., by passage of the Employment Act of 1946, which officially recognized that it was "the continuing policy and responsibility of the Federal Government . . . to promote maximum employment, production, and purchasing power."[21]

But, along with many far-reaching social and economic reforms, the New Deal made many mistakes and fell short of many liberal hopes, especially in the area of economic planning. Although labor had been granted a long overdue bill of rights, the importance of the consumer-worker whose economic function of mass consumption had grown more and more vital as technology increased the complexity and velocity of mass production had been generally overlooked; and no serious attempt had been made to adjust wages, not to a dwindling sum of toil, but to the growing total of consumption. A timid beginning had been made toward social security, but health was omitted, and provisions against the great hazards of unemployment and old age were mean and niggardly. The initial effect of New Deal economic policies had been to inaugurate four years of steady and rapid

On Memorial Day 1937, a peaceful crowd of C.I.O. sympathizers, including women and children, demonstrating before the non-union Republic Steel plant in Chicago were fired upon by police, and in the subsequent massacre ten demonstrators were killed and more than seventy-five injured.

Wide World Photos

recovery—industrial production in this period doubled and real income increased more than fifty percent, both regaining the 1929 peak—but hasty and ill-advised fiscal and monetary policies brought recovery to a halt in 1937. Roosevelt's deficiencies as an economist were in the opinion of Robert Heilbroner as striking as his triumphs as a politician. In many cases, as Thurman Arnold, a former New Dealer, complained, "measures were improvised and hurled at symptoms" without thorough diagnosis. Often where vigorous and decisive action was called for, the Roosevelt administration settled for halfway measures, especially when it came to deficit spending. For all the cry against government spending, the sums laid out by the New Deal for social welfare and public works were pitifully meager, far too small to "prime the pump" of a great economy. As a result, by 1939, although conditions had vastly improved, there were still 9.5 million Americans, about 17 percent of the labor force, without work.[22]

At last resort, it was primarily the demands of approaching war, not New Deal policy, which increased government spending and led to full production and employment. Ironically, the war expanded civilian consumption fifty percent. While the New Deal had created technical devices for governing the economy, it not only had not learned how to use them effectively but found it ideologically impossible to put them to full use because of the still prevailing popular distrust of compensatory government spending in times of peace. With the coming of World War II, however, the nation moved rapidly, and without undue sentimental shock, into a planned prosperity which was based upon huge government expenditures for arms and which necessitated tight controls over production and distribution, wages and prices, profits, rents, and consumer spending. What democracy and humanitarianism had been unable to accomplish in the name of a better life, patriotism and militarism easily achieved when the goal was mass slaughter.

Readings:

Collapse of the Old Order

Thomas Nixon Carver (1865-1961)

A respected orthodox economist, he was professor of economics at Oberlin College from 1894 to 1900, then at Harvard until his retirement in 1937. He specialized in the sociological aspects of economics, taking the point of view that the full development of the capitalistic system would not be reached until practically everyone has become a capitalist.

WHAT CAPITALISM IS AND WHAT IT DOES

Whatever may be said against capitalism it has at least abolished famine in every country where it has been permitted to develop freely. That is more than can be said of any noncapitalistic system that ever existed. The worst that can be said against the capitalistic system is that it has not yet abolished inequality of wealth. Those inequal-

From *The Present Economic Revolution in the United States* (Boston: Little, Brown & Co., 1925), pp. 209–12, 215–21. Copyright Thomas Nixon Carver; reprinted by permission of Mrs. Ruth Ripley Carver.

ities which still persist, however, are not essential to the capitalistic system. In fact, where capitalism is given a chance to develop freely, unhampered by social and political obstacles, it tends to eliminate its own inequalities and secure not only great abundance for everybody, but to distribute the best things of life more evenly than any other system has ever succeeded in doing.

In spite of all the inequalities which persist under capitalism the masses of the people are better off under it than they have ever been under any other system. In fact, they are better fed, clothed, housed, and supplied with the adornments and embellishments of life than any but the rulers and a few hereditary aristocrats in any noncapitalistic country. . . .

It is an observed fact that laborers seldom migrate from a capitalistic to a noncapitalistic country, unless lured by free land or undeveloped mines, forests, or other natural resources. When these natural resources are once occupied and no longer free, the migration turns toward those places where capital has accumulated in largest quantities. That is where they find the best jobs, the highest wages, and the best living conditions. . . . Either the laborers are very unwise in doing this or there is a sound reason why they should do so.

These reasons are perfectly clear to anyone who understands what capitalism really is. The difficulty is that the word capitalism has been pronounced with such a wry face by so many persons. This has caused many of us to feel that it is necessarily bad. Those who feel that way about it have never really tried to understand it, but have tried, rather, to find new epithets to apply to it.

One difficulty in the way of a proper understanding of capitalism is the tendency to judge it by its superficial or temporary aspects rather than by its fundamental and permanent aspects. Strictly speaking, capitalism is not a system at all. It is merely a fact that grows out of the suppression of violence. Wherever violence is repressed, capital comes automatically into existence. Where violence is repressed, the man who has made a thing, or found it before anyone else has gained possession of it, cannot be dispossessed without his consent. No government can repress violence without automatically creating property as a result. Of course, this is only the beginning of our present system of property. This germ that is created by the mere repression of violence has been cultivated and developed by many other acts of government. Rightful possession has to be defined; what constitutes valid possession, a valid transfer, a valid contract, and many other questions of like character, have to be determined by government through its courts before any modern system of property is complete. Nevertheless, property would exist, in a simple and undeveloped form, even if government did nothing in the world except repress all violence. . . .

The so-called system of private property, therefore, is not a system in itself; it is a natural and unavoidable result of the repression of violence. . . .

The safety which comes from the repression of violence not only encourages accumulation but also invention. In fact, mechanical inventions and accumulations of capital go together like the two blades of a pair of scissors. Neither is of much use without the other. Where there are no mechanical inventors, no matter how many savers or accumulators there are, such accumulations of wealth as are possible must largely be in the form of hoards of money, jewels and other consumers' goods rather than of producers' goods. Where there are no savers and accumulators, there is no one who is willing to invest labor or money in expensive machines. No matter how many inventive geniuses there may be, productive inventions will not be used. If conditions are so unsafe as to discourage savings and accumulations, goods whose uses extend over the distant future are not likely to be accumulated at all because everyone is uncertain as to whether he will get the use of them or not. Mechanical inventions, especially of the larger and more productive sort, can seldom yield an immediate product sufficient to pay the cost. They must be kept for a long time before they will pay for themselves. In short, they are among the forms of accumulation which depend most closely upon safe conditions. No one will invest money or labor in such things unless he has confidence that they will not be taken away from him without his consent. . . .

The vast accumulation of machines and other expensive forms of capital that results from the permanent suppression of violence is very impressive. It seems to be one of the outstanding features of the present economic situation. It is not surprising, therefore, that a great deal of attention should be concentrated upon it, nor that they who concentrate their attention upon it should sometimes fail to see the underlying fact which produced it. The great tree is more impressive to the casual passer-by than the conditions which permitted it to grow.

These accumulations of powerful mechanisms, however, do not constitute the real capitalistic system. They are merely the visible manifestations of it. The real system was created when possession was protected by the suppression of violence. Wherever that fact exists, the outward and visible manifestations of it, such as the accumulation of wealth in durable forms and the development of powerful engines of production, will come into existence. These things will not go out of existence until possession is no longer protected. . . .

The existence of fraud or deception may still remain a factor unless the same power that defends the possessor against violence also defends him against fraud. When both fraud and violence are effectively repressed, industry and foresight, or general productive power, become the chief factors in prosperity. Differences in prosperity are based largely upon differences in the power to produce and in the foresight that leads to accumulation.

Even this situation is not free from danger. They who have, for any reason, failed to accumulate may envy those who have succeeded. Others may sympathize with the envious ones and invent apologies and excuses for them. If this envy grows strong enough, it is very likely to lead to acts of violence either by individuals or classes. Class war is especially dangerous and destructive of civilization. So long as the government succeeds in repressing violence, possessors remain safe in their possession. When, for any reason, the government fails to repress violence, possession ceases to be property. Possessions must then be defended by the prowess of their possessors or else the possessors will lose them to those who have the power to take by force what they want.

Sometimes the very engine, namely, government, that began by repressing violence becomes itself the engine of violence. Instead of defending the possessors, it uses its superior power to dispossess them. There is always danger of this if those who have not accumulated anything grow envious enough and numerous enough to gain control of the government. They may then use it as a means of taking accumulations away from those who accumulated them. The wealth thus taken away from its accumulators may then be disposed of in two ways. One is to give it to the nonaccumulators, the other is for the government to hold it and give the income derived from it to all without regard to the degree of foresight exercised by different individuals. Under these conditions, the foreseeing and the thoughtless fare alike. Foresight would not be rewarded at all because the individual would be given no opportunity to exercise it, or to accumulate the results of his foresight. If he tried to exercise it he would be dispossessed of his accumulations by the government. The very power which we now rely upon to protect us against being dispossessed without our consent would then be perverted to the performance of that which it was designed to repress.

It was pointed out earlier that a highly capitalistic country . . . always attracts laborers from noncapitalistic countries. They come because wages and other conditions are better than they were in their noncapitalistic homes. These good wages and good living conditions which attract immigrants also encourage the multiplication of thoughtless and thriftless people at home. There is, therefore, a strong probability that a considerable propertyless class will develop. It may become so large as to be dangerous. If it should be able to outvote the class of savers and accumulators, it may gain control of the government and use it as an engine for the dispossession of those who have managed to accumulate. The safety of modern civilization requires that these nonaccumulating classes shall be kept few in number.

The full development of the so-called capitalistic system will not be reached until practically everyone has become a capitalist, that is, an owner or part owner of some of the instruments of production called capital. The suppression of violence took power out of the hands of those who were willing and able to prosper by the use of violence. This made it possible for those who were too gentle or too weak physically to profit by violence to prosper by means of their industry and foresight. When everyone takes advantage of this opportunity, the full benefits of the suppression of violence will be realized. All real progress in the past has aimed in this direction, and all real progress in the future must lie in the same direction. No forcible leveling of the industrious and the idle is progressive; it is retrogressive. Any forcible leveling of the thrifty and the thriftless, of the forethoughtful and the nonforethoughtful, is equally retrogressive.

The crisis of civilization is reached whenever civilized people face this question. When the nonaccumulators refuse to respect the laws for the repression of violence, and begin to take by violence what others have peacefully accumulated, conditions are bad enough. In so far as they succeed in defying the efforts of the government to preserve law and order, to that extent must civilization decline. Conditions are much worse, however, when the nonaccumulators, instead of resisting the government, become numerous enough to gain control of it and unscrupulous enough to use it as the means of violence, that is, as the agency for the forcible dispossession of the peaceful accumulators. This is vastly more destructive of civilization than merely resisting government.

Stuart Chase (1888–   )

Born into an old New England family, he graduated cum laude *from Harvard in 1910 and entered his father's accounting firm. His interest in social problems began the day he picked up Henry George's* Progress and Poverty. *In the 1920's, under the influence of Thorstein Veblen, he joined the staff of the Technical Alliance (nucleus of a later and more famous organization called Technocracy) and in 1927 helped found Consumers' Research. Although he has written many books, a single theme runs through them all, namely the impact of the machine on human beings.*

WHAT IS AN ECONOMIC SYSTEM FOR?

John Maynard Keynes tells us that in one hundred years there will be no economic problem. He is probably right. We have already largely solved the problem of production, in the sense that the nations of America and Western Europe are equipped to produce more than enough to go around. In a few years Russia will undoubtedly join them. We have left the economy of scarcity behind and entered

From *A New Deal* (New York: The Macmillan Co., 1932), pp. 1–5, 21–3. Copyright Stuart Chase; reprinted by permission of the author.

the economy of abundance—though very few of us realize this, and most of our thinking is still in terms of scarcity economics, a cultural lag which we shall presently discuss. A billion and a half horses of mechanical energy, added to the time-honored stock of man and animal power, have at last put us in the position where, if we care to concentrate our energy, we can raise more food than we can eat, build more houses than we can inhabit, fabricate more clothing than we can wear out. Only by wasting and even deliberate destruction—such as the burning of cotton, corn, and coffee—can we dispose of the present output under the prevailing price system.

Distribution, the other wing of the economic problem, is *not* solved, as the present depression bears eloquent testimony. We can pile up the goods in the warehouse with an efficiency hitherto unknown to homo sapiens, but there they stick. We cannot get them out in sufficient volume either to keep the productive plant functioning steadily, and thus economically, or to keep the general population adequately fed, sheltered, and clothed. At times—as in America from 1922 to 1929—the flow, while far below capacity, leaving many millions on the ragged edge, is relatively better. At other times—as in 1921, and from 1930 to the present date—it is totally inadequate. Warehouses bulge and children cry for food.

That we have solved the main outlines of production—the inflow—does not help us much. Unless distribution—the outflow—can be directed, the misery which springs from economic causes will tend to continue unabated. Though we have entered the economy of abundance, its practical effects must be confined to certain classes in certain periods called "prosperity," unless the dam which impounds the warehoused products can be channeled. Strangely enough the dam, stubborn as it is, is made of paper. Goods do not flow out because there is insufficient purchasing power available to call them forth. Gradually students of economics are being forced to the conclusion—and this depression has helped to force them—that a dependable supply of purchasing power provides one basic answer to the riddle of distribution.

Why is purchasing power inadequate, why do we Western peoples fail to gain the full benefits of an economy of abundance; why must we go through such scarifying periods of mental panic and physical deprivation as the present? How can they be avoided? . . .

Certainly one fundamental cause of the failure of distribution is the prevailing attitude towards the methods whereby we are, if lucky, fed, sheltered and clothed. What is an economic system for? By and large it is regarded either as a means to achieve power and prestige, or as an amusing game to be played, the counters being those same pieces of paper which form purchasing power. Says John Dewey:

> The psychology and morale of business are based on trading in insecurity. They are criticised by serious moralists as if the animating spirit were that of acquisition. The accusations do not reach the mark. . . . It is the excitement of the game which counts. . . . We hunt the dollar, but hunting is hunting, not dollars.

The element of gambling enters into even the soberest and most orthodox of financial calculations. Profit is the reward of *risk*, the classical economists tell us. When the market is not rigged in advance, this is often true. Risk means something not sure, upon which one takes a chance, in short, a game.

It is assumed, in a left-handed way, that in accumulating the power, or in playing the game, we contrive somehow to grease the wheels of industry and serve a social purpose. Occasionally such is indeed the case, but normally this reasoning is pure rationalization. What man, starting in business, asks himself with any care whether the work he proposes to do will strengthen or weaken the economic system; whether it will serve a social function; whether it will increase or decrease the evil effects of the business cycle; whether it will choke or expand the flow of purchasing power? Such questions are normally undreamed of, and are displaced by others: is there money in the venture? or, is there fun in it? . . .

The cardinal questions simply are not asked. Hardly anybody bothers to inquire what an economic system is for. Certain rules and procedures have grown up. These are taken for granted, and within their limits, those responsible for directing economic activity, primarily the business man and the banker, attempt to satisfy their egos and appetites, and to play their games. This would be all very well if there were a divine providence looking after the system, insuring, while men sought to amuse themselves, an automatic and dependable output of goods. But providence, we ought by now to realize, displays not the slightest interest in steering a mechanism men neglect.

Out of the human need for nourishment, a mechanism has been established, simple among handicraft peoples, exceedingly complicated among peoples of the machine age. In broad outline it may be compared to the human body, where the cooperation of millions of cells is essential to the efficient functioning which means health and life. When a group of cells refuses to cooperate, becomes unduly imbued with what might be called anatomical rugged individualism, we have a cancer and, in the end, death. Persistent irritations are often responsible for cancers. Fortunately the body has an automatic nervous system which normally keeps the cells in order with little or no conscious control. The economic body has no such biological protection; it lies defenseless against abuse. . . .

What is an economic system for? We return to the original point. Is it . . . primarily to be manipulated for some individual's profit, power or amusement? This brings us to a very important consideration, one frequently overlooked by critics of the established order. It is not the profit which the fortune hunter actually takes which makes the bulk of the trouble; it is *the waste and maladjustment he creates in trying to take it.* For every success there are scores of failures, and most of the failures are responsible for at least as much dislocation as the successes. In an economy of abundance, properly organized, we could probably stand the cash drain on purchasing power caused by the profiteers and absentee owners. What no system can bear indefinitely is the continual roweling of its vitals by those who are trying to get rich. It makes little difference whether they succeed or fail; the operation is disastrous in either case. If we took all the income away from the wealthy and distributed it to the rest of the population, the standard of living of the latter would be increased, according to Professor Bowley, only some ten percent. But if we could eliminate the gyrations of those who are trying to become wealthy, we could abolish poverty and double the standard of living, virtually over night.

The defenders of the existing system roll their eyes to heaven at the thought of limiting these gyrations—with qualifications, perhaps, in respect to the more outré forms of racketeering and graft; but speculation they defend as providing some mystical variety of balance wheel. The pursuit of individual profit, they insist, is the force which keeps the mechanism going; progress, civilization itself, would collapse without it. . . . [This] is nonsense. Such activities throttle genuine progress.

Well, what *is* an economic system for? It is to provide a means, without excessive waste and loss, whereby those who live under it may eat. It has a function, and the function is to provide food, shelter, clothing and comforts in as dependable and adequate quantities as natural resources and the state of the technical arts permit, just as the function of human physiology is to supply every cell with enough oxygen and nutriment. When used as a channel for personal aggrandizement, a system's function and meaning collapse. It becomes an industrial whirlpool, throwing out a certain amount of goods and services as a byproduct, but susceptible to frightful stoppages, reverse twists, and even complete draining out. We have come in 1932 perilously close to the last.

From the functional point of view, economic activity takes on an entirely new meaning. It becomes at once more serious and less omnipotent. Order, discipline, the consciousness of definite social aim are needed to insure a dependable flow of goods from the earth to the ultimate consumer, but when that discipline—and it is largely one of engineering— is established, economic activity, with its four to six hours of work a day, becomes, if not a minor, at least a subordinate consideration. More important will be the problem of how to live; how to use fruitfully one's leisure time; how to improve the biological stock; how to educate; how to love and marry without the emotional miseries which now beset us; how to develop the arts; how to get the most out of life. These are the real problems of a civilized people who have yoked a billion of mechanical horse power. To go on stumbling through economic pits and mires, under a sky recurrently black with the horror of insecurity and even starvation, is tragic and needless waste.

Herbert Hoover (1874–1964)

Thirty-first President of the United States, he worked his way through Stanford University, and then engaged in mining operations abroad, first in Australia, then in China, Africa, Central and South America, and Russia. Between the Boxer Rebellion (1900) and World War I he built a $6 million fortune as an international consulting engineer. Because he left the country in the days of McKinley Republicanism not to return until the Harding administration, he entirely missed the Progressive period with its campaigns for political and social reform which,

*if experienced, might have tempered his in-
flexible individualism.*

ECONOMIC INDIVIDUALISM

That high and increasing standards of living and comfort
should be the first of considerations in public mind and in
government needs no apology. We have long since realized
that the basis of an advancing civilization must be a high
and growing standard of living for all the people, not for a
single class; that education, food, clothing, housing, and the
spreading use of what we so often term non-essentials, are
the real fertilizers of the soil from which spring the finer
flowers of life. The economic development of the past
fifty years has lifted the general standard of comfort far
beyond the dreams of our forefathers. The only road to
further advance in the standard of living is by greater invention, greater elimination of waste, greater production
and better distribution of commodities and services, for by
increasing their ratio to our numbers and dividing them
justly we each will have more of them.

The superlative value of individualism through its impulse
to production, its stimulation to invention, has, so far as I
know, never been denied. Criticism of it has lain in its
wastes but more importantly in its failures of equitable
sharing of the product. In our country these contentions
are mainly over the division to each of his share of the
comforts and luxuries, for none of us is either hungry or
cold or without a place to lay his head—and we have much
besides. In less than four decades we have added electric
lights, plumbing, telephones, gramophones, automobiles,
and what not in wide diffusion to our standards of living.

From *American Individualism* (Garden City: Doubleday, Page & Co., 1922),
pp. 32–40, 44–5. Reprinted by permission of Mr. Frank E. Mason.

Each in turn began as a luxury, each in turn has become so commonplace that seventy or eighty per cent of our people participate in them.

To all practical souls there is little use in quarreling over the share of each of us until we have something to divide. So long as we maintain our individualism we will have increasing quantities to share and we shall have time and leisure and taxes with which to fight out proper sharing of the "surplus." The income tax returns show that this surplus is a minor part of our total production after taxes are paid. Some of this "surplus" must be set aside for rewards to saving for stimulation of proper effort to skill, to leadership and invention—therefore the dispute is in reality over much less than the total of such "surplus." While there should be no minimizing of a certain fringe of injustices in sharing the results of production or in the wasteful use made by some of their share, yet there is vastly wider field for gains to all of us through cheapening the costs of production and distribution through the eliminating of their wastes, from increasing the volume of product by each and every one doing his utmost, than will ever come to us even if we can think out a method of abstract justice in sharing which did not stifle production of the total product.

It is a certainty we are confronted with a population in such numbers as can only exist by production attuned to a pitch in which the slightest reduction of the impulse to produce will at once create misery and want. If we throttle the fundamental impulses of man our production will decay. The world in this hour is witnessing the most overshadowing tragedy of ten centuries in the heart-breaking life-and-death struggle with starvation by a nation with a hundred and fifty millions of people. In Russia under the new tyranny a group, in pursuit of social theories, have destroyed the primary self-interest impulse of the individual to production. . . .

But those are utterly wrong who say that individualism

has as its only end the acquisition and preservation of private property—the selfish snatching and hoarding of the common product. Our American individualism, indeed, is only in part an economic creed. It aims to provide opportunity for self-expression, not merely economically, but spiritually as well. Private property is not a fetish in America. The crushing of the liquor trade without a cent of compensation, with scarcely even a discussion of it, does not bear out the notion that we give property rights any headway over human rights. Our development of individualism shows an increasing tendency to regard right of property not as an object in itself, but in the light of a useful and necessary instrument in stimulation of initiative to the individual; not only stimulation to him that he may gain personal comfort, security in life, protection to his family, but also because individual accumulation and ownership is a basis of selection to leadership in administration of the tools of industry and commerce. It is where dominant private property is assembled in the hands of the groups who control the state that the individual begins to feel capital as an oppressor. Our American demand for equality of opportunity is a constant militant check upon capital becoming a thing to be feared. Out of fear we sometimes even go too far and stifle the reproductive use of capital by crushing the initiative that makes for its creation. . . .

The domination by arbitrary individual ownership is disappearing because the works of today are steadily growing more and more beyond the resources of any one individual, and steadily taxation will reduce relatively excessive individual accumulations. The number of persons in partnership through division of ownership among many stockholders is steadily increasing—thus 100,000 to 200,000 partners in a single concern are not uncommon. The overwhelmingly largest portion of our mobile capital is that of our banks, insurance companies, building and loan associations, and the vast majority of all this is the aggregated small

savings of our people. Thus large capital is steadily becoming more and more a mobilization of the savings of
the small holder—the actual people themselves—and its
administration becomes at once more sensitive to the moral
opinions of the people in order to attract their support.
The directors and managers of large concerns, themselves
employees of these great groups of individual stockholders,
or policy holders, reflect a spirit of community responsibility. . . .

Today business organization is moving strongly toward
cooperation. There are in the cooperative great hopes that
we can even gain in individuality, equality of opportunity,
and an enlarged field for initiative, and at the same time
reduce many of the great wastes of over-reckless competition in production and distribution. Those who either congratulate themselves or those who fear that cooperation
is an advance toward socialism need neither rejoice or
worry. Cooperation in its current economic sense represents
the initiative of self-interest blended with a sense of service, for nobody belongs to a cooperative who is not striving to sell his products or services for more or striving to
buy from others for less or striving to make his income
more secure. Their members are furnishing the capital for
extension of their activities just as effectively as if they
did it in corporate form and they are simply transferring
the profit principle from joint return to individual return.
Their only success lies where they eliminate waste either
in production or distribution—and they can do neither if
they destroy individual initiative. Indeed this phase of development of our individualism promises to become the
dominant note of its 20th Century expansion. But it will
thrive only in so far as it can construct leadership and a
sense of service, and so long as it preserves the initiative
and safeguards the individuality of its members.

Adolf A. Berle, Jr. (1895–   )

*Lawyer, teacher, diplomat, writer, and corpora-
tion expert, he was one of President Roosevelt's
brain trusters. An apprentice and friend of
Louis D. Brandeis, he refused to carry on
Brandeis' famous battle against the curse of
bigness in business, contending that it was a
"liberal stereotype" rather than a rational appraisal of the facts. Big business, in his view,
was one of the major forces steadily and almost
unintentionally transforming American life—
and doing this, he maintained, with less agony,
less noise, and less waste than was the case in
any other twentieth-century revolution.*

Gardiner C. Means (1896–   )

*An influential economist with a doctorate from
Harvard, he was, like Berle, associated with the
New Deal in an advisory capacity. From 1933 to
1935 he served as economic adviser to the Secretary of Agriculture and then with the National
Resources Planning Board until the end of the
decade. Significantly, the statistics on corporate
concentration quoted by President Roosevelt in
the Commonwealth Club address of 1932 were
drawn from research done by Means while at
Columbia.*

ECONOMIC ORGANIZATION

Underlying the thinking of economists, lawyers and business

men during the last century and a half has been the picture of economic life so skillfully painted by Adam Smith. Within his treatise on the "Wealth of Nations" are contained the fundamental concepts which run through most modern thought. Though adjustments in his picture have been made by later writers to account for new conditions, the whole has been painted in the colors which he supplied. Private property, private enterprise, individual initiative, the profit motive, wealth, competition,—these are the concepts which he employed in describing the economy of his time and by means of which he sought to show that the pecuniary self-interest of each individual, if given free play, would lead to the optimum satisfaction of human wants. Most writers of the Nineteenth Century built on these logical foundations, and current economic literature is, in large measure, cast in such terms.

Yet these terms have ceased to be accurate, and therefore tend to mislead in describing modern enterprise as carried on by the great corporations. Though both the terms and the concepts remain, they are inapplicable to a dominant area in American economic organization. New terms, connoting changed relationships, become necessary. . . .

Private Property

To Adam Smith and to his followers, private property was a unity involving possession. He assumed that ownership and control were combined. Today, in the modern corporation, this unity has been broken. *Passive property,*—specifically, shares of stock or bonds,—gives its possessors an interest in an enterprise but gives them practically no control over it, and involves no responsibility. *Active property,*—plant, good will, organization, and so forth which make up the actual enterprise,—is controlled by individuals who, almost invariably, have only minor ownership interests in it. In terms of relationships, the present situation can be described as including:—(1) "passive property," consisting of a set of relationships between an individual and an enterprise, involving rights of the individual toward the enterprise but almost no effective powers over it; and (2) "active property," consisting of a set of relationships under which an individual or set of individuals hold powers over an enterprise but have almost no duties in respect to it which can be effectively enforced. When active and passive property relationships attach to the same individual or group, we have private property as conceived by the older economists. When they attach to different individuals, private property in the instruments of production disappears. Private property in the share of stock still continues, since the owner possesses the share and has power to dispose of it, but his share of stock is only a token representing a bundle of ill-protected rights and expectations. It is the possession of this token which can be transferred, a transfer which has little if any influence on the instruments of production. Whether possession of active property,—power of control over an enterprise, apart from ownership,—will ever be looked upon as private property which can belong to and be disposed of by its possessor is a problem of the future, and no prediction can be made with respect to it. Whatever the answer, it is clear that in dealing with the modern corporation we are not dealing with the old type of private property. Our description of modern economy, in so far as it deals with the quasi-public corporation, must be in terms of the two forms of property, active and passive, which for the most part lie in different hands.

Wealth

In a similar way, the concept "wealth" has been changed and divided. To Adam Smith, wealth was composed of tangible things,—wheat and land and buildings, ships and merchandise,—and for most people wealth is still thought of in physical terms. Yet in connection with the modern corporation, two essentially different types of wealth exist. To the holder of passive property, the stockholder, wealth consists, not of tangible goods,—factories, railroad stations, machinery,—but of a bundle of expectations which have a market value and which, if held, may bring him income and, if sold in the market, may give him power to obtain some other form of wealth. To the possessor of active property,—the "control"—wealth means a great enterprise which he dominates, an enterprise whose value is for the most part composed of the organized relationship of tangible properties, the existence of a functioning organization of workers and the existence of a functioning body of consumers. Instead of having control over a body of tangible wealth with an easily ascertainable market value, the group in control of a large modern corporation is astride an organism which has little value except as it continues to function, and for which there is no ready market. Thus, side by side, these two forms of wealth exist:—on the one hand passive wealth,—liquid, impersonal and involving no responsibility, passing from hand to hand and constantly appraised in the market place; and on the other hand, active wealth,—great, functioning organisms dependent for their lives on their security holders, their workers and consumers, but most of all on their mainspring,—"control." The two forms of wealth are not different aspects of the same thing, but are essentially and functionally distinct.

Private Enterprise

Again, to Adam Smith, private enterprise meant an individual or a few partners actively engaged and relying in large part on their own labor or their immediate direction. Today we have tens and hundreds of thousands of owners, of workers and of consumers combined in single enterprises. These great associations are so different from the small, privately owned enterprises of the past as to make the concept of private enterprise an ineffective instrument of analysis. It must be replaced with the concept of corporate enterprise, enterprise which is the organized activity of vast bodies of individuals, workers, consumers and suppliers of capital, under the leadership of the dictators of industry, "control."

Individual Initiative

As private enterprise disappears with increasing size, so also does individual initiative. The idea that an army operates on the basis of "rugged individualism" would be ludicrous. Equally so is the same idea with respect to the modern corporation. Group activity, the coordinating of the different steps in production, the extreme division of labor in large scale enterprise necessarily imply not individualism but cooperation and the acceptance of authority almost to the point of autocracy. Only to the extent that any worker seeks advancement within an organization is there room for individual initiative,—an initiative which can be exercised only within the narrow range of function he is called on to perform. At the very pinnacle of the hierarchy of organization in a great corporation, there alone, can individual initiative have a measure of free play. Yet even there a limit is set by the willingness and ability of subordinates to carry out the will of their superiors. In modern industry, individual liberty is necessarily curbed.

The Profit Motive

Even the motivation of individual activity has changed its aspect. For Adam Smith and his followers, it was possible to abstract one motive, the desire for personal profit, from all the motives driving men to action and to make this the key to man's economic activity. They could conclude that, where true private enterprise existed, personal profit was an effective and socially beneficent motivating force. Yet we have already seen how the profit motive has become distorted in the modern corporation. To the extent that profits induce the risking of capital by investors, they play their customary role. But if the courts, following the traditional logic of property, seek to insure that all profits reach or be held for the security owners, they prevent profits from reaching the very group of men whose action is most important to the efficient conduct of enterprise. Only as profits are diverted into the pockets of control do they, in a measure, perform their second function.

Nor is it clear that even if surplus profits were held out as an incentive to control they would be as effective an instrument as the logic of profits assumes. Presumably the motivating influence of any such huge surplus profits as a modern corporation might be made to produce would be subject to diminishing returns. Certainly it is doubtful if the prospect of a second million dollars of income (and the surplus profits might often amount to much larger sums) would induce activity equal to that induced by the prospect of the first million or even the first hundred thousand. Profits in such terms bear little relation to those envisaged by earlier writers.

Just what motives are effective today, in so far as control is concerned, must be a matter of conjecture. But it is probable that more could be learned regarding them by studying the motives of an Alexander the Great, seeking new worlds to conquer, than by considering the motives of a petty tradesman of the days of Adam Smith.

Competition

Finally, when Adam Smith championed competition as the great regulator of industry, he had in mind units so small that fixed capital and overhead costs played a role so insignificant that costs were in large measure determinate and so numerous that no single unit held an important position in the market. Today competition in markets dominated by a few great enterprises has come to be more often either cut-throat and destructive or so inactive as to make monopoly or duopoly conditions prevail. Competition between a small number of units each involving an organization so complex that costs have become indeterminate does not satisfy the condition assumed by earlier economists, nor does it appear likely to be as effective a regulator of industry and of profits as they had assumed.

In each of the situations to which these fundamental concepts refer, the Modern Corporation has wrought such a change as to make the concepts inapplicable.° New concepts must be forged and a new picture of economic relationships created. . . .

Most fundamental to the new picture of economic life must be a new concept of business enterprise as concentrated in the corporate organization. In some measure a concept is already emerging. Over a decade ago, Walter Rathenau wrote concerning the German counterpart of our great corporation:

"No one is a permanent owner. The composition of the thousandfold complex which functions as lord of the undertaking is in a state of flux. . . . This condition of things signifies that ownership has been depersonalized. . . . The depersonalization of ownership simultaneously implies the objectification of the thing owned. The claims to ownership are subdivided in such a fashion, and are so mobile, that the enterprise assumes an independent life, as if it belonged to no one; it takes an objective existence, such as in earlier days was embodied only in state and church, in a municipal corporation, in the life of a guild or a religious order. . . . The depersonalization of ownership, the objectification of enterprise, the detachment of property from the possessor, leads to a point where the enterprise becomes transformed into an institution which resembles the state in character." †

The institution here envisaged calls for analysis, not in

°It is frequently suggested that economic activity has become vastly more complex under modern conditions. Yet it is strange that the concentration of the bulk of industry into a few large units has not simplified rather than complicated the economic process. It is worth suggesting that the apparent complexity may arise in part from the effort to analyze the process in terms of concepts which no longer apply.

†"Von Kommenden Dingen," Berlin, 1918, trans. by E. & C. Paul ("In Days to Come"), London, 1921, pp. 120-1.

terms of business enterprise but in terms of social organization. On the one hand, it involves a concentration of power in the economic field comparable to the concentration of religious power in the mediaeval church or of political power in the national state. On the other hand, it involves the interrelation of a wide diversity of economic interests,— those of the "owners" who supply capital, those of the workers who "create," those of the consumers who give value to the products of enterprise, and above all those of the control who wield power.

Such a great concentration of power and such a diversity of interest raise the long-fought issue of power and its regulation—of interest and its protection. A constant warfare has existed between the individuals wielding power, in whatever form, and the subjects of that power. Just as there is a continuous desire for power, so also there is a continuous desire to make that power the servant of the bulk of the individuals it affects. The long struggles for the reform of the Catholic Church and for the development of constitutional law in the states are phases of this phenomenon. Absolute power is useful in building the organization. More slow, but equally sure is the development of social pressure demanding that the power shall be used for the benefit of all concerned. This pressure, constant in ecclesiastical and political history, is already making its appearance in many guises in the economic field.

Observable throughout the world, and in varying degrees of intensity, is this insistence that power in economic organization shall be subjected to the same tests of public benefit which have been applied in their turn to power otherwise located. In its most extreme aspect this is exhibited in the communist movement, which in its purest form is an insistence that *all* of the powers and privileges of property, shall be used only in the common interest. In less extreme forms of socialist dogma, transfer of economic powers to the state for public service is demanded. In the strictly capitalist countries, and particularly in time of depression, demands are constantly put forward that the men controlling the great economic organisms be made to accept responsibility for the well-being of those who are subject to the organization, whether workers, investors, or consumers. In a sense the difference in all of these demands lies only in degree. . . .

. . . Neither the claims of ownership nor those of control can stand against the paramount interests of the community. The present claims of both contending parties now in the field have been weakened by the developments described. It remains only for the claims of the community to be put forward with clarity and force. Rigid enforcement of property rights as a temporary protection against plundering by control would not stand in the way of the modification of these rights in the interest of other groups. When a convincing system of community obligations is worked out and is generally accepted, in that moment the passive property right of today must yield before the larger interests of society. Should the corporate leaders, for example, set forth a program comprising fair wages, security to employees, reasonable service to their public, and stabilization of business, all of which would divert a portion of the profits from the owners of passive property, and should the community generally accept such a scheme as a logical and human solution of industrial difficulties, the interests of passive property owners would have to give way. Courts would almost of necessity be forced to recognize the result, justifying it by whatever of the many legal theories they might choose. It is conceivable,—indeed it seems almost essential if the corporate system is to survive,—that the "control" of the great corporations should develop into a purely neutral technocracy, balancing a variety of claims by various groups in the community and assigning to each a portion of the income stream on the basis of public policy rather than private cupidity.

❀   ❀   ❀   ❀   ❀   ❀   ❀   ❀   ❀

In still larger view, the modern corporation may be regarded not simply as one form of social organization but potentially (if not yet actually) as the dominant institution of the modern world. In every age, the major concentration of power has been based upon the dominant interest of that age. The strong man has, in his time, striven to be cardinal or pope, prince or cabinet minister, bank president or partner in the House of Morgan. During the Middle Ages, the Church, exercising spiritual power, dominated Europe and gave to it a unity at a time when both political and economic power were diffused. With the rise of the modern state, political power, concentrated into a few large units, challenged the spiritual interest as the strongest bond of human society. Out of the long struggle between church and state which followed, the state emerged victorious; nationalist politics superseded religion as the basis of the major unifying organization of the western world. Economic power still remained diffused.

The rise of the modern corporation has brought a concentration of economic power which can compete on equal terms with the modern state—economic power versus political power, each strong in its own field. The state seeks in some aspects to regulate the corporation, while the corporation, steadily becoming more powerful, makes every effort to avoid such regulation. Where its own interests are concerned, it even attempts to dominate the state. The future may see the economic organism, now typified by the corporation, not only on an equal plane with the state, but possibly even superseding it as the dominant form of social organization. The law of corporations, accordingly, might well be considered as a potential constitutional law for the new economic state, while business practice is increasingly assuming the aspect of economic statesmanship.

Walter Lippmann (1889–   )

*A well-known political essayist and newspaper
columnist, he was reportedly one of the most
brilliant undergraduates ever to attend Harvard.
There he came under the influence of the
philosophers George Santayana and William
James, but neither affected him as did the
visiting British Socialist Graham Wallas, who
taught him to accept the fact that man often
acts irrationally and to recognize the importance of looking at politics from that skeptical
point of view. After racing through college in
three years, he began in 1910 as an investigator
for Lincoln Steffens, then served as an editor of
the* New Republic *from 1914 to 1919. Afterward
he went to the newspapers and wrote a syndicated column for the* Herald-Tribune *from 1931
to its demise in 1966. From a youthful liberal
with distinctly leftist tendencies, he became in
his late forties a conservative, shocking his old
associates in 1936 by openly declaring himself
a Republican.*

THE SERVILE STATE

Although all the known examples of collectivism have had
their origin in war or have as their objective the preparation for war, it is widely believed that a collectivist order
could be organized for peace and for plenty. "It is nonsense," says Mr. George Soule, "to say that there is any
physical impossibility of doing for peace purposes the sort
of thing we actually did for war purposes." If the state can
organize for war, it is asked, why can it not organize for
peace and plenty? If it can mobilize against a foreign en-

From *The Good Society* (Boston: Little, Brown & Co., 1937), pp. 91, 93, 101–5,
385–7. Reprinted by permission of the author.

emy, why not against poverty, squalor, and the hideous social evils that attend them?

It is plain enough that a dictated collectivism is necessary if a nation is to exert its maximum military power: very evidently its capital and labor must not be wasted on the making of luxuries; it can tolerate no effective dissent, nor admit that men have any right to the pursuit of private happiness. No one can dispute that. The waging of war must be authoritarian and collectivist. The question we must now consider is whether a system which is essential to the conduct of war can be adapted to the civilian ideal of peace and plenty. Can this form of organization, historically associated with military purposes and necessities, be used for the general improvement of men's condition? . . .

A call to arms is specific and everyone understands it. The cry that the enemy is at the gates, even the cry that beyond the deserts and mountains of Africa lies the promised land, needs little explaining. This is a very different thing from blowing the bugles and summoning the people to the abundant life to be achieved by "capacity operation of its plant, on the balanced load principle." Anyone can imagine an enemy and hate him; but to talk about an abundant life is merely to begin an interminable argument. This is the reason, based on deep psychological compulsion, why the socialist propaganda has always relied more upon an appeal to class war than upon the vision of a socialist society, why the effective leaders from Marx to Lenin have always derided as "unscientific" and "utopian" any detailed concern with the nature of a socialist society. Their intuition has surely been sound. For it is the war spirit that most readily imposes unanimity for collective action among masses of men. When men are at peace, they have an incorrigible tendency, if one likes collectivism, a noble tendency if one dislikes it, to become individuals. . . .

The primary factor which makes civilian planning incalculable is the freedom of the people to spend their income. Planning is theoretically possible only if consumption is rationed. For a plan of production *is* a plan of consumption. If the authority is to decide what shall be produced, it has already decided what shall be consumed. In military planning that is precisely what takes place: the authorities decide what the army shall consume and what of the national product shall be left for the civilians. No economy can, therefore, be planned for civilians unless there is such scarcity that the necessities of existence can be rationed. As productivity rises above the subsistence level, free spending becomes possible. A planned production to meet a free demand is a contradiction in terms and as meaningless as a square circle.

It follows, too, that a plan of production is incompatible with voluntary labor, with freedom to choose an occupation. A plan of production is not only a plan of consumption, but a plan of how long, at what, and where the people shall work. By no possible manipulation of wage rates could the planners attract to the various jobs precisely the right number of workers. Under voluntary labor, particularly with consumption rationed and standardized, the unpleasant jobs would be avoided and the good jobs overcrowded. Therefore the inevitable and necessary complement of the rationing of consumption is the conscription of labor, either by overt act of law or by driving workers into the undesirable jobs by offering them starvation as the alternative. This is, of course, exactly what happens in a thoroughly militarized state.

The conscription of labor and the rationing of consumption are not to be regarded as transitional or as accidental devices in a planned economy. They are the very substance of it. To make a five-year plan of what a whole nation shall produce is to determine how it shall labor and what it shall receive. It can receive only what the plan provides. It can obtain what the plan provides only by doing the work which the plan calls for. It must do that work or the plan is a failure; it must accept what the plan yields in the way of goods or it must do without.

All this is perfectly understood in an army or in war time when a whole nation is in arms. The civilian planner cannot avoid the rationing and the conscription, for they are the very essence of his proposal. There is no escape. If the people are free to reject the rations, the plan is frustrated; if they are free to work less or at different occupations than those prescribed, the plan cannot be executed. Therefore their labor and their standards of living have to be dictated by the planning board or by some sovereign power superior to the board. In a militarized society that sovereign power is the general staff.

But who, in a civilian society, is to decide what is to be the specific content of the abundant life? It cannot be the people deciding by referendum or through a majority of their elected representatives. For if the sovereign power to pick the plan is in the people, the power to amend it is there also at all times. Now a plan subject to change from month to month or even from year to year is not a plan; if the decision has been taken to make ten million cars at $500 and one million suburban houses at $3000, the people cannot change their minds a year later, scrap the machinery to make the cars, abandon the houses when they are partly built, and decide to produce instead skyscraper apartment houses and underground railroads.

There is, in short, no way by which the objectives of a planned economy can be made to depend upon popular decision. They must be imposed by an oligarchy of some sort,* and that oligarchy must, if the plan is to be carried through, be irresponsible in matters of policy. Individual oligarchs might, of course, be held accountable for breaches of the law just as generals can be court-martialed. But their policy can no more be made a matter of continuous accountability to the voters than the strategic arrangements of the generals can be determined by the rank and file. The planning board

---

*Which may, of course, let the people ratify the plan once and irrevocably by plebiscite, as in the German and Italian plebiscites.

or their superiors have to determine what the life and labor of the people shall be.

Not only is it impossible for the people to control the plan, but, what is more, the planners must control the people. They must be despots who tolerate no effective challenge to their authority. Therefore civilian planning is compelled to presuppose that somehow the despots who climb to power will be benevolent—that is to say, will know and desire the supreme good of their subjects. This is the implicit premise of all the books which recommend the establishment of a planned economy in a civilian society. They paint an entrancing vision of what a benevolent despotism could do. They ask—never very clearly, to be sure—that somehow the people should surrender the planning of their existence to "engineers," "experts," and "technologists," to leaders, saviors, heroes. This is the political premise of the whole collectivist philosophy: that the dictators will be patriotic or class-conscious, whichever term seems the more eulogistic to the orator. It is the premise, too, of the whole philosophy of regulation by the state, currently regarded as progressivism. Though it is disguised by the illusion that a bureaucracy accountable to a majority of voters, and susceptible to the pressure of organized minorities, is not exercising compulsion, it is evident that the more varied and comprehensive the regulation becomes, the more the state becomes a despotic power as against the individual. For the fragment of control over the government which he exercises through his vote is in no effective sense proportionate to the authority exercised over him by the government.

Benevolent despots might indeed be found. On the other hand they might not be. They may appear at one time; they may not appear at another. The people, unless they choose to face the machine guns on the barricades, can take no steps to see to it that benevolent despots are selected and the malevolent cashiered. They cannot select their despots. The despots must select themselves, and, no matter whether they are good or bad, they will continue in office as long as they can suppress rebellion and escape assassination.

Thus, by a kind of tragic irony, the search for security and a rational society, if it seeks salvation through political authority, ends in the most irrational form of government imaginable—in the dictatorship of casual oligarchs, who have no hereditary title, no constitutional origin or responsibility, who cannot be replaced except by violence. The reformers who are staking their hopes on good despots, because they are so eager to plan the future, leave unplanned that on which all their hopes depend. Because a planned society must be one in which the people obey their rulers, there can be no plan to find the planners: the selection of the despots who are to make society so rational and so secure has to be left to the insecurity of irrational chance. . . .

[Aristotle's] argument that "some persons are slaves, other are freemen by appointment of nature," is the ultimate doctrine upon which every apologist of oppression must rely in order to make the law of the jungle take on the guise of rationality to civilized men. No doubt it seems like a long jump from Aristotle's apology for chattel slavery to the collectivists in democratic countries who dream of a rationally administered economy. But what conception of men as personalities does Mr. Stuart Chase, for example, have when he tells us that "a working dictatorship over industry is indicated, if the plant is to be efficiently operated" . . . that "the industrial discipline must be accepted—all of it—or it must be renounced" because "technological imperative is impersonal, amoral, and non-ethical"? I know that Mr. Chase is a civilized man. So was Aristotle. Are not Mr. Chase's regimented citizens mere "living instruments" of his glorified technicians? And as such, because they are less than men, are material to be fabricated by his engineers, have they not been stripped of their defenses against oppression? Have not the technicians who are to be their masters been relieved of all restraint? If the technological imperatives of his technocrats are so impersonal, so amoral, and so non-ethical, then how can they ever be challenged? Against these imperatives there are no human rights, not even the right of revolution.

Of the many rationalizations of tyranny the subtlest is that which teaches the individual that he is a cog in a corporate machine or a cell in a collective organism. Men have learned to defend themselves against personal sovereigns, against the doctrine that as slaves they belong to their lord, as subjects to their king. But in the presence of the anonymous master, the super-organism of the collectivists, they do not so easily discern its inhuman pretensions and brutalizing dominion.

For the demand that men be subordinated and submerged in the mass is easily mistaken for the ideal of a fellowship of free individuals in which the human personality realizes some of its noblest possibilities. It is not always easy to distinguish between the patriotism of the collectivist who sacrifices the individual and the patriotism of free men who sacrifice themselves voluntarily; or to distinguish between social obligation which is the respect of persons for the legal and equitable rights of others and social discipline which means that men's lives are to be planned and administered by their superiors. The counterfeit resembles the real thing just enough to be deeply confusing. Thus many cannot even distinguish between the plebiscites by which dictators ratify their supremacy and the elections by which free men choose their public servants, between the acquiescence which the dictators obtain when individuals are cowed, corrupted, and without recourse, and the consent of self-governing societies.

But the distinctions, though often obscured, are radical. In the social discipline of all collectivists the inviolability of men is somewhere denied. Men are not fully persons. They are things to be used for purposes which others, be they Aristotle or Mr. Stuart Chase, deem desirable. They are conscripts under commanders; in Mr. Hilaire Belloc's penetrating phrase, they are subjects of the Servile State. On the other hand, in the discipline of a free society, it is the inviolability of all individuals which determines the social obligations of each individual, of the official no less than the citizen. They are citizens who are consulted and consent. And their consent has meaning because they are protected in the right to withhold consent. The lives of such individuals cannot be administered. In their transactions justice can be dispensed, and that justice has its criterion and its sanction in the fact that they are inviolable individuals dealing wih other inviolable individuals.

So it is here, on the nature of man, between those who would respect him as an autonomous person and those who would degrade him to a living instrument, that the issue is joined. From these opposing conceptions are bred radically different attitudes towards the whole of human experience, in all the realms of action and of feeling, from the greatest to the smallest.

Franklin D. Roosevelt (1882–1945)

Thirty-second President of the United States, he came from an old and aristocratic New York family but, as Eric Goldman said, throughout his life showed "an upperdog concern for the underdog." He revealed in this campaign speech delivered at the Commonwealth Club in San Francisco in 1932 not only his concern that every man should have a right to life and a comfortable living but also a daringly new economic and social philosophy which contrasted sharply with Hoover's hollow assurances that the foundations of the economy were still sound. The speech, which expressed the essence of the New Deal creed, had been written by Adolf A. Berle with some help from Rexford Tugwell, and re-

my friends, and we cannot deny that their experience had warranted some measure of fear. The most brilliant, honest and able exponent of this point of view was Hamilton. He was too impatient of slow-moving methods. Fundamentally he believed that the safety of the republic lay in the autocratic strength of its Government, that the destiny of individuals was to serve that Government, and that fundamentally a great and strong group of central institutions, guided by a small group of able and public spirited citizens, could best direct all Government.

But Mr. Jefferson, in the summer of 1776, after drafting the Declaration of Independence turned his mind to the same problem and took a different view. He did not deceive himself with outward forms. Government to him was a means to an end, not an end in itself; it might be either a refuge and a help or a threat and a danger, depending on the circumstances. We find him carefully analyzing the society for which he was to organize a Government. "We have no paupers. The great mass of our population is of laborers, our rich who cannot live without labor, either manual or professional, being few and of moderate wealth. Most of the laboring class possess property, cultivate their own lands, have families and from the demand for their labor, are enabled to exact from the rich and the competent such prices as enable them to feed abundantly, clothe above mere decency, to labor moderately and raise their families."

These people, he considered, had two sets of rights, those of "personal competency" and those involved in acquiring and possessing property. By "personal competency" he meant the right of free thinking, freedom of forming and expressing opinions, and freedom of personal living, each man according to his own lights. To insure the first set of rights, a Government must so order its functions as not to interfere with the individual. But even Jefferson realized that the exercise of the property rights might so interfere with the rights of the individual that the Government, without whose assistance the property rights could not exist, must intervene, not to destroy individualism, but to protect it.

You are familiar with the great political duel which followed; and how Hamilton and his friends, building toward a dominant centralized power, were at length defeated in the great election of 1800, by Mr. Jefferson's party. Out of that duel came the two parties, Republican and Democratic, as we know them today.

So began, in American political life, the new day, the day of the individual against the system, the day in which individualism was made the great watchword of American life. The happiest of economic conditions made that day long and splendid. On the Western frontier, land was substantially free. No one, who did not shirk the task of earning a living, was entirely without opportunity to do so. Depressions could, and did, come and go; but they could not alter the fundamental fact that most of the people lived partly by selling their labor and partly by extracting their livelihood from the soil, so that starvation and dislocation were practically impossible. At the very worst there was always the possibility of climbing into a covered wagon and moving west where the untilled prairies afforded a haven for men to whom the East did not provide a place. So great were our natural resources that we could offer this relief not only to our own people, but to the distressed of all the world; we could invite immigration from Europe, and welcome it with open arms. Traditionally, when a depression came a new section of land was opened in the West; and even our temporary misfortune served our manifest destiny.

It was in the middle of the nineteenth century that a new force was released and a new dream created. The force was what is called the industrial revolution, the advance of steam and machinery and the rise of the forerunners of the modern industrial plant. The dream was the dream of an economic machine, able to raise the standard of living for everyone; to bring luxury within the reach of the humblest; to annihilate distance by steam power and later by electricity, and to release everyone from the drudgery of the heaviest manual toil. It was to be expected that this would necessarily affect Government. Heretofore, Government had merely been called upon to produce conditions within which people could live happily, labor peacefully, and rest secure. Now it was called upon to aid in the consummation of this new dream. There was, however, a shadow over the dream. To be made real, it required use of the talents of men of tremendous will and tremendous ambition, since by no other force could the problems of financing and engineering and new developments be brought to a consummation.

So manifest were the advantages of the machine age, however, that the United States fearlessly, cheerfully, and, I think, rightly, accepted the bitter with the sweet. It was thought that no price was too high to pay for the advantages which we could draw from a finished industrial system. The history of the last half century is accordingly in large measure a history of a group of financial Titans, whose methods were not scrutinized with too much care, and who were honored in proportion as they produced the results, irrespective of the means they used. The financiers who pushed the railroads to the Pacific were always ruthless, often wasteful, and frequently corrupt; but they did build railroads, and we have them today. It has been estimated that the American investor paid for the American railway system more than three times over in the process; but despite this fact the net advantage was to the United States. As long as we had free land; as long as population was growing by leaps and bounds; as long as our industrial plants were insufficient to supply our own needs, society chose to give the ambitious man free play and unlimited reward provided only that he produced the economic plant so much desired.

During this period of expansion, there was equal opportunity for all and the business of Government was not to interfere but to assist in the development of industry. This was done at the request of business men themselves. The tariff was originally imposed for the purpose of "fostering our infant industry," a phrase I think the older among you will remember as a political issue not so long ago. The railroads were subsidized, sometimes by grants of money, oftener by grants of land; some of the most valuable oil lands in the United States were granted to assist the financing of the railroad which pushed through the Southwest. A nascent merchant marine was assisted by grants of money, or by mail subsidies, so that our steam shipping might ply the seven seas. Some of my friends tell me that they do not want the Government in business. With this I agree; but I wonder whether they realize the implications of the past. For while it has been American doctrine that the Government must not go into business in competition with private enterprises, still it has been traditional, particularly in Republican administrations, for business urgently to ask the Government to put at private disposal all kinds of Government assistance. The same man who tells you that he does not want to see the Government interfere in business—and he means it, and has plenty of good reasons for saying so—is the first to go to Washington and ask the Government for a prohibitory tariff on his product. When things get just bad enough, as they did two years ago, he will go with equal speed to the United States Government and ask for a loan; and the Reconstruction Finance Corporation is the outcome of it. Each group has sought protection from the Government for its own special interests, without realizing that the function of Government must be to favor no small group at the expense of its duty to protect the rights of personal freedom and of private property of all its citizens. . . .

A glance at the situation today only too clearly indicates that equality of opportunity as we have known it no longer exists. Our industrial plant is built; the problem just now is whether under existing conditions it is not overbuilt. Our last frontier has long since been reached, and there is practically no more free land. More than half of our people do not live on the farms or on lands and cannot derive a living by cultivating their own property. There is no safety valve in the form of a Western prairie to which those thrown out of work by the Eastern economic machines can go for a new start. We are not able to invite the immigration from Europe to share our endless plenty. We are now providing a drab living for our own people. . . .

Just as freedom to farm has ceased, so also the opportunity in business has narrowed. It still is true that men can start small enterprises, trusting to native shrewdness and ability to keep abreast of competitors; but area after area has been preempted altogether by the great corporations, and even in the fields which still have no great concerns, the small man starts under a handicap. The unfeeling statistics of the past three decades show that the independent business man is running a losing race. Perhaps he is forced to the wall; perhaps he cannot command credit; perhaps he is "squeezed out," in Mr. Wilson's words, by highly organized corporate competitors, as your corner grocery man can tell you. Recently a careful study was made of the concentration of business in the United States. It showed that our economic life was dominated by some six hundred odd corporations who controlled two-thirds of American industry. Ten million small business men divided the other third. More striking still, it appeared that if the process of concentration goes on at the same rate, at the end of another century we shall have all American industry controlled by a dozen corporations, and run by perhaps a hundred men. Put plainly, we are steering a steady course toward economic oligarchy, if we are not there already.

Clearly, all this calls for a re-appraisal of values. A mere builder of more industrial plants, a creator of more railroad systems, an organizer of more corporations, is as likely to be a danger as a help. The day of the great promoter or the financial Titan, to whom we granted anything if only he would build, or develop, is over. Our task now is not discovery or exploitation of natural resources, or necessarily producing more goods. It is the soberer, less dramatic business of administering resources and plants already in hand, of seeking to reestablish foreign markets for our surplus production, of meeting the problem of underconsumption, of adjusting production to consumption, of distributing wealth and products more equitably, of adapting existing economic organizations to the service of the people. The day of enlightened administration has come.

Just as in older times the central Government was first a haven of refuge, and then a threat, so now in a closer economic system the central and ambitious financial unit is no longer a servant of national desire, but a danger. I would draw the parallel one step farther. We did not think because national Government had become a threat in the 18th century that therefore we should abandon the principle of national Government. Nor today should we abandon the principle of strong economic units called corporations, merely because their power is susceptible of easy abuse. In other times we dealt with the problem of an unduly ambitious central Government by modifying it gradually into a constitutional democratic Government. So today we are modifying and controlling our economic units.

As I see it, the task of Government in its relation to business is to assist the development of an economic declaration of rights, an economic constitutional order. This is the common task of statesman and business man. It is the minimum requirement of a more permanently safe order of things.

Happily, the times indicate that to create such an order not only is the proper policy of Government, but it is the only line of safety for our economic structures as well. We know, now, that these economic units cannot exist unless prosperity is uniform, that is, unless purchasing power is well distributed throughout every group in the Nation. That is why even the most selfish of corporations for its own interest would be glad to see wages restored and unemployment ended and to bring the Western farmer back to his accustomed level of prosperity and to assure a permanent safety to both groups. That is why some enlightened industries themselves endeavor to limit the freedom of action of each man and business group within the industry in the common interest of all; why business men everywhere are asking a form of organization which will bring the scheme of things into balance, even though it may in some measure qualify the freedom of action of individual units within the business.

The exposition need not further be elaborated. It is brief and incomplete, but you will be able to expand it in terms of your own business or occupation without difficulty. I think everyone who has actually entered the economic struggle—which means everyone who was not born to safe wealth—knows in his own experience and his own life that we have now to apply the earlier concepts of American Government to the conditions of today.

The Declaration of Independence discusses the problem of Government in terms of a contract. Government is a relation of give and take, a contract, perforce, if we would follow the thinking out of which it grew. Under such a contract rulers were accorded power, and the people consented to that power on consideration that they be accorded certain rights. The task of statesmanship has always been the re-definition of these rights in terms of a changing and growing social order. New conditions impose new requirements upon Government and those who conduct Government. . . .

I feel that we are coming to a view through the drift of our legislation and our public thinking in the past quarter century that private economic power is, to enlarge an old phrase, a public trust as well. I hold that continued enjoyment of that power by any individual or group must depend upon the fulfillment of that trust. The men who have reached the summit of American business life know this best; happily, many of these urge the binding quality of this greater social contract.

The terms of that contract are as old as the Republic, and as new as the new economic order.

Every man has a right to life; and this means that he has also a right to make a comfortable living. He may by sloth or crime decline to exercise that right; but it may not be denied him. We have no actual famine or dearth; our industrial and agricultural mechanism can produce enough and to spare. Our Government formal and informal, political and economic, owes to everyone an avenue to possess himself of a portion of that plenty sufficient for his needs, through his own work.

Every man has a right to his own property; which means a right to be assured, to the fullest extent attainable, in the safety of his savings. By no other means can men carry the burdens of those parts of life which, in the nature of things, afford no chance of labor; childhood, sickness, old age. In all thought of property, this right is paramount; all other property rights must yield to it. If, in accord with this principle, we must restrict the operations of the speculator, the manipulator, even the financier, I believe we must accept the restriction as needful, not to hamper individualism but to protect it.

These two requirements must be satisfied, in the main, by the individuals who claim and hold control of the great industrial and financial combinations which dominate so large a part of our industrial life. They have undertaken to be, not business men, but princes of property. I am not prepared to say that the system which produces them is wrong. I am very clear that they must fearlessly and competently assume the responsibility which goes with the power. So many enlightened business men know this that the statement would be little more than a platitude, were it not for an added implication.

This implication is, briefly, that the responsible heads of finance and industry instead of acting each for himself, must work together to achieve the common end. They must, where necessary, sacrifice this or that private advantage; and in reciprocal self-denial must seek a general advantage. It is here that formal Government—political Government, if you choose—comes in. Whenever in the pursuit of this objective the lone wolf, the unethical competitor, the reckless promoter, the Ishmael or Insull whose hand is against every man's, declines to join in achieving an end recognized as being for the public welfare, and threatens to drag the industry back to a state of anarchy, the Government may properly be asked to apply restraint. Likewise, should the group ever use its collective power contrary to the public welfare, the Government must be swift to enter and protect the public interest.

The Government should assume the function of economic regulation only as a last resort, to be tried only when private initiative, inspired by high responsibility, with such assistance and balance as Government can give, has finally failed. As yet there has been no final failure, because there has been no attempt; and I decline to assume that this Nation is unable to meet the situation.

The final term of the high contract was for liberty and the pursuit of happiness. We have learned a great deal of both in the past century. We know that individual liberty and individual happiness mean nothing unless both are ordered in the sense that one man's meat is not another man's poison. We know that the old "rights of personal competency," the right to read, to think, to speak, to choose and live a mode of life, must be respected at all hazards. We know that liberty to do anything which deprives others of those elemental rights is outside the protection of any compact; and that Government in this regard is the maintenance of a balance, within which every individual may have a place if he will take it; in which every individual may find safety if he wishes it; in which every individual may attain such power as his ability permits, consistent with his assuming the accompanying responsibility.

CHAPTER FOUR

The Materialistic Faith

I

As business reached a higher level of sophistication in the 1920's, the aspirations of the American cult of success also changed. There was the same ingenuous love of money, and money still defined success, but the day was past when simple country boys could become the sole owners of large enterprises. For, as Irvin G. Wyllie noted, "With chances for success controlled by the corporations and by the widows and orphans who owned them, the trick now was to rise into the managerial elite." While Andrew Carnegie could become his own boss, the most a bright young man in the twenties might aspire to was to become the hired manager of a great industrial organization. Likewise, with the advance of technology, the uneducated, practical man was in less demand than the professionally trained executive who not only understood something of engineering or chemistry but who was also versed in business administration, salesmanship, and public relations. Business, in short, was becoming a profession, and to fill the great demand for scientific business training most of the large universities opened business schools. "These roaring mills of the new learning," the *American Mercury* reported, offered a wide field of study. "Thus, Cornell lists Hotel Supervision, and Syracuse bills Hotel Management, Store

221

Management, and Practical Table Service. Columbia offers
Bond Salesmanship, the New York Money Market, and the
Business of the Theatre. Southern California reveals the
mysteries of Apartment House Management, Traffic Management, and Real Estate Advertising, with special highly
scientific lectures on Billboards, Trips to Property, Golf
Links, Country Clubs, and Model Homes." Besides its
famous Oil Executives' Course, New York University was
said to have also had on draft a course on Hosiery and
Underwear for the training of buyers and executives. For
good or bad, the effect of this academic enterprise upon
higher education was to suggest that learning was a mer-
chandisable commodity and that business instruction was to
take precedence over scholarship as the goal of university
training because it was allegedly more useful.[1]

The intrusion of businesslike ideals, aims, and methods
into the temples of learning reflected the ruling interest
of American society. "Of course," the President of the
United States told American editors, "the accumulation of
wealth cannot be justified as the chief end of existence.
But we are compelled to recognize it as a means to well-
nigh every desirable achievement." Beyond doubt the ruling
interest in the twenties was pecuniary gain. And training
for business, Veblen observed, stood to this ruling interest
of the modern community "in a relation analogous to that
in which theology . . . stood to the ruling interest in those
earlier times when the salvation of men's souls was the
prime object of solicitude." The business school had a
place in the modern university similar to that of the divinity
school in nineteenth-century America. Both schools were
equally extraneous to that "intellectual enterprise" which
was ostensibly the function of the university, but while the
divinity school belonged to the old order and was losing out,
the "seminary of business" belonged to the new order and
was gaining ground. Plainly, for most Americans, the primacy among man's interests was passing from religion to
business.[2]

Indicative of the new priorities, the most popular religious ideas in the twenties were those which sustained the dominant business values. Not only were religious spokesmen generally complaisant to the business point of view, but some gave divine sanction to the materialistic creed by suggesting that "it pays to pray." The Reverend Shailer Mathews, dean of the Divinity School of the University of Chicago and a former president of the Federal Council of Churches of Christ in America, when asked "Could a man make more money if now and then he prayed about his business?" replied, "I think so—if he is honest and serious." The Swedish Immanuel Congregational Church in New York, according to the *American Mercury*, recognized the supremacy of the business over the spiritual appeal by offering to all who contributed one hundred dollars to its building fund "an engraved certificate of investment in preferred capital stock in the Kingdom of God." And a church billboard in the same city issued the persuasive call: "Come to Church. Christian Worship Increases Your Efficiency. Christian F. Reisner, Pastor."[3]

Under the gospel of Service, a pragmatic variation of the Christian principle of brotherly love, a new American religion was created on the material plane. Instead of trafficking in divinely beneficial intangibles, it was based upon faith in the miracles of the existent commercial order and promises, not of divine glory, but of human ease. On these grounds, business was acclaimed "the sanest religion" by a popular journalist, Edward Earle Purinton.[*] According to this businesslike creed, the office or factory was the temple, work was worship, and salvation was success. "For the true believer, its commandment was Service, its sacrament the weekly lunches of fellowship at Kiwanis or Rotary, its ritual the collective chanting of cheerful songs," and its high priests the advertising men who with unflagging devotion publicized American business as the fount from

[*]Edward Earle Purinton, *The New American Religion*. See page 238.

which all blessings flow. It was hardly coincidence that the most popular religious book of the twenties and the non-fiction best-seller for 1925 and 1926 was Bruce Barton's *The Man Nobody Knows.* An advertising executive, Barton propagandized the faith by portraying Jesus as a "great advertiser" and "the founder of modern business." This simple "boy from a country village" had succeeded because he used "the principles of modern salesmanship." "He would be a national advertiser today." Jesus, the book revealed, was not only "the most popular dinner guest in Jerusalem" but a great executive. "He picked up twelve men from the bottom ranks of business and forged them into an organization that conquered the world." That the same principles of salesmanship should be found good and profitable for business and religion did not seem in the least profane to Barton, but rather to show how truly daily business carried on the business of the Lord. For as Barton wrote, "All work is worship, all useful service prayer." In this connection Veblen wryly noted that the Godfearing businessmen who administered the nation's affairs appeared to realize this congruity between sacred and secular salesmanship "so much so that they have on due consideration found that investment in commercial advertising is rightfully exempt from the income tax, very much as the assets and revenues of the churches are tax-exempt. The one line of publicity, it appears, is intrinsic to the good of man, as the other is essential to the continued Glory of God."[4]

Americans had come at last to openly worship a great machine for making money, but to put it so bluntly would have made believers uncomfortable. So, as in medieval days when faith was thought better than reason, the actual functioning of the economic system like the ways of God was something to be accepted but never openly questioned. As Edmund Wilson affirmed at the time, "The newspapers will not deal with this subject; even the philosophers try to get around it; and if you bring it into a conversation, you are guilty of an act of bad taste comparable to joking

In American mythology the predominant figure was the businessman. All virtues were ascribed to him. He was, at the same time, a hard-boiled trader, a scholar, a patron of the arts, a thrifty housewife, a philanthropist, a statesman, a patriot, and a sentimental protector of widows and orphans.

about Scripture in the presence of a devout old lady."[5] Instead, Americans preferred to deal with symbols and myths that transformed the ugly facts of economic life into ideal aspirations. In dollar theology selfishness became service, profit the means of individual redemption, and success the reward of virtue. Thus, the virtuous man was a free individual who sought salvation by accumulating money. By extending this sacred symbolism to the corporation—treating great industrial organizations as inviolable persons before the law—business theologians, judges and lawyers, established taboos which made any attempt to regulate huge corporations appear as a profane attack upon the religion of capitalism. The effect of this twentieth-century version of the doctrine of the two swords, observed Thurman Arnold, a Yale professor of law, was to place the spiritual realm of business beyond the temporal jurisdiction of government; and thus when, as during the depression, necessity demanded government intervention, dogma denied it, hampering effective action at every turn.°

II

If most Americans had come to worship at the shrine of business, there were still a few heretics who were not ready to accept business values as the standard of civilization. Though the businessman might live in a palace, ride in the most luxurious limousines, and fill his mansion with old masters and the costliest manuscripts, so long as he cared more for material things than intellectual and spiritual values, he was—from their point of view—not civilized but what the Greeks properly called a "barbarian." Under such circumstances, the businessman was "merely a purveyor and not a creator of the real values of a civilization." Civilizations rest fundamentally upon ideas, and in the United States where the dominant idea was profit the owner of a cigar-store chain, said James Truslow Adams, was "infinitely more valuable to humanity than a Keats"—even though from every past civilization the only things which remained of value to humanity were "the creative works of those who were not businessmen." But while Adams seriously questioned whether a great civilization could be built upon the philosophy of profit, Sinclair Lewis in his popular novels *Main Street* (1920) and *Babbitt* (1922) lampooned the American businessman as a clumsy, well-meaning "boob" trapped in sleazy middle-class philistinism. With vitriolic pen Lewis caricatured George F. Babbitt, a hustling, successful, all-American barbarian, to whom Keats was just another one

°Thurman Arnold, *The Theology of Capitalism.* See page 242.

of those "shabby bums living in attics and feeding on booze and sphagetti" and who had no use for "a lot of moth-eaten, mildewed, out-of-date, old, European dumps" that "aren't producing anything but bootblacks and scenery and booze, that haven't got one bathroom per hundred people!" Through the hapless Babbitt who congratulated himself on belonging to the new generation of Standardized Americans—"fellows with hair on their chests and smiles in their eyes and adding machines in their offices"—Lewis satirized "that clean fighting determination to win Success" that had produced in America "punchful prosperity," paved streets, bathrooms, vacuum cleaners, and all the other signs of civilization—minus the civilization.[6]

Certainly in a technically advanced nation such as America there was a strong temptation to regard the products and paraphernalia of technology as synonymous with civilization. Because of machines the average American in the 1920's enjoyed more power, more comforts, more amusements, and more leisure than any people had ever known. Airplanes and automobiles broke down barriers of space and gave him mastery over time; movies and radios extended his sensory powers and opened distant worlds once beyond sight and sound. New inventions and improved technology enabled American factories to provide him with a never-ending flow of automobiles, radios, refrigerators, telephones, typewriters, adding machines, rayon stockings, and countless other gadgets for his pleasure and convenience at popular prices. The constant endeavor of business was to get him to fill up his life with things—things that could be made and sold—and through advertising to foster the belief that there was a close relation between his well-being and the number of bathtubs, automobiles, and similar machine-made products that he might possess. Nor was the average American hard to convince, for the unprecedented abundance of goods was to him visible evidence of progress. And when he reflected further that the machine promised not only to lift the burden of poverty but also to emancipate him from a lifetime of drudgery, it was easy for him to believe in the beneficence of the machine.

Intellectuals, for the most part, were not so readily disposed to accept the machine as the paragon of progress. To these dissenters, the compulsive urge to produce and sell, to mechanize life—even when the results of mechanization were plainly disastrous—was destructive of human values. In America, said Edmund Wilson, "life had become a stampede to produce and sell all sorts of commodities— the question was not whether people really needed or wanted these things but whether by any means they could be induced to buy them." For himself, he was unable to accept an ideal of happiness based solely on the possession of things, nor recognize as valid a conception of civilization that "glorifies the United States as an inexhaustible market." Such a society functioned admirably in the large production of cheap automobiles, dollar watches, and safety razors. But the trouble was, according to Sinclair Lewis, "it is not satisfied until the entire world also admits that the end and joyous purpose of living is to ride in flivvers, to make advertising-pictures of dollar watches, and in the twilight to sit talking not of love and courage but of the convenience of safety razors." Such "purposeless materialism" —the American tendency not to satisfy the physical and aesthetic needs of living but to multiply indefinitely the physical accessories of life—was deplored by Ralph Borsodi as a misuse of the machine and a tragic waste of human energy. From his viewpoint happiness was dependent not upon producing as much as possible but as little as was "compatible with the enjoyment of the superior life."[7]

But these few voices of protest were drowned in the crash and clatter of the assembly line, for the majority of Americans appeared to be in thorough agreement with Henry Ford, world champion of mass production, that man's happiness was dependent upon an unending increase of machines and goods. Though the famed mechanical and industrial genius repeatedly insisted that machines were but means to an end and criticized Americans for being too wrapped up in the things they were doing and not enough concerned with the reasons why they did them, Ford nevertheless dismissed as "mushy sentimentalism" the notion that man might be happier producing less. "The purpose of a factory is to produce, and it ill serves the community in general unless it does produce to the utmost of its capacity." Ford proclaimed machinery "The New Messiah," and declared it was accomplishing in the world what man had failed to do by preaching, propaganda, or the written word. Agreeing with the Detroit manufacturer, Glenn Frank, president of the University of Wisconsin, praised the machine as "one of humanity's most promising instruments of emancipation."° Taking his cue from Henry Ford's statement, "Hard labor is for machines, not for men," Frank claimed to find the germ of a new civilization hidden in that simple sentence, the first line of a new Magna Carta for mankind. "There are a hundred unwritten Iliads in it. There is the birthright of a new Shakespeare in it. It is the charter of new art galleries. It foreshadows a new birth of education. There is unreleased music in it. It is a sort of secular 'Let There Be Light' for a new kind of world."[8]

By the thirties Americans had become much less enthusiastic about the machine-made millennium. The decline of this absolute faith resulted from a number of causes. The development and multiplication of highly destructive machines of war, without an accompanying development of higher social purposes, had served in many people's minds only to magnify the possibilities of depravity and barbarism. The airplane, instead of merely speeding up travel and intercourse between countries, had intensified their fear of each other. As an instrument of war, in combination with the latest advancements in explosives and poison gas, it promised "a ruthlessness of extermination that man has here-

---

°Glenn Frank, *Our Machine Civilization.* See page 247.

tofore not been able to apply to either bugs or rats." In mechanizing swiftly and heedlessly, men had failed to assimilate the machine and to coordinate it with human capacities and human needs. The automobile, for instance, which in 1924 was hailed as "the very acme of human aspiration," had soon proven to be a most lethal weapon—a mechanized killer that slaughtered more Americans on streets and highways than had been slain on the nation's battlefields. Finally, as the depression made so painfully clear to millions of Americans, the machine had not been

---

The automobile, instead of speeding up travel, created monumental traffic-jams, and the rising tide of traffic fatalities made it painfully clear, as the *New York Times* remarked, that these fuming monsters had not yet been brought "within the restraints of a decent civilization."

United Press International Photo

integrated into society. Instead of adjusting the use and rhythm of the machine to fit the actual needs of the community, the human gains of mechanization had been largely forfeited to the demands of private profit. Under the industrial regimen of the machine, man had been treated as a waste product and regarded like Mr. Zero in Elmer Rice's play *The Adding Machine* as nothing more than a slave to a contraption of steel and iron. It was these symptoms of social danger and cultural decay, according to Lewis Mumford, that had weakened the absolute faith in the machine. As a result, the absolute validity of the machine had become a conditioned validity.[9] While Mumford was hopeful of both man's destiny and that of the machine, he believed it imperative that the human question must always outweigh the question of profit or mechanical feasibility. It was his further conviction that once the objective of industry was diverted from profit-making, private aggrandizement, crude exploitation, the economy would function on a broader and more intelligently socialized basis. As social life became more mature, the nature and function of the mechanical environment would change, and the machine would fall into its proper place of servant, not master.°

III

If quantitatively the American achievement was impressive, qualitatively it was openly challenged. It was, said Ezra Pound, "admirable as far as it goes. . . . But where does this get us? For everything above comfortable brute existence there is a vacuum." For himself, Pound—along with some of the best of American poets and novelists—had sought a more congenial atmosphere for the development of his creative talents by joining the postwar exodus to Europe. But, at home, indictment of America's spiritual emptiness was sustained by a few sturdy novelists, poets, and by a small but persevering group of academic critics known as Humanists who believed that with commercialism "laying its great greasy paw upon everything," there was no place in this country for "the true artist," no chance for development of the "inner life." "What must one think of a country," asked Irving Babbitt of Harvard, who with Paul Elmer More led the movement, "whose most popular orator is W. J. Bryan, whose favorite actor is Charlie Chaplin, whose most widely read novelist is Harold Bell Wright, whose best-known evangelist is Billy Sunday, and whose representative journalist is William Randolph Hearst?" What one must think of such a country, said Babbitt, was that it not only lacked "true" standards but suffered also from an inversion of what few standards it had. The end result of American materialism, in his opinion, was "a huge mass of standardized mediocrity."[10]

Taking issue with this bleak view, the philosopher George Santayana expressed his admiration for the materialistic

°Lewis Mumford, *The Diminution of the Machine*. See page 254.

"get up and go" of modern America and his distaste for the gloomy pundits whose oracular "humanism" was to him mere egotism or moralism.° As a hard, non-humanistic materialist of the Ionian school, he was able to stand aloof from both sides in America, criticizing the one for trying to "apply" culture to this raw vital energy and looking rather benevolently upon the primitivism of the other which he believed held promise of a new intellect and spirit. The distinctive quality of Americanism he admired was its ability to combine "unity in work with liberty of spirit," and he declared "that art, etc., has a better soil in the ferocious 100% America than in the Intelligentsia of New York. It is veneer, rouge, aestheticism, art museums, new theatres, etc., that make America impotent. The good things are football, kindness, and jazz bands."[11]

In America after 1932, however, when everything seemed to be breaking down at once, that "moral materialism" upon which Santayana had hopefully smiled appeared impotent in the face of disaster. It was, Alfred Kazin remarked, a "material failure which could not be understood in material terms alone." This economic disaster "was so manifestly something more" that to bewildered Americans it seemed that the very bottom had dropped out of things. The foundation of capitalism had been materialism, and when it failed to "deliver the goods," its social support crumbled, for its promise and ideology no longer had any meaning. Looking into the apparently bottomless pit of depression, intellectuals were already writing the obituary of capitalism. "If one cannot yet call capitalism dead," wrote Lewis Mumford in *Common Sense*, "it is only because no body can be treated as dead so long as the worms are actively crawling around in it. Attacks on capitalism are like wasting ammunition on a creature that has fatally poisoned itself. All our efforts should be concentrated, not in listening to the gasps and groans of this dying creature

°George Santayana, *The Genteel Tradition at Bay*. See page 262.

and in pointing reproachful fingers at it: our efforts should go into the task of creating a new order."[12]

In contrast to the dreary spectacle of a failing capitalism, the Soviet Union during the early thirties appeared to be a boom country. The difference between the two lands was to the American novelist Theodore Dreiser "fantastic." Here, on the one hand, was America, a scene of "poverty, frustration, and defeat of the many"; on the other, "that great, sound and by now successful experiment, the Soviet Union with all it has achieved in merging into one colossal entity the intellect and the naturally creative impulses and inventive vigors of all its immense population, and the using of those for the development as well as the permanent comfort of that population." The well-publicized achievements of the U.S.S.R. had an especial appeal for jobless workers who heard there was no unemployment in Russia and for American intellectuals who were "trying to escape from a feeling of isolation and ineffectuality." Dispatriated intellectuals, whether of fact or fancy—most of the "literary exiles" of the decade before returned home in the thirties—found in Communism a faith and an acceptance denied them under the capitalist system. As Malcolm Cowley, a repatriate and "fellow-traveler," confirmed, they were not as much interested in Marx as a philosopher or economist as "a prophet calling for a day of judgment and new heaven on earth." To writers and artists who had never liked the "Big Business system" and "always resented its crowding out of everything they cared about," these were exhilarating years. "One couldn't help being exhilarated at the sudden unexpected collapse of that stupid gigantic fraud," wrote Edmund Wilson. "It gave us a new sense of freedom; and it gave us a new sense of power to find ourselves carrying on while the bankers for a change were taking a beating." Beguiled by the "essential oneness" of Marx's vision of a "whole cultural revolution," the American intelligentsia piously embraced a new religion of materialism. Under the magic spell of Marxism, the thirties became an

In the gloomy days of depression, as breadlines lengthened on city streets, everything seemed to be breaking down at once. With the world gone awry, poverty and frustration made new converts for Communism.

"Age of Faith," and in Daniel Aaron's words, it "turned college professors into union leaders, philosophers into politicians, novelists into agitators, poets into public speakers."[13]

Although in its purely materialistic and economic aspects Communism merely claimed to be in the long run a superior technical instrument for obtaining the same materialistic benefits as capitalism, its considerable appeal lay, as John Maynard Keynes noted, in "a combination of two things which Europeans have kept for some centuries in different compartments of the soul—religion and business. We are shocked because the religion is new, and contemptuous because the business, being subordinated to the religion instead of the other way round, is highly inefficient." Like other successful religions, Russian Communism exalted the common man and made him everything. Here was nothing new. But, Keynes pointed out, Communism—"though absolutely, defiantly non-supernatural"—was a new religion in the sense that it involved a revolution in ways of thinking and feeling about money. Unlike American Capitalism with "its habitual appeal to the Money Motive in nine-tenths of the activities of life," Russian Communism proposed to construct a framework of society in which materialistic motives, while not forsaken, should have a lesser importance, in which social approbation should be differently accorded, and where money-making, which previously was normal and respectable, should be no longer either the one or the other. When compared with an irreligious capitalism which had fallen short of economic paradise, the new religion was bound to hold tremendous attraction for those who had always felt an antipathy toward money-making and who normally, as a matter of course, placed moral above material advantage.[14]

The theory of the class struggle thus became for infatuated intellectuals the key to understanding the ultimate social reality that the Communists alone had been able to penetrate. When these Americans were converted to Communism in the 1930's, the one basic article of faith, they discovered, was the revolutionary nature of the proletariat and the counter-revolutionary nature of the middle class: "The proletariat was the revolutionary hero, the middle class the reformist villain. The proletariat was the guarantee of the ultimate goal, the middle class the corrupting influence of immediate demands. The proletariat was dedicated to the class struggle, the middle class to class collaboration." In *The Decline of American Capitalism* (1934) Lewis Corey, who as Louis C. Fraina had broken with the Communist party in 1922 but remained a Marxist, explained in rigidly orthodox terms that the mass of Americans exploited by "bankers' capitalism" had been thrust downward so that the few might live in ease and luxury. Though even in prosperity the working class, the driving force of the industrial system, had been victimized and tormented by the antagonisms and repressions of capitalism, their fate in depression was unbearable. For the inevitable collapse of capitalism had turned the American dream of well-being into a nightmare.* So, aroused intellectuals, embarrassed by their middle-class origins and synthetic social consciousness, belatedly aligned themselves with the "proletariat" and went forth to battle, in speech and on paper, for a workers' dictatorship.[15]

*Lewis Corey, *Decline of American Capitalism*. See page 267.

Readings:

The Materialistic Faith

Edward Earle Purinton (1878-   )

*A popular writer and business publicist, he
specialized in self-help articles written in the
Horatio Alger spirit. Among his publications, for
example, were such titles as* How to Be Happy
(1909), Efficient Living *(1915), and* Personal
Efficiency in Business *(1919).*

THE NEW AMERICAN RELIGION

Among the nations of the earth today America stands for
one idea: *Business.* National opprobrium? National opportunity. For in this fact lies, potentially, the salvation of
the world.

Thru business, properly conceived, managed and conducted, the human race is finally to be redeemed. How and
why a man works foretells what he will do, think, have,
give and be. And real salvation is in doing, thinking, having, giving and being—not in sermonizing and theorizing.

I shall base the facts of this article on the personal tours
and minute examinations I have recently made of twelve
of the world's largest business plants: U. S. Steel Corpora-

From "Big Ideas from Big Business," *Independent,* April 16, 1921, pp. 375–6.

tion, International Harvester Company, Swift & Company, E. I. du Pont de Nemours & Company, National City Bank, National Cash Register Company, Western Electric Company, Sears, Roebuck & Company, H. J. Heinz Company, Peabody Coal Company, Statler Hotels, Wanamaker Stores.

These organizations are typical, foremost representatives of the commercial group of interests loosely termed "Big Business." A close view of these corporations would reveal to any trained, unprejudiced observer a new conception of modern business activities. Let me draw a few general conclusions regarding the best type of business house and business man.

What is the finest game? Business. The soundest science? Business. The truest art? Business. The fullest education? Business. The fairest opportunity? Business. The cleanest philanthropy? Business. The sanest religion? Business.

You may not agree. That is because you judge business by the crude, mean, stupid, false imitation of business that happens to be located near you.

The finest game is business. The rewards are for everybody, and all can win. There are no favorites—Providence always crowns the career of the man who is worthy. And in this game there is no "luck"—you have the fun of taking chances but the sobriety of guaranteeing certainties. The speed and size of your winnings are for you alone to determine; you needn't wait for the other fellow in the game—it is always your move. And your slogan is not "Down the Other Fellow!" but rather "Beat Your Own Record!" or "Do It Better Today!" or "Make Every Job a Masterpiece!" The great sportsmen of the world are the great business men.

The soundest science is business. All investigation is reduced to action, and by action proved or disproved. The idealistic motive animates the materialistic method. Hearts as well as minds are open to the truth. Capital is furnished for the researches of "pure science"; yet pure science is not regarded pure until practical. Competent scientists are suitably rewarded—as they are not in the scientific schools.

The truest art is business. The art is so fine, so exquisite, that you do not think of it as art. Language, color, form, line, music, drama, discovery, adventure—all the components of art must be used in business to make it of superior character.

The fullest education is business. A proper blend of study, work and life is essential to advancement. The whole man is educated. Human nature itself is the open book that all business men study; and the mastery of a page of this educates you more than the memorizing of a dusty tome from a library shelf. In the school of business, moreover, you teach yourself and learn most from your own mistakes. What you learn here you live out, the only real test.

The fairest opportunity is business. You can find more, better, quicker chances to get ahead in a large business house than anywhere else on earth. The biographies of champion business men show how they climbed, and how you can climb. Recognition of better work, of keener and quicker thought, of deeper and finer feeling, is gladly offered by the men higher up, with early promotion the rule for the man who justifies it. There is, and can be, no such thing as buried talent in a modern business organization.

The cleanest philanthropy is business. By "clean" philanthropy I mean that devoid of graft, inefficiency and professionalism, also of condolence, hysterics and paternalism. Nearly everything that goes by the name of Charity was born a triplet, the other two members of the trio being Frailty and Cruelty. Not so in the welfare departments of leading corporations. Savings and loan funds; pension and insurance provisions; health precautions, instructions and safeguards; medical attention and hospital care; libraries, lectures and classes; musical, athletic and social features of all kinds; recreational facilities and financial opportunities—these types of "charitable institutions" for employees add to the worker's self-respect, self-knowledge and self-improvement, by making him an active partner in the welfare program, a producer of benefits for his employer and associates quite as much as a recipient of bounty from the company. I wish every "charity" organization would send its officials to school to the heads of the welfare departments of the big corporations; the charity would mostly be transformed into capability, and the minimum of irreducible charity left would not be called by that name.

The sanest religion is business. Any relationship that forces a man to follow the Golden Rule rightfully belongs amid the ceremonials of the church. A great business enterprise includes and presupposes this relationship. I have seen more Christianity to the square inch as a regular part of the office equipment of famous corporation presidents than may ordinarily be found on Sunday in a verbalized but not vitalized church congregation. A man is not wholly religious until he is better on week-days than he is on Sunday. The only ripened fruits of creeds are deeds. You can fool your preacher with a sickly sprout or a wormy semblance of character, but you can't fool your employer. I would make every business house a consultation bureau for the guidance of the church whose members were employees of the house.

I am aware that some of the preceding statements will be challenged by many readers. I should not myself have made them, or believed them, twenty years ago, when I was a pitiful specimen of a callow youth and cocksure professional man combined. A thoro knowledge of business has implanted a deep respect for business and real business men.

The future work of the business man is to teach the teacher, preach to the preacher, admonish the parent, advise the doctor, justify the lawyer, superintend the statesman, fructify the farmer, stabilize the banker, harness the dreamer, and reform the reformer. Do all these needy

persons wish to have these many kind things done to them
by the business man? Alas, no. They rather look down
upon him, or askance at him, regarding him as a mental
and social inferior—unless he has money or fame enough
to tilt their glance upward. . . .

The biggest thing about a big success is the price. It
takes a big man to pay the price. You can measure in advance the size of your success by how much you are willing to pay for it. I do not refer to money. I refer to the
time, thought, energy, economy, purpose, devotion, study,
sacrifice, patience, care, that a man must give to his life
work before he can make it amount to anything.

The business world is full of born crusaders. Many of
the leaders would be called martyrs if they weren't rich.
The founders of the vast corporations have been, so far as
I know them, fired with zeal that is supposed to belong only
to missionaries.

Of all the uncompromising, untiring, unsparing idealists
in the world today, none surpass the founders and heads of
the business institutions that have made character the cor-
nerstone. The costliest thing on earth is idealism.

Thurman W. Arnold (1891-   )

*After growing up in the Wild West (Wyo-
ming), he was educated at Princeton and Harvard Law School. Appointed Professor of Law at
Yale in 1930, he joined the revolt against the
narrowness of the traditional legal curriculum.
His attempt to study legal institutions from the
point of view of public psychology led to his
first two books—The Symbols of Government
and The Folklore of Capitalism. The latter led to
his appointment by President Roosevelt in 1938
as Assistant Attorney General in charge of the
Anti-trust Division. While he had earlier dis-*

*paraged the anti-trust laws, he became known
as the nation's "number one trust-buster," filing
more than two hundred suits in five years.*

THE THEOLOGY OF CAPITALISM

In the United States the mythology used to be very simple.
The predominant figure was the American Businessman.
Warriors were respected, but they had a distinctly minor
place. The National Government had to imitate the American Businessman. Whenever it failed, people became
alarmed. A businessman balances his budget. Hence the un-
balanced budget which was actually pulling us out of the depression was the source of greater alarm than administrative
failures which were actually much more dangerous. The
American Businessman bosses his employees. Hence the encouragement of the C.I.O. was thought to be the forerunner
of a revolution, in spite of the fact that never had industrial
unrest been followed with less actual disorder.

The creed of the American Businessman was celebrated in
our institutions of learning. Since the American Scholar was
a minor divinity, some of his characteristics had to be assumed by the great industrial organization. Therefore colleges were endowed to prove that the predominant divinity
was supported by reason and scholarship. All the Christian
virtues were also ascribed to him—for the selfishness of
business was an enlightened selfishness which resulted in the
long run in unselfish conduct if it were only let alone.

The American Businessman was independent of his fellows. No individual could rule him. Hence the "rule of law
above men" was symbolized by the Constitution. This meant
that the American Businessman was an individual who was
free from the control of any other individual and owed allegiance only to the Constitution. However, he was the only

From *The Folklore of Capitalism* (New Haven: Yale University Press, 1937),
pp. 35–6, 185–90. Reprinted by permission of the publisher.

individual entitled to this kind of freedom. His employees were subject to the arbitrary control of this divinity. Their only freedom consisted in the supposed opportunity of laborers to become American businessmen themselves.

It is this mythology, operating long after the American Businessman has disappeared as an independent individual, which gives the great industrial organization an established place in our temporal government. Every demand on these great industrial structures is referred to the conception of the American Businessman as a standard.

Thus pension systems for great corporations are all right provided businessmen inaugurate them. Economic coercion is permitted provided these heroes accomplish it. Boondoggling of every kind is subject to no criticism if businessmen finance it. Charity and welfare work, provided they are used to portray businessmen in their softer and more sentimental moods, are lovely things. When undertaken by the Government, they are necessary evils because such activity impairs the dignity and prestige of our great national ideal type. The businessman is the only divinity supposed to conduct such affairs. Therefore one never hears a community chest spoken of as a necessary evil as the dole is. Private charity even in times when it is an obvious failure is supposed to be more efficient than government relief.

In this mythology are found the psychological motives for the decisions of courts, for the timidity of humanitarian action, for the worship of states rights and for the proof by scholars that the only sound way of thinking about government is a fiscal way of thinking. Move Communism or any other kind of creed into this country, keep the present national hierarchy of tutelary divinities, and one would soon find that the dialecticians and priests were ingenious enough to make communistic principles march the same way as the old ones. So long as the American Businessman maintains his present place in this mythological hierarchy, no practical inconvenience is too great to be sacrificed to do him honor— every humanitarian impulse which goes counter to the popular conception of how the businessman should act is soft and effeminate. . . .

One of the essential and central notions which give our industrial feudalism logical symmetry is the personification of great industrial enterprise. The ideal that a great corporation is endowed with the rights and prerogatives of a free individual is as essential to the acceptance of corporate rule in temporal affairs as was the ideal of the divine right of kings in an earlier day. Its exemplification, as in the case of all vital ideals, has been accomplished by ceremony. Since it has been a central ideal in our industrial government, our judicial institutions have been particularly concerned with its celebration. Courts, under the mantle of the Constitution, have made a living thing out of this fiction. Men have come to believe that their own future liberties and dignity are tied up in the freedom of great industrial organizations from restraint, in much the same way that they thought their salvation in the future was dependent on their reverence and support of great ecclesiastical organizations in the Middle Ages. This ideal explains so many of our social habits, rituals, and institutions that it is necessary to examine it in some detail.

The origin of this way of thinking about organization is the result of a pioneer civilization in which the prevailing ideal was that of the freedom and dignity of the individual engaged in the accumulation of wealth. The independence of the free man from central authority was the slogan for which men fought and died. The free man was a trader, who got ahead by accumulating money. . . . There was nothing in that philosophy which justified far-flung industrial empires. Indeed, the great organization in which most men were employees, and a few at the top were dictators, was a contradiction of that philosophy. The great organization came in as a result of mechanical techniques which specialized the work of production so that men could not operate by themselves. Nothing could stop the progress of such organization, and therefore in order to tolerate it, men had to pretend that corporations were individuals. When faced with the fact that they were not individuals, they did not seek to control, but denounced and tried to break them up into smaller organizations. Those who did not choose to dissent, however, sought refuge in transferring the symbolism of the individual to the great industrial armies in which they were soldiers. . . .

It was this identification of great organizations with the dignities, freedom, and general ethics of the individual trader which relieved our federation of industrial empires from the hampering restrictions of theology which always prevent experiment. Men cheerfully accept the fact that some individuals are good and others bad. Therefore, since great industrial organizations were regarded as individuals, it was not expected that all of them would be good. Corporations could therefore violate any of the established taboos without creating any alarm about the "system" itself. Since individuals are supposed to do better if let alone, this symbolism freed industrial enterprise from regulation in the interest of furthering any current morality. The *laissez faire* religion, based on a conception of a society composed of competing individuals, was transferred automatically to industrial organizations with nation-wide power and dictatorial forms of government.

This mythology gave the Government at Washington only a minor part to play in social organization. It created the illusion that we were living under a pioneer economy composed of self-sufficient men who were trading with each other. In that atmosphere the notion of Thomas Jefferson, that the best government was the one which interfered the least with individual activity, hampered any control of our industrial government by our political government. We were slower, therefore, in adopting the measures of control of industrial organization than a country like England. The Government at Washington gradually changed into what was essentially a spiritual government whose every action was designed to reconcile the conflict between myth and reality which men felt when a creed of individualism was applied to a highly organized industrial world. Government in Washington was supposed to act so as to instil "confidence" in great business organizations. The Supreme Court of the United States, because it could express better than any other institution the myth of the corporate personality, was able to hamper Federal powers to an extent which foreigners, not realizing the emotional power of the myth, could not understand. This court invented most of the ceremonies which kept the myth alive and preached about them in a most dramatic setting. It dressed huge corporations in the clothes of simple farmers and merchants and thus made attempts to regulate them appear as attacks on liberty and the home. So long as men instinctively thought of these great organizations as individuals, the emotional analogies of home and freedom and all the other trappings of "rugged individualism" became their most potent protection.

Glenn Frank (1887-1940)

Editor, publicist, and university president, he began his career as a protégé of the socially minded Boston merchant Edward A. Filene. Later he became editor of Century magazine, which provided him with a forum for his liberal ideas. In 1925 he was appointed president of the University of Wisconsin. While there his most talked-about undertaking was the Experimental College, headed by Alexander Meiklejohn, which sought to find some workable departure from the traditional methods of higher education. But the experiment, besides being expensive, had little faculty support and was abandoned.

OUR MACHINE CIVILIZATION

Must we smash our machines in order to save our souls? The social mystics of the slower-paced Orient are sure that we must. Every energy of the frail body and flaming spirit of Mahatma Gandhi is invested in the attempt to convince the Western world that it must emancipate itself from the machine if it is to avert the downfall of its civilization. To him, the application of machine power to production meant the entrance of the serpent into the Eden of a handicraft world. To this wistful ascetic of India, the spinning-wheel is a symbol of salvation for our machine civilization.

To Gandhi and his kind, machine civilization must always mean the centralization of production in great industrial cities where congestion breeds its ugly offspring; a narcotic monotony of factory routine that turns masters of tools into servants of machines; a mass production that puts quantity above quality; a standardization of processes and products that will not stop until it has ironed out the mind and manners and morals of mankind into a sterile sameness, the death alike of the inventive skill and the independent spirit of the worker; an overspeeding that will leave mankind spiritually out of breath; and a subtle conspiracy against beauty that will end by making ugliness and utility interchangeable terms.

The business man of the Western world might dismiss all this as but the natural reaction of the mystical East if it came alone from Mahatma Gandhi, seated at his spinning-wheel, clothed only in his loin-cloth, and his longing for a premachine economy. But Gandhi and his fellow rebels against the machine are winning converts in the West.

These Western converts to the social mysticism of the

East are what the late Walter Rathenau, distinguished head of the *Allgemeine Deutsche Elektrische Gesellschaft,* called "the Shepherds of Arcady." Herr Rathenau was at once a social prophet and a successful profit-maker, seer, and business man in one. He had little patience and less confidence to give to men who, face to face with the admitted materialism and muddling of our machine civilization, had no remedy to offer save a cowardly retreat into some Arcadian simplicity of life which is possible only to a select few of the saints and seers. Herr Rathenau was willing to let these Shepherds of Arcady run away from the challenge of our machine civilization if they chose, but he preferred to buckle down to the practical task of wresting health and happiness and security and serenity from our machine civilization for the vast masses of men and women who cannot and will not run away from modern society to the haven of some private paradise.

Mahatma Gandhi is not more keenly aware of the perils of machine civilization than Herr Rathenau was; but Herr Rathenau was more keenly aware of the promise of machine civilization than Mahatma Gandhi is. Gandhi thinks mankind must emancipate itself from the machine; Rathenau thought mankind must emancipate itself through the machine. . . .

I am willing to grant to Mahatma Gandhi and his Western converts that to date our machine civilization has much to its discredit. It has too often subjected men to the new and more terrible drudgery of soul-killing speed of work. Its savings have not always been put to work for the improvement of its service. It has sometimes been guilty of the short-sighted business policy of paying its men the least they would stand for and charging its customers the most they would stand for. It has built and crowded into hideously ugly industrial centers. It has often forgotten beauty and frowned upon quality. It has often produced for sale rather than for use. And so on to the end of an indictment I shall not undertake to contradict.

But—and this is the nub of the matter—these are sins of a pioneer period. We must remember that our machine civilization is a mere fledgling among the social schemes of history. These sins will, in time, disappear from our machine civilization. In fact, they are disappearing more rapidly than appears to the side-line onlooker. And they are disappearing, not because business men have received a sudden baptism of brotherly love, but simply because it is becoming daily more evident that such sins are bad business.

And as a result of all this—if I may put it bluntly—I think that the masses have more to hope for from great engineers, great inventors, and great captains of industry than from the social reformers who woo them with their panaceas. The greatest social progress of the next 50 years is likely to come as a by-product of technical progress. Our most potent revolutionists are the really far-sighted manufacturers. . . .

My hopes respecting the future of our machine civilization rest neither upon outside reformers nor upon any internal reform of the human nature of business men, which, I suspect, has not materially changed since the American Indians passed their wampum from hand to hand.

I believe that the steady advance of technical progress, plus the increasingly intelligent effort of business men to find the soundest and most profitable forms of organization, processes of production, and methods of distribution will, without any "hifalutin" declaration of unselfish social purpose, correct the existing evils of our machine civilization and produce a social and business order the normal functioning of which will in itself be the highest social service.

Let me condescend to details and suggest some of the ways in which I think our machine civilization is correcting its more obvious shortcomings—the correction coming as an incidental by-product of technical progress and of business men's search for the soundest and most profitable ways of doing business. I can, of course, do little more than report a few tendencies by way of illustration.

First of all, there are technical and economic forces, making for an extensive decentralization of American industry, which bid fair to correct most of the evils of centralization and congestion against which muck-rakers and mystics have been railing for a generation. It is only a question of time until American industry will stop the complete manufacture and assembly of all the parts of complicated machines in great industrial centers. The parts will be manufactured in factories located at the source of the raw materials used in their manufacture.

For a time great industrial centers will persist as points at which the parts, manufactured elsewhere, are assembled and from which they are shipped to local markets. Ultimately the great congested industrial centers will disappear even as points of assembly, for in the end we shall ship parts to the very doorways of local markets for assembly.

This revolutionary industrial change—and the equally revolutionary social effects that will follow—will come, not because of any Utopian reformer's crusade, but as the result of technical progress in the field of superpower. Heretofore we have had to build our factories at the sources of motive power. The production of steel has stuck close by the coal mines of Pennsylvania. The production of flour has pitched its tent near the waterfalls of Minneapolis. And so on. Heretofore the flour industry has had to operate near the waterfalls, not near the wheat fields. Heretofore the iron industry has had to operate near the coal mines, not near the iron mines. All this will be changed as we perfect a nation-wide interlocking power system.

The critics of our machine civilization have assumed that we could not have mass production without centralization, and so they have said that we could not remedy the evils of centralization without renouncing mass production. They knew that we would not renounce mass production, so they have pronounced the evils of centralization as incurable. But now the outlook is that we shall ultimately find it possible to carry on mass production more profitably in a decentralized than in a centralized industry. When this is achieved many of the ugly social problems that have followed in the wake of industrial centralization will automatically disappear. . . .

Then, too, I am not sure that standardization of production processes, with all the factory routine that it implies, is the unmixed evil its critics assert. I realize the deadening effect that the monotonous repetition of a single specialized movement has upon the worker. It is true that, by and large, the man who makes one forty-secondth part of a watch is likely to become one forty-secondth of a watchmaker.

Standardized machine production does not make for creative craftsmanship in the worker. But it is not every worker who is a suppressed artist champing at the bit to "create." The brutal truth is that there is a vast amount of mediocrity in the human breed. And standardized machine production has given mediocrity its first chance to make a better living than the ancient artist-craftsman made. The mediocre workman, thanks to machine production, today has a cottage and a car; in a handicraft world he would be living in a hovel and walking.

And in the machine civilization of the next 50 years, I doubt that the craftsman blessed with the creative urge will be so badly off. The further development of mass production will give him two inestimable boons—leisure and means.

The outstanding fact of mass production and mass distribution is that its effective administration enables the manufacturer to do four apparently contradictory things at one and the same time—raise wages, lower prices, shorten hours, and increase total profits. And the first three mean leisure and means for the workman whose spirit is bigger than the set task he does in the factory. . . .

Even the most creative craftsman must face the necessity of living in a machine civilization. It is gratifying, therefore, to know that our machine civilization, in the normal perfection of its processes, is making for shorter hours and higher pay, thus staking out in the lives of the rank and file of workers larger and larger areas of leisure in which they may laugh and love and adventure among things of the mind and the spirit. When machine civilization has produced this leisure and means it will remain for the worker to prove that he has it in him to make as intelligent use of his opportunity for a broad and free life as the peasant and craftsman of other days made of a similar opportunity.

So much for the problem of standardization and the individual. What about the effect of standardization upon our civilization in general? I have broken my lance innumerable times in fights against the standardization of the American mind. But there has been a vast amount of sheer silliness spent upon a wholesale condemnation of all standardization.

A certain amount of standardization is necessary to the effective living of our lives. If we did not standardize and render more or less automatic the processes of shaving, dressing, and eating, we should have to spend most of our time in the bathroom and in the dining-room. I know men who do most of their creative business and professional planning while they are shaving and dressing. These processes have become so automatic that their energies are free for bigger things.

The same thing can be true of a civilization. The vast processes of production of necessities can become so standardized and automatic that the major energies of a people can be freed for bigger things. . . .

And, finally, our machine civilization is escaping from its earlier enslavement to ugliness. Machine industry is finding that beauty is not the foe but the friend of utility. Machine production is coming out of its gawky age. It is no longer enough that an automobile shall run well. It must also look well. And it is significant, I think, that the $600 car is aspiring to beauty of form and color as well as the $6,000 car. Machine industry has committed high crimes against beauty, but one look at the exquisitely beautiful period cabinet of a 1927 talking-machine shows that some-

thing revolutionary has happened since the days of the
first talking-machine with its hideously ugly horn jutting
out into the room like a steamer funnel. . . .

And the beauty born of a machine age promises to have
greater social significance than the beauty born of the premachine age. The machine industry of the future promises to
bring to the common man everywhere prosperity in the
wages he receives and beauty in the things he sees and
touches and handles day by day. This will be something
new under the sun. . . .

Modern industry is leading to a time when men will bring
the same beauty to the manufacturing of commodities that
medieval religion brought to the building of cathedrals.
And it will no longer be the case of beautiful cathedrals
looking down upon sordid serfdoms. The new beauty of the
machine age will be a democratized beauty. . . .

All in all, I prefer to take my stand with the Rathenaus
rather than with the Gandhis, for it seems to me that our
machine civilization is carrying about in its own processes the cures of all the evils that have afflicted it in its
adolescence.

Lewis Mumford (1895–   )

*At the age of twelve, he built his first radio set
and was soon writing short articles for popular
technical magazines. Though he later attended
City College and the New School for Social
Research in New York, admittedly the most
important influence in his life was Patrick
Geddes, the Scottish biologist and civic planner,
whose writings first turned his attention to social
ecology, the interplay between man and his
environment. Putting this theme to work, he
published in 1934 a study of technics and
civilization in which, among other things, he*

pointed out that all the critical instruments of modern technology had existed in other cultures, but what was new was the fact that these technical functions had been projected and embodied in organized forms which dominated every aspect of modern existence.

THE DIMINUTION
OF THE MACHINE

Most of the current fantasies of the future, which have been suggested by the triumph of the machine, are based upon the notion that our mechanical environment will become more pervasive and oppressive. Within the past generation, this belief seemed justified: Mr. H. G. Wells's earlier tales of The War of the Worlds and When the Sleeper Wakes, predicted horrors, great and little, from gigantic aerial combats to the blatant advertisement of salvation by go-getting Protestant churches—horrors that were realized almost before the words had left his mouth.

The belief in the greater dominance of mechanism has been reenforced by a vulgar error in statistical interpretation: the belief that curves generated by a past historic complex will continue without modification into the future. Not merely do the people who hold these views imply that society is immune to qualitative changes: they imply that it exhibits uniform direction, uniform motion, and even uniform acceleration—a fact which holds only for simple events in society and for very minor spans of time. The fact is that social predictions that are based upon past experience are always retrospective: they do not touch the real future. That such predictions have a way of justifying themselves from time to time is due to another fact: namely that in what Professor John Dewey calls judgments of practice the hypothesis itself becomes one of the determining elements in the working out of events: to the extent that it is seized and acted upon it weights events in its favor. The doctrine of mechanical progress doubtless had such a rôle in the nineteenth century.

What reason is there to believe that the machine will continue to multiply indefinitely at the rate that characterized the past, and that it will take over even more territory than it has already conquered? While the inertia of society is great, the facts of the matter lend themselves to a different interpretation. The rate of growth in all the older branches of machine production has in fact been going down steadily: Mr. Bassett Jones even holds that this is generally true of all industry since 1910. In those departments of mechanical industry that were well-established by 1870, like the railroad and the textile mill, this slowing down applies likewise to the critical inventions. Have not the conditions that forced and speeded the earlier growth— namely, the territorial expansion of Western Civilization and the tremendous increase in population—been diminishing since that point?

Certain machines, moreover, have already reached the limit of their development: certain areas of scientific investigation are already completed. The printing press, for example, reached a high pitch of perfection within a century after its invention: a whole succession of later inventions, from the rotary press to the linotype and monotype machines, while they have increased the pace of production, have not improved the original product: the finest page that can be produced today is no finer than the work of the sixteenth-century printers. The water turbine is now ninety per cent efficient; we cannot, on any count, add more than ten per cent to its efficiency. Telephone transmission is practically perfect, even over long distances; the best the engineers can now do is to multiply the capacity of the wires and to extend the inter-linkages. Distant speech and vision cannot be transmitted faster than they are transmitted today by electricity: what gains we can make are in cheapness and ubiquity. In short: there are bounds to mechanical progress within the nature of the physical world itself. It is only by ignoring these limiting conditions that a belief in the automatic and inevitable and limitless expansion of the machine can be retained.

And apart from any wavering of interest in the machine, a general increase in verified knowledge in other departments than the physical sciences already threatens a large curtailment of mechanical practices and instruments. It is not a mystic withdrawal from the practical concerns of the world that challenges the machine so much as a more comprehensive knowledge of phenomena to which our mechanic contrivances were only partial and ineffective responses. Just as, within the domain of engineering itself, there has been a growing tendency toward refinement and efficiency through a nicer inter-relation of parts, so in the environment at large the province of the machine has begun to shrink. When we think and act in terms of an organic whole, rather than in terms of abstractions, when we are concerned with life in its full manifestation, rather than with the fragment of it that seeks physical domination and that projects itself in purely mechanical systems, we will no longer require from the machine alone what we should demand through a many-sided adjustment of every other aspect of life. A finer knowledge of physiology reduces the number of drugs and nostrums in which the physician places confidence: it also decreases the number and scope of surgical operations—those exquisite triumphs of machine-technics!—so that although refinements in technique have increased the number of potential operations that can be resorted to, competent physicians are tempted to exhaust the resources of nature before utilizing a mechanical shortcut. In general, the classic methods of Hippocrates have begun to displace, with a new certitude of conviction, both the silly potions prescribed in Molière's Imaginary Invalid and the barbarous intervention of Mr. Surgeon Cuticle. Similarly, a sounder notion of the human body has relegated to the scrapheap most of the weight-lifting apparatus of late Victorian gymnastics. The habit of doing without hats and petticoats and corsets has, in the past decade, thrown whole industries into limbo: a similar fate, through the more decent attitude toward the naked human body, threatens the bathing suit industry. Finally, with a great part of the utilities, like railroads, power lines, docks, port facilities, automobiles, concrete roads which we constructed so busily during the last hundred years, we are now on a basis where repair and replacement are all that is required. As our production becomes more rationalized, and as population shifts and regroups in better relationship to industry and recreation, new communities designed to the human scale are being constructed. This movement which has been taking place in Europe during the last generation is a result of pioneering work done over a century from Robert Owen to Ebenezer Howard. As these new communities are built up the need for the extravagant mechanical devices like subways, which were built in response to the disorganization and speculative chaos of the megalopolis, will disappear.

In a word, *as social life becomes mature, the social unemployment of machines will become as marked as the present technological unemployment of men.* Just as the ingenious and complicated mechanisms for inflicting death used by armies and navies are marks of international anarchy and painful collective psychoses, so are many of our present machines the reflexes of poverty, ignorance, disorder. The machine, so far from being a sign in our present civilization of human power and order, is often an indication of ineptitude and social paralysis. Any appreciable improvement in education and culture will reduce the amount of machinery devoted to multiplying the spurious mechanical substitutes for knowledge and experience now provided through the channels of the motion picture, the tabloid newspaper, the radio, and the printed book. So, too, any appreciable improvement in the physical apparatus of life, through better nutrition, more healthful housing, sounder forms of recreation, greater opportunities for the natural enjoyments of life, will decrease the part played by mechanical apparatus in salvaging wrecked bodies and broken minds. Any appreciable gain in personal harmony and balance will be recorded in a decreased demand for compensatory goods and services. The passive dependence upon the machine that has characterized such large sections of the Western World in the past was in reality an abdication of life. Once we cultivate the arts of life directly, the proportion occupied by mechanical routine and by mechanical instruments will again diminish.

Our mechanical civilization, contrary to the assumption of those who worship its external power the better to conceal their own feeling of impotence, is not an absolute. All its mechanisms are dependent upon human aims and desires: many of them flourish in direct proportion to our failure to achieve rational social cooperation and integrated personalities. Hence we do not have to renounce the machine completely and go back to handicraft in order to abolish a good deal of useless machinery and burdensome routine: we merely have to use imagination and intelligence and social discipline in our traffic with the machine itself. In the last century or two of social disruption, we were tempted by an excess of faith in the machine to do everything by means of it. We were like a child left alone with a paint brush who applies it impartially to unpainted wood, to varnished furniture, to the tablecloth, to his toys, and to his own face. When, with increased knowledge and judgment, we discover that some of these uses are inappropriate, that others are redundant, that others are inefficient substitutes for a more vital adjustment, we will contract the machine to those areas in which it serves directly as an instrument of human purpose. The last, it is plain, is a large area: but it is probably smaller than that now occupied by the machine. One of the uses of this period of indiscriminate mechanical experiment was to disclose unsuspected points of weakness in society itself. Like an old-fashioned menial, the arrogance of the machine grew in proportion to its master's feebleness and folly. With a change in ideals from material conquest, wealth, and power to life, culture, and expression, the machine like the menial with a new and more confident master, will fall back into its proper place: our servant, not our tyrant.

Quantitatively, then, we shall probably be less concerned with production in future than we were forced to be during the period of rapid expansion that lies behind us. So, too, we shall probably use fewer mechanical instruments than we do at present, although we shall have a far greater range to select from, and shall have more skillfully designed, more finely calibrated, more economical and reliable contrivances than we now possess. The machines of the future, if our present technics continue, will surpass those in use at present as the Parthenon surpassed a neolithic wood-hut: the transformation will be both toward durability and to refinement of forms. The dissociation of production from the acquisitive life will favor technical conservatism on a high level rather than a flashy experimentalism on a low level.

But this change will be accompanied by a qualitative change in interest, too: in general a change from mechanical interest to vital psychic and social interests. This potential change in interest is generally ignored in predictions about the future of the machine. Yet once its importance is grasped it plainly alters every purely quantitative prediction that is based upon the assumption that the interests which for three centuries have operated chiefly within a mechanical framework will continue to remain forever within that framework. On the contrary, proceeding under the surface in the work of poets and painters and biological scientists, in a Goethe, a Whitman, a von Mueller, a Darwin, a Bernard, there has been a steady shift in attention from the mechanical to the vital and the social: more and more, adventure and exhilarating effort will lie here, rather than within the already partly exhausted field of the machine.

Such a shift will change the incidence of the machine and profoundly alter its relative position in the whole complex of human thought and activity. Shaw, in his Back to Methuselah, put such a change in a remote future; and risky though prophecy of this nature be, it seems to me that it is probably already insidiously at work. That such a movement could not take place, certainly not in science and its technical applications, without a long preparation in the inorganic realm is now farily obvious: it was the relative simplicity of the original mechanical abstractions that enabled us to develop the technique and the confidence to approach more complicated phenomena. But while this movement toward the organic owes a heavy debt to the machine, it will not leave its parent in undisputed possession of the field. In the very act of enlarging its dominion over human thought and practice, the machine has proved to a great degree self-eliminating: its perfection involves in some degree its disappearance—as a communal watersystem, once built, involves less daily attention and less expense on annual replacements than would a hundred thousand domestic wells and pumps. This fact is fortunate for the race. It will do away with the necessity, which Samuel Butler satirically pictured in Erewhon, for forcefully extirpating the dangerous troglodytes of the earlier mechanical age. The old machines will in part die out, as the great saurians died out, to be replaced by smaller, faster, brainier, and more adaptable organisms, adapted not to the mine, the battlefield and the factory, but to the positive environment of life.

George Santayana (1863-1952)

While the better part of his life was spent in the United States, and his books were written in the English language, he never relinquished his Spanish nationality. From the Boston Latin School he went to Harvard and then after two years in Berlin taught philosophy there from 1889 to 1912. Afterward he lived the rest of his life in Europe. Though he never had any illusions about the world's being rationally guided or true to any ideals, he thought it possible to live nobly in this world only if one lived in another world ideally.

THE GENTEEL TRADITION AT BAY

Twenty years ago the genteel tradition in America seemed ready to melt gracefully into the active mind of the country. There were few misgivings about the perfect health and the all-embracing genius of the nation: only go full speed ahead and everything worth doing would ultimately get done. The churches and universities might have some pre-American stock-in-trade, but there was nothing stubborn or recalcitrant about them; they were happy to bask in the golden sunshine of plutocracy; and there was a feeling abroad—which I think reasonable—that wherever the organisation of a living thing is materially perfected, there an appropriate moral and intellectual life will arise spontaneously. But the gestation of a native culture is necessarily long, and the new birth may seem ugly to an eye accustomed to some other form of excellence. Will the new life ever be as beautiful as the old? Certain too tender or too learned minds may refuse to credit it. Old Harvard men will remember the sweet sadness of Professor Norton. He would tell his classes, shaking his head with a slight sigh, that the Greeks did not play football. In America there had been no French cathedrals, no Venetian school of painting, no Shakespeare, and even no gentlemen, but only gentlemanly citizens. The classes laughed, because that recital of home truths seemed to miss the humour of them. It was jolly to have changed all that; and the heartiness of the contrary current of life in everybody rendered those murmurs useless and a little ridiculous. In them the genteel tradition seemed to be breathing its last. Now, however, the worm has turned. We see it raising its head more admonishingly than ever, darting murderous glances at its enemies, and protesting that it is not genteel or antiquated at all, but orthodox and immortal. Its principles, it declares, are classical, and its true name is Humanism.

The humanists of the Renaissance were lovers of Greek and of good Latin, scornful of all that was crabbed, technical, or fanatical: they were pleasantly learned men, free from any kind of austerity, who, without quarrelling with Christian dogma, treated it humanly, and partly by tolerance and partly by ridicule hoped to neutralise all its metaphysical and moral rigour. Even when orthodoxy was reaffirmed in the seventeenth century and established all our genteel traditions, some humanistic leaven was mixed in: among Protestants there remained a learned unrest and the rationalistic criticism of tradition: among Catholics a classical eloquence draping everything in large and seemly folds, so that nothing trivial, barbaric, or ugly should offend the cultivated eye. But apart from such influences cast upon orthodoxy, the humanists continued their own labours. Their sympathy with mankind was not really universal, since it stopped short at enthusiasm, at sacrifice, at all high passion or belief; but they loved the more physical and comic aspects of life everywhere and all curious knowledge, especially when it could be turned against prevalent prejudices or abuses. They believed in the sufficient natural goodness of mankind, a goodness humanised by frank sensuality and a wink at all amiable vices; their truly ardent morality was all negative, and flashed out in their hatred of cruelty and oppression and in their scorn of imposture. This is still the temper of revolutionaries everywhere, and of philosophers of the extreme Left. These, I should say, are more truly heirs to the humanists than the merely academic people who still read, or pretend to read, the classics, and who would like to go on thrashing little boys into writing Latin verses. . . .

Why not frankly rejoice in the benefits, so new and extraordinary, which our state of society affords? We may not possess those admirable things which Professor Norton pined for, but at least (besides football) haven't we Einstein and Freud, Proust and Paul Valéry, Lenin and Mussolini? For my part, though a lover of antiquity, I should certainly congratulate myself on living among the moderns, if the moderns were only modern enough, and dared to face nature with an unprejudiced mind and a clear purpose. . . .

So far, then, the gist of modern history would seem to be this: a many-sided insurrection of the unregenerate natural man, with all his physical powers and affinities, against the regimen of Christendom. He has convinced himself that his physical life is not as his ghostly mentors asserted, a life of sin; and why should it be a life of misery? Society has gradually become a rather glorious, if troubled, organisation of matter, and of man for material achievements. Even our greatest troubles, such as the late war, seem only to accelerate the scientific bridling of matter: troubles do not cease, but surgery and aviation make remarkable progress. Big Business itself is not without its grave worries: wasted production, turbulent labour, rival bosses, and an inherited form of government, by organised parties and elections, which was based on revolutionary maxims, and has become irrelevant to the true work of the modern world if not disastrous for it. Spiritual distress, too, cannot be banished by spiritual anarchy; in obscure privacy and in the sordid tragedies of doubt and of love, it is perhaps more desperate than ever. We live in an age of suicides. Yet this spiritual distress may be disregarded, like bad dreams, so long as it remains isolated and does not organise any industrial revolt or any fresh total discouragement and mystic withdrawal, such as ushered in the triumph of Christianity. For the present, Big Business continues to generate the sort of intelligence and loyalty which it requires: it favours the most startling triumphs of mind in abstract science and mechanical art, without any philosophic commitments regarding their ultimate truth or value. Indeed, mechanical art and abstract science are other forms of Big Business, and congruous parts of it. They, too, are instinctive undertakings, in which ambition, co-operation, and rivalry keep the snowball rolling and getting bigger and bigger. Some day attention will be attracted elsewhere, and the whole vain thing will melt away unheeded. But while the game lasts and absorbs all a man's faculties, its rules become the guides of his life. In the long run, obedience to them is incompatible with anarchy, even in the single mind. Either the private anarchy will ruin public order, or the public order will cure private anarchy.

The latter, on the whole, has happened in the United States, and may be expected to become more and more characteristic of the nation. There, according to one of the new humanists, "The accepted vision of a good life is to make a lot of money by fair means; to spend it generously; to be friendly; to move fast; to die with one's boots on." This sturdy ideal has come to prevail naturally, despite the preachers and professors of sundry finer moralities; it includes virtue and it includes happiness, at least in the ancient and virile sense of these words. We are invited to share an industrious, cordial, sporting existence, self-imposed and self-rewarding. There is plenty of room, in the margin and in the pauses of such a life, for the intellectual tastes which anyone may choose to cultivate; people may associate in doing so; there will be clubs, churches, and colleges by the thousand; and the adaptable spirit of Protestantism may be relied upon to lend a pious and philosophical sanction to any instinct that may deeply move the national mind. Why should anyone be dissatisfied? Is it not enough that millionaires splendidly endow libraries and museums, that the democracy loves them, and that even the Bolsheviks prize the relics of Christian civilisation when laid out in that funereal documentary form? Is it not enough that the field lies open for any young professor in love with his subject to pursue it hopefully and ecstatically, until perhaps it begins to grow stale, the face of it all cracked and wrinkled with little acrid controversies and perverse problems? And when not pressed so far, is it not enough that the same studies should supply a pleasant postscript to business, a congenial hobby or night-cap for ripe rich elderly people? May not the ardent humanist still cry (and not in the wilderness): Let us be well-balanced, let us be cultivated, let us be high-minded; let us control ourselves, as if we were wild; let us chasten ourselves, as if we had passions; let us learn the names and dates of all famous persons; let us travel and see all the pictures that are starred in Baedeker; let us establish still more complete museums at home, and sometimes visit them in order to show them to strangers; let us build still more immense libraries, containing all known books, good, bad, and indifferent, and let us occasionally write reviews of some of them, so that the public, at least by hearsay, may learn which are which.

Why be dissatisfied? . . . Big Business is an amiable monster, far kindlier and more innocent than anything Machiavelli could have anticipated, and no less lavish in its patronage of experiment, invention, and finery than Bacon could have desired. The discontent of the American humanists would be unintelligible if they were really humanists in the old sense; if they represented in some measure the soul of that young oak, bursting the limits of Christendom. Can it be that they represent rather the shattered urn, or some one of its fragments? The leaders, indeed, though hardly their followers, might pass for rather censorious minds, designed by nature to be the pillars of some priestly orthodoxy; and their effort, not as yet very successful, seems to be to place their judgments upon a philosophical basis. After all, we may actually be witnessing the demise of the genteel tradition, though by a death more noble and glorious than some of us had looked for. Instead of expiring of fatigue, or evaporating into a faint odour of learning and sentiment hanging about Big Business, this tradition, in dying, may be mounting again to its divine source.

Lewis Corey [Louis C. Fraina] (1894–1953)

A self-taught intellectual and Marxist economist, he was born in Italy and grew up in the poverty and filth of New York's East Side. At the age when other boys were struggling through high school, he was already a full-fledged revolutionary, delivering radical speeches on street corners for De Leon's Socialist Labor party. After the Russian Revolution of 1917, he became director of the American Bolshevik Bureau of Information, and when the Communist Party of America was formed in 1919, he served as a member of the Central Executive Committee and as editor of the official party organ, The Communist.

Then, in 1922, after a strange series of accusa-
tions, exonerations, and counter-accusations, he
was repudiated by the party, although he still
considered himself an orthodox Marxist.

DECLINE
OF AMERICAN CAPITALISM

Underlying the class-ideological crisis created by the decline
of capitalism is a crisis of faith in the old order. More concretely, it is a crisis of the constituent ideals which animate
the faith. The ideals of the American dream—the trinity of
liberty, opportunity, and progress—were becoming, long
before the crisis of the capitalist system, increasingly restricted in scope and unrealizable in practice. They lin-
gered on primarily as a cultural lag: for ideals may persist
and affect social action after the material conditions of
their origin are no more. Now the breakdown of the ideals
is startlingly revealed by the decline of capitalism. The
faith of the million-masses begins to crumble.

The stubborn cultural lag identified with the ideals of
the American dream is proof of their former vigor and
measurable reality. They were, it is true, ideals forged in
the fires of the bourgeois revolution in Europe, but they
acquired greater scope and realization in the American
scene because of the frontier and the absence of feudal
hangovers, resulting in more favorable social-economic
relations for the practice of liberty, opportunity, and progress. The American dream assumed definite shape and
flourished most vigorously in the 1820's–50's. An enormous
mass of settlers was absorbed by the frontier, creating an
agrarian democracy whose independence and rebellious
spirit strongly colored American life. Industry developed

From *The Decline of American Capitalism* (New York: Covici-Friede, 1934),
pp. 517–9, 525–6, 535–8.

rapidly, and it was in the small-scale stage which made it "open to all the talents." Restrictions on the right of labor to organize were overthrown. Remnants of semi-feudal tenure in the colonial land system were destroyed. The older aristocracy was breaking down, the new not yet entrenched in power. Free public education was enacted into law, and it measurably included higher learning. The ideals of the American revolution and of Jeffersonian democracy seemed wholly realizable. . . .

[But] developments after the Civil War constantly restricted the reality of the American dream: its ideals disintegrated, were limited in practice, or assumed a different character. Most of the libertarian spirit evaporated. Independence was increasingly replaced by insecurity. Class lines began to harden and government to usurp more repressive powers. Individualism was submerged, except for the freedom granted to capitalist buccaneers, as a constantly greater proportion of the population became direct employees or general dependents of large-scale corporate industry dominated by the financial oligarchy. Opportunity for the mass was more and more limited to survival or slightly improving one's lot within the new institutional set-up. The dream became primarily a faith in mere material progress; its old cultural promise was destroyed. But the dream was still vigorous and profoundly affected American life, mainly because of cultural lag, partly because there was still progress in many directions and capitalism, by and large, still "delivered the goods."

The American dream lingers on, for the lag is stubborn. But it now experiences a crisis more serious than any in the past. For former crises did not shatter the dream; they merely destroyed some of its ideals, increasingly limited the realization of others, and gave still others new, if vulgar and unsatisfactory, forms of expression. Material progress and reform helped to sustain the dream's cultural lag; but these very forces (the one ending in monopoly capitalism and imperialism, the other making them acceptable to the mass of the people) prepared the conditions of the decline of capitalism, which turns the American dream into a nightmare. . . .

Mass well-being has become the most important ideal of the American dream for the workers, because of their occupational inflexibility resulting from constantly more rigid class stratification. The ideal was not, however, of bourgeois origin; it was created primarily by the upthrust of the masses and the ideology of the labor movement arising out of the conditions of capitalist development. Bourgeois revolutions called the masses to action but suppressed them after the conquest of power, disregarding their well-being. The industrial revolution was accompanied by increasing mass misery; improvement of the workers' lot in the epoch of capitalist upswing was offset by increasing misery in newly developing industrial nations and in colonial lands. Yet capitalism, by and large, raised considerably the level of mass well-being as a by-product of economic expansion and necessity and in response to the struggles of labor. Not as much, of course, as among other classes; not as much as was possible in view of the immensely augmented productive forces of society. There were recurrent depressions when mass well-being was submerged, and periods of prosperity when the workers did not share in the gains of material progress or saw their relative share decreased. Nor was poverty abolished, although its abolition has been possible these many, many years. But the tendency was upward, if slowly, interruptedly, agonizingly, and there was always the hope of better things to come. Now the hope is killed by the decline of capitalism and its crisis of the system, by mass disemployment, lower wages, and lower standards of living.

The shattering of the ideal of continuously greater mass well-being is of the utmost significance, as the great mass of workers have increasingly interpreted the American dream in terms of improvement on the job. Now jobs become scarce and working conditions worse. Mass well-being is replaced with mass misery, the ideal of the abolition of poverty with a new and wholly unnecessary poverty. Capitalism returns to the epoch of increasing misery. . . .

The bourgeoisie wrought the idea of progress, a concept of the utmost creative significance. It arose out of the struggle waged by the new bourgeois class against feudalism on all fronts: economic, political, cultural. Social relations had to become different, to change, to *move*. But not mere motion: it was a concept of development, of continuous upward movement to new objectives. As the bourgeois revolution thrust its ideals beyond immediate class objectives, so the idea of progress soared beyond its class-economic origins. It released the forces of the human will, created a new approach to the world, made man feel himself capable of mastering his fate.

Faith in progress was particularly vital in the American dream. It was invigorated by a new world taking shape in the wilderness, by an almost complete shattering of the fetters of the past, by an extraordinary economic development and its progressive accompaniments. The ideal arising out of these conditions is thus expressed by Dr. Charles A. Beard:

"Underlying all is a belief that the lot of mankind can be continuously improved by research, invention, and taking thought. This is the philosophy of progress. . . . All legislation, all community action, all individual effort are founded on the assumption that evils can be corrected, problems solved, the ills of life minimized and its blessings multiplied by rational methods, intelligently applied. Essentially by this faith is American civilization justified."

This ideal was always limited and distorted in practice. It is now, in its bourgeois form, a mere pitiable echo of what has been and a tragic ignoring of what might be. For Dr. Beard speaks (in 1932!) as if the ideal was now in action: but what a mockery of progress, of the rational and intelligent, is the social-economic breakdown created by the crisis of the capitalist system! Dr. Beard speaks as if capitalism is identified with progress everlasting: but capitalism, limiting progress even in the epoch of upswing, now in its decline openly revolts against progress and all its works, because they undermine the existing order.

The revolt against progress originates in the movement of economic forces. . . . Production and realization of surplus value move downward because of the increasingly higher composition of capital and mass disemployment. The productivity of labor creates an abundance which presses upon contracting markets and endangers profit. Industrialization of new regions is either completed or prevented by the contradictions of monopoly capitalism. Capitalism is undermined by the very productive forces it called into being. The formerly relative self-destructive character of capitalist production now becomes absolute. It resorts to limitation of output on a mass scale: repression of the productive forces of society. Out of decline and decay arises the capitalist revolt against economic progress.

The revolt against economic progress becomes an ideological revolt. Progress means the continuous upward movement of society. But capitalism is not eternal; it is not immune to the law of social succession. Basing himself on the idea of progress and its manifestations in the dialectical movement of capitalist production, Marx saw the relations of a new social order developing within the shell of the old. Capitalism created collective or social forms of production, the objective basis of socialism. The capitalist bourgeoisie moved and had its being by creating the industrial proletariat, the objective carrier of socialism. As this dialectical movement appeared more clearly, threatening the old order, the bourgeois idea of progress began to change. Where formerly it included the revolutionary transformation of an old social order by the new, progress was now limited to mere change and pedestrian reform within the existing order. Among small but important intellectual groups a whole philosophy arose embodying a reaction against progress: limiting, scoffing, rejecting, mobiliz-

ing all the resources of the human mind to prove that
progress was a delusion and a snare. Now the philosophy
opposed to progress is seized upon by the capitalist class.
For capitalism has outlived its historical utility. It is in the
epoch of decline and decay. Progress is now realizable only
in a form which endangers capitalist rule, by socialism re-
leasing the creative social-economic forces of society, by
the revolutionary struggle for power of the proletariat and
its allies. Hence capitalism reacts against progress on all
fronts: economic, political, cultural. Progress now again
means the necessity of revolutionary change.

State capitalism clings to progress in words. But where
is it in practice? The real job of state capitalism is to prop
up the old order, to make it more resistant to progress, or
socialism. State capitalism merely tries to "freeze" the
breakdown and decay of capitalist decline. This eventually
manifests itself in the fascist repudiation of the idea of
progress. Fascism fuses into a system all the old reactionary
ideas opposed to progress and deliberately moves backward to revival of a mixture of Cæsarism and medievalism,
which was emphatically rejected by the revolutionary
bourgeoisie. Reaction becomes a faith and retrogression its
works.

New and finer fulfillments? They are doomed by capitalist
decline and decay. New and finer fulfillments of progress
are potential only in the revolutionary struggle for power,
for socialism and communism.

Thus capitalism is driven to revolt against progress and
all the other ideals of the American dream and of the
bourgeois revolution. Now, in ideological form, the forces
which sustained capitalism turn into their opposites and
become its antagonists. For the ideals, seizing upon great
masses, are an historical force. The masses believe in them
and want them realized, having measurably identified them
with their own mixed, groping, yet definitely plebeian
aspirations. Cultural lag is identified with the bourgeois
form of the ideals, with faith in the possibility of their

realization in the existing order. As capitalist decline increasingly limits their already incomplete realization and moves toward their destruction, including destruction of the concrete democratic rights of the workers, the ideals become dangerous, for it is impressed upon the masses that they are realizable only in new forms and in a new social order.

This is the crisis of the American dream, underlying the class-ideological crisis created by the decline of capitalism. The crisis prepares the subjective conditions of fundamental social change. For the objective clash between the old and the new order must become a conscious class struggle, which transforms the quantity of accumulated social-economic changes into the quality of revolutionary action for the new social order. A class, in this case the proletariat, cannot become revolutionary and perform its historic task, cannot carry on the struggle for power, until it has broken the ideological fetters of the old order: it must replace the old faith with its own consciousness and ideals, and make the new world they express acceptable to the other exploited elements of society.

CHAPTER FIVE

Liberalism and Democracy

I

In a society which placed such disproportionate emphasis on the production of material goods there was little room for liberal intellectuals. Business success was by common consent regarded as conclusive evidence of ability, intelligence, and wisdom, even in matters having no relation to economic affairs. "Give out the news that one has just made a killing in the stock market, or robbed some confiding widow of her dower, or swindled the government in some patriotic enterprise," gibed Mencken, "and at once one will discover that one's shabbiness is a charming eccentricity, and one's judgment of wines worth hearing, and one's political hallucinations worthy of attention." On the other hand, the "long-haired gentry" who called themselves "liberals" and "radicals" and "non-partisan" and "intelligentsia" and—"God only knows how many other trick names"—were looked down upon as fault-finders and knockers. As George F. Babbitt told the annual Get-Together Fest of the Zenith Real Estate Board, the ideal of American manhood and culture was not "a lot of cranks sitting around chewing the rag about their Rights and their Wrongs, but a God-fearing, hustling, successful two-fisted Regular Guy" ready to sell efficiency and to whoop it up for national prosperity and whose answer to his critics was a "square-toed boot that'll teach the grouches and smart alecks to respect the He-man and get out and root for Uncle Samuel, U.S.A.!" In such a hostile atmosphere where the good life was calculated in dollars and cents, the dissident intellectual unable to find comfort in the flivver, the telephone, the radio, the movies, and the funnies was an outsider who either fled to Europe with Ernest Hemingway and F. Scott Fitzgerald or stayed to scoff with those modern disciples of Diogenes, Sinclair Lewis and Henry L. Mencken. To the normal American Babbitt, his critics were freaks who deliberately disliked their neighbors because they were comfortable and contented, and though stung by their ridicule, he took comfort in his more practical role. As a commercial rimester put it:

> Babbitts—though we jeer and flout them—
> We could never do without them.
> Artists all—we would be beggars
> Were it not for Butter 'n' Eggers.
>
> For though Art is very swell, it
> Hardly pays unless you sell it.
> And the artist—ain't it funny?—
> Like the Babbitt, values money.
>
> Also rather likes to grab it
> From the much-enduring Babbitt.
> Babbitts great and Babbitts small
> Speaking frankly "Aren't we all?"°

The modern-day Diogenes gained a great reputation jeer-

°Berton Braley, "Babbitt Ballads," *Nation's Business*, XVI (Jan., 1928), 29. Reprinted by permission of the publisher, The Chamber of Commerce of the United States.

ing at useful citizens, said *Nation's Business*, but for all
his talk how much time and money did he give to charity
and to the upbuilding of his community?[1]

In contrast to the exuberant materialism of Babbitt and
his associates, the liberals appeared on the verge of exhaustion. Tired radicals who had gone through the "disillu-
sionizing" process of war seemed to be victims of what
John Dewey described as the "post-war mind." "With the
let up of war, with the issue determined, the tension re-
laxes, and the immediate present regains with added force
its command. Not the arduous labor of reconstruction but
enjoyment of the present, of the gains to be snatched from
using the opportunities of pleasure and profit in things as
they are, captures the mind."[2] Just as the fierce outburst
of materialistic money-making that followed in the immediate wake of the war was due in part to a release from the
unnatural strain of war, so the post-war relaxation of liberal endeavor can be explained as a natural human response.
When the stress of war was removed, the crusading zeal,
the spiritual exhilaration it generated could no longer be
sustained. Liberals who earlier had dreamed of remaking
the world turned at the end of the war with a sigh of relief to the homelier and less exciting satisfactions of peace.
To men in such a mood, the dull, commonplace virtues of
the American businessman no longer seemed contemptuous.
For all his foolishness, his smug faith in comfort and service, Babbitt was not wholly bad. Those who like Walter
Weyl had worn themselves out in the cause of humanity
now appreciated Babbitt's simple joy in the conveniences
of his life and his home. Reform and revolution, Weyl discovered as he grew older, were not everything, and if one
could find satisfaction in the "little busy-nesses" of everyday
experience, the good life was in way of being achieved.°

Others, however, took a less sanguine view of the de-

°Walter Weyl, *Tired Radicals*. See page 290.

cline of liberalism. While personally Weyl might attribute
loss of the liberal fighting spirit to the mellowing of age,
Floyd Dell, who also belonged to the pre-war generation,
contended that the liberal movement had simply reached
the point of bankruptcy. When its few tangible social
achievements were matched against the enormous obligations incurred in the name of peace and reform, there
remained an overwhelming deficit which few men had the
courage to face. Because of this defeatist psychosis, Dell
concluded, the liberals had fallen into a numbed state of
"intellectual shell-shock." As a result, said Vernon Louis
Parrington, middle-aged liberals, "whose hair is growing
thin and the lines of whose figures are no longer what they
were," found themselves "in the unhappy predicament of
being treated as mourners at their own funerals." But, insisted Parrington, they were celebrating the wrong funeral
—he and his generation were not yet authentic corpses. It
was the faith of America that was dead, and Babbitt, "an
empty soul," was symbol of that common emptiness.

For a hundred and fifty years America had sustained its
hopes on the rich nourishment provided by the Enlightenment. "Faith in the excellence of man, in the law of progress, in the ultimate reign of justice, in the conquest of
nature, in the finality and sufficiency of democracy, faith in
short in the excellence of life, was the great driving force in
those earlier, simpler days." But this "noble dream" had
been slowly dissipated by an encompassing materialism in
which "faith in machinery came to supersede faith in man."
And now, in the twenties, Parrington lamented, America
had fallen so low that "our faith in justice, progress, the
potentialities of human nature, the excellence of democracy, is stricken with pernicious anemia, and even faith
in the machine is dying." By 1925 liberalism had grown so
infirm and politically impotent that Glenn Frank, editor
and President of the University of Wisconsin, reported that
he found very few "realistically minded liberals" who re-

tained any confidence in the "practical possibilities of office-holding liberalism." With the conservatives firmly in power, the future looked dark for liberalism.[3]

Then, unexpectedly, with the coming of the depression and the election of Roosevelt, the liberals were catapulted into power. Though the Democratic party was a working coalition of liberals, conservatives, and machine politicians, President Franklin Roosevelt declared at the outset that his party was to be "the party of militant liberalism," and in the years immediately after 1933 the liberal outlook prevailed. While undeniably there was a pragmatic and opportunistic streak in New Deal liberalism, it was nevertheless consistent in its view that government should help the people "to gain a larger social justice." As Richard Hofstadter has noted, "Where Progressivism had capitalized on a growing sense of the ugliness under the successful surface of American life, the New Deal flourished on a sense of the human warmth and the technological potentialities that could be found under the surface of its inequities and its post-depression poverty." But like Progressivism, the liberalism of the thirties was a reaffirmation of faith in America. Just as Herbert Croly warned the nation at the beginning of the century that the fulfillment of the American national promise demanded a hard and inextinguishable faith, so Henry A. Wallace, Secretary of Agriculture and Vice-President under Roosevelt, reminded his countrymen in 1934 that the reforms of the New Deal would never succeed unless they were inspired in their hearts by "a larger vision than the hard-driving profit motives of the past."* Yet, frank and realistic, Wallace agreed with Croly that faith was no substitute for good works. Good intentions were not enough—there must be set up such social machinery as would give the human heart opportunity for translating its aspirations into practical action.[4]

---

*Henry A. Wallace, *The New Frontier.* See page 295.

Tennessee Valley Authority

Through innovation the New Deal searched for acceptable solutions to problems rather than imposing preconceived solutions. Its most "socialistic" undertaking, the Tennessee Valley Authority, caused private enterprise to flourish in an area where previously it had barely existed.

II

Though the New Deal reaffirmed democratic principles, back in the 1920's democracy had come under slashing attack. In the cynicism that followed the war, wrote Parrington, "the democratic liberalism of 1917 was thrown away like an empty whiskey-flask." Clever young men and beardless philosophers who had recently discovered Nietzsche began to poke fun at democracy. Their leader was the irreverent Henry L. Mencken, who defined democracy as "that system of government under which the people, having sixty million native-born adult whites to choose from, including thousands who are handsome and many who are wise, pick out a Coolidge to be head of the state." A recent convert to behaviorism, Mencken had discovered that psychology had some amusing comments to make on politics. From army intelligence tests he had picked up the concept of the moron which he used as a bludgeon to flay democracy.° Flippantly defining democracy as "boobocracy," he suggested that the mob—the raw material of democracy—was composed in the main of "men and women who have not got beyond the ideas and emotions of childhood, hovers, in mental age, around the time of puberty, and chiefly below it." According to Mencken, the minds of these permanent adolescents could not grasp even the simplest abstractions; their so-called thinking was "purely a bio-chemical process exactly comparable to what goes on in a barrel of cider." Since all their thought was on the level of a few primitive appetites and emotions, it was a sheer impossibility to educate them, and therefore they could only be governed by playing upon their fears and prejudices.[5]

For all his flippancy and sarcasm, Mencken's was a serious indictment of democracy. If the masses were never to rise above sex appeals and belly needs, then there was not much hope for a democratic society. Certainly the belief that the majority of the people were unable to think for themselves found support in higher military and business circles. A U.S. Army *Training Manual* issued in 1928 defined democracy as "a government of the masses. Authority derived through mass meeting or any other forms of 'direct' expression. Results in mobocracy. Attitude toward property is communistic—negating property rights. Attitude toward law is that the will of the majority shall regulate, whether

°Henry L. Mencken, *Democratic Man*. See page 302.

In the thirties there were some who thought the answer to America's problems was a fascist dictatorship. Disillusionment with democracy and admiration for Hitler and his methods led to formation of the German-American Bund with its swastikas and Nazi salutes.

it be based upon deliberation or governed by passion, prejudice, and impulse, without restraint or regard to consequences. Results in demagogism, license, agitation, discontent, anarchy." In similar vein, the members of the National Association of Manufacturers were informed that the "working masses" constituted "a great class below" their employers. Left alone, the masses instinctively held to "right principles," but at the same time they were "unwittingly susceptible" to the demogogic appeals of agitators and "professional uplifters." From the viewpoint of its critics, the great problem in a democracy was the real and ever-present danger of the irresponsible masses dominating the "thinking people." As evidence of the perils of mass power, businessmen were asked to consider the mob's irrational demands: "Hear the chorused voice of the multitude screaming for an increase of compensation in direct proportion to a reduction in hours of labor. Listen to the strange philosophies of the living-wage, the check-off system, the minimum wage, government controlled children, the closed union shop, and the socialistic redistributions of wealth." In their deep antipathy for democracy, business spokesmen initially hailed the Fascist coup in Italy as "the most creditable development in human history," and Mussolini was praised as a "fine type of business executive." Some hoped the "same sound philosophy" was developing in America.[6]

Such disparagements of democracy did not go unchallenged. Nor were the majority of Americans convinced, for as Charles A. Beard pointed out, nothing was easier than the game of attacking democracy by citing scandalous incidents, absurd episodes, and the idiotic antics of some elected persons. It merely turned against democracy the weapons once employed against monarchy—the scurrilous reporting of authentic cases of imbecility, murder, poison, arson, adultery, bastardy, corruption, drunkenness, useless wars, and other examples of royal misconduct. Although eighteenth-century republican agitators thought they had made an unanswerable argument for their cause, in the end, said the historian, it produced nothing more important than amusement. If the United States were composed as Mencken asserted almost exclusively of beings without courage, ability, aspiration, or honor, then, reasoned Edmund Wilson, they could never have settled the West nor even made "the effort necessary to sustain a single street of shops," much less establish a great nation. Likewise dissenting, G. K. Chesterton, the British writer, accused the elitists and Menckenites of persecuting the common man and contended their anti-democracy was "as much stuffed with cant as their democracy." It was easy to weary of democracy and to cry out for an intellectual aristocracy. But, said Chesterton, "the trouble is that every intellectual aristocracy seems to have been utterly unintellectual." Although it was the fad to say that most modern blunders were due to the common man, it was his opinion that the most appalling had in fact been due to the uncommon man. For example, Adam

Smith, whom he cited as an uncommon man, advanced a theological theory that Providence had so made the world that men might be happy through their selfishness, a doctrine held sacred by the business elite of the twenties. But "the common man soon found out just how happy—in the slums where they left him and in the slump to which they led him."[7]

Most of those who argued against democracy in theory did so from their dislike of it in practice. They condemned democracy because it was too democratic. Since the practice was precisely what the theory intended, those critics were not arguing logically, but merely expressing a prejudice. For a long time, at least since the beginning of the national existence, America had been trying to improve the condition of the masses. Over the years the nation had been steadily gaining on this ideal, but "instead of celebrating the victory, the fastidious withdraw their skirts, anxious housewives deplore the passing of 'the good, old-fashioned servant,' and uneasy employers complain of the increase of wages and the standard of living." So argued Professor Ralph Barton Perry of Harvard, who found that while democracy had not been an unqualified success, neither had it proved a complete failure.[*] In his opinion the charge of failure was due in part to unrealistic expectations of success. Democracy had been expected to work miracles almost automatically. But as the depression taught, democracy was dependent on knowledge and wisdom beyond all other forms of government. Democracy, as the jurist Felix Frankfurter explained, "seeks to prevail" when the complexities of modern industrial life "make a demand upon knowledge and understanding never made before, and when the forces inimical to the play of reason have power and subtlety unknown in the past." Those who were filled with doleful forebodings about democracy not only overlooked the fact that the most brilliant civilization in recorded his-

[*]Ralph Barton Perry, *The Alleged Failure of Democracy.* See page 308.

tory was a civilization born under a pure democracy at Athens, but in their desire for an easy way out proposed to go back and begin over again, modeling modern American institutions on those ancient forms which their revolutionary ancestors had denounced as tyrannical. Yet, as was becoming increasingly apparent in the thirties, the Fascist governments of Mussolini and Hitler had not discovered any panaceas for the perplexing problems of modern industrial life, but had only "created out of disorder by terror of disorder" a brutal government of gangs. If the real test of any government was "what does it do for the average man?"—then compared to these reactionary tyrannies with their militarism, violence, and regimentation, democracy in America was a stupendous success.[8]

III

The reactionary and materialistic temper of the twenties made all progressive and liberal programs seem sentimental, inept, and rather hopelessly out of touch with things. "The decadent religion of Liberalism" was denounced by the Right for having no "standards," and dismissed by the Left as a "flabby relativism" based upon a want of conviction. "It was useless," conceded the disillusioned muckraker Lincoln Steffens, "to fight for the right under our system; petty reforms in politics, wars without victories, just peace, were impossible." In the vanguard of liberal reform in prewar days, Steffens had written countless exposures of the shame of the cities, states, and corporate business between 1900 and 1910—as he said, "narrating rather bitterly the defeated struggles of heroic leaders to reform politics and government." If, after the war and the peace, he had forsaken the heroic course of the old muckraking days and had lost his "illusion about democracy as the road to democracy," Steffens proved a notable exception to the general rule that old reformers became "tired radicals." For he cast aside his liberalism only to embrace Communism. After

viewing the Russian Revolution at first hand, he came to
the conclusion that the Communists would "win out" and
"save the world." Despairing of the "good" people and
evolutionary reform, Steffens abandoned his role of "sentimental rebel" to become a prophet of revolution. He con-
veyed his vision in an historical parable called *Moses in
Red* (1926) which treated the revolt of Israel under Moses
as the classic pattern of revolution.* Since he himself had
been corrupted by "the easy life of the old culture," Steffens felt obliged to admire the revolution from a distance.
But, like Moses, he pointed the way to the Promised Land.
By the beginning of the thirties, as a home-grown radical,
he had become something of a hero; and when his *Autobiography* appeared in 1931, it was accepted as "almost a
textbook of revolution" and doubtless helped persuade
many idealistic young Americans to take a pro-Communist
position.[9]

Among these fighting young Communists, being a Socialist—like being a liberal—meant the person was "not really
thinking" in realistic terms of the class struggle. In seeking
"a New Deal for the world," they believed fervently in
the power of historical forces to move the mass of mankind
inexorably toward the glorious world of pure Communism.
As sectarian ideologues, they were rigidly committed to the
Soviet Union, the Communist Party, and the Marxist dox-
ology. To them "human aims seemed more important than
national goals," and they "talked more about the hope for
an ideal society than the benefits of the existing one." The
movement proved a haven for intellectuals who preferred
theories to facts, and much time was wasted in "endless
meetings" and "passionate speeches" about such unreal
subjects as the "culture of the working class." Yet, as Howard Zinn has said, it is all too easy to be witty at their
expense. "The stage whispering, the posturing, the dogma,
the in-fighting; the Talmudic debates among Trotskyists,

*Lincoln Steffens, *Why I Am a Leninist.* See page 315.

Communists, Lovestonites, old Wobblies; the hypocrisy, the self-righteousness" appear ridiculous today. But when measured against the evils which the Left faced in the 1930's: "the hungry children, the evicted families shivering in the streets, the men standing in long lines for a day's work, the Negroes lynched in the South and jammed into filthy ghettos in the North" and "overseas, the Japanese butchering China, Mussolini's tanks rumbling toward Ethiopian farmers carrying spears, German warplanes bombing Barcelona, Hitler beginning the deadly roundup of the Jews"—then these young Quixotes appear more realistic, for they at least took a stand against the crimes, here and abroad, and joined the fight against Fascism before it became respectable.[10]

Most important for American intellectuals was the indisputable fact that the Communists had assumed the leadership in the world struggle against international Fascism. A month after Hitler seized power in Germany, the *Daily Worker* called for "A United Front to Fight Fascism," and shortly afterward the *New Masses* published a manifesto against the Nazis. Hatred of Fascism, in the opinion of Daniel Aaron, brought many American writers and intellectuals into the Communist orbit who otherwise might never have had anything to do with the movement. The high point of anti-Fascist sentiment in the thirties was the Spanish Civil War in which the Loyalist cause was enthusiastically accepted by an overwhelming majority of the American intelligentsia as the cause of humanity against the brutish powers of darkness.[11]

Although a considerable number of American writers and intellectuals turned Left in the thirties, not all were caught by the Marxist dialectic. Some, derisively dubbed "fellow travelers," merely sympathized with Communism and adopted a pro-Soviet attitude; others, more independent, joined John Dewey in the call for a new radical party. A perennial liberal, Dewey in 1934 believed a second American Revolution loomed ahead. While it might not be *the* Revolution to the disciples of Marx, at the same time Dewey insisted there was to be "no truckling to capitalism." What Dewey actually proposed was, in the words of Norman Thomas, "an intellectualized version of a watered-down socialism," but it was never Communism. For Communism held no fascination for Dewey.° As early as 1928, reporting on a trip to the Soviet Union in the *New Republic*, he pronounced the Revolution "a great success" but wrote off Communism as "a frost."[12]

The first rift between American intellectuals and Communism opened at the time of the Moscow trials of 1936–38, during which Stalin methodically purged thousands of so-called "enemies of the people." They were deeply shocked to discover that Leninism was, after all, "the faith of a persecuting and propagating minority of fanatics led by hypocrites" and Stalin a Mahomet, not a Debs. According to Irving Howe and Lewis Coser, the mass treason trials "marked a major step in the collapse of morale among radical American intellectuals," for it was sensed by everyone involved that the moral fate of radicalism was at stake. The Leftist intellectual world was ripped into bitter factions. The anti-Stalinists sponsored a "Commission of Inquiry" headed by John Dewey which cross-examined Leon Trotsky in Mexico City and concluded that Soviet charges of counter-revolution were false. Party leaders, while pretending all was well in the "workers' fatherland," viciously denounced "renegade" intellectuals and summarily excommunicated doubting fellow travelers. But the final break, "the moment of truth," came in the summer of 1939 when Stalin signed a non-aggression pact with Hitler. For Lewis Corey, author of *The Decline of American Capitalism* and the leading Marxist economist in the country, the shock was so great that it not only cooled his Communist sympathies but destroyed his belief in Marxism itself. Since the flirtation of a great many American writers and

°John Dewey, *Why I Am Not a Communist*. See page 327.

intellectuals with the Communist party had been built upon anti-Fascism, when the Soviet Union deserted the fight against Fascism, they became disenchanted once and for all—for them, Marxism had proved a failure and the mission of the proletariat a delusion.[13]

The epitaph, however, was written, not by a disillusioned American intellectual of the thirties, but by an unknown expatriate in Paris in 1928: "Russia . . . I think . . . will become a sort of fat, complaisant, second-rate United States. It is rapidly adopting the American economic vision because the revolution cleared a way for it. When the country becomes properly Americanized, say in fifty years, it will be producing hordes and hordes of Russian Harold Bell Wrights and Edgar Guests, while the one time Dostoievskys will have become merely classical legends, like Shakespeare in England today. . . . The country will become industrialized, radioized, movieized, and standardized, the huge population of illiterate peasants will be taught how to read advertisements, newspapers, and bibles, the country will placidly settle down to the preoccupation of money grubbing."[14]

Readings:

Liberalism and Democracy

Walter Weyl (1873-1919)

A veteran Progressive, he gained a national reputation with the publication in 1912 of The New Democracy. *One of the really significant books of the day, it called for a liberal, non-utopian program of democratic reform which would emphasize social rather than private ethics, common rather than individual responsibility. As one of the founding editors of the* New Republic, *he was slow to catch the war fever, but the appeal of the Wilson formula of "peace without victory" finally won him over. Though the war always taxed his conscience, the peace brought complete disillusionment, and he retreated from politics and reform to private life and personal consolations.*

TIRED RADICALS

I once knew a revolutionist who thought that he loved

From *Tired Radicals and Other Papers* by Walter Weyl, pp. 9–15. Copyright 1921 by B. W. Huebsch, Inc., 1949, by The Viking Press, Inc. Reprinted by permission of The Viking Press, Inc.

Humanity but for whom Humanity was merely a club with which to break the shins of the people he hated. He hated all who were comfortable and all who conformed. He hated the people he opposed and he hated those who opposed his opponents in a manner different from his. Zeal for the cause was his excuse for hating, but really he was in love with hate and not with any cause.

The war came, and this vibrant, humorless man, this neurotic idealist who was almost a genius, found a wider vent for his emotion. His hatred, without changing its character, changed its incidence. He learned to hate Germans, Bolshevists, and radicals. He completed the full circle and soon was consorting most incongruously with those whom he had formerly attacked. Today nothing is left of his radicalism or his always leaky consistency; nothing is left but his hatred. At times he hates himself. He would always hate himself could he find no one else to hate. He is becoming half-reactionary, half-cynical. He will end— But who knows how anyone will end?

Radicalism loses little in the defection of this unconsciously sadistical agitator, for despite his stormy eloquence he was always less embarrassing to his enemies than his friends. His case, however, suggests an inherent weakness in radical movements, an inevitable mortality among radicals, traceable to wars and other calamities, but due chiefly to the manner in which radicals are recruited and the kind of men they are.

There are two large, but not sharply defined groups of radicals: radicals by environment and radicals by temperament. The first are usually the slower and surer-footed because their course is controlled by the rut in which they live; the latter are quicker, more violent, more uncompromising, less realistic, because their radicalism springs from within. They would be rebels in Paradise and reformers in the Garden of Eden. They do not depend on environment for their passion but on their own psychological disequilibrium, their unsatisfied emotions, their agonizing perceptions of the gulf between their ideals and a world that is always out of joint. These men hate all dogmas and conventions that press down on them and they possess the gift of rebellion. But many of them are ill-grounded in their beliefs, for they have chosen a philosophy to suit their nerves, as one chooses a wall-paper. Give them a war or some other excitement and their emotion is deflected, and their radical ideas "cease upon the midnight without pain."

There are epochs in history when humanity becomes tired and emotions age quicker than usual, and radicals disappear. In the last centuries of the Western Roman Empire, discouraged reformers retired within themselves. Our own Civil War depleted the store of our emotion and for a generation put an end to American idealism. So, also, the aborted Russian Revolution of 1905, which destroyed Russian radicalism for a decade, or at least drove it underground. In such periods of reaction men who might have been rebels become saints or debauchés, depending on temperament and circumstances. At times this day of reaction is brief, a flicker of darkness, a thin black line in a brilliant spectrum. In all these periods, long or short, radicalism declines and radicals fall away.

At worst, however, it is not a unique calamity, for even in good times age deals harshly with radicals. Adolescence is the true day for revolt, the day when obscure forces, as mysterious as growth, push us, trembling, out of our narrow lives into the wide throbbing life beyond self. But one cannot forever remain adolescent and long before a man's arteries begin to harden, he sees things more as his father and grandfather saw them. Once he becomes an ancestor he imbibes respect for ancestors and for what they thought. As young radicals grow older they marry pleasant wives, beget interesting children, and begin to build homes in the country, and their zeal cools. Life, they now think, is more than reform or revolution. There are the lilies of the field, as sweet to radicals as to conservatives, and as

softly beautiful as in the days of Solomon's glory. Life is
old and tenaciously conservative, and so is Nature—the
stars, the sea, the mountains—and so is Society; and what
we are trying to do is only what futile generations long
dead and rotted also tried to do. What is the use of these
endless efforts to budge the immovable Earth? What use
even to look ahead? You "wished to know the secrets of
the future"? So Sylvestre Bonnard apostrophizes the perverse beauty, Leuconöé, dead these nineteen hundred years.
"That future is now the past, and we know it well. Of a
truth you were foolish to worry yourself about so small a
matter."

After all, thinks the tired radical, each of us is bounded
by his own tight skin, and his life is wrapped up in his
own sensations. If I must have a world revolution to amuse
me so much the worse; he is happier who can dig his
garden and be content. Why fret? Let God in His own
appointed time reform the world that He has been rash
enough to create.

Such is the course from radical thought and action, from
intense preoccupation with the affairs of humanity, to self—
self-culture, self-indulgence. Those who return to self after
wandering through a wilderness of altruism, acquire anew
something of the child's fresh relish for simple experiences.
They find all sorts of important little busy-nesses and discover in the small world all the absorbing interests in minia-
ture that they abandoned in the great world. The wearied
Charles the Fifth, abdicating as Holy Roman Emperor, takes
up life again in a pleasant little garden in Estremadura. The
deposed statesman who is sent to jail recovers his interest
in life from a solitary blade of grass forcing its way up between the flagstones of the prison yard. So the tired radical
in his smaller way applies his grand passion for Universal
Housekeeping to a microscopic farm, and he who aspired
to overturn Society (that obese, ponderous and torpid Society that hates to be overturned) ends by fighting in a dull

Board of Directors of a village library for the inclusion of certain books. To what little uses do we descend and how gratefully!

If I were the United States of America I would give a few acres, an agreeable wife, two or three docile children and a sufficient tale of kine and swine to every discouraged radical, replenishing him suitably like Job after his trials. I would make him sovereign over these acres and leave him there and forget him. I would not let him loose on the path which he had tired of treading. For progress is halted by these tired radicals who do not know that they have ceased to be radicals. They turn into pillars of salt. There they stand, aging every moment as though aging were all they had to do. Unconsciously they become sensible, glacially sensible. They become expert in the science of Impossibles; they know better than anyone else why everything is impossible because have they not failed in everything? Oh, how preternaturally practical they become! How they grow enamored of the Indifferent because better than the Bad, and of the Bad because better than the Worse! How they decline into feeble, dwarfed enthusiasms, the pale ghosts of their former ambitions! But let their decline be smooth and their transition easy. Let them tranquilly convince themselves that "every nation has the government it deserves," that "progress comes by good will alone," that the world will better itself or that it is past bettering, and let them accept all the other sedative aphorisms that end gently in a quietistic philosophy. Let them even grow into clever reactionaries, or after shedding all ideals, become absorbed in business, practical politics or pleasure, retaining only an ironical, half-regretful pity for their callow days of radicalism. Let them go peacefully into the great monastery of Effortlessness, where things are left to God or Inevitable Social Evolution, and whence strife and conflict and zeal are banished.

There is no use crying over those who are graduated out of Radicalism, for the young trees grow where the old trees die. In truth it is the growth of the young that kills the old. The aging, tiring radical, who has unwittingly given hostages to Society and knows what butcher's bills and baker's bills and the wife's dress and the children's shoes cost and what a steady job means, and who has learned in the course of the years what slow monotonous things revolutions are, is also discouraged by the radical fledglings who being younger and more ignorant are also more untrammeled, vehement and appealing than he. After all, radicalism is a young man's job and only a few older guides are needed, men who preserve an even balance between imagination and judgment, between enthusiasm and experience, and who though old are young. Every radical movement is a relay race in which a fresh runner seizes the torch from the hand of him who lags. It is better that the tired radicals who have run their course should drop out of the race. Let us therefore not berate them and let us beware of charging them with inconsistency, for they are consistent with the way of life and the law of growth. Let us rather give thanks to them and wish them Godspeed for the youngest of us in time may go their way.

Henry A. Wallace (1888-1965)

An Iowa farmer and one of the most controversial figures of American politics, he took to Washington his own vision of the promised land, a determination to slay whatever dragons stood in his way, and an intense hunger for social justice. As Secretary of Agriculture under Roosevelt, he introduced many programs which eventually became firm elements of modern farm and foreign policy—output controls, price supports, easy-term sales on surpluses to needy countries, and so on. Although he was Roosevelt's running mate in

*1940, he broke with the administration over the
Cold War. Deserted by the New Dealers, he
continued to argue for friendliness toward
Russia, first as an editor of the* New Republic,
*then as the unsuccessful Presidential candidate
of the Progressive party in 1948.*

THE NEW FRONTIER

When those forty thousand undisciplined slaves, the Children of Israel, left Egypt, it was possible for them to reach their promised land within a few months. But they were not fit to march a straight course, enter and take possession. The older men and women among them thought of everything in terms of the fleshpots of Egypt. Before the promised land could be attained it was necessary for the younger generation, hardened by travels in the wilderness, to come to maturity.

We have been forced away from the fleshpots. When our stock market crashed in 1929 it was plain that we would have to abandon them. We, too, know something about a new land and how it may be reached, but we are not yet fit to go in and take possession. Too many of us would like one last round with those fleshpots and golden calves. It may be that many of our younger people have been sufficiently hardened by suffering in our economic wilderness. But all will have to come to a more effective maturity before the new land can be fully possessed. Advance guards sent out to estimate the cost of the march tell us that there are giants in the way.

I am sometimes accused of undue idealism; but I know very well that it will not do to hope too much of the generation of which I am a part. It is simply impossible for us to let go overnight of the habits and beliefs of a life-

From *New Frontiers* (New York: Reynal & Hitchcock, 1934), pp. 269–77. Reprinted by permission of Mrs. Ila B. Wallace, Executrix.

time. Younger people, if they will, can easily accomplish changes which seem impossible to older people.

Unfortunately, many of the oncoming generation now in our schools, or idling in our homes, are handicapped by an inheritance of past concepts, bitterly complicated by the present stalemate. They are stirred into potentially menacing forms of protest by the fact that the present world does not seem to want their services. If misled by demagogues and half-baked educators, they may be inclined to assume more and more that the world owes them not only a living but a limousine. Their restlessness and present disillusionment can be fatal or infinitely constructive, depending upon which side they wake up on.

After all, we middle-aged, middle-course, people have some hard thinking and many hard jobs to do, before we can reasonably expect to arouse our young to hope for an enduring democracy. Talk alone will not lead them to consolidate the position we now strive to hold, and push forward to something better.

The Children of Israel's problems did not come to an end after they had crossed the borders, or even after they had taken possession of their promised land. Their real troubles as a people had then only begun. They had put behind them a vague, nomadic wandering, but they still had to adapt themselves in some measure to the commercial features of the Canaanite civilization. Their old frontier was gone. They had to work on new frontiers. These problems, in many respects strikingly modern, provoked the strife and turmoil which resulted in the tremendous literature of the prophets and the historical records contained in Chronicles and Kings. Amos, that farmer prophet of the hill country of Judah, first raised in dramatic form the problem of social justice, fair treatment of debtors, and balanced prices.

Physically, and in other ways also, the basic structure of our land of yesterday had been torn to pieces. By the raw pioneer rules of first stakes we have encamped as migrants and have taken greedily and unevenly of its wealth. A few

of us, in consequence, have much more than we can comfortably or decently spend or handle; yet most of us have
too little for comfort, decency and hope of a general progress. . . .

The old frontier was real. There were Indians and fear
of foreign conquest. People in the older Colonies or States
had to stand together against actual perils on the edge of
a new civilization.

Their determination to stand together was continually
renewed by romantic tales of many unknown kinds of
wealth out on the frontier, of precious metals, and fertile
valleys, although as a matter of fact, the old frontier was
all too often a place of ragged, barbed-wire fences, dusty
roads, unpainted shacks. Nevertheless, the hopes and fears
that existed in the old frontier furnished a unity to our
national life. For a hundred and fifty years we felt it was
manifest destiny to push onward, until the Pacific Coast
was reached, until all the fertile lands between had been
plowed and bound together by railroads and paved highways.

The obvious physical task to which we set ourselves has
been accomplished; and in so doing, we have destroyed in
large measure the thing which gave us hope and unity as
a people.

We now demand a new unity, a new hope. There are
many spiritual and mental frontiers yet to be conquered,
but they lead in many different directions and our hearts
have not yet fully warmed to any one of them. They do not
point in an obvious single direction as did that downright
physical challenge which, for so many generations, existed
on the Western edge of our life. Now we have come to the
time when we must search our souls and the relationship
of our souls and bodies to those of other human beings.

Can we build up a unified, national cultural life, unique,
outstanding, one that will reinforce the cultural life of
the entire world? Can we leave something that contributes

toward giving life meaning, joy and beauty for generations to come?

During the sixteenth, seventeenth, eighteenth and nineteenth centuries, ideas took possession of our fathers and grandfathers which made them resolute hard workers, men of iron, equally good as Indian fighters, pioneer farmers, and captains of industry. They suffered and forged ahead in the world, believing that there was something prophetically worthy in all they did. Progress Westward, land-ward, and wealth-ward was their continual urge. They exploited not only natural resources but the generations which came after. We glorify these men, grabbers and exploiters that they were, and marvel at their conquests. But they did not know how to live with each other and they did not know how to teach the American nation to live with other nations.

The keynote of the new frontier is cooperation just as that of the old frontier was individualistic competition. The mechanism of progress of the new frontier is social invention, whereas that of the old frontier was mechanical invention and the competitive seizure of opportunities for wealth. Power and wealth were worshiped in the old days. Beauty and justice and joy of spirit must be worshiped in the new.

Many of the most lively, intimate expressions of spirit spring from the joyous, continuous contact of human beings with a particular locality. They feel the age-long spirit of this valley or that hill each with its trees and rocks and special tricks of weather, as the seasons unfold in their endless charm. If life can be made secure in each community and if the rewards of the different communities are distributed justly, there will flower in every community not only those who attain joy in daily, productive work well done; but also those who paint and sing and tell stories with the flavor peculiar to their own valley, well-loved hill, or broad prairie. And so we think of cooperative communities not merely in a competent commercial sense but also from the standpoint of people who are helping unfold each other's lives in terms of the physical locality and tradition of which they are a part.

In this way, every community can become something distinctly precious in its own right. Children will not try to escape as they grow up. They will look ahead to the possibility of enriching the traditions of their ancestors. They will feel it is a privilege to learn to live with the soil and the neighbors of their fathers. Such communities will be strung like many-colored beads on the thread of the nation and the varied strings of beads will be the glory of the world.

The pettiness of small communities will disappear as their economic disadvantages disappear. The people of small communities, rid of the pettiness which grows of economic fear, will be free to realize that community success may be truly measured only in terms of contribution to a spirit of world unity, even though political and economic ties may be very loose.

In the old days, we could not trust ourselves with joy and beauty because they ran counter to our competitive search for wealth and power. Men of the old days, whether Protestant or Catholic, accepted implicitly the discipline of the Protestant Ethic (see Weber's *The Protestant Ethic and the Spirit of Capitalism*). The men of the new day must have their social discipline comparable in its power with that of the inner drive toward the hard-working, competitive frugality of the old frontier. People may actually work harder than they did on the old frontier, but their motive will be different. They may make and use more mechanical inventions. They may do more to increase the wealth-producing power of the race.

But their efforts will, of necessity, be continually moved by the spirit of cooperative achievement. They will devise ways in which the monetary mechanism can be modified to distribute the rewards of labor more uniformly. They will work with disinterested spirit to modify the governmental and political machinery so that there is a balanced relationship between prices, an even flow of employment, and a far-wider possibility of social justice and social charity.

So enlisted, men may rightfully feel that they are serving a function as high as that of any minister of the Gospel. They will not be Socialists, Communists or Fascists, but plain men trying to gain by democratic methods the professed objectives of the Communists, Socialists and Fascists: security, peace, and the good life for all.

In their efforts they will not allow their work to be divided or embittered by the dogma or prejudice of any narrow, superficially logical, political or religious sect.

Some will seek for the fountains of an abundant life in renewed artistic, religious, and scientific inspiration. They will not, I trust, accept the animal view of human nature, put forth by the biologists and the economists of the 19th century. Of necessity, they will recognize competitive individualists and competitive nations and deal with them, as the anachronisms they are, treating them kindly, firmly, and carefully.

But the new frontiersman will be continually seeking for his fellows those satisfactions which are mutually enriching. The nature of these satisfactions can only be faintly shadowed now. They exist in a land as strange and far as was America in 1491. In this land of ageless desire we are all striving newcomers. It is not a mushy, sentimental frontier, but one of hard realities, requiring individual and social discipline beyond that of the old frontiers. It lies within us and all about us. A great seer of the human heart who lived nineteen hundred years ago called it the Kingdom of Heaven. He knew that the tiny spark of divine spirit found in each individual could be fanned into an all-consuming flame, an intense passion for

fair play, man to man, and man to woman, in the little
time that we are here. In the Sermon on the Mount, He
spoke of the rules of the Kingdom of Heaven.

The land beyond the new frontier will be conquered by
the continuous social inventions of men whose hearts are
free from bitterness, prejudice, hatred, greed and fear; by
men whose hearts are aflame with the extraordinary beauty
of the scientific, artistic and spiritual wealth now before
us, if only we reach out confidently, together.

Henry L. Mencken (1880–1956)

*A lifelong newspaperman, he was temperamen-
tally a "censor-baiting" subversive individualist
and fundamentally a sentimental middle-class
German-American who loved music, beer, and
cigars. From 1906 on he wrote for the Baltimore
Sun but held several "left-hand jobs," becoming
in 1914 an editor of the Smart Set and from
1924 to 1933 serving as editor of the American
Mercury. Hiding "a conservative's taste under a
firebrand's vocabulary," he exerted a tremendous
influence over the literary-minded youth of the
1910's and early 1920's.*

DEMOCRATIC MAN

Democracy came into the Western World to the tune of
sweet, soft music. There was, at the start, no harsh bawl-
ing from below; there was only a dulcet twittering from
above. Democratic man thus began as an ideal being, full
of ineffable virtues and romantic wrongs—in brief, as Rous-

From *Notes on Democracy*, by H. L. Mencken, pp. 3–11, 15–7. Copyright 1926
by Alfred A. Knopf, Inc., and renewed 1954 by H. L. Mencken. Reprinted by
permission of the publisher.

seau's noble savage in smock and jerkin, brought out of the tropical wilds to shame the lords and masters of the civilized lands. The fact continues to have important consequences to this day. It remains impossible, as it was in the Eighteenth Century, to separate the democratic idea from the theory that there is a mystical merit, an esoteric and ineradicable rectitude, in the man at the bottom of the scale—that inferiority, by some strange magic, becomes a sort of superiority—nay, the superiority of superiorities. Everywhere on earth, save where the enlightenment of the modern age is confessedly in transient eclipse, the movement is toward the completer and more enamoured enfranchisement of the lower orders. Down there, one hears, lies a deep, illimitable reservoir of righteousness and wisdom, unpolluted by the corruption of privilege. What baffles statesmen is to be solved by the people, instantly and by a sort of seraphic intuition. Their yearnings are pure; they alone are capable of a perfect patriotism; in them is the only hope of peace and happiness on this lugubrious ball. The cure for the evils of democracy is more democracy!

This notion, as I hint, originated in the poetic fancy of gentlemen on the upper levels—sentimentalists who, observing to their distress that the ass was over-laden, proposed to reform transport by putting him into the cart. A stale Christian bilge ran through their veins, though many of them, as it happened, toyed with what is now called Modernism. They were the direct ancestors of the more saccharine Liberals of to-day, who yet mouth their tattered phrases and dream their preposterous dreams. I can find no record that these phrases, in the beginning, made much impression upon the actual objects of their rhetoric. Early democratic man seems to have given little thought to the democratic ideal, and less veneration. What he wanted was something concrete and highly materialistic—more to eat, less work, higher wages, lower taxes. He had no apparent belief in the acroamatic virtue of his own class,

and certainly none in its capacity to rule. His aim was not
to exterminate the baron, but simply to bring the baron
back to a proper discharge of baronial business. When,
by the wild shooting that naturally accompanies all mob
movements, the former end was accidentally accomplished,
and men out of the mob began to take on baronial airs,
the mob itself quickly showed its opinion of them by butchering them deliberately and in earnest. Once the pikes
were out, indeed, it was a great deal more dangerous to
be a tribune of the people than to be an ornament of
the old order. The more copiously the blood gushed, the
nearer that old order came to resurrection. The Paris
proletariat, having been misled into killing its King in
1793, devoted the next two years to killing those who had
misled it, and by the middle of 1796 it had another King
in fact, and in three years more he was King *de jure,* with
an attendant herd of barons, counts, marquises and dukes,
some of them new but most of them old, to guard, sym-
bolize and execute his sovereignty. And he and they were
immensely popular—so popular that half France leaped
to suicide that their glory might blind the world.

Meanwhile, of course, there had been a certain seeping
down of democratic theory from the metaphysicians to
the mob—obscured by the uproar, but still going on. Rhetoric, like a stealthy plague, was doing its immemorial work.
Where men were confronted by the harsh, exigent realities of battle and pillage, as they were everywhere on the
Continent, it got into their veins only slowly, but where
they had time to listen to oratory, as in England and, above
all, in America, it fetched them more quickly. Eventually,
as the world grew exhausted and the wars passed, it began to make its effects felt everywhere. Democratic man,
contemplating himself, was suddenly warmed by the spectacle. His condition had plainly improved. Once a slave,
he was now only a serf. Once condemned to silence, he
was now free to criticize his masters, and even to flout
them, and the ordinances of God with them. As he gained

skill and fluency at that sombre and fascinating art, he began to heave in wonder at his own merit. He was not only, it appeared, free to praise and damn, challenge and remonstrate: he was also gifted with a peculiar rectitude of thought and will, and a high talent for ideas, particularly on the political plane. So his wishes, in his mind, began to take on the dignity of legal rights, and after a while, of intrinsic and natural rights, and by the same token the wishes of his masters sank to the level of mere ignominious lusts. By 1828 in America and by 1848 in Europe the doctrine had arisen that all moral excellence, and with it all pure and unfettered sagacity, resided in the inferior four-fifths of mankind. In 1867 a philosopher out of the gutter pushed that doctrine to its logical conclusion. He taught that the superior minority had no virtues at all, and hence no rights at all—that the world belonged exclusively and absolutely to those who hewed its wood and drew its water. In less than half a century he had more followers in the world, open and covert, than any other sophist since the age of the Apostles.

Since then, to be sure, there has been a considerable recession from that extreme position. The dictatorship of the proletariat, tried here and there, has turned out to be—if I may venture a prejudiced judgment—somewhat impracticable. Even the most advanced Liberals, observing the thing in being, have been moved to cough sadly behind their hands. But it would certainly be going beyond the facts to say that the underlying democratic dogma has been abandoned, or even appreciably overhauled. To the contrary, it is now more prosperous than ever before. The late war was fought on its name, and it was embraced with loud hosannas by all the defeated nations. Everywhere in Christendom it is now official, save in a few benighted lands where God is temporarily asleep. Everywhere its fundamental axioms are accepted: (a) that the great masses of men have an inalienable right, born of the very nature of things, to govern themselves, and (b) that they are competent to do it. Are they occasionally detected in gross and lamentable imbecilities? Then it is only because they are misinformed by those who would exploit them: the remedy is more education. Are they, at times, seen to be a trifle naughty, even swinish? Then it is only a natural reaction against the oppressions they suffer: the remedy is to deliver them. The central aim of all the Christian governments of to-day, in theory if not in fact, is to further their liberation, to augment their power, to drive ever larger and larger pipes into the great reservoir of their natural wisdom. That government is called good which responds most quickly and accurately to their desires and ideas. That is called bad which conditions their omnipotence and puts a question mark after their omniscience.

So much for the theory. It seems to me, and I shall here contend, that all the known facts lie flatly against it—that there is actually no more evidence for the wisdom of the inferior man, nor for his virtue, than there is for the notion that Friday is an unlucky day. There was, perhaps, some excuse for believing in these phantasms in the days when they were first heard of in the world, for it was then difficult to put them to the test, and what cannot be tried and disproved has always had a lascivious lure for illogical man. But now we know a great deal more about the content and character of the human mind than we used to know, both on high levels and on low levels, and what we have learned has pretty well disposed of the old belief in its congenital intuitions and inherent benevolences. It is, we discover, a function, at least mainly, of purely physical and chemical phenomena, and its development and operation are subject to precisely the same natural laws which govern the development and operation, say, of the human nose or lungs. There are minds which start out with a superior equipment, and proceed to high and arduous deeds; there are minds which never get any further than a sort of insensate sweating, like that of a kidney. We not only observe such differences; we also begin to chart them with more or less accuracy. Of one mind we may say with some confidence that it shows an extraordinary capacity for function and development—that its possessor, exposed to a suitable process of training, may be trusted to acquire the largest body of knowledge and the highest skill at ratiocination to which *Homo sapiens* is adapted. Of another we may say with the same confidence that its abilities are sharply limited—that no conceivable training can move it beyond a certain point. In other words, men differ inside their heads as they differ outside. There are men who are naturally intelligent and can learn, and there are men who are naturally stupid and cannot. . . .

The concept of arrested development has caused an upheaval in psychology, and reduced the arduous introspections of the old-time psychologists to a series of ingenious but unimportant fancies. Men are *not* alike, and very little can be learned about the mental processes of a congressman, an ice-wagon driver or a cinema actor by studying the mental processes of a genuinely superior man. The difference is not only qualitative; it is also, in important ways, quantitative. One thus sees the world as a vast field of greased poles, flying gaudy and seductive flags. Up each a human soul goes shinning, painfully and with many a slip. Some climb eventually to the high levels; a few scale the dizziest heights. But the great majority never get very far from the ground. There they struggle for a while, and then give it up. The effort is too much for them; it doesn't seem to be worth its agonies. Golf is easier; so is joining Rotary; so is Fundamentalism; so is osteopathy; so is Americanism.

In an aristocratic society government is a function of those who have got relatively far up the poles, either by their own prowess or by starting from the shoulders of their fathers—which is to say, either by God's grace or by God's grace. In a democratic society it is the function of all, and hence mainly of those who have got only a few spans from the ground. Their eyes, to be sure, are still thrown toward the stars. They contemplate, now bitterly, now admiringly, the backsides of those who are above them. They are bitter when they sense anything rationally describable as actual superiority; they admire when what they see is fraud. Bitterness and admiration, interacting, form a complex of prejudices which tends to cast itself into more or less stable forms. Fresh delusions, of course, enter into it from time to time, usually on waves of frantic emotion, but it keeps its main outlines. This complex of prejudices is what is known, under democracy, as public opinion. It is the glory of democratic states.

Ralph Barton Perry (1876–1957)

After graduate study at Harvard, where he was a pupil and close friend of William James, he taught briefly at Williams and Smith, then returned to Harvard in 1902 to teach philosophy and remained there until his retirement. An outstanding authority on James, his own philosophic system was a sort of extension of pragmatism called neo-realism. In the thirties, he was a vigorous spokesman against Fascism.

THE ALLEGED FAILURE OF DEMOCRACY

The rejection of democracy is nowadays regarded as evidence of superior wisdom. Although it is still customary, for political purposes, to pay it lip service, "between friends," or in the judgment of the hard-boiled fact-finder, it is often supposed to be an exploded myth—a practical

---

From "The Alleged Failure of Democracy," *The Yale Review*, XXIV (Spring, 1934), 37, 40, 49–51. Reprinted by permission of *The Yale Review*.

failure as well as a theoretical fallacy. Opinion has been veering so swiftly in this direction that while a few years ago the defense of democracy would have been condemned as hackneyed and banal, one who undertakes it now is suspected of seeking notoriety. . . .

We are here concerned primarily with the charge that democracy has broken down—that, owing to human nature and the complexities of life, it has proved a failure. In replying to this form of attack I would not for a moment argue, or seem to argue, that democracy has been an unqualified success. That it has in some measure failed is indisputable, and this partial failure has been, no doubt, in some measure due to the complacent assumption of success. Sound criticism, however, will know how to pass beyond complacency or rhetorical eulogy without leaping to the other and equally futile extreme of reckless despair.

The adverse judgment which the present age is disposed to pronounce on the success of democracy has, in the first place, to be qualified by the reflection that all human institutions are failures as judged by standards of perfection. They all leave room for improvement. There is what may be called a constant of failure in all great enterprises, arising out of the complexity of the problem, the weaknesses of mankind, and the weight of the obstacles to be overcome. Marriage is a failure, agriculture and industry are failures, religion is a failure, education is a failure. Government, being peculiarly difficult, is perhaps the greatest failure of all. But it would be equally true to say that government is a remarkable achievement. It all depends upon the height of your expectation; and if it be legitimate to remark how badly it is done, it is equally legitimate and sometimes more wholesome to wonder that it should be done at all. From time to time some particular institution becomes the symbol of human failure in general, and has to bear the brunt of human discontent. There are signs that economic institutions are taking their turn as such a symbol and that the sins of government may soon be deemed less scandalous.

In fairness, then, we should admit this constant of human failure, and at the same time eliminate it from the specific bill of indictment brought against democracy. Besides this ordinary failure, to be seen in every phase of human development, there is also an extraordinary failure peculiar to the times in which we live. It seems safe to predict that when the curve of human fortunes is charted by the historians of the future, it will show a pronounced dip between 1914 and some year later than 1934. Here again, we are likely to charge the whole account against some single factor such as democracy on which attention happens at the moment to be focussed. But nobody, so far as I know, has proved that democracy was responsible for the Great War, or for the economic prostration and lowered morale which have followed it; for the price of raw materials, or technological unemployment, or economic nationalism, or bank failures, or the increase of divorce, or the decline of religion and the arts. The fact is that with few exceptions everything has worked badly since 1914; and it is just as unnatural and unreasonable to hold a particular political institution wholly responsible for this as it is to charge every evil against the political party that happens to be in power. Thus so much of the failure of democracy as is shared by other institutions, whether it be the normal failure which attends all human affairs or the abnormal failure of this particular historic crisis, should be discounted. Let us now examine the evidence.

First, precisely what is it that is supposed to have failed? The answer is that it is *political democracy*. Social democracy has not failed, for the good and sufficient reason that it has never had the chance. The point is this. Political democracy is a form of government designed to produce a desirable social result. According to Aristotle the state exists for the sake of "the good life," and all parties to the discussion would doubtless agree upon the truth of that saying. Most proponents of political democracy believe that the good life, or desirable social result, which the state should promote, is an individualistic, free, and, in some sense, equalitarian society. The name we usually give to this standard is social democracy. It is not this which has failed, for social democracy is itself the ideal. By what shall it be judged a failure? To say that it has failed would be like saying that justice, goodness, or happiness has failed. The fact is that critics of democracy have not, as a rule, distinguished between democracy as a political means and democracy as a social end. Making the charitable assumption that they know what they mean, they probably mean that political democracy has failed to provide that minimum of security and order which conditions *any* form of the good life, including social democracy. Is this charge well-founded? Or, if it be conceded that mankind has recently suffered from insecurity and disorder, is this the fault of political democracy?

There is here, I think, at least that degree of reasonable doubt which is supposed to justify acquittal. Writing about the Great War in 1929, Professor G. G. Benjamin put the question, "What, then, do the source materials, the memoirs and monographs produced since the armistice, prove?" The third of the five summary conclusions with which he answers his question is, that "the failure of Germany was the failure of absolute power." I do not see how anbody who reads the history of Europe during the years immediately preceding the war can fail to be impressed by the stupidity and feebleness of the three great military monarchies, Germany, Russia, Austria. It is to be observed, furthermore, that these three governments were swept away by the war, and that the three nations which emerged victorious and are now the most powerful, England, France, and the United States, are all political democracies.

If we examine the charge more closely, we find that what is supposed to have failed is not political democracy in general, but only parliamentary government of a specific kind. Political democracy has a good many more tricks in its bag. There is, for example, representative government in the old-fashioned sense intended by the framers of the Federal

Constitution. There are alternative electoral and party methods, alternative forms of the legislative body, and of its relation to the executive. I am not qualified to propose a remedy, but I do not for a moment believe that therapeutic invention is exhausted or that institutional development is at a standstill. The failures of political democracy, even if they be granted, would suggest not that democracy in general be abandoned but that in respect of certain specific mechanisms it be varied and improved.

It is true that outside of England, France, and the United States there has been a very general abandonment or rejection of democratic institutions. The general trend towards political democracy that was so clearly marked in the last century has lately been checked or diverted. The most notable governments that have arisen since the war, Communistic Russia, Fascist Italy, and Nazi Germany, are blatant dictatorships. Turkey, Yugoslavia, Poland, Hungary, and Austria are dictatorships in substance, if not in form. Japan is in the throes of political reaction. The facts are indisputable. How shall they be interpreted? I submit that they are the effects of emergency rather than of constructive development.

In times of stress or national calamity, when heroic measures are necessary, when swift, remedial action is important at all costs—in times of civil war, actual or threatening, and in times of panic or desperation—in such times political procedure must be temporarily altered. A demand arises for unified and authoritative control. Liberty of action must give way for the term of the emergency to discipline, and discussion to obedience. There is nothing new in this. It happens in every country in event of war, in every community in case of flood or earthquake, in every family in case of accident or illness, in every individual in moments of crisis. There is then a temporary stripping for action and a massing of energies where the danger threatens, with sacrifice, abridgment, paralysis elsewhere. There are, in other words, peculiar modes of organization and control which are required for emergencies. But it would be a grave mistake to define our norms and ideals by such requirements. An emergency is by definition something out of the ordinary, requiring extraordinary measures. Their use is to keep one alive until the better life can be resumed. When one's leg is broken one puts it in a plaster cast, but one does not therefore conclude that freely moving limbs are a failure and should be permanently abolished. The ultimate purpose of the rigid cast is to restore the usual freedom of movement. . . .

The rejection of democracy as a practical failure implies a willingness to accept some alternative. What are the alternatives to democracy? There should be a law compelling every destructive critic to provide an alternative. The alternatives to political democracy have been tried, and it was because they had been tried unsuccessfully that political evolution up to 1914 moved in the direction of democracy. Jefferson remarked in his First Inaugural Address: "Sometimes it is said that man cannot be trusted with the government of himself. Can he, then, be trusted with the government of others? Or have we found angels in the forms of kings to govern him? Let history answer this question." I, for one, if I should withdraw my support from democracy, should not know where to find any other political investment that I would not distrust more, unless, as seems unlikely, an Almighty, All-wise, and All-benevolent God could be induced to assume the government himself.

It is a curious thing that those who turn in their thoughts from democracy to dictatorship forget that dictatorship consists to a large extent in the evils of a democracy without its merits. If anyone who is weary of democracy were asked to name its most intolerable abuse, he would no doubt name the demagogue. But, as Plato pointed out a good many years ago, the tyrant is essentially a great demagogue, who is so artful and unscrupulous in his demagoguery that he drives out all the little demagogues and monopolizes the business for himself.

An editorial writer in "The Manchester Guardian" recently recalled Bismarck's saying that "any fool can govern by martial or semi-martial law. . . ." "It is a mistake," the writer continued, "to suppose that a dictatorship brings the able men to the top. The exact opposite is true—it eliminates the courageous, the critical, the intelligent. . . . No premier in any European democracy has so many catch-phrases as Mussolini or Pilsudski [and he might have added, Hitler] to call forth popular applause so blind and hysterical."

There is no commoner form of sentimentalism than that with which we color those forms of government under which we are not obliged to live. The man who longs for a dictatorship usually imagines that *he* is the dictator, or at any rate that he is the dictator's best friend and most trusted counsellor. He thinks of the system as a means of getting done, promptly and thoroughly, what he himself believes ought to be done. But the fact is that for most people most of the time dictatorship consists not in dictating but in being dictated to; not in getting done what one thinks ought to be done, but in being compelled to submit helplessly to what one thinks ought not to be done. It is true that we are living in an age when non-democratic forms of government are being revived and modernized. But instead of weakening our allegiance to democratic institutions this should rather confirm our faith by presenting the odious alternatives in their stark reality.

Any government has in the last analysis to be justified by the quality of the life which it promotes. A political democracy claims to secure more than that bare minimum of security and order which may be rightly demanded of any social system. Those who adhere to it as a political creed commonly do so because of an equalitarian social ideal.

This ideal means that a man should have his chance to rise as high in attainment as his energy and natural capacity will carry him. It is not implied that attainment shall be equal. There is only one way by which this could be brought about—by penalizing superiority and so reducing life to the level of the least competent. The ideal of social democracy implies a spirit that is rarer and more generous—a magnanimity which will respect genuine superiority wherever it appears, and prefer a pyramid of excellence to a plane of mediocrity. It will recognize the unalterable inequalities of endowment, and the inevitable inequalities of attainment; and will encourage eminence for the enrichment of the common life.

But the cult of social democracy is not satisfied with a vicarious equality, a merely theoretical equality of rights, or an unattainable equality of aspiration. In the common human faculties and the common human lot it discovers actual equalities. It focusses attention on these equalities, and from them it proposes to form the essential bond between man and man, believing that a society founded on mutual respect is the fundamental condition of the best life. Political democracy is both a means to this social end and one of its chief embodiments.

Lincoln Steffens (1866-1936)

After graduation from the University of California in 1889, he spent three years studying at Berlin, Heidelberg, Leipzig, and the Sorbonne. During the nineties as a police reporter and later city editor of the New York Evening Post, he met Theodore Roosevelt and Jacob Riis and first became interested in social questions. One of the greatest muckrakers, he was considered an enfant terrible who shocked people because he asked forthright questions and came to candid conclusions. Contradictory and paradoxical by nature, he liked people, including "honest crooks" and "good bad capitalists." In his last years he was subjected to constant persecution because of his Communist affiliations.

WHY I AM A LENINIST

Revolutions, like wars, are social-economic explosions due to human (political) interference with natural (and, therefore, divine) laws and forces which make for the gradual growth or constant change called evolution.

"I believe in evolution, not revolution," says the righteous citizen. So would the revolutionist prefer evolution, if he had his choice. Nobody likes revolutions; they are violent, messy, stormlike affairs which are almost impossible to manage and direct. The revolutionist would rather work out his reforms in the comparative quietude of evolution. But that is quite impossible. The "evolutionist" won't permit it. The "evolutionist" works always for revolution, not knowingly, of course. He does not do anything knowingly. But the fact that he unwittingly uses the methods of violence he deplores only exasperates the honest reformer who would willingly go slow if only he were allowed to go. The "evolutionist" will not go at all. There is a definition of a pessimist as a man who has just met an optimist. In that spirit, revolutionists are reformers who have been up against the righteous political evolutionists. For evolution, if it means anything in political economy, is a process of reformation of old laws, customs and institutions to make them conform to the social, economic, and psychological changes that are occurring all the time. When society passes, however unintentionally, from hand-labor to machinery, man-made laws, constitutions and customs must be altered and should be allowed to change consciously and easily. It is this that the conservative blocks. He does not know it because, being righteous, he has to believe

From *Moses in Red* (Philadelphia: Dorrance & Co., 1926), pp. 18–28, 33–9.

that he is for reform in general; he merely happens to find himself (and his interest) against each and every particular reform that strikes at the root of his old "rights" and privileges. What he cannot see is that the effect in general of his resistance in particular is to incite the maddened revolutionists and the mad revolution.

A revolution is a natural phenomenon, as natural and as understandable as a flood, a fire or a war, a financial depression, an epidemic of disease or a pimple on the nose. It has its causes and its natural history. And it should be preventable, therefore, but not by prayer and not by force. God obeys His own laws. Arresting revolutionists does not arrest the revolution any more than prohibition stops drinking. Force only puts off the red day as a warlike peace treaty carries on the process of war. The prayerful but impious pacifists, who do not seek the causes of war but would only forbid the arming of nations, should bring up their boys to be, not soldiers, perhaps—soldiers get killed—but officers. Pacifists rank with the evolutionists who fight the revolutionists with police force; they both are, like Pharaoh in the story of Moses, fellow-conspirators for the explosion which must break through all merely righteous conservatism —lest the people perish, as the Egyptians did, and the Greeks and the Romans, leaving only their names behind. The modern Egyptians, the modern Greeks, and the Italians in Rome today, are fit survivors of their "moral culture," which is ours. But, then, there is another culture growing up amongst us, a culture that tells us how to avoid the fate of the ancients.

The scientific culture that is coming in spite of the opposition of the righteous, teaches us that what we have to do to prevent revolutions, wars and all our so-called evils, is to study the forces involved in them, trace their workings back to their original, continuing misuse, correct that and so deal scientifically with causes. We followed this method when we examined the lightning and turned its terrors into electric light and power. We discovered then that what we had dreaded as an evil was good. And whenever we have looked reverently (scientifically) into a "bad" thing, we have found it made up of "good" elements. It is the pious belief of the high priests of science that there is no evil; that all the forces and all the laws of nature are good, *i.e.*, beneficent of God and blessings to man, if he will but learn to understand and use them. Legislators should be or they should consult, not lawyers, but biologists, chemists and economists. Lawyers study and live upon man-made laws. The scientists alone look for and learn the laws of God. Not the priests any more, and not yet the historians and political critics; they take the moral point of view, talk in the terms of superstition, and judge men and events by their standards of right and wrong. According to science, which is the only living religion in the world today, all nature is a book of revelations, every laboratory experiment is a worship and every natural phenomenon—whether it be a chemical reaction or a poem, a war or a revolution—is a sign of the hand, the voice and the knowledge of God, and as such to be respected; and so described.

The Bible sets an example. The Old Testament story of the revolt and the exodus of Israel is the history of a revolution, and it has the hand of God acting and His voice speaking all through it; literally. Jehovah is a character; He is the leading person in the plot of that great drama. The theologians dispute whether to read it literally or symbolically, but that makes no essential difference. The story rings true in the way that the New Testament gospels of Jesus ring true. The narrative follows the course of a typical revolution. Let Jehovah personify and speak for Nature; think of Moses as the uncompromising Bolshevik; Aaron as the more political Menshevik; take Pharaoh as the ruler who stands for the Right (the conservative "evolutionist"), and the Children of Israel as the people—any people; read the Books of Moses thus and they will appear as a revolutionary classic. Anyone that has gone through a revolution will recognize, not only the *dramatis personæ* of the story, but the regular stages of its progress, the typical individual and mob psychology, the tragic disappointments and excesses, and the comic criticisms and excuses of every such crisis in the affairs of men.

It seems necessary, however, to go through a revolution to see this. It was for me. . . .

When the World War broke in 1914, I was in Europe, preparing to muckrake England, France, Germany and Italy. I had gone far enough in my secret investigations to see that the same system of corruption which reigned in all American cities, states and business corporations, dominated Europe, too. There was some law at work, parallels of identical forces which made the social problem one and the same problem everywhere. The only difference between the United States and Europe was that due to time. The process of corruption was farther advanced abroad than at home, and old Italy was deeper in it than France, which was as much farther gone than England as France is older in experience and culture than England. Germany was the least corrupted, the nearest to the United States—the best of the big "bad" world governments I had studied, because it is the youngest. All of them, however, were so corrupt that—according to my theory—they could not be saved by reforms. Nothing but the revolution could adjust them to the economic changes that had occurred in our civilization and the strain of the war would precipitate THE revolution. I did not, therefore, go to the front. I went to the rear. I decided to make a study of revolutions. I took a boat and went to Mexico because there was a revolution there. On a theory again.

If one corrupted city was like every other city, if all states were alike and all countries—all governments in one and the same process of corruption; if one reform movement, whether in New York, San Francisco or Jerusalem was typical of all reforms, then, I reasoned, one revolution would furnish me with the key to all revolutions. The Mexican revolution would prepare me for the European

revolution. And, that a human mind has to be thus prepared by experience to see straight, was illustrated the
moment I landed at Vera Cruz. I met there a committee
of socialists, sent from Italy, France and Spain to report
whether the Mexican revolution was a "true" revolution,
worthy of the sympathy and support of the Latin revolutionists of Europe. They had made their investigation and were
about to sail for home to report against the Mexican revolt.
Why?

It was not according to Marx! It had occurred, not in a
highly capitalized country, but in a backward country with
an undeveloped industrial system among an unorganized,
illiterate people who knew nothing of socialism and little
of labor unions. It had no clearly defined Socialist purposes;
it was all mixed up: politics, economics, civil wars and
graft; it was guilty of all sorts of cruel excesses, worse
than the evils a revolution was intended to correct.

I went on through the Mexican revolution, most of the
time on the inside among the leaders, and I found that
all the counts of that Socialist Committee were true; and
more beside, many more. From Mexico I went off to Russia
when the revolution occurred there, and I have been following it ever since, that and the other revolutionary
movements in Europe. I cannot say whether the Mexican
or even the Russian revolution is a true Marxian revolution,
because I do not know any more what is meant by that
phrase. My own theory of "the" revolution and most of
the written theories suffered in the revolutions I saw very
much as the governments did that they exploded under.
Theory was blown all to pieces. But I did what Marx did,
when, after writing at length about "the" revolution, he
witnessed the Paris Commune. He altered his theory to
conform to the facts; I acted upon the same pious scientific
principle that, whenever an actual experience in nature
runs counter to our expectations, it is probable that Nature
is right and that our theory was wrong.

Regardless, then, of theory, mine, Marx's and everybody

else's; regardful only of the facts, I say with assurance that the Mexican and the Russian revolutions revolved in their courses as like as two stars.

There is in that statement, if true, a basis for a science of revolution; there is in it an implication that revolutions are governed by some natural (economic-psychological-social) laws which make them alike and, therefore, understandable and perhaps manageable, if not avoidable. Having seen this parallel of two revolutions, I went back and read again the classic accounts of the other great historical revolutions and I found that they were, in all essentials, like the Russian and the Mexican revolutions. The laws held; whatever they are, the natural laws of revolution were always obeyed and they were not recognized by the historians, critics and statesmen only because they knew but one revolution or none. When I knew New York alone, I could only see and write that Boss Croker was to blame for the corruption. It was not till I knew St. Louis and saw there another boss with another name, but the same backers, methods and effects as Croker in New York, that I could describe the Boss as an institution and the boss system as a natural development out of the conditions common to all cities at a certain stage of growth under our universal culture.

When I had seen two revolutions and had understood several more, I looked around for some classic revolutions which everybody was familiar with. An incident recalled the Books of Moses. I took up the Bible and I reread once more the story of the Exodus of the Children of Israel, and lo and behold, there it was: The Revolution. I knew (in my bones) now, that that famous old story was a true report of an historical event. No doubt about it. The original tellers of the tale may have twisted it in the telling; that happens in a revolution always. . . .

Making every allowance for errors, priestcraft and politics in the Books of Moses, however, I hold to my thesis that they give an essentially true account of a typical revolution and that they are therefore worth studying as such. We have to make a science of sociology and we cannot do that so long as we look upon some social events with horror. The mind of man shies at revolutions, wars and other disasters in history, especially in the news of the day. We behave like a cab-horse that I saw meet the first automobile in New York. The new vehicle was coming swiftly towards him. He saw it suddenly when it was close upon him. The poor beast stopped in his tracks and, from terror or amazement, collapsed. His hind legs sprawled from under him and he actually sat down, his mouth open, his eyes and his ears fixed upon that new and unknown apparition. All Europe and North America sat down on their haunches before the Russian revolution; they haven't stood up to it yet. Able observers have gone into Russia to investigate it, as the Labor Socialists went into Mexico, and most of them have come out and reported that the Russian revolution was not according to Marx, or not up to their own expectations of a revolution. This is one of the incidents common to all revolutions: the outside world does not like them. People see only the excesses of it, and these they exaggerate. Moses had his experience with the investigators. The committee of chiefs he sent to spy out the Land of Promise came back with a majority report that the country was full of giants and that it would take hard fighting and long labor to make of it the heaven on earth that they had dreamed of. They preferred to go back to Egypt and servitude, and the people were with the pessimists. Jehovah, who, like Nature, was offering them not a heaven on earth but only an opportunity to make one, saw their uselessness and commanded them to wander off into the wilderness and die. Only their children, brought up in liberty, should inherit the land and liberty. . . .

"What we need," said Lenin to me in 1919, "is a revision of all our theories in the light of the war, the peace and this and the other revolutions. I can't undertake it. I can't even change my own ideas very much. When you are in action you cannot stop to theorize; it is difficult even to think. I have to live in the country to think clear. But if there were scientific men outside, in America, England—Europe—they could look on and they could study, think and tell us. We need criticism. The captains in all crises really need the counsel of wise, thoughtful, sympathetic observers safely, quietly out of the storm center. But there is no such criticism; there are no such critics. All we get is the ignorant horror at the signs of our distress, the height of the waves, the discipline of the crew and the number of poor devils washed overboard. That is no help. We feel all this, more than our critics do. What we want to know is how to get through the difficulties to an objective, which is the aim of all men who have a purpose in life. We differ about the route; we agree on the port— all of us."

The horrors of a revolution are never singular; they are the ever-recurring symptoms and signs of the natural phenomenon they accompany—always. This one can see by observing that they occur regularly in all revolutions, some of them in all social crises. There are killings and terrors, loot and destruction, in a war or a strike. The side or the leaders blamed for them do not always wish for and command them. They also deplore them. When I asked Lenin officially about the terror, he whirled on me fiercely.

"Who wants to ask us about our killings?" he demanded.

"Paris," I said, meaning, as he well understood, the Peace Conference.

"Do you mean to tell me that those men who have just generaled the slaughter of seventeen millions of men in a purposeless war are concerned over the few thousands that have been killed in a revolution which has a conscious aim—to get out of the necessity of war and—and armed peace?"

He stood a moment facing me with his blazing eyes, then quieting down, he said:

"But never mind, do not deny the terror. Don't minimize any of the evils of a revolution. They occur. They must be counted upon. If we have to have a revolution, we have to pay the price of it."

That is the point. The evils of revolution happen in a revolution. They have to be studied, therefore; not merely shied at, but examined and then, perhaps, when they are understood scientifically, they can be avoided or used. Take a few of them, for example: the "excesses" that shocked not only the public opinion of the world, but the theoretical minds of the scientists and even of some revolutionists. Take the dictatorship, democracy, the terror, and "liberty."

Both the Mexican and the Russian revolutions ran straight to a dictatorship. Looking back in history it appears that all other revolutions took on the form of an autocracy. Moses was the chief, the absolute ruler of the Exodus. But so do all great social crises develop into dictatorships. The Jews, the Russians and the Mexicans had lived under that form of government; it was the arrangement they were accustomed to. It might be peculiar to them to return to it. But during the World War all the modern governments changed from their old "democratic" to the autocratic form. Great Britain made Lloyd George a dictator, France ended up with Clemenceau as the absolute ruler, and the United States, for all its fixed representative form and hard and fast Constitution, let President Wilson be king. Having seen this happen, it would seem that the scientific observer might infer, not that the Russian dictatorship was bad and that therefore the Russian revolution was to be condemned, but that our theories, our wishes for democracy, had led us astray in our thinking. We might, if we had used our eyes and our memories, have been helped to a revision of our opinions, which is always good—progressive, evolutionary—and so have reached a tentative statement of some such general law as this:

In revolutions, in wars and in all such disorganizing,

fear-spreading crises in human affairs, nations tend to return to the first, the simplest, and perhaps the best form of government: a dictatorship.

For, after all, the original form of government is that of the chief and the tribe, seen in the gang organizations of savages, boys, criminals, politicians, financiers and morons. American cities, despite their carefully drawn charters for representative democracies, all had the boss and his gang as actual rulers. And, after the war, when the crisis of revolution approached Italy, Mussolini saw the empty throne of fear, leaped into it like the brave man he was, and found himself welcomed by enough of organized society to hold him in his dictatorship.

A dictatorship, then, is neither red nor white, good nor bad—it is a natural development out of a situation in which a people is so frightened that it huddles back into the herd state. Knowing this, as Lenin did before the Russian revolution, he could anticipate it, "seize power" and have the chance he sought to try to direct a revolution toward the achievement of economic democracy. Whether he succeeded or not, he was at any rate a wiser leader than the Mexican Madera, a liberal, who had democratic theories which made him hate his dictatorship and purposely share his power with the leading good citizens who, finally, had him murdered. Lenin was a more scientific historian than the liberals of Europe and a better revolutionist than those revolutionists, who, believing that the objective of a revolution is democracy and liberty, expected it to be free and popular from the beginning, and turned against it because it started off, like all revolutions, to go through the regular stages and forms of the revolutionary process.

Liberty and democracy may not be the objectives of a revolution, but even if they are, it is apparent in history and in the news of our day, that neither of these two human desires can be set up by the will of man or the law of a land. The United States, England—most civilized governments give Constitutional guarantees of free speech, free press, free assemblage. These free laws do not stand up under the pressure of war, panic or fear of a revolution.

This is a disappointment to liberals; all disillusionment is bitter. But there is a principle of disillusionment, too. My experience is that whenever I am losing an illusion, I need but make a study of the facts and the forces that are destroying it; these will provide me with another—illusion, no doubt. But that way lies progress. When I examined the causes and the advantages of a dictatorship, I lost my illusion about democracy as the road to democracy, but by watching the Russian people give up their power, with a sigh of relief, to Lenin; and by watching him, the dictator, introduce necessary economic changes so complicated and subtle that no people can understand (and vote for) them— I could see that a dictatorship may be able to deal with the causes of evil more easily and scientifically than a representative legislature can.

So with democracy. The Russian people did rule for the first six months of the Russian revolution, and they enacted idealistic laws. But nothing happened, nothing was done. The laws were not executed. It's a long story, but as I witnessed that first democratic phase of the revolution, I was convinced that political democracy simply cannot exist until after economic democracy has been set up and got to going well. Democracy and a free people are effects, not causes; ends, not beginnings.

And so, third: it was hard to see liberty go at the end of the first six months and tyranny come. But the sight of the abuse of the free press, free speech and free assemblage was so obviously a menace to a people which had to decide upon some one course and, for better or worse, unite upon it, that one was reconciled when the mob itself turned itself and its liberties out and chose to follow the leader. Taking that experience, and that of all the peoples in the war, I would offer (to liberals especially) this very liberal statement of a natural law of freedom:

Liberty is a state of freedom which, related in some way

to the state of the public mind, increases in some ratio
with the general sense of security and decreases in some
similar ratio with the general sense of danger—regardless of
man-made laws and soul-felt idealism.

Under this natural law freedom will be the last achievement of man. Liberty will arrive after a free, unprivileged
system of economics has been laid as a basis of a society,
which has lived on it long enough to have no fear of
tyranny or abuse. In other words: liberty, democracy, justice
—all our universally desired human ideals are conditions
subject to some natural (economic-psychological) laws
which we must understand and conform to before we can
establish them, as ends.

John Dewey (1859-1952)

Son of a small-town storekeeper in Vermont, he
received his Ph.D. in 1884 at Johns Hopkins
and in 1904 went to Columbia, where he taught
philosophy long past the usual retirement age.
Father of the Progressive School movement, a
leader in the fight for civil and academic free-
dom, he was in the 1930's the chief living ex-
ponent of Pragmatism. Anything but the retiring
professor, he participated actively in the rough-
and-tumble of politics and at the age of seventy
became chairman of the League for Independent
Political Action.

WHY I AM NOT A COMMUNIST

I begin by emphasizing the fact that I write with reference
to being a Communist in the Western world, especially

From *The Modern Monthly*, VIII (April, 1934).

here and now in the United States, and a Communist after the pattern set in the U.S.S.R.

1. *Such* Communism rests upon an almost entire neglect of the specific historical backgrounds and traditions which have operated to shape the patterns of thought and action in America. The autocratic background of the Russian Church and State, the fact that every progressive movement in Russia had its origin in some foreign source and has been imposed from above upon the Russian people, explain much about the form Communism has taken in that country. It is therefore nothing short of fantastic to transfer the ideology of Russian Communism to a country which is so profoundly different in its economic, political, and cultural history. Were this fact acknowledged by Communists and reflected in their daily activities and general program, were it admitted that many of the practical and theoretical features of Russian Communism (like belief in the plenary and verbal inspiration of Marx, the implicit or explicit domination of the Communist party in every field of culture, the ruthless extermination of minority opinion in its own ranks, the verbal glorification of the mass and the actual cult of the infallibility of leadership) are due to local causes, the character of Communism in other countries might undergo a radical change. But it is extremely unlikely that this will take place. For official Communism has made the practical traits of the dictatorship *of* the proletariat and *over* the proletariat, the suppression of the civil liberties of all non-proletarian elements as well as of dissenting proletarian minorities, integral parts of the standard Communist faith and dogma. It has imposed and not argued the theory of dialectic materialism (which in the U.S.S.R. itself has to undergo frequent restatement in accordance with the exigencies of party factional controversy) upon all its followers. Its cultural philosophy, which has many commendable features, is vitiated by the absurd attempt to make a single and uniform entity out of the "proletariat."

2. Particularly unacceptable to me in the ideology of

official Communism is its monistic and one-way philosophy of history. This is akin to the point made above. The thesis that all societies must exhibit a uniform, even if uneven, social development from primitive communism to slavery, from slavery to feudalism, from feudalism to capitalism, and from capitalism to socialism, and that the transition from capitalism to socialism must be achieved by the same way in all countries, can be accepted only by those who are either ignorant of history or who are so steeped in dogma that they cannot look at a fact without changing it to suit their special purposes. From this monistic philosophy of history, there follows a uniform political practice and a uniform theory of revolutionary strategy and tactics. But where differences in historic background, national psychology, religious profession and practice are taken into account —and they must be considered in every scientific theory— there will be corresponding differences in political methods, differences that may extend to general policies as well as to the strategy of their execution. For example, as far as the historic experience of America is concerned, two things among many others are overlooked by official Communists whose philosophy has been projected on the basis of special European conditions. We in the United States have no background of a dominant and overshadowing feudalism. Our troubles flow from the oppressive exercise of power by financial over-lords and from the failure to introduce new forms of *democratic* control in industry and government consonant with the shift from individual to corporate economy. It is a possibility overlooked by official Communists that important social changes in the direction of democratization of industry may be accomplished by groups working *with* the working-class although, strictly speaking, not *of* them. The other point ignored by the Communists is our deeply-rooted belief in the importance of individuality, a belief that is almost absent in the Oriental world from which Russia has drawn so much. Not to see that this attitude, so engrained in our habitual ways of thought and action, demands a very different set of policies and methods from those embodied in official Communism, verges to my mind on political insanity.

3. While I recognize the existence of class-conflicts as one of the fundamental facts of social life to-day, I am profoundly skeptical of class war as *the* means by which such conflicts can be eliminated and genuine social advance made. And yet this is a basic point in Communist theory and is more and more identified with the meaning of dialectic materialism as applied to the social process. Historically speaking, it may have been necessary for Russia in order to achieve peace for her war-weary soldiers, and land for her hungry peasants, to convert incipient class-war into open civil war culminating in the so-called dictatorship of the proletariat. But nonetheless Fascism in Germany and Italy cannot be understood except with reference to the lesson those countries learned from the U.S.S.R. How Communism can continue to advocate the kind of economic change it desires by means of civil war, armed insurrection and iron dictatorship in face of what has happened in Italy and Germany I cannot at all understand. Reliable observers have contended that the communist ideology of dictatorship and violence together with the belief that the communist party was the foreign arm of a foreign power constituted one of the factors which aided the growth of Fascism in Germany. I am firmly convinced that imminent civil war, or even the overt threat of such a war, in any western nation, will bring Fascism with its terrible engines of repression to power. Communism, then, with its doctrine of the necessity of the forcible overthrow of the state by armed insurrection, with its doctrine of the dictatorship of the proletariat, with its threats to exclude all other classes from civil rights, to smash their political parties, and to deprive them of the rights of freedom of speech, press and assembly—which Communists *now* claim for themselves under capitalism—Communism is itself, an unwitting, but nonetheless, powerful factor in bringing about Fascism.

As an unalterable opponent of Fascism in every form, I cannot be a Communist.

4. It is not irrelevant to add that one of the reasons I am not a Communist is that the emotional tone and methods of discussion and dispute which seem to accompany Communism at present are extremely repugnant to me. Fair-play, elementary honesty in the representation of facts and especially of the opinions of others, are something more than "bourgeois virtues." They are traits that have been won only after long struggle. They are not deep-seated in human nature even now—witness the methods that brought Hilterism to power. The systematic, persistent and seemingly intentional disregard of these things by Communist spokesmen in speech and press, the hysteria of their denunciations, their attempts at character assassination of their opponents, their misrepresentation of the views of the "liberals" to whom they also appeal for aid in their defense campaigns, their policy of "rule or ruin" in their so-called united front activities, their apparent conviction that what they take to be the end justifies the use of *any* means if only those means promise to be successful—all these, in my judgment, are fatal to the very end which official Communists profess to have at heart. And if I read the temper of the American people aright, especially so in this country.

5. A revolution effected solely or chiefly by violence can in a modernized society like our own result only in chaos. Not only would civilization be destroyed but the things necessary for bare life. There are some, I am sure, now holding and preaching Communism who would be the first to react against it, if in this country Communism were much more than a weak protest or an avocation of literary men. Few communists are really aware of the far-reaching implications of the doctrine that civil war is the *only* method by which revolutionary economic and political changes can be brought about. A comparatively simple social structure, such as that which Russia had, may be able to recover

from the effects of violent, internal disturbance. And Russia, it must be remembered, had the weakest middle class of any major nation. Were a large scale revolution to break out in highly industrialized America, where the middle class is stronger, more militant and better prepared than anywhere else in the world, it would either be abortive, drowned in a blood bath, or if it were victorious, would win only a Pyrrhic victory. The two sides would destroy the country and each other. For this reason, too, I am not a Communist.

I have been considering the position, as I understand it, of the orthodox and official Communism. I cannot blind myself, however, to the perceptible difference between communism with a small c, and Communism, official Communism, spelt with a capital letter.

The Modern Ethic

I

At the beginning of the twenties the forces of prudery and restraint appeared victorious in their effort to keep America free, white, pure, Protestant, and sober. Their repressive legions swarmed over the land—the Ku Klux Klan to keep America white and Nordic, 100% Americans to censor school books (they began by excluding Bolshevist ideas and ended by banning Voltaire's *Candide*), fundamentalist ministers to wage holy war on evolution, prohibition agents to trap unwary drinkers, Will Hays to keep movies pure and beautiful, plus assorted Puritans and "blue-noses" eager to battle with sex, Sunday ball games, the devil, and Sigmund Freud. But at this very time there erupted a revolt of flaming youth that shook the hearthstones in respectable homes across the nation.

Although rebellious tendencies had been detected among the young intelligentsia shortly before the war, as Henry F. May has shown, they had never been widespread nor attracted a sizeable following. It was still, the *Nation* remarked at the time, only a revolt, not a revolution. Not until after the war did the "fluttering tastes of the half-baked intellectuals" infect most of the younger generation and capture the nation's youth (and some of the old) by storm. The "innocent rebellion" of 1912–17 had never at-

The "flapper" was a symbol of the revolt of flaming youth in the 1920's. As modern as the Charleston and the one-piece bathing suit, she discarded surplus clothes and surplus manners with the same enthusiasm she devoted to acquiring gin and cigarettes.

"Do you think the flapper is passing out?"
He—Well, I've had lots of them pass out on me.

Culver Pictures, Inc., from *Judge*, December 29, 1923

tained popular proportions, but the new revolt was decidedly different in temper and tone. Where the earlier rebellion had been somewhat furtive, even modest, the revolution of the twenties was open and shameless. It was, as John Flynn said, doubtless the most violent revolution against established manners and ideas of morality and religion this country had ever seen. "The flapper, the flivver, Freud, and gin ran wild over the land."[1]

Most revealing was the radically changed role of the young woman. Where the "emancipated" young woman of the previous decade had taken the lead in attempting to wipe out prostitution, abolish the saloon, and trying in general to raise the social standards of men to her own, the "flapper"—the free-wheeling female of the twenties—ran serious competition to the prostitute. She invaded the saloon not with raised axe but with lifted elbow, and she tried her best to beat the man on his own level. Though it is true Mencken had described the "flapper" as early as 1915, bringing the word into public use, his flapper had been an eccentric; in the 1920's she became a convention. She was, moreover, a different girl from her mother. Mother's skirt had "just reached her very trim and pretty ankles" and her newly coiled hair "exposed the ravishing whiteness of her neck," but daughter wore her hair in a short bob and her skimpy dress soared above the knees, revealing her rolled stockings and at times a fleeting glimpse of white thighs. Rather than Christabel Pankhurst and Omar Khayyam, she read Freud and F. Scott Fitzgerald and worried not about the evils of white slavery but the comparative merits of contraceptives. Discreetly sipping wine by candlelight was not for her; she smoked cigarettes and drank in public and got "blotto" on bathtub gin, preferring to take her booze like a man from a hip-flask or with one foot on the brass rail in a basement speakeasy. Instead of the romantic violin and the exotic tango, she chose the skittish saxophone and the boisterous Charleston; and after midnight, instead of returning to a garret in Greenwich Village to talk until dawn of Strindberg, Ibsen, Shaw, and Wells, she drove off in an automobile for a "petting party" down some dark side-street or country lane while her mother lay awake and worried. To be sure, not all "nice" girls behaved as she did, but there were enough of them who did to make the younger generation a topic of anxious discussion from coast to coast.[2]

Behind the flagrant change in manners was an even more radical change in morals. As with all great social revolutions, it was cumulative rather than catastrophic, compound rather than simple in origins. Beyond doubt, the war played a part, shaking many young people loose from settled moorings and deranging moral and religious values. But while war accelerated change, it was only a catalyst, not the major determining force. The old culture had collapsed not because of the war but because the war, combined with various scientific and intellectual developments, brought to light its inadequacies.

It was a "botched" civilization, and no one saw it more clearly than the young. His generation had emerged from the war, said F. Scott Fitzgerald, "to find all Gods dead, all wars fought, all faiths in man shaken." For the younger generation, the "war to end war" had turned out to be a "cockeyed lunatic asylum," destroying all the ideals and principles they most believed in. War, as one of its victims concluded in John Dos Passos' novel *1919*, was "a dirty goldbrick game put over by governments and politicians for their own selfish interests" and "crooked from A to Z." In a world "knocked to pieces," all deceptions were out. If "these wild young people" shocked their elders who could not see what all the concern was about, if they were harsh, reckless, and sometimes wicked, it was because —as one of them explained—the break-up of things was no time for "little tin-pot ideals."° If they were mocking and irreverent and took established institutions very lightly, it was because the civilization they inherited was, in the words of Ezra Pound, "an old bitch, gone in the teeth."³

Irritation at things as they were and disgust at the continual frustrations and aridities of American life led those young people who could not escape to seek fresh values. They could accept neither the war nor the Puritanical reaction that followed. Yet it was not Puritanism so much as complacency that they fought. As Carol, the youthful heroine of *Main Street*, made clear, it was the savorless quality of the traditional pattern of life that the more intelligent young people revolted against. They deplored the "unimaginatively standardized background," the "sluggishness of speech and manners," the "rigid ruling of the spirit by the desire to appear respectable." To the young such a life was "the contentment of the quiet dead, who are scornful of the living for their restless walking." It was "negation canonized as the one positive virtue." It was "the prohibition of happiness," "slavery self-sought and self-defended." It was "dullness made God." Yet, said Randolph Bourne, defending the young rebels, these malcontents were not barbarians and had no intention of being cultural vandals, but simply sought the vital and the sin-

°John F. Carter, *These Wild Young People*. See page 353.

The most celebrated institution of the Jazz Age was the "speak-easy." In 1929, there were 32,000 speakeasies in New York City, double the number of saloons in the old days. Drunkenness, as F. Scott Fitzgerald said, became a mark "of the superior status of those who are able to afford the indulgence."

cere everywhere. "All they want is a new orientation of
the spirit that shall be modern," an orientation to accompany that scientific and technical apparatus which the war
accelerated and which was fast coming to dominate civilization. "So they are likely to go ahead beating their heads
at the wall until they are either bloody or light appears."[4]

Most of them found that "new orientation of the spirit"
through the popularized ideas of Sigmund Freud. In a time
of growing skepticism about civilization and morality,
Freud taught the primacy of natural desire, seeming to
uphold the world of nature against the hypocrisies and
cruelties of the world of man. The sexual urge was the
primordial force of man's nature, the fundamental drive
of life, and civilization was built upon the heroic sacrifice of man's desire. While Freud recognized that civilization required the repression or sublimation of sexuality, he
also warned that the continuous sacrifice of nature that
was demanded by civilization held great peril for the individual. "Experience teaches us that for most people there
is a limit beyond which their constitution cannot comply
with the demands of civilization. All who wish to be more
noble-minded than their constitution allows fall victims to
neurosis; they would have been more healthy if it could
have been possible for them to be less good."[5]

Early in 1922, Harold Stearns diagnosed the ills of
American society in just such Freudian terms. The intellectual life in America was sour and sterile because it had
"lost its earthy roots, its sensuous fulness." Scorning its
biological history and emotional setting, the American intellect had failed to reach its own proper dignity and effec-
tiveness because it made an "ascetic divorce between the
passions and the intellect, the emotions and the reason,"
where instead it should have tried to function "in some
kind of rational relationship with the more clamorous instincts of the body."[6]

Far from counseling license, however, Freud was a man
whose ideal was to control passion by reason and who, in

his own attitude toward sex, lived up to the Victorian sexual morality. Yet always implicit in his writing about the conflict between the natural urges of man and the conventions of society was the question whether "civilized" morality was worth the price. Though insisting sexual satisfaction was not in itself a universal remedy for the ills of civilization, his conclusion in *Civilization and Its Discontents* was that "our so-called civilization itself is to blame for a great part of our misery, and we should be happier if we were to give it up and go back to primitive conditions."[7]

The explicit primitivism of Freud appealed greatly to culturally jaded Americans who seized upon the idea that surrender to impulse was the scientific way to individual fulfillment, satisfaction, and happiness. Whether Freud intended it or not, Freudianism as popularly interpreted in the United States in the 1920's meant unrestrained sexuality. Not only was it regarded as healthful and expedient to get rid of one's "repressions," but to throttle the instincts on outdated moral grounds was to arouse suspicions that one was inhibited or neurotic and, among the more sophisticated, to invite social condemnation. The wide and pervasive obsession with sex which infected the older as well as the younger generation excited considerable indignation among the clergy and other righteous citizens of the republic. Cried a leading churchman, "The morale of the whole country has been lowered, minds have been polluted, tongues loosened from their decent reticencies, youth perverted, marriages dissolved, by this vicious theory flaunting itself under the name of Science. The psychoanalyst interprets everything in terms of sex." And, as he rightly lamented, so did a good many Americans.[8]

The new view of sex was applauded by George Jean Nathan on behalf of the *avant garde* in the *American Mercury*, of which he was co-editor. "It used to be thought pretty generally that sex was a grim, serious and ominous business, to be entered into only by those duly joined in holy wedlock or by those lost souls already in thrall to the devil. Sex was synonymous with danger, tragedy, woe, or at its best, with legalized baby carriages. This view of sex has gone out of style with such other contemporary delusions as French altruism, the making of the world safe for democracy and the evil of Bolshevist government." Though Nathan did not dispute that "back in the cow pastures of the Republic" the old view of sex still prevailed, he argued that "wherever lights are brighter" and "wherever a band, however bad, plays on Saturday nights, there you will find a change in the old order." The change in approach to the sex question, Nathan explained, had not been an arbitrary one but was based upon "a thoroughly clear and intelligent view of sex." In the past sex had been overrated. Through an "idiotic conspiracy" the world had been made to accept it as something of paramount consequence in the life of man. Yet the reflective man had long known that, as a matter of fact, sex was a relatively trivial and inconsequential event and of considerably less importance in life than his tobacco or his *Schnapps*. "Sex is, purely and simply, the diversion of man, a pastime for his leisure hours and, as such, on the same plane with his other pleasures. The civilized man," said Nathan, "knows little difference between his bottle of vintage champagne, his Corona Corona, his seat at the 'Follies' and the gratification of his sex impulse." Sex was "simply something always amusing and sometimes beautiful" and to be taken no more seriously than a symphony concert.[9]

Freudianism and Sex became a big business in America. Exploiting the sexually repressed, advertisements in the illustrated magazines sold pretty girls along with the product, conveying the impression that the curvaceous bathing-beauty went with the car or suggesting that to smoke a certain brand of cigarettes was the next thing to an orgasm with a dazzlingly better-than-life flapper or gigolo. "Chiropractors of the subconscious," as Nathan called them, began to flourish in every community that boasted a brick rail-

road station and a gilt movie parlor. The public craze for
analysis, a conscience-stricken physician confessed in the
New Republic, had permitted him to double, then triple
his fees. As the demand was greater than the supply of
trained analysts, the lucrative market was soon invaded by
hucksters and shysters whose only qualifications were a
secondhand couch, a straggly beard, and an *ersatz* German
accent. In polite society, parlor Bolshevists made way for
parlor analysts who found the Freudian slip a sure con-
versational gambit as well as a superior technique for se-
duction. In the greedy hands of popularizers such as Harvey
O'Higgins, American history was rewritten in Freudian
terms, and great figures of the past, the free man and the
exceptional man, were converted into Freudian cases.[10]

Freudian psychoanalysis invaded almost every conceivable field of American thought and conduct. Anthropology,
sociology, religion, penology, jurisprudence, pedagogy,
medicine, art, and literature all succumbed in some degree
to the blandishments of the Viennese sage. At the same
time, there was no question that in the twenties Freudianism degenerated into a fad. "If there is anything you do
not understand in human life," wrote Sherwood Anderson
in *Dark Laughter,* "consult the works of Dr. Freud." And
Americans did, for in the long list of books published on
this subject before 1928 there were not only *Psychology
and Common Life, Psychology and Sex Life, Psychology
and Business Efficiency,* but also *Psychology of Golf,
Psychology of Murder, Psychology of Package Labels.* A
"great wave of mind culture" swept the United States, and
Freudianism, which in its inception was a clinical method
for carefully trained psychiatrists, became a sophisticated,
fashionable jargon for debunking American life. The *New
York Times Magazine,* for example, carried an erudite
article explaining the enormous popularity of the then current song "Yes, We Have No Bananas" in terms of a national inferiority complex. In its popularized version, at
least, one must agree with Aldous Huxley that Freudianism

was in a class with phrenology, physiognomy, animal magnetism, and other pseudo-scientific fads of bygone years.[11]

Sex had been the great scientific discovery of the century, and, as Nathan said, could be more easily handled than relativity and was equally profound. The accepted panacea for every ill during the middle twenties, popular Freudianism was in full retreat by the early thirties. After the depression failed to yield to psychoanalysis, people began to poke fun at "sexology," and popular acceptance of such books as the facetious symposium *Whither, Whither or After Sex What?* and James Thurber's and E. B. White's droll *Is Sex Necessary?* confirmed the change in temper. So complete was the reaction against Freudianism that the *Atlantic* in 1934 could publish a serious article called "The Rise and Fall of Psychology." Its downfall had come about, the author explained, because in the modern mind science was a form of magic, and the magic of Freud had failed: "Psychoanalysis, for all its theories, has performed no miracles. It has renamed our emotions 'complexes' and our habits 'conditioned reflexes,' but it has neither changed our habits nor rid us of our emotions. We are the same blundering folk that we were twelve years ago, and far less sure of ourselves."[12]

By 1926, according to F. Scott Fitzgerald, the universal preoccupation with sex had become a nuisance. Sex, as the title of one of his books *All the Sad Young Men* suggested, had not proved the master-key to happiness. Uninhibited young men and women, world-weary at twenty-two, had rediscovered the Victorian truism that love and sex were not identical. Fitzgerald himself, who epitomized the Jazz Age both in his life and writings, suffered a nervous breakdown in the thirties, and his once gay young wife ended life tragically in a sanitarium for the mentally ill. Like his sad young men, Fitzgerald learned to his discomfiture that spiritual distress cannot be banished by

spiritual anarchy.° "What most distinguishes the generation who have approached maturity since the *débâcle* at
the end of the war," wrote Walter Lippmann in 1929, "is
not their rebellion against the religion and the moral code
of their parents, but their disillusionment with their own
rebellion."[13]

II

The dilemma of the younger generation was a consequence of their having inherited worn and broken ideals
which failed to meet the practical test of daily life. Not
only had the soldiers and statesmen left things in a terrible
muddle, but the preachers and philosophers in trying to
explain the ugliness and chaos of life made things seem
only more hopelessly chaotic and unintelligible. However,
when in their frantic search for a serviceable plan of existence to replace the shabby old generalities they turned
to the scientists, they seemed to find a very different state
of affairs.

The scientific activities of man, unlike his other intellectual activities, apparently had not suffered shell-shock.
Life to the scientist, so it seemed, was not chaos at all
but a realm in whose apparent disorder he found a definite kind of order. For instance, out of those very aspects
of human life that had in the past seemed a hopeless jangle
of contradictions, the science of psychology had created
"an intelligible and practically demonstrable theoretic
unity." By what he claimed to find in the seemingly
chaotic jumble of the "unconscious," the psychologist was
enabled to correlate and explain all sorts of bewildering
and painful discrepancies in human conduct, previously
inexplicable. "Our mortification and our painful disillusionment on account of the uncivilized behavior of our

°F. Scott Fitzgerald, *Echoes of the Jazz Age*. See page 359.

fellow-citizens of the world during this war," Freud explained, "were unjustified. They were based on an illusion which had to give way. In reality our fellow-citizens have not sunk so low as we feared, because they had never risen so high as we believed. . . . The demands we make . . . should be far more modest." But of even greater import than a scientific explanation of disenchantment was the promise of Freudian science to undertake therapeutically the task of bringing harmony, order, and happiness into inharmonious, disorderly, and futile lives.[14]

In a world of uncertainties and half-certainties, science seemed to promise modern man a practical guide to a universe freed from the superstition of religion and the perplexity of philosophy. Although scientists warned of the dangers of oversimplification and deplored the public's habit of accepting the findings of science with too much reverence, a great many people—in their desperate desire to escape the discomfort of bewilderment—found in science "a plausible substitute for the simplicity of the Sunday sermon, an interpretation of reality at once convincing and easy to grasp." With the result, as Frederick J. Hoffman has described it, that "the genuinely popular religion in America in the 1920's was the religion of practical consequences—in short, science as it was known through its results, multiplied by efficient industrial means, and distributed over the extensive reaches of a democratic population."[15]

The apotheosis of science created a need for a modern scientific ethic which would bring human ethics into "active partnership with human science." Such was the contention of the distinguished mathematician and philosopher, Alfred North Whitehead of Harvard, who asserted that the business of philosophy was to fuse religion and science into one rational scheme of thought. In *Science and the Modern World* (1925) he began to construct a system of ideas which would "bring the aesthetic, moral, and religious interests into relation with those concepts of the world which have their origin in natural science." In his view modern science had imposed on the human mind the necessity for wandering. Its progressive thought and its progressive technology made the transition through time, from generation to generation, a true spiritual adventure. While he admitted modern science was destructive of faith in God as "an all-powerful arbitrary tyrant," Whitehead believed science was contributing to the development of religion by freeing it from the bonds of outdated imagery and thus helping to reveal its own genuine message.° It was his profound belief that once religion adopted the progressive spirit of science, it would regain its old power.[16]

Because science was popularly acclaimed as a new revelation, it attracted cults which "attached themselves to scientific hypotheses as fortune-tellers to a circus." These cults were an attempt to fit the working theories of science to the common man's desire for salvation, but sooner or later they ran into difficulty. For the great obstacle in the way of the conversion of modern science into a popular faith, as Lippmann saw, lay precisely in its "rejection of the belief, which is at the heart of all popular religions, that the forces which move the stars and atoms are contingent upon the preferences of the human heart." Where the science of Aristotle and the medieval scholars had been a truly popular science in the sense that they read into the cause and goal of the universe the experience and needs of ordinary men, the radical novelty of modern science, as Whitehead observed, was the fact that "scientific theory is outrunning common sense." Rather than providing an explanation of reality in terms of human desire and sense-experience, modern science disinterestedly describes the universe as a series of highly abstract relationships. Once this fact was perceived, science became useless to the unscientific man as an ethical or religious account of human destiny.[17]

° Alfred North Whitehead, *Religion and Science.* See page 370.

For the ordinary man in the twenties science proved a false messiah, and the disillusion with Freudianism was indicative of a larger disillusionment with modern science as a pseudo-religion. Popular Freudianism, as popular Darwinism earlier, had served to break down traditional moral and religious barriers by dissolving the age-old distinction between man and nature and had attempted to bring man back to nature, not only by teaching that man, like every other animal, was in reality in bondage to natural forces, but also by inferring that human virtues were biologic vices. In practice, however, the Freudian analysis with its deterministic emphasis on naturalism and primitivism had shown serious limitations, proving in many cases to be the disease it purported to cure. For as the painful experience of the Jazz Age had confirmed, the means of nature did not necessarily lead to human ends. On the contrary, as Fitzgerald's sad young men belatedly perceived, somewhere along the line a choice had to be made between an essentially animal existence or a life oriented toward human, as opposed to natural, values.[18]

It was here that Joseph Wood Krutch located the source of modern man's discontent. A young intellectual writing just before the depression, Krutch took an opposite view to Whitehead's, contending that science had proven progressively destructive of all ethical and human values. The universe revealed by science was one in which the human spirit could not find a comfortable home, because that spirit flourished only in a world where human values were of supreme importance. Men needed to believe, argued Krutch, that right and wrong were real, that love was more than a biological function, that the human brain was capable of reason rather than merely of rationalization, and that it had the power to will and choose instead of being compelled merely to react in the fashion predetermined by its conditioning. Since science had seemingly exposed those beliefs as delusions, Krutch concluded that man must either surrender his humanity by adjusting to the natural world or live some kind of tragic existence in a universe alien to the deepest needs of his nature.°

III

Not all Americans succumbed to scientism and the Freudian demonology. The worth, the dignity, the soul of man also had champions in the twenties, but their unfashionable counsel of spiritual discipline and social cooperation ran counter to the dominant ideas of the time: scientific naturalism and economic individualism. The Protestant clergy generally deplored the reduction of theology to psychology, the majority being in agreement with Harry Emerson Fosdick that "What the Freudians call religion Jesus of Nazareth called sin." But perhaps the most resolute champion of the spiritual and altruistic side of human nature was Harry F. Ward, a clergyman and teacher of Christian ethics as well as an aggressive leader of the newly formed American Civil Liberties Union. To Ward the most hopeful fact of the immediate postwar era was that humanity was becoming conscious of itself as an organic unity and was seeking to come together as a whole. Though a man of utopian vision, Ward was well aware that the new social order would not come about by wishing and praying; and though a social evolutionist with strong Marxist sympathies, he never saw it simply as a project in social engineering. What was called for, in his opinion, was no mere tinkering with the machinery of society but a tremendous upheaval—a revolution in social ethics founded upon a conscious choice of the highest, most difficult end for human life. Social progress, Ward insisted, demanded a vital change in approach to the human personality. Hence he rejected the vulgar appeal of materialism, because he regarded man as vastly more than a goods-producing and goods-consuming creature. Neither did he yield to the prev-

°Joseph Wood Krutch, *Disillusion with the Laboratory.* See page 377.

A Suggestion for Our Cathedral Builders

Proposed Design for a Memorial Window to Moral Turpitude

Culver Pictures, Inc., from *Life*, March 11, 1926, p. 17

In the twenties a few brave Protestant ministers tried to revive the "social gospel"—the union of religion and social action—but their optimistic program of social redemption found little support in a money-minded society.

alent urge to find a mechanistic explanation for everything, nor resort to the heuristic fictions of the unconscious, the libido, id, and ego, for he believed any new social order must reckon with the immortal spark within man that refused to be satisfied with animal pleasures and creature comforts and that ever pursued the impossible. It was this spiritual aspect of human nature, rather than the instinctual, which must be freed and given expression and development in all social or economic arrangements. Once the supremacy of personality was established, Ward expected social progress to follow almost automatically.° For in his view the social order was not a framework external to humanity but was composed of humanity itself, and if the individuals composing society mastered their egoistic im-

°Harry F. Ward, *A New Social Order*. See page 384.

pulses and chose the promotion of the common welfare of humanity as the end of life, the new order would come into being.[19]

Viewing the world in 1932 during the darkest days of depression, Reinhold Niebuhr—unlike Ward—saw little hope for either the social gospel or its optimistic program of social redemption. Not only had human intelligence seemingly abdicated in face of social disaster, but the old brutal forces of economic and military coercion were everywhere in ascendancy. A Protestant minister and theologian, Niebuhr had been actively involved in the industrial and interracial difficulties of Detroit, and from his experience there had reached a conclusion similar to that of Krutch—that between technology and science, man was caught in a depersonalized society building up in a depersonalized universe. Although he conceded that social gospelists such as Ward realistically appraised the contemporary social situation, recognizing that modern civilization threatened man with reduction to machine-life, in Niebuhr's view they persistently erred in their romantic overestimate of human virtue and moral capacity. But what Niebuhr found lacking most among these modern religious idealists was an understanding of the profound difference between the moral and social behavior of individuals and of social groups.[20]

For Niebuhr the contradiction between the individual conscience and that of the group was dramatized by World War I: the moral man in 1916 was the protestant, the man of individual conscience; immoral society, the nation at war. The war convinced Niebuhr that, contrary to the social gospel, religion could be effective only if it resisted the embraces of civilization. The inferior morality of groups he explained by the fact that the collective egoism, compounded of the egoistic impulses of individuals, was harder to control and its cumulative impact when united in common impulse was more violent and exaggerated than when expressed separately. Though individuals might achieve a degree of reason and sympathy which would enable them to see and understand the interests of others as vividly as they understood their own and a moral goodwill which would prompt them to uphold the rights of others as vigorously as they upheld their own, such an ideal was beyond the capacity of society as a whole. Since the immorality of society might be mitigated but never overcome, the relations between groups must therefore always be political rather than ethical, that is, they will in the end be determined by power. ¯

But, Niebuhr cautioned, this inevitable conflict between the individual and society should not make for moral cynicism but rather for a more realistic approach to the problem of social ethics. The hope of an ethical civilization rested not upon the possibility of making power completely ethical but upon the possibility of creating enough intelligence and conscience among the holders of power to make a gradual equalization of power possible. If society were to be morally regenerated, men of goodwill must combine the "wisdom of serpents" with the "guilelessness of doves."°

Niebuhr's refutation of unpolitical social idealism exposed the vast gulf between the ethical views of the 1920's and the 1930's. Just as the comfortable and uncritical materialism of the earlier decade easily overrode the crabbed moralism that strained to keep an expansive society within the narrow confines of Prohibition and Fundamentalism, so the practical political ethic of the thirties by its awareness of man's willfulness and self-interest sharply contradicted the sentimental and superficial notions current to the twenties that the individual could save himself and society simply by following his animal instincts or by responding to his Christian reflexes. It would be an oversimplification to attribute this radical reorientation entirely to economic factors, but they nevertheless played a major role. For the depression forced Americans to radically revise their ideas and painfully readjust their values. Prosperity, as Frederick

°Reinhold Niebuhr, *Moral Man and Immoral Society.* See page 394.

Lewis Allen observed, had been more than an economic condition—it was also a state of mind. "There was hardly a man or woman in the country whose attitude toward life had not been affected by it in some degree and was not now affected by the sudden and brutal shattering of hope." Certainly the most conspicuous evidence of the change in intellectual climate was the change in charisma.[21]

If Freud was the oracle of the Jazz Age, Marx was the culture-god of the depression year. Each, in a sense, was exalted by the *zeitgeist* of the times. In the comfortable twenties, food, clothes, and warmth were accepted as instruments, and the most eager attention was directed, not toward attaining them, but toward the gratifications of status and emotional well-being which men are able to pursue when necessities are granted. So complacent men spurned Christian asceticism for the intemperate ethic of Freudianism which, because it was a purely subjective system of morality based upon self-indulgence of the individual's instincts and material aims, was better suited to the profligate temper of the twenties. But the depression-ridden thirties brought a fundamentally different atmosphere. Food, clothes, and warmth were in short supply, and now instead of being considered as means to an end became ends in themselves. In a world beset with the more urgent problems of work and hunger, the psychoanalytic couch lost its magic. The whole machinery of sexual symbolism, the exciting quest for phallic images and dream equivalents of fornication, now seemed so fantastic as to be quite unbelievable—especially when compared to Marx's realistic insight that, not sexual hunger, but a more basic hunger for material satisfactions was the driving force in life. Acting upon the Marxist assumption that the only maladjustments from which men suffer are social, the comrades of depression threw out psychological individualism to embrace a social ethic based upon an objective evaluation of the collective material needs of mankind. But, ironically, bemused by the belief that in a perfect economy all men will be perfectly happy, the true-believers of the thirties refused to remember what the sad young men of the twenties had learned—though Fitzgerald reminded them—that physical well-being is no guarantee of felicity.

As ethical formulas for the Good Society, both Freudianism and Marxism turned out to be egregious failures. Because of their single-minded insistence on strictly and abstractly doctrinal approaches to the problems of the individual or society, they failed to translate even their valid discoveries and criticisms into social practice. Both betrayed a lack of social responsibility. In face of capitalistic greed and injustice, the Marxists begged the question of social reform by claiming the thirties was a time of "intellectual preparation" for revolution, not of radical social change. So, likewise, the Freudians who, having discovered the pathological effect of sexual repression on the human spirit, failed to follow through by either ridding society of its neuroses or providing a brave new morality to replace the "hush-hush ethics" of an ascetic Christianity. What prevailed in the end was the old pragmatic alliance between humanistic democracy and materialistic capitalism, the two disparate faiths once again reunited by war.

Readings:

The Modern Ethic

John F. Carter, Jr. (1897–   )

*Son of an Episcopal clergyman and a member
of the class of 1920, he was at Yale with Stephen
Vincent Benét, Thornton Wilder, and Archibald
MacLeish. A serious infection in childhood left
him with bad eyes and a leaky heart, so he
learned to write, as he said, in self-defense. A
foreign correspondent and then a political
journalist, he wrote a brilliant, well-informed,
syndicated pro-New Deal column, "We, the
People," under the pseudonym Jay Franklin.*

THESE WILD YOUNG PEOPLE

For some months past the pages of our more conservative
magazines have been crowded with pessimistic descriptions
of the younger generation, as seen by their elders and, no
doubt, their betters. Hardly a week goes by that I do not
read some indignant treatise depicting our extravagance,
the corruption of our manners, the futility of our existence,

John F. Carter, Jr., "'These Wild Young People' by One of Them," *Atlantic
Monthly*, CXXVI (Sept., 1920), 301–4. Reprinted by permission of the *Atlantic
Monthly*.

poured out in stiff, scared, shocked sentences before a sympathetic and horrified audience of fathers, mothers, and maiden aunts—but particularly maiden aunts.

In the May issue of the *Atlantic Monthly* appeared an article entitled "Polite Society," by a certain Mr. Grundy, the husband of a very old friend of my family. In kindly manner he

> Mentioned our virtues, it is true,
> But dwelt upon our vices, too.

"Chivalry and Modesty are dead. Modesty died first," quoth he, but expressed the pious hope that all might yet be well if the oldsters would but be content to "wait and see." His article is one of the best-tempered and most gentlemanly of this long series of Jeremiads against "these wild young people." It is significant that it should be anonymous. In reading it, I could not help but be drawn to Mr. Grundy personally, but was forced to the conclusion that he, like everyone else who is writing about my generation, has very little idea of what he is talking about. . . .

I would like to say a few things about my generation.

In the first place, I would like to observe that the older generation had certainly pretty well ruined this world before passing it on to us. They give us this Thing, knocked to pieces, leaky, red-hot, threatening to blow up; and then they are surprised that we don't accept it with the same attitude of pretty, decorous enthusiasm with which they received it, 'way back in the eighteen-nineties, nicely painted, smoothly running, practically fool-proof. "So simple that a child can run it!" But the child couldn't steer it. He hit every possible telegraph-pole, some of them twice, and ended with a head-on collision for which *we* shall have to pay the fines and damages. Now, with loving pride, they turn over their wreck to us; and, since we are not properly overwhelmed with loving gratitude, shake their heads and sigh, "Dear! dear! We were so much better-mannered than these wild young people. But then we had the advantages of a good, strict, old-fashioned bringing-up!" How intensely *human* these oldsters are, after all, and how fallible! How they always blame us for not following precisely in their eminently correct footsteps!

Then again there is the matter of outlook. When these sentimental old world-wreckers were young, the world was such a different place—at least, so I gather from H. G. Wells's picture of the nineties, in *Joan and Peter.* Life for them was bright and pleasant. Like all normal youngsters, they had their little tin-pot ideals, their sweet little visions, their naïve enthusiasms, their nice little sets of beliefs. Christianity had emerged from the blow dealt by Darwin, emerged rather in the shape of social dogma. Man was a noble and perfectible creature. Women were angels (whom they smugly sweated in their industries and prostituted in their slums). Right was downing might. The nobility and the divine mission of the race were factors that led our fathers to work wholeheartedly for a millennium, which they caught a glimpse of just around the turn of the century. Why, there were Hague Tribunals! International peace was at last assured, and according to current reports, never officially denied, the American delegates held out for the use of poison gas in warfare, just as the men of that generation were later to ruin Wilson's great ideal of a league of nations, on the ground that such a scheme was an invasion of American rights. But still, everything, masked by ingrained hypocrisy and prudishness, seemed simple, beautiful, inevitable.

Now my generation is disillusionized, and, I think, to a certain extent, brutalized, by the cataclysm which *their* complacent folly engendered. The acceleration of life for us has been so great that into the last few years have been crowded the experiences and the ideas of a normal lifetime. We have in our unregenerate youth learned the practicality and the cynicism that is safe only in unregenerate old age. We have been forced to become realists overnight, instead of idealists, as was our birthright. We have seen man at his lowest, woman at her lightest, in the terrible moral chaos of Europe. We have been forced to question, and in many cases to discard, the religion of our fathers. We have seen hideous peculation, greed, anger, hatred, malice, and all uncharitableness, unmasked and rampant and unashamed. We have been forced to live in an atmosphere of "tomorrow we die," and so, naturally, we drank and were merry. We have seen the rottenness and shortcomings of all governments, even the best and most stable. We have seen entire social systems overthrown, and our own called in question. In short, we have seen the inherent beastliness of the human race revealed in an infernal apocalypse.

It is the older generation who forced us to see all this, which has left us with social and political institutions staggering blind in the fierce white light that, for us, should beat only about the enthroned ideal. And now, through the soft-headed folly of these painfully shocked Grundys, we have that devastating wisdom which is safe only for the burned-out embers of grizzled, cautious old men. We may be fire, but it was they who made us play with gunpowder. And now they are surprised that a great many of us, because they have taken away our apple-cheeked ideals, are seriously considering whether or no *their* game be worth *our* candle.

But, in justice to my generation, I think that I must admit that most of us have realized that, whether or no it be worth while, we must all play the game, as long as we are in it. And I think that much of the hectic quality of our life is due to that fact and to that alone. We are faced with staggering problems and are forced to solve them, while the previous incumbents are permitted a graceful and untroubled death. All my friends are working and working hard. Most of the girls I know are working. In one way or another, often unconsciously, the great burden put upon us is being borne, and borne gallantly, by that immodest, unchivalrous set of ne'er-do-wells, so delightfully portrayed by Mr. Grundy and the amazing young Fitzgerald. A keen interest in political and social problems, and a determination to face the facts of life, ugly or beautiful, characterizes us, as it certainly did not characterize our fathers. We won't shut our eyes to the truths we have learned. We have faced so many unpleasant things already, —and faced them pretty well,—that it is natural that we should keep it up.

Now I think that this is the aspect of our generation that annoys the uncritical and deceives the unsuspecting oldsters who are now met in judgment upon us: our devastating and brutal frankness. And this is the quality in which we really differ from our predecessors. We are frank with each other, frank, or pretty nearly so, with our elders, frank in the way we feel toward life and this badly damaged world. It may be a disquieting and misleading habit, but is it a bad one? We find some few things in the world that we like, and a whole lot that we don't, and we are not afraid to say so or to give our reasons. In earlier generations this was not the case. The young men yearned to be glittering generalities, the young women to act like shy, sweet, innocent fawns—toward one another. And now, when grown up, they have come to believe that they actually were figures of pristine excellence, knightly chivalry, adorable modesty, and impeccable propriety. But I really doubt if they were so. Statistics relating to, let us say, the immorality of college students in the eighteen-eighties would not compare favorably with those of the present. However, now, as they look back on it, they see their youth through a mist of muslin, flannels, tennis, bicycles, Tennyson, Browning, and the Blue Danube waltz. The other things, the ugly things that we know about and talk about, must also have been there. But our elders didn't care or didn't dare to consider them, and now they are forgotten. We talk about them unabashed, and not necessarily with Presbyterian disapproval, and so they jump to the conclusion that we are thoroughly bad, and keep pestering us to make us good.

The trouble with them is that they can't seem to realize that we are busy, that what pleasure we snatch must be incidental and feverishly hurried. We have to make the most of our time. We actually haven't got so much time for the noble procrastinations of modesty or for the elaborate rigmarole of chivalry, and little patience for the lovely formulas of an ineffective faith. Let them die for a while! They did not seem to serve the world too well in its black hour. If they are inherently good they will come back, vital and untarnished. But just now we have a lot of work, "old time is still a-flying," and we must gather rose-buds while we may.

Oh! I know that we are a pretty bad lot, but has not that been true of every preceding generation? At least we have the courage to act accordingly. Our music is distinctly barbaric, our girls are distinctly *not* a mixture of arbutus and barbed-wire. We drink when we can and what we can, we gamble, we are extravagant—but we work, and that's about all that we can be expected to do; for, after all, we have just discovered that we are all still very near to the Stone Age. The Grundys shake their heads. They'll *make* us be good. Prohibition is put through to stop our drinking, and hasn't stopped it. Bryan has plans to curtail our philanderings, and he won't do any good. A Draconian code is being hastily formulated at Washington and elsewhere, to prevent us from, by any chance, making any alteration in this present divinely constituted arrangement of things. The oldsters stand dramatically with fingers and toes and noses pressed against the bursting dykes. Let them! They won't do any good. They can shackle us down, and still expect us to repair their blunders, if they wish. But we shall not trouble ourselves very much about them any more. Why should we? What have they done? They have made us work as they never had to work in all their padded lives—but we'll have our cakes and ale for a' that.

For now we know our way about. We're not babes in the wood, hunting for great, big, red strawberries, and confidently expecting the Robin Red-Breasts to cover us up with pretty leaves if we don't find them. We're men and women, long before our time, in the flower of our full-blooded youth. We have brought back into civil life some of the recklessness and ability that we were taught by war. We are also quite fatalistic in our outlook on the tepid perils of tame living. All may yet crash to the ground for aught that we can do about it. Terrible mistakes will be made, but *we* shall at least make them intelligently and insist, if we are to receive the strictures of the future, on doing pretty much as we choose now.

Oh! I suppose that it's too bad that we aren't humble, starry-eyed, shy, respectful innocents, standing reverently at their side for instructions, playing pretty little games, in which they no longer believe, except for us. But we aren't, and the best thing the oldsters can do about it is to go into their respective backyards and dig for worms, great big pink ones—for the Grundy tribe are now just about as important as they are, and they will doubtless make company more congenial and docile than "these wild young people," the men and women of my generation.

F. Scott Fitzgerald (1896-1940)

From a prosperous midwestern family, he went to Princeton where for four years he "wasted his time scribbling." His first novel, This Side of Paradise *(1920), at once established him as the spokesman of his generation in the Jazz Age. After a gay and precocious beginning—youth, charm, money, celebrity—he "cracked up" in early middle-age and spent his last years in Hollywood almost forgotten.*

ECHOES OF THE JAZZ AGE

November, 1931

It is too soon to write about the Jazz Age with perspective, and without being suspected of premature arteriosclerosis. Many people still succumb to violent retching when they happen upon any of its characteristic words—words which have since yielded in vividness to the coinages of the underworld. It is as dead as were the Yellow Nineties in 1902. Yet the present writer already looks back to it with nostalgia. It bore him up, flattered him and gave him more money than he had dreamed of, simply for telling people that he felt as they did, that something had to be done with all the nervous energy stored up and unexpended in the War.

The ten-year period that, as if reluctant to die outmoded in its bed, leaped to a spectacular death in October, 1929, began about the time of the May Day riots in 1919. When the police rode down the demobilized country boys gaping at the orators in Madison Square, it was the sort of measure bound to alienate the more intelligent young men from the prevailing order. We didn't remember anything about the Bill of Rights until Mencken began plugging it, but we did know that such tyranny belonged in the jittery little countries of South Europe. If goose-livered business men had this effect on the government, then maybe we had gone to war for J. P. Morgan's loans after all. But, because we were tired of Great Causes, there was no more than a short outbreak of moral indignation, typified by Dos Passos' *Three Soldiers*. Presently we began to have slices of the national cake and our idealism only flared up when the newspapers made melodrama out of such stories as Harding and the Ohio Gang or Sacco and Vanzetti. The events of 1919 left us cynical rather than revolutionary, in spite of the fact that now we are all rummaging around in our trunks wondering where in hell we left the liberty cap—"I know I *had* it"—and the moujik blouse. It was characteristic of the Jazz Age that it had no interest in politics at all.

It was an age of miracles, it was an age of art, it was an age of excess, and it was an age of satire. A Stuffed Shirt, squirming to blackmail in a lifelike way, sat upon the throne of the United States; a stylish young man hurried over to represent to us the throne of England. A world of girls yearned for the young Englishman; the old American groaned in his sleep as he waited to be poisoned by his wife, upon the advice of the female Rasputin who then made the ultimate decision in our national affairs. But such matters apart, we had things our way at last. With Americans ordering suits by the gross in London, the Bond Street tailors perforce agreed to moderate their cut to the American long-waisted figure and loose-fitting taste, something subtle passed to America, the style of man. During the Renaissance, Francis the First looked to Florence to trim his leg. Seventeenth-century England aped the court of France, and fifty years ago the German Guards officer bought his civilian clothes in London. Gentlemen's clothes —symbol of "the power that man must hold and that passes from race to race."

We were the most powerful nation. Who could tell us any longer what was fashionable and what was fun? Isolated during the European War, we had begun combing the unknown South and West for folkways and pastimes, and there were more ready to hand.

The first social revelation created a sensation out of all proportion to its novelty. As far back as 1915 the unchaperoned young people of the smaller cities had discovered the mobile privacy of that automobile given to young Bill at sixteen to make him "self-reliant." At first petting was a desperate adventure even under such favorable conditions, but presently confidences were exchanged and the old commandment broke down. As early as 1917 there were references to such sweet and casual dalliance in any number of the *Yale Record* or the *Princeton Tiger*.

But petting in its more audacious manifestations was confined to the wealthier classes—among other people the old standard prevailed until after the War, and a kiss meant that a proposal was expected, as young officers in strange cities sometimes discovered to their dismay. Only in 1920 did the veil finally fall—the Jazz Age was in flower.

Scarcely had the staider citizens of the republic caught their breaths when the wildest of all generations, the generation which had been adolescent during the confusion of the War, brusquely shouldered my contemporaries out of the way and danced into the limelight. This was the generation whose girls dramatized themselves as flappers, the generation that corrupted its elders and eventually overreached itself less through lack of morals than through lack of taste. May one offer in exhibit the year 1922! That was the peak of the younger generation, for though the Jazz Age continued, it became less and less an affair of youth.

The sequel was like a children's party taken over by the elders, leaving the children puzzled and rather neglected and rather taken aback. By 1923 their elders, tired of watching the carnival with ill-concealed envy, had discovered that young liquor will take the place of young blood, and with a whoop the orgy began. The younger generation was starred no longer.

A whole race going hedonistic, deciding on pleasure. The precocious intimacies of the younger generation would have come about with or without prohibition—they were implicit in the attempt to adapt English customs to American conditions. (Our South, for example, is tropical and early maturing—it has never been part of the wisdom of France and Spain to let young girls go unchaperoned at sixteen and seventeen.) But the general decision to be amused that began with the cocktail parties of 1921 had more complicated origins.

The word jazz in its progress toward respectability has meant first sex, then dancing, then music. It is associated with a state of nervous stimulation, not unlike that of big cities behind the lines of a war. To many English the War still goes on because all the forces that menace them are still active—Wherefore eat, drink and be merry, for tomorrow we die. But different causes had now brought about a corresponding state in America—though there were entire classes (people over fifty, for example) who spent a whole decade denying its existence even when its puckish face peered into the family circle. Never did they dream that they had contributed to it. The honest citizens of every class, who believed in a strict public morality and were powerful enough to enforce the necessary legislation, did not know that they would necessarily be served by criminals and quacks, and do not really believe it today. Rich righteousness had always been able to buy honest and intelligent servants to free the slaves or the Cubans, so when this attempt collapsed our elders stood firm with all the stubbornness of people involved in a weak case, preserving their righteousness and losing their children. Silver-haired women and men with fine old faces, people who never did a consciously dishonest thing in their lives, still assure each other in the apartment hotels of New York and Boston and Washington that "there's a whole generation growing up that will never know the taste of liquor." Meanwhile their granddaughters pass the well-thumbed copy of *Lady Chatterley's Lover* around the boarding-school and, if they get about at all, know the taste of gin or corn at sixteen. But the generation who reached maturity between 1875 and 1895 continue to believe what they want to believe.

Even the intervening generations were incredulous. In 1920 Heywood Broun announced that all this hubbub was nonsense, that young men didn't kiss but told anyhow. But very shortly people over twenty-five came in for an intensive education. Let me trace some of the revelations vouchsafed them by reference to a dozen works written for various types of mentality during the decade. We begin with the suggestion that Don Juan leads an interesting life (*Jurgen*, 1919); then we learn that there's a lot of sex around if we only knew it (*Winesburg, Ohio*, 1920), that adolescents lead very amorous lives (*This Side of Paradise*, 1920), that there are a lot of neglected Anglo-Saxon words (*Ulysses*, 1921), that older people don't always resist sudden temptations (*Cytherea*, 1922), that girls are sometimes seduced without being ruined (*Flaming Youth*, 1922), that even rape often turns out well (*The Sheik*, 1922), that glamorous English ladies are often promiscuous (*The Green Hat*, 1924), that in fact they devote most of their time to it (*The Vortex*, 1926), that it's a damn good thing too (*Lady Chatterley's Lover*, 1928), and finally that there are abnormal variations (*The Well of Loneliness*, 1928, and *Sodom and Gomorrah*, 1929).

In my opinion the erotic element in these works, even *The Sheik* written for children in the key of *Peter Rabbit*, did not one particle of harm. Everything they described, and much more, was familiar in our contemporary life. The majority of the theses were honest and elucidating— their effect was to restore some dignity to the male as opposed to the he-man in American life. ("And what is a 'He-man'?" demanded Gertrude Stein one day. "Isn't it a large enough order to fill out to the dimensions of all that 'a man' has meant in the past? A '*He*-man'!") The married woman can now discover whether she is being cheated, or whether sex is just something to be endured, and her compensation should be to establish a tyranny of the spirit, as her mother may have hinted. Perhaps many women found that love was meant to be fun. Anyhow the objectors lost their tawdry little case, which is one reason why our literature is now the most living in the world.

Contrary to popular opinion, the movies of the Jazz Age had no effect upon its morals. The social attitude of the producers was timid, behind the times and banal—for example, no picture mirrored even faintly the younger generation until 1923, when magazines had already been started to celebrate it and it had long ceased to be news. There were a few feeble splutters and then Clara Bow in *Flaming Youth;* promptly the Hollywood hacks ran the theme into its cinematographic grave. Throughout the Jazz Age the movies got no farther than Mrs. Jiggs, keeping up with its most blatant superficialities. This was no doubt due to the censorship as well as to innate conditions in the industry. In any case, the Jazz Age now raced along under its own power, served by great filling stations full of money.

The people over thirty, the people all the way up to fifty, had joined the dance. We graybeards (to tread down F. P. A.) remember the uproar when in 1912 grandmothers of forty tossed away their crutches and took lessons in the Tango and the Castle-Walk. A dozen years later a woman might pack the Green Hat with her other affairs as she set off for Europe or New York, but Savonarola was too busy flogging dead horses in Augean stables of his own creation to notice. Society, even in small cities, now dined in separate chambers, and the sober table learned about the gay table only from hearsay. There were very few people left at the sober table. One of its former glories, the less sought-after girls who had become resigned to sublimating a probable celibacy, came across Freud and Jung in seeking their intellectual recompense and came tearing back into the fray.

By 1926 the universal preoccupation with sex had become a nuisance. (I remember a perfectly mated, contented young mother asking my wife's advice about "having an affair right away," though she had no one especially in mind, "because don't you think it's sort of undignified when you get much over thirty?") For a while bootleg Negro records with their phallic euphemisms made everything suggestive, and simultaneously came a wave of erotic plays—young girls from finishing-schools packed the galleries to hear about the romance of being a Lesbian and George Jean Nathan protested. Then one young producer lost his head entirely, drank a beauty's alcoholic bath-water and went to the penitentiary. Somehow his pathetic attempt at romance belongs to the Jazz Age, while his contemporary in prison, Ruth Snyder, had to be hoisted into it by the tabloids—she was, as *The Daily News* hinted deliciously to gourmets, about "to cook, *and sizzle, AND FRY!*" in the electric chair.

The gay elements of society had divided into two main streams, one flowing toward Palm Beach and Deauville, and the other, much smaller, toward the summer Riviera. One could get away with more on the summer Riviera, and whatever happened seemed to have something to do with art. From 1926 to 1929, the great years of the Cap d'Antibes, this corner of France was dominated by a group quite distinct from that American society which is dominated by Europeans. Pretty much of anything went at Antibes— by 1929, at the most gorgeous paradise for swimmers on the Mediterranean no one swam any more, save for a short hang-over dip at noon. There was a picturesque graduation of steep rocks over the sea and somebody's valet and an occasional English girl used to dive from them, but the Americans were content to discuss each other in the bar. This was indicative of something that was taking place in the homeland—Americans were getting soft. There were signs everywhere: we still won the Olympic games but with champions whose names had few vowels in them—teams composed, like the fighting Irish combination of Notre Dame, of fresh overseas blood. Once the French became really interested, the Davis Cup gravitated automatically to their intensity in competition. The vacant lots of the

Middle-Western cities were built up now—except for a short period in school, we were not turning out to be an athletic people like the British, after all. The hare and the tortoise. Of course if we wanted to we could be in a minute; we still had all those reserves of ancestral vitality, but one day in 1926 we looked down and found we had flabby arms and a fat pot and couldn't say boop-boop-a-doop to a Sicilian. Shades of Van Bibber!—no utopian ideal, God knows. Even golf, once considered an effeminate game, had seemed very strenuous of late—an emasculated form appeared and proved just right.

By 1927 a wide-spread neurosis began to be evident, faintly signalled, like a nervous beating of the feet, by the popularity of cross-word puzzles. I remember a fellow expatriate opening a letter from a mutual friend of ours, urging him to come home and be revitalized by the hardy, bracing qualities of the native soil. It was a strong letter and it affected us both deeply, until we noticed that it was headed from a nerve sanitarium in Pennsylvania.

By this time contemporaries of mine had begun to disappear into the dark maw of violence. A classmate killed his wife and himself on Long Island, another tumbled "accidently" from a skyscraper in Philadelphia, another purposely from a skyscraper in New York. One was killed in a speak-easy in Chicago; another was beaten to death in a speak-easy in New York and crawled home to the Princeton Club to die; still another had his skull crushed by a maniac's axe in an insane asylum where he was confined. These are not catastrophes that I went out of my way to look for—these were my friends; moreover, these things happened not during the depression but during the boom.

In the spring of '27, something bright and alien flashed across the sky. A young Minnesotan who seemed to have had nothing to do with his generation did a heroic thing, and for a moment people set down their glasses in country clubs and speakeasies and thought of their old best dreams.

Maybe there was a way out by flying, maybe our restless blood could find frontiers in the illimitable air. But by that time we were all pretty well committed; and the Jazz Age continued; we would all have one more.

Nevertheless, Americans were wandering ever more widely—friends seemed eternally bound for Russia, Persia, Abyssinia and Central Africa. And by 1928 Paris had grown suffocating. With each new shipment of Americans spewed up by the boom the quality fell off, until toward the end there was something sinister about the crazy boatloads. They were no longer the simple pa and ma and son and daughter, infinitely superior in their qualities of kindness and curiosity to the corresponding class in Europe, but fantastic neanderthals who believed something, something vague, that you remembered from a very cheap novel, I remember an Italian on a steamer who promenaded the deck in an American Reserve Officer's uniform picking quarrels in broken English with Americans who criticised their own institutions in the bar. I remember a fat Jewess, inlaid with diamonds, who sat behind us at the Russian ballet and said as the curtain rose, "Thad's luffly, dey ought to baint a bicture of it." This was low comedy, but it was evident that money and power were falling into the hands of people in comparison with whom the leader of a village Soviet would be a gold-mine of judgment and culture. There were citizens travelling in luxury in 1928 and 1929 who, in the distortion of their new condition, had the human value of Pekinese, bivalves, cretins, goats. I remember the Judge from some New York district who had taken his daughter to see the Bayeux Tapestries and made a scene in the papers advocating their segregation because one scene was immoral. But in those days life was like the race in *Alice in Wonderland*, there was a prize for every one.

The Jazz Age had had a wild youth and a heady middle age. There was the phase of the necking parties, the Leopold-Loeb murder (I remember the time my wife was arrested on Queensborough Bridge on the suspicion of being the "Bob-haired Bandit") and the John Held Clothes. In the second phase such phenomena as sex and murder became more mature, if much more conventional. Middle age must be served and pajamas came to the beach to save fat thighs and flabby calves from competition with the one-piece bathing-suit. Finally skirts came down and everything was concealed. Everybody was at scratch now. Let's go—

But it was not to be. Somebody had blundered and the most expensive orgy in history was over.

It ended two years ago,° because the utter confidence which was its essential prop received an enormous jolt, and it didn't take long for the flimsy structure to settle earthward. And after two years the Jazz Age seems as far away as the days before the War. It was borrowed time anyhow—the whole upper tenth of a nation living with the insouciance of grand ducs and the casualness of chorus girls. But moralizing is easy now and it was pleasant to be in one's twenties in such a certain and unworried time. Even when you were broke you didn't worry about money, because it was in such profusion around you. Toward the end one had a struggle to pay one's share; it was almost a favor to accept hospitality that required any travelling. Charm, notoriety, mere good manners, weighed more than money as a social asset. This was rather splendid, but things were getting thinner and thinner as the eternal necessary human values tried to spread over all that expansion. Writers were geniuses on the strength of one respectable book or play; just as during the War officers of four months' experience commanded hundreds of men, so there were now many little fish lording it over great big bowls. In the theatrical world extravagant productions were carried by a few second-rate stars, and so on up the scale into politics, where it was difficult to interest good men in

° 1929

positions of the highest importance and responsibility, importance and responsibility far exceeding that of business executives but which paid only five or six thousand a year.

Now once more the belt is tight and we summon the proper expression of horror as we look back at our wasted youth. Sometimes, though, there is a ghostly rumble among the drums, an asthmatic whisper in the trombones that swings me back into the early twenties when we drank wood alcohol and every day in every way grew better and better, and there was a first abortive shortening of the skirts, and girls all looked alike in sweater dresses, and people you didn't want to know said "Yes, we have no bananas," and it seemed only a question of a few years before the older people would step aside and let the world be run by those who saw things as they were—and it all seems rosy and romantic to us who were young then, because we will never feel quite so intensely about our surroundings any more.

Alfred North Whitehead (1861-1947)

An Englishman and one of the leading mathematical theorists of the day, he went in 1924 to Harvard, where he was a professor of philosophy until his retirement in 1937. Primarily a mathematical philosopher using symbols as means of expression, he was also fundamentally a religious man, having an almost mystical attitude toward science. To him the discoveries of modern science supplied a basis for regenerative philosophy, but he protested against taking scientific abstractions out of their setting and treating them as if they were antecedent existences defining "reality."

RELIGION AND SCIENCE

The difficulty in approaching the question of the relations
between Religion and Science is, that its elucidation requires that we have in our minds some clear idea of what
we mean by either of the terms, "religion" and "science."
Also I wish to speak in the most general way possible, and
to keep in the background any comparison of particular
creeds, scientific or religious. We have got to understand the
type of connection which exists between the two spheres,
and then to draw some definite conclusions respecting the
existing situation which at present confronts the world.

The *conflict* between religion and science is what naturally occurs to our minds when we think of this subject.
It seems as though, during the last half-century, the results
of science and the beliefs of religion had come into a position of frank disagreement, from which there can be no
escape, except by abandoning either the clear teaching of
science, or the clear teaching of religion. This conclusion
has been urged by controversialists on either side. Not by
all controversialists, of course, but by those trenchant in-
tellects which every controversy calls out into the open.

The distress of sensitive minds, and the zeal for truth, and
the sense of the importance of the issues, must command our
sincerest sympathy. When we consider what religion is
for mankind, and what science is, it is no exaggeration to
say that the future course of history depends upon the decision of this generation as to the relations between them.
We have here the two strongest general forces (apart from
the mere impulse of the various senses) which influence
men, and they seem to be set one against the other—the

force of our religious intuitions, and the force of our impulse to accurate observation and logical deduction.

A great English statesman once advised his countrymen to use large-scale maps, as a preservative against alarms, panics, and general misunderstanding of the true relations between nations. In the same way in dealing with the clash between permanent elements of human nature, it is well to map our history on a large scale, and to disengage ourselves from our immediate absorption in the present conflicts. When we do this, we immediately discover two great facts. In the first place, there has always been a conflict between religion and science; and in the second place, both religion and science have always been in a state of continual development. In the early days of Christianity, there was a general belief among Christians that the world was coming to an end in the lifetime of people then living. We can make only indirect inferences as to how far this belief was authoritatively proclaimed; but it is certain that it was widely held, and that it formed an impressive part of the popular religious doctrine. The belief proved itself to be mistaken, and Christian doctrine adjusted itself to the change. Again in the early Church individual theologians very confidently deduced from the Bible opinions concerning the nature of the physical universe. In the year A.D. 535, a monk named Cosmas wrote a book which he entitled, *Christian Topography*. . . . In this book, basing himself upon the direct meaning of Biblical texts as construed by him in a literal fashion, he denied the existence of the antipodes, and asserted that the world is a flat parallelogram whose length is double its breadth.

In the seventeenth century the doctrine of the motion of the earth was condemned by a Catholic tribunal. A hundred years ago the extension of time demanded by geological science distressed religious people, Protestant and Catholic. And today the doctrine of evolution is an equal stumbling-block. These are only a few instances illustrating a general fact.

But all our ideas will be in a wrong perspective if we think that this recurring perplexity was confined to contradictions between religion and science; and that in these controversies religion was always wrong, and that science was always right. The true facts of the case are very much more complex, and refuse to be summarised in these simple terms. . . .

Science is even more changeable than theology. No man of science could subscribe without qualification to Galileo's beliefs, or to Newton's beliefs, or to all his own scientific beliefs of ten years ago.

In both regions of thought, additions, distinctions, and modifications have been introduced. So that now, even when the same assertion is made today as was made a thousand, or fifteen hundred years ago, it is made subject to limitations or expansions of meaning, which were not contemplated at the earlier epoch. We are told by logicians that a proposition must be either true or false, and that there is no middle term. But in practice, we may know that a proposition expresses an important truth, but that it is subject to limitations and qualifications which at present remain undiscovered. It is a general feature of our knowledge, that we are insistently aware of important truths; and yet that the only formulations of these truths which we are able to make presuppose a general standpoint of conceptions which may have to be modified. . . .

I will give you [an] example taken from the state of modern physical science. Since the time of Newton and Huyghens in the seventeenth century there have been two theories as to the physical nature of light. Newton's theory was that a beam of light consists of a stream of very minute particles, or corpuscles, and that we have the sensation of light when these corpuscles strike the retinas of our eyes. Huyghens' theory was that light consists of very minute waves of trembling in an all-pervading ether, and that these waves are travelling along a beam of light. The two theories are contradictory. In the eighteenth century Newton's theory was believed, in the nineteenth century Huyghens' theory was believed. Today there is one large group of phenomena which can be explained only on the wave theory, and another large group which can be explained only on the corpuscular theory. Scientists have to leave it at that, and wait for the future, in the hope of attaining some wider vision which reconciles both.

We should apply these same principles to the questions in which there is a variance between science and religion. We would believe nothing in either sphere of thought which does not appear to us to be certified by solid reasons based upon the critical research either of ourselves or of competent authorities. But granting that we have honestly taken this precaution, a clash between the two on points of detail where they overlap should not lead us hastily to abandon doctrines for which we have solid evidence. It may be that we are more interested in one set of doctrines than in the other. But, if we have any sense of perspective and of the history of thought, we shall wait and refrain from mutual anathemas.

We should wait: but we should not wait passively, or in despair. The clash is a sign that there are wider truths and finer perspectives within which a reconciliation of a deeper religion and a more subtle science will be found.

In one sense, therefore, the conflict between science and religion is a slight matter which has been unduly emphasised. A mere logical contradiction cannot in itself point to more than the necessity of some readjustments, possibly of a very minor character on both sides. Remember the widely different aspects of events which are dealt with in science and in religion respectively. Science is concerned with the general conditions which are observed to regulate physical phenomena; whereas religion is wholly wrapped up in the contemplation of moral and aesthetic values. On the one side there is the law of gravitation, and on the other the contemplation of the beauty of holiness. What one side sees, the other misses; and vice versa.

Consider, for example, the lives of John Wesley and of Saint Francis of Assisi. For physical science you have in these lives merely ordinary examples of the operation of the principles of physiological chemistry, and of the dynamics of nervous reactions: for religion you have lives of the most profound significance in the history of the world. Can you be surprised that, in the absence of a perfect and complete phrasing of the principles of science and of the principles of religion which apply to these specific cases, the accounts of these lives from these divergent standpoints should involve discrepancies? It would be a miracle if it were not so.

It would, however, be missing the point to think that we need not trouble ourselves about the conflict between science and religion. In an intellectual age there can be no active interest which puts aside all hope of a vision of the harmony of truth. To acquiesce in discrepancy is destructive of candour, and of moral cleanliness. It belongs to the self-respect of intellect to pursue every tangle of thought to its final unravelment. If you check that impulse, you will get no religion and no science from an awakened thoughtfulness. The important question is, In what spirit are we going to face the issue? There we come to something absolutely vital.

A clash of doctrines is not a disaster—it is an opportunity. . . .

In formal logic, a contradiction is the signal of a defeat: but in the evolution of real knowledge it marks the first step in progress towards a victory. This is one great reason for the utmost toleration of variety of opinion. Once and forever, this duty of toleration has been summed up in the words, "Let both grow together until the harvest." The failure of Christians to act up to this precept, of the highest authority, is one of the curiosities of religious history. . . .

For over two centuries religion has been on the defensive, and on a weak defensive. The period has been one of unprecedented intellectual progress. In this way a series of novel situations have been produced for thought. Each such occasion has found the religious thinkers unprepared. Something, which has been proclaimed to be vital, has finally, after struggle, distress, and anathema, been modified and otherwise interpreted. The next generation of religious apologists then congratulates the religious world on the deeper insight which has been gained. The result of the continued repetition of this undignified retreat, during many generations, has at last almost entirely destroyed the intellectual authority of religious thinkers. Consider this contrast: when Darwin or Einstein proclaim theories which modify our ideas, it is a triumph for science. We do not go about saying that there is another defeat for science, because its old ideas have been abandoned. We know that another step of scientific insight has been gained.

Religion will not regain its old power until it can face change in the same spirit as does science. Its principles may be eternal, but the expression of those principles requires continual development. This evolution of religion is in the main a disengagement of its own proper ideas from the adventitious notions which have crept into it by reason of the expression of its own ideas in terms of the imaginative picture of the world entertained in previous ages. Such a release of religion from the bonds of imperfect science is all to the good. It stresses its own genuine message. The great point to be kept in mind is that normally an advance in science will show that statements of various religious beliefs require some sort of modification. It may be that they have to be expanded or explained, or indeed entirely restated. If the religion is a sound expression of truth, this modification will only exhibit more adequately the exact point which is of importance. This process is a gain. In so far, therefore, as any religion has any contact with physical facts, it is to be expected that the point of view of those facts must be continually modified as scientific knowledge advances. In this way, the exact relevance of these facts for religious thought will grow more and more clear. The progress of science must result in the unceasing codification of religious thought, to the great advantage of religion.

Joseph Wood Krutch (1893–   )

Drama critic of the Nation *from 1924 to 1950 and formerly professor of English at Columbia, he has generally taken a pessimistic view of life, literature, and Western civilization as a whole. Though his "gallant despair" has mellowed somewhat during the years, and he no longer believes that the mechanistic, materialistic, and deterministic findings of science have to be accepted as a fact, he still foresees only two rather dismal choices before man. Either he embraces the creed of atheistical existentialism, which is the tragic solution proposed in* The Modern Temper, *or he turns optimistically to social psychology for the creation of a Robot Utopia, "whose well-adjusted citizens will have comfortably forgotten that their forefathers believed themselves to be Men."*

DISILLUSION WITH THE LABORATORY

We went to science in search of light, not merely upon the nature of matter, but upon the nature of man as well, and though that which we have received may be light of a sort, it is not adapted to our eyes and is not anything by which we can see. Since thought began we have groped in the

dark among shadowy shapes, doubtfully aware of land-
marks looming uncertainly here and there—of moral principles, human values, aims, and ideals. We hoped for an
illumination in which they would at last stand clearly and
unmistakably forth, but instead they appear even less certain and less substantial than before—mere fancies and illusions generated by nerve actions that seem terribly remote
from anything we can care about or based upon relativities
that accident can shift. We had been assured that many
troublesome shadows would flee away, that superstitious
fears, irrational repugnances, and all manner of bad dreams
would disappear. And so in truth very many have. But we
never supposed that most of the things we cherished
would prove equally unsubstantial, that all the aims we
thought we vaguely perceived, all the values we pursued,
and all the principles we clung to were but similar shadows, and that either the light of science is somehow deceptive or the universe, emotionally and spiritually, a vast
emptiness.

Hopes are disappointed in strange and unexpected ways.
When first we embrace them we fear, if we fear at all,
some miscarriage in the details of our plan. We are anxious
lest we should not be able to go where we hope to go,
acquire what we hope to own, or gain the distinction we
hope to win. But it is not thus that we are most frequently
or most bitterly disappointed. We accomplish the journeys,
assume the possessions, and receive the distinctions, but
they are not what we thought them, and in the midst of
success it is failure that we taste. It is not the expected
thing but the effect that is lost, the advantages of possession
or the joys of achievement which fail to materialize, in
spite of the fact that it was never at that point that we
feared a failure. And so it has been with modern science.
It has marched from triumph to triumph, winning each
specific victory more completely and more expeditiously
than even its most enthusiastic prophet predicted, but those

specific victories do not bear the fruits expected. Less follows than once seemed inevitable and we are disillusioned with success.

Your scientist, impatient and a little scornful of the speculations, dreams, and fancies which have occupied the man ignorant of the laboratory and its marvels, is inclined to feel sure of his superiority when he insists that it is with *realities* that he deals; but it may be that by that statement he is destroying himself, since the contact of the human mind with reality is so slight that two thousand years of epistemology have not been able to decide exactly what the nexus is, and it is easier to argue that our consciousness exists in utter isolation than to prove that it is actually aware of the external phenomena by which it is surrounded. Nor need we, in order to demonstrate this fact, confine ourselves to the consideration of such intangible things as those which have just been discussed, since the physical world of which we are aware through the senses is almost equally remote from that which the laboratory reveals.

The table before which we sit may be, as the scientist maintains, composed of dancing atoms, but it does not reveal itself to us as anything of the kind, and it is not with dancing atoms but a solid and motionless object that we live. So remote is this "real" table—and most of the other "realities" with which science deals—that it cannot be discussed in terms which have any human value, and though it may receive our purely intellectual credence it cannot be woven into the pattern of life as it is led, in contradistinction to life as we attempt to think about it. Vibrations in the ether are so totally unlike, let us say, the color purple that the gulf between them cannot be bridged, and they are, to all intents and purposes, not one but two separate things of which the second and less "real" must be the most significant for us. And just as the sensation which has led us to attribute an objective reality to a nonexistent thing which we call "purple" is more important for human life than the conception of vibrations of a certain frequency, so too the belief in God, however ill founded, has been more important in the life of man than the germ theory of decay, however true the latter may be.

We may, if we like, speak in consequence, as certain mystics love to do, of the different levels or orders of truth. We may adopt what is essentially a Platonistic trick of thought and insist upon postulating the existence of external realities which correspond to the needs and modes of human feeling and which, so we may insist, have their being in some part of the universe unreachable by science. But to do so is to make an unwarrantable assumption and to be guilty of the metaphysical fallacy of failing to distinguish between a truth of feeling and that other sort of truth which is described as a "truth of correspondence," and it is better perhaps, at least for those of us who have grown up in an age of scientific thought, to steer clear of such confusions and to rest content with the admission that, though the universe with which science deals is the real universe, yet we do not and cannot have any but fleeting and imperfect contacts with it; that the most important part of our lives—our sensations, emotions, desires, and aspirations—takes place in a universe of illusions which science can attenuate or destroy, but which it is powerless to enrich.

But once we have made that admission we must guard ourselves against the assumption, hastily embraced by those who make the admission too gladly, that we have thereby liberated ourselves from all bondage to mere fact and freed the human spirit so that it may develop in its own way. The human world is not completely detached and autonomous. Since mind can function only through body, the one world is interpenetrated by the other. The two clash from time to time, and when they do so it is always the solider which must prevail, so that we dare not attempt to deny its existence. The world which our minds have created to meet our desires and our needs exists precariously and on sufferance; it is shadowy and insubstantial for the very reason that there is nothing outside itself to correspond with it, and hence it must always be fragile and imperfect.

Science, to be sure, has sometimes imagined a wholly scientific man of the future, and the more thoroughgoing sort of scientist has sometimes predicted that the time would come when the world of the human mind would be precisely the world of the laboratory and nothing more. Conceiving a daily life far more thoroughly mechanized than that of today—of a society that sped through the air at incredible speed, that took its nourishment in the form of concentrated pellets, and generated its children from selected seeds in an annealed glass womb—he has imagined a man possessed of a soul fit for such surroundings. To him the needs and emotions referred to in this essay as distinctly human are merely troublesome anachronisms destined to pass away when we have accustomed ourselves more completely to things as they are, and it is our business to get rid of them as rapidly as possible in order to hasten the coming of the happy being to whom the roar of wheels will be the sweetest melody and a laboratory the only tabernacle for which he feels any need.

But it must be remembered that before such a creature could come into being changes more fundamental than are sometimes imagined would have to take place, since, even if we confine our attention to his physical surroundings only, he would have to be one who lived no longer, as all of us do, in the world of appearances, but one for whom vibrations were more real than colors because the spectroscope and the interferometer were more natural than the eye. For him the table in its most intimate aspect would have to be a swarm of dancing atoms, and not only all the art but all the thought and feeling of past humanity alien nonsense. We could understand him no more than we now understand the ant on the one hand or the dynamo on the other, and he would feel no kinship with us. And hence, though we may admit the possibility that the future belongs to him, we cannot feel any delight in it or make its possessor any concern of ours. It is to our humanity that we cling, because it is the thing which we recognize as ourselves, and if it is lost, then all that counts for us is lost with it.

What we have come to realize, then, is that the scientific optimism of which Huxley may be taken as a typical exponent was merely a new variety of faith, resting upon certain premises which are no more unassailable than those which have supported other vanished religions of the past. It has as its central dogma the assumption that truths (of correspondence) were necessarily useful, and that the human spirit flowered best in the midst of realities clearly perceived. After the manner of all religions, it instinctively refrained from any criticism of this essential dogma, and it was left to us in an age troubled by a new agnosticism to perceive how far this first article of the scientific creed is from being self-evidently true. Experience has taught us that the method of the laboratory has its limitation and that the accumulation of scientific data is not, in the case of all subjects, useful. We have learned how certain truths—intimate revelations concerning the origin and mechanism of our deepest impulses—can stagger our souls, and how a clear perception of our lonely isolation in the midst of a universe which knows nothing of us and our aspirations paralyzes our will. We are aware, too, of the fact that art and ethics have not flowered anew in the light, that we have not won a newer and more joyous acceptance of the universe, and we have come to realize that the more we learn of the laws of that universe—in which we constitute a strange incongruity—the less we shall feel at home in it.

Each new revelation fascinates us. We would not, even if we dared, remain ignorant of anything which we can learn, but with each new revelation we perceive so much the more clearly that half—perhaps the most important half—of all we are and desire to be can find no comfort or support in such knowledge, that it is useless to seek for correspondences between our inner world and the outer one when we know that no such correspondences exist. Many of the things which we value most have a relation to external nature no more intimate than the relation of purple to vibrations of the ether, and the existence of such a relation can never be to us more than an academic fact. We are disillusioned with the laboratory, not because we have lost faith in the power of those findings but because we have lost faith in the power of those findings to help us as generally as we had once hoped they might help. . . .

Nor is there any reason why we should fail to realize the fact that the acceptance of such despair as must inevitably be ours does not, after all, involve a misery so acute as that which many have been compelled to endure. Terror can be blacker than that and so can the extremes of physical want and pain. The most human human being has still more of the animal than of anything else and no love of rhetoric should betray one into seeming to deny that he who has escaped animal pain has escaped much. Despair of the sort which has here been described is a luxury in the sense that it is possible only to those who have much that many people do without, and philosophical pessimism, dry as it may leave the soul, is more easily endured than hunger or cold.

Leaving the future to those who have faith in it, we may survey our world and, if we bear in mind the facts just stated, we may permit ourselves to exclaim, a little rhetorically perhaps,

> Hail, horrors, hail,
> Infernal world! and thou profoundest hell,
> Receive thy new possessor.

If Humanism and Nature are fundamentally antithetical, if the human virtues have a definite limit set to their development, and if they may be cultivated only by a process which renders us progressively unfit to fulfill our biological duties,

then we may at least permit ourselves a certain defiant satisfaction when we realize that we have made our choice
and that we are resolved to abide by the consequences.
Some small part of the tragic fallacy may be said indeed to
be still valid for us, for if we cannot feel ourselves great
as Shakespeare did, if we no longer believe in either our
infinite capacities or our importance to the universe, we
know at least that we have discovered the trick which has
been played upon us and that whatever else we may be we
are no longer dupes.

Rejuvenation may be offered to us at a certain price.
Nature, issuing her last warning, may bid us embrace
some new illusion before it is too late and accord ourselves once more with her. But we prefer rather to fail in
our own way than to succeed in hers. Our human world may
have no existence outside of our own desires, but those
are more imperious than anything else we know, and we will
cling to our own lost cause, choosing always rather to know
than to be. Doubtless fresh people have still a long way
to go with Nature before they are compelled to realize
that they too have come to the parting of the ways, but
though we may wish them well we do not envy them. If
death for us and our kind is the inevitable result of our
stubbornness then we can only say, "So be it." Ours is a
lost cause and there is no place for us in the natural universe, but we are not, for all that, sorry to be human. We
should rather die as men than live as animals.

Harry F. Ward (1873-   )

*An ordained minister, he was regarded as the
"stormy petrel of Methodism." From his "stock-
yards" church in Chicago he served as executive
secretary of the Methodist Federation for Social
Service, and the later shift of Federation per-*

spective from a prewar emphasis upon social
service and reform to an outright opposition to
capitalism was his doing. Although he deplored
class conflict and espoused the social gospel as
a means of avoiding it, as head of the American
Civil Liberties Union in the twenties he defended
the political rights of Communist leaders. Unable
to surrender his idealism as had many other dis-
appointed Progressives, he embraced the utopian
vision of Marxism. Yet, despite his seem-
ingly uncompromising anti-capitalistic po-
sition, his social views in the end rested upon
a pure abstract revivalism.

A NEW SOCIAL ORDER

So far in our industrial society, efficiency has been interpreted too exclusively in terms of wealth production, and
the danger is that it will be so interpreted. To offset this
is the fact that many educators and social workers are
strenuously endeavoring to give social efficiency its real
content, to take it far beyond the field of wealth production into the wider ranges of human living. They are facing the question of the end of human living in order that
the means of life may be truly determined. They are asking
not only in what respects, but for what purpose, is humanity
to be efficient.

That, of course, is one of the old questions of philosophy,
both for individual and social living; but as the world
life becomes organized in such a way that humanity can
in fellowship choose its ends and work toward them, this
question of philosophy becomes a very practical issue for
the common people. The question of what the social organization is driving at is, after all, a very concrete question. Here is a scientific, mechanical age trying its best to

From *The New Social Order* (New York: The Macmillan Company, 1922), pp.
131-2, 135-8, 146-9, 151-3. Reprinted by permission of the author.

get its machinery adapted to certain immediate ends with the utmost possible perfection, without any general vision of the final end of human endeavor. So that after all the toil and struggle of social organization, the spirit of humanity remains unsatisfied and often defeated. In the most advanced communities there is still much cynicism and not a little despondency. . . .

Unless this state of affairs can be changed, history moves on to its supreme tragedy: the development of all the resources of knowledge and all the powers of civilization and their application to no other than material needs and sensuous enjoyments on the part of the majority of the people. Either humanity must find a higher goal than that for its energy, or perish, either from the diseases developed by the indulgence of its appetites or from the conflicts incident to such a mode of life. . . .

If, to the average person who does not know much about science or history or philosophy, the question is put, "What is the most valuable thing in the universe for you?" in what terms will the answer be likely to come? Will it not be in terms of personality? If it happens to be a particularly self-centered person it may possibly be in terms of their own existence, but for the ordinary run of persons it will be some other person or persons who hold for them the supreme values of life by ties of kinship or the choice of a supreme affection; some other person or persons for whom they are perfectly willing at any time to lose their own life. On the train quite constantly I see traveling men pull out their watches and in a big majority of cases there is a photograph of a person or a family group on the inside of the case, and that picture is their answer to the question of supreme values. As life enlarges its interests and associations the estimate of value in terms of personality is made in group forms; men value the family more than themselves, the state more than their family, and humanity above the state, because these groupings are really an enlargement of personality, with the power to increase its values.

If the question of supreme values is put to human institutions, the answer comes also in terms of personality. Ask the state and the school and the church what they are trying to do, and they will tell you they are trying to develop people; their end is to produce a certain type of individual and a certain kind of associated living. One of the greatest words of philosophy is that no human being must ever be treated as a means, but always as an end. The greatest teacher of religion asks, "What shall it profit a man if he gain the whole world and lose his own soul,"— that is, destroy his own personality? He declares: "I am come that they may have life; and that they may have it more abundantly."

Without the key of the meaning and value of personality, the universe is an insoluble riddle and man sinks into despair. With that key in his possession, he becomes, if need be, independent of the physical universe. For the development of personality in time and space, of course, he depends upon the environment of nature; but if he so will, he can defy the world, he can blow it to pieces about his head and with his body smashed to fragments go out into the future in a supreme assertion of himself.

It does not lie within our present purpose to define personality, but simply to point out that the new order must recognize and attempt to realize its supreme worth and value. It must be said, however, that personality is increasingly defined in social terms, its values are discovered and realized in fellowship. We shall be able to add a great deal to what the philosophers have told us about personality by experimentally discovering in social action what personality may become. If there is a greater sense of the dignity and worth of the common run of people today than there was a thousand years ago, it is due to the fact that improvements in social organization have developed and actually realized greater values in the common run of people. Thus the process of social development continually defines and enlarges the nature of personality. It becomes increasingly clear that the meaning and end of individual life and of social living is reciprocal and inter-dependent; that each feeds upon, enlarges and completes the other. The more the individual values the community, the more he contributes to it, and thereby enlarges his own life; the higher the community regards its constituent members, the more it provides for their development, the stronger and richer is its own life.

It follows, therefore, that the new order must seek for its chosen end and goal the development of personality. The things of the spirit and not material goods must be the ultimate and supreme object of its endeavor. This is not simply idealism, not merely a question of imagining, wishing and choosing a high goal; it is also a question of understanding the trend and direction of the evolutionary social process, of accepting and working with it. The social order is not spiritualized by injecting something into it, but rather by discovering what are its inherent spiritual values and then consciously developing them. This is the process of ethical and spiritual development for the individual. As he comes to consciousness he chooses certain values, he embraces certain ends; thus his understanding of life becomes moral and his actions religious. . . .

Institutions ought to be reverenced in so far as they serve to develop persons, and so make for the progress of society. They have a right to loyalty in the proportion to which they do these things. But the test must always be the extent to which they serve the life of all the people and not simply the degree to which they benefit those who belong to them. We ought not to wait to criticise our institutions until they begin to limit us, we ought to criticise them whenever it appears to us that they are in any degree limiting the development of personality anywhere. In other words, our institutions must be always a means and not ever an end; and they must always be a means to the general good, not merely to the good of a few. If they are the means to develop the social whole, they will then be an instrument for the development of the personality of those who compose them, giving these persons their proper social expression and function. The principle is this then, that men must serve institutions only in order that institutions may serve men. Personality must ever maintain itself supreme over the machinery it has created, lest in these latter days, imagining itself free from all false gods, it may unknowingly bind itself once again in utter bondage to the work of its own hands.

If institutions are to be tested by what they do to persons, if they exist for people and not people for them, then a state that permits a privileged few to live off the people is like some great Minotaur devouring their lives, it is a state against which the people must rebel. The state does that when it is the organization of a military autocracy; it equally does it when it is the organization of an economic autocracy. This generation has concluded that the autocratic state, demanding the sacrifice of the people, putting itself beyond morals and above God, is an outrageous blasphemy against human personality. But what about the tyranny of a majority in the democratic state? Should it repress and coerce dissenters? May not that too, become such a repression of personality as to be a violation of the individual and therefore an offense against the common good? If there is one thing above any other which the English people have contributed to the progress of humanity, it is their tradition of respect and reverence for individual rights, for the sacredness of persons, even of the meanest and lowest. It is the tradition of the English state that their voice may be heard, their rights and liberties protected. But that tradition is in danger, in the development of democracy. It is in danger in the increase of our social organization. The spirit of democracy may be threatened by mere bureaucratic routine. The state may become such a great cumbersome machine that persons are tied to the wheels, even ground up in it. The democratic state, even under the development of economic democracy, may become nothing but bureaucratic industrialism in which, in rigidly ordered routine, the people go through their monotonous lives. The problem is to make cooperation increase freedom. It is the province of democracy to enlarge personality. This is accomplished only when the people voluntarily give their best endeavor to the collective life. Such a condition is not yet even approximately approached in our industrial civilization. The test for the church and for educational organization, just as much as for industry, is whether it is leading the people into a larger life through its machinery or merely driving them into a lock step treadmill of routine. If the other social institutions are to fully promote personality, it is necessary for the institutions of education and religion to show the way. Those who operate them must see that they are given a continuous opportunity for the expression and development of their personality, that they do not become mere routine workers going through the same mechanical operations day after day like those who attend an automatic machine in a factory. They must see to it that these institutions reverence human life as a whole and that all their operations tend to develop human life as a whole. The meaning and value of church and state and school can be seen and measured in the last and lowest child within the sphere of their influence. By what they do to it; by whether they leave it neglected and dirty, weak and uneducated, or whether they give it care and protection and continuous unfolding, do they stand judged. This is the final test.

The urgent consideration for an industrial civilization is that personality must not be sacrificed to property, for in an industrial order, property becomes the major interest and increasingly determines the character and course of all the associations and institutions of life. In these days personality has to assert itself most of all in the conflict with property.

Harry F. Ward

Our forefathers fought against institutions, both church and state, and well they fought for human freedom. Our fight is mainly against property, but not against property for its own sake, only in so far as it limits personality. The task before us is to establish the supremacy of personality in a civilization that is largely given over to materialism. The present order is a machine order and has produced a mechanistic mode of thought which has overlooked some of the essential factors and problems of life. The nineteenth century has been called the wonderful century because of its discoveries and inventions, but it left us the same social evils that troubled Babylon and Nineveh. Because it centered human energy upon the production and acquisition of material wealth, because, as Bertrand Russell has pointed out, it enlarged the possessive at the expense of the creative instinct, it raised in more crucial form than ever the old question of the choice between God and Mammon. With all its gains in knowledge, its social organization predominantly expressed a philosophy of life which has no outlook and no outreach beyond the things of time and space. It failed to organize civilization around the infinite, measureless possibilities of human life.

The question which man has to face today is whether in his great industrial civilization, he has made first a machine to enslave him and then a God to devour him. The plain fact that property enslaves people is every day to be seen. It enslaves both those who have it and those who have it not, and it is an open question which of them are more thrown into bondage by the increased concentration of property ownership. Property is today the goal of the strong and its possession is the sign of power. In the old order, property in land went to the strong in arms; in the modern order, property in capital goes to the strong of brain. On the one hand are many wage slaves, and the phrase is not rhetorical, held in bondage to the institution of property; on the other hand the owners of that property are also bound in chains, almost as strong, to the things which they own. The struggle for "these things," land in the old order and capital in the new, is not for property's sake, but for the sake of the domination over others that property gives. The miser is a rare bird, the capitalist a numerous species. The acquisitive instinct becomes socially dangerous as it is allied with and strengthens the instinct for dominance, which finally becomes a more consuming God than the passion to hoard. Man becomes a predatory being, not for the sake of gorging upon the possessions of others, nor to wantonly destroy them, but in order to exert control over others. Competitive industrialism is a struggle for power just as was militarism and is therefore likely to renew that ancient evil. . . .

There is another ideal of civilization which never got expression in wide organizations; it is contained in the teachings of the Hebrew law, the prophets and Jesus. Their ideal was to form a community life in which human rights were set above property rights, and property was made subordinate to the development of personality. The day has now come for the widespread organization of that scale of values. Mankind is about to value the creator of social values above the possessor, and to organize that valuation into social arrangements. The principles which the Hebrews have taken with them all over the earth, which the Christian teaching in its true form has still further developed, are sooner or later going to get a world-wide expression. . . .

The western world is about to make important changes in the institution of human property in order to secure a larger measure of freedom for all the people. The changes must go deeper than a wider distribution of income and a democratic control of the sources of income, both of which are needed for the enlargement of personality. They must rest upon the social control of the acquisitive instinct, for the failure to control this instinct, and not any external system or class is the real cause of the subordination of the people to property interests. What is needed is a true conception of the relation of property to personality. It is perfectly possible, in emancipating the working class in one form from the institution of property to enslave them to it in another, as the property class is now enslaved. From the bondage of improper production they may pass to the bondage of improper consumption. Mankind has yet to learn how to make property the servant and not the master of life. The beginning of the lesson is the fundamental principle that things are to be sought not for their own sake, not for self-gratification and power over others, but for common use and service. The problem of controlling the acquisitive instinct is to be solved by devising those measures which shall express the principle: "property for use and not for power." When production is organized for this purpose, and distribution democratically controlled to this end, then property in its creation will express personality and in its possession will develop personality, both individually and socially. Not until we accept this principle of common use and service, with whatever modifications are necessary to protect individuality, do things become the means to the development of personality. An economic order exists to produce wealth not for wealth's sake, but for the upbuilding of the people. To that end, and in whatever forms will best promote it, wealth production and wealth ownership and distribution must be socialized; they must be carried on for the common good. When they are carried on for the individual good their effect is always to break down and finally overthrow the standard of the supremacy of personality. But when they are safeguarded by common control for the common purpose, society comes to value creation above acquisition, the economic machinery is adjusted to produce life, and goods only as they increase life. Then the increase of personality becomes the supreme objective of social organization while property falls into its proper place as the base upon which man stands to derive from it the nourishment for his spiritual development.

Reinhold Niebuhr (1892–   )

*Born in a little backwoods town in Missouri, he
became perhaps the most intellectually sophisticated of American theologians. Ordained a
Lutheran minister in 1915, he started out in
Detroit where his Socialist views and reformist
zeal made him unpopular with employers.
Between 1919 and 1938 his experience led him to
reject almost all the liberal theological views
with which he had begun. In his opinion
modern liberals had been led astray by a too
optimistic interpretation of human nature and,
for this reason, had been unable to cope with
their immediate problems, much less with
ultimate religious problems. Advocating a return
to basic Christian orthodoxy, he contended that
religion, in order to survive, must extricate itself
from the prejudices and illusions of a sinking
culture.*

MORAL MAN
AND IMMORAL SOCIETY

Though human society has roots which lie deeper in history than the beginning of human life, men have made
comparatively but little progress in solving the problem of
their aggregate existence. Each century originates a new
complexity and each new generation faces a new vexation
in it. For all the centuries of experience, men have not
yet learned how to live together without compounding their

Reprinted with the permission of Charles Scribner's Sons from pages 1–7, 8–9,
and 79–81 of *Moral Man and Immoral Society* by Reinhold Niebuhr. Copyright
1932 Charles Scribner's Sons; renewal copyright © 1960 Reinhold Niebuhr. British
rights by permission of SCM Press, Ltd.

vices and covering each other "with mud and with blood." The society in which each man lives is at once the basis for, and the nemesis of, that fulness of life which each man seeks. However much human ingenuity may increase the treasures which nature provides for the satisfaction of human needs, they can never be sufficient to satisfy all human wants; for man, unlike other creatures, is gifted and cursed with an imagination which extends his appetites beyond the requirements of subsistence. Human society will never escape the problem of the equitable distribution of the physical and cultural goods which provide for the preservation and fulfillment of human life.

Unfortunately the conquest of nature, and the consequent increase in nature's beneficences to man, have not eased, but rather accentuated, the problem of justice. The same technology, which drew the fangs of nature's enmity of man, also created a society in which the intensity and extent of social cohesion has been greatly increased, and in which power is so unevenly distributed, that justice has become a more difficult achievement. Perhaps it is man's sorry fate, suffering from ills which have their source in the inadequacies of both nature and human society, that the tools by which he eliminates the former should become the means of increasing the latter. That, at least, has been his fate up to the present hour; and it may be that there will be no salvation for the human spirit from the more and more painful burdens of social injustice until the ominous tendency in human history has resulted in perfect tragedy.

Human nature is not wanting in certain endowments for the solution of the problem of human society. Man is endowed by nature with organic relations to his fellow-men; and natural impulse prompts him to consider the needs of others even when they compete with his own. With the higher mammals man shares concern for his offspring; and the long infancy of the child created the basis for an organic social group in the earliest period of human history.

Gradually intelligence, imagination, and the necessities of social conflict increased the size of this group. Natural impulse was refined and extended until a less obvious type of consanguinity than an immediate family relationship could be made the basis of social solidarity. Since those early days the units of human co-operation have constantly grown in size, and the areas of significant relationships between the units have likewise increased. Nevertheless conflict between the national units remains as a permanent rather than a passing characteristic of their relations to each other; and each national unit finds it increasingly difficult to maintain either peace or justice within its common life.

While it is possible for intelligence to increase the range of benevolent impulse, and thus prompt a human being to consider the needs and rights of other than those to whom he is bound by organic and physical relationship, there are definite limits in the capacity of ordinary mortals which makes it impossible for them to grant to others what they claim for themselves. Though educators ever since the eighteenth century have given themselves to the fond illusion that justice through voluntary co-operation waited only upon a more universal or a more adequate educational enterprise, there is good reason to believe that the sentiments of benevolence and social goodwill will never be so pure or powerful, and the rational capacity to consider the rights and needs of others in fair competition with our own will never be so fully developed as to create the possibility for the anarchistic millennium which is the social utopia, either explicit or implicit, of all intellectual or religious moralists.

All social co-operation on a larger scale than the most intimate social group requires a measure of coercion. While no state can maintain its unity purely by coercion neither can it preserve itself without coercion. Where the factor of mutual consent is strongly developed, and where standardised and approximately fair methods of adjudicating and resolving conflicting interests within an organised group have been established, the coercive factor in social life is frequently covert, and becomes apparent only in moments of crisis and in the group's policy toward recalcitrant individuals. Yet it is never absent. Divergence of interest, based upon geographic and functional differences within a society, is bound to create different social philosophies and political attitudes which goodwill and intelligence may partly, but never completely, harmonise. Ultimately, unity within an organised social group, or within a federation of such groups, is created by the ability of a dominant group to impose its will. Politics will, to the end of history, be an area where conscience and power meet, where the ethical and coercive factors of human life will interpenetrate and work out their tentative and uneasy compromises. The democratic method of resolving social conflict, which some romanticists hail as a triumph of the ethical over the coercive factor, is really much more coercive than at first seems apparent. The majority has its way, not because the minority believes that the majority is right (few minorities are willing to grant the majority the moral prestige of such a concession), but because the votes of the majority are a symbol of its social strength. Whenever a minority believes that it has some strategic advantage which outweighs the power of numbers, and whenever it is sufficiently intent upon its ends, or desperate enough about its position in society, it refuses to accept the dictates of the majority. Military and economic overlords and revolutionary zealots have been traditionally contemptuous of the will of majorities. Recently Trotsky advised the German communists not to be dismayed by the greater voting strength of the fascists since in the inevitable revolution the power of industrial workers, in charge of the nation's industrial process, would be found much more significant than the social power of clerks and other petty bourgeoisie who comprised the fascist movement.

There are, no doubt, rational and ethical factors in the democratic process. Contending social forces presumably use the forum rather than the battleground to arbitrate their differences in the democratic method, and thus differences are resolved by moral suasion and a rational adjustment of rights to rights. If political issues were really abstract questions of social policy upon which unbiased citizens were asked to commit themselves, the business of voting and the debate which precedes the election might actually be regarded as an educational programme in which a social group discovers its common mind. But the fact is that political opinions are inevitably rooted in economic interests of some kind or other, and only comparatively few citizens can view a problem of social policy without regard to their interest. Conflicting interests therefore can never be completely resolved; and minorities will yield only because the majority has come into control of the police power of the state and may, if the occasion arises, augment that power by its own military strength. Should a minority regard its own strength, whether economic or martial, as strong enough to challenge the power of the majority, it may attempt to wrest control of the state apparatus from the majority, as in the case of the fascist movement in Italy. Sometimes it will resort to armed conflict, even if the prospects of victory are none too bright, as in the instance of the American Civil War, in which the Southern planting interests, outvoted by a combination of Eastern industrialists and Western agrarians, resolved to protect their peculiar interests and privileges by a forceful dissolution of the national union. The coercive factor is, in other words, always present in politics. If economic interests do not conflict too sharply, if the spirit of accommodation partially resolves them, and if the democratic process has achieved moral prestige and historic dignity, the coercive factor in politics may become too covert to be visible to the casual observer. Nevertheless, only a romanticist of the purest water could maintain that a national group ever arrives at a "common mind" or becomes conscious of a "general will" without the use of

either force or the threat of force. This is particularly true
of nations, but it is also true, though in a slighter degree,
of other social groups. Even religious communities, if they
are sufficiently large, and if they deal with issues regarded
as vital by their members, resort to coercion to preserve
their unity. Religious organisations have usually availed
themselves of a covert type of coercion (excommunication
and the interdict) or they have called upon the police
power of the state.

The limitations of the human mind and imagination,
the inability of human beings to transcend their own interests sufficiently to envisage the interests of their fellow-
men as clearly as they do their own makes force an inevitable part of the process of social cohesion. But the
same force which guarantees peace also makes for injustice. "Power," said Henry Adams, "is poison"; and it
is a poison which blinds the eyes of moral insight and lames
the will of moral purpose. The individual or the group
which organises any society, however social its intentions
or pretensions, arrogates an inordinate portion of social
privilege to itself. . . . Any kind of significant social power
develops social inequality. Even if history is viewed from
other than equalitarian perspectives, and it is granted that
differentials in economic rewards are morally justified and
socially useful, it is impossible to justify the degree of inequality which complex societies inevitably create by the
increased centralisation of power which develops with more
elaborate civilisations. The literature of all ages is filled
with rational and moral justifications of these inequalities,
but most of them are specious. If superior abilities and services to society deserve special rewards it may be regarded
as axiomatic that the rewards are always higher than the
services warrant. No impartial society determines the rewards. The men of power who control society grant these
perquisites to themselves. Whenever special ability is not
associated with power, as in the case of the modern professional man, his excess of income over the average is

ridiculously low in comparison with that of the economic overlords, who are the real centres of power in an industrial society. Most rational and social justifications of unequal privilege are clearly afterthoughts. The facts are created by the disproportion of power which exists in a given social system. The justifications are usually dictated by the desire of the men of power to hide the nakedness of their greed, and by the inclination of society itself to veil the brutal facts of human life from itself. This is a rather pathetic but understandable inclination; since the facts of man's collective life easily rob the average individual of confidence in the human enterprise. The inevitable hypocrisy, which is associated with all of the collective activities of the human race, springs chiefly from this source: that individuals have a moral code which makes the actions of collective man an outrage to their conscience. They therefore invent romantic and moral interpretations of the real facts, preferring to obscure rather than reveal the true character of their collective behavior. Sometimes they are as anxious to offer moral justifications for the brutalities from which they suffer as for those which they commit. The fact that the hypocrisy of man's group behavior . . . expresses itself not only in terms of self-justification but in terms of moral justification of human behavior in general, symbolises one of the tragedies of the human spirit: its inability to conform its collective life to its individual ideals. As individuals, men believe that they ought to love and serve each other and establish justice between each other. As racial, economic and national groups they take for themselves, whatever their power can command. . . .

The evolutionary optimism of the eighteenth and nineteenth century, and the sentimentalisation of the moral and social problem in romanticism, have affected religious idealism with particular force in America, because they suited the mood of a youthful and vigorous people, youth usually being oblivious of the brutality which is the inevitable concomitant of vitality. Furthermore the expanding economy of America obscured the cruelties of the class struggle in our economic life, and the comparative isolation of a continent made the brutalities of international conflict less obvious. Thus we developed a type of religious idealism, which is saturated with sentimentality. In spite of the disillusionment of the World War, the average liberal Protestant Christian is still convinced that the kingdom of God is gradually approaching, that the League of Nations is its partial fulfillment and the Kellogg Pact its covenant, that the wealthy will be persuaded by the church to dedicate their power and privilege to the common good and that they are doing so in increasing numbers, that the conversion of individuals is the only safe method of solving the social problem, and that such ethical weaknesses as religion still betrays are due to its theological obscurantism which will be sloughed off by the progress of enlightenment.

It might be added that when the cruelties of economic and political life are thus obscured, and when the inertia, which every effort toward social justice must meet in any society, however religious or enlightened, remains unrecognised, there is always a note of hypocrisy, as well as sentimentality, in the total view. Those who benefit from social injustice are naturally less capable of understanding its real character then those who suffer from it. They will attribute ethical qualities to social life, if only the slightest gesture of philanthropy hides social injustice. If the disinherited treat these gestures with cynicism and interpret unconscious sentimentality as conscious hypocrisy, the privileged will be properly outraged and offended by the moral perversity of the recipients of their beneficences. Since liberal Protestantism is, on the whole, the religion of the privileged classes of Western civilization, it is not surprising that its espousal of the ideal of love, in a civilisation reeking with social injustice, should be cynically judged and convicted of hypocrisy by those in whom bitter social experiences destroy the sentimentalities and illusions of the comfortable.

Religion, in short, faces many perils to the right and to

the left in becoming an instrument and inspiration of social justice. Every genuine passion for social justice will always contain a religious element within it. Religion will always leaven the idea of justice with the ideal of love. It will prevent the idea of justice, which is a politico-ethical ideal, from becoming a purely political one, with the ethical element washed out. The ethical ideal which threatens to become too purely religious must save the ethical ideal which is in peril of becoming too political. Furthermore there must always be a religious element in the hope of a just society. Without the ultrarational hopes and passions of religion no society will ever have the courage to conquer despair and attempt the impossible; for the vision of a just society is an impossible one, which can be approximated only by those who do not regard it as impossible. The truest visions of religion are illusions, which may be partially realised by being resolutely believed. For what religion believes to be true is not wholly true but ought to be true; and may become true if its truth is not doubted.

Yet the full force of religious faith will never be available for the building of a just society, because its highest visions are those which proceed from the insights of a sensitive individual conscience. If they are realised at all, they will be realised in intimate religious communities, in which individual ideals achieve social realisation but do not conquer society. To the sensitive spirit, society must always remain something of the jungle, which indeed it is, something of the world of nature, which might be brought a little nearer the kingdom of God, if only the sensitive spirit could learn, how to use the forces of nature to defeat nature, how to use force in order to establish justice. Knowing the peril of corruption in this strategy, the religious spirit recoils. If that fear can be overcome religious ideals may yet achieve social and political significance.

influence was thrown on the side of unneutrality and war—was still exhibiting timidity and voicing qualms, but the Progressive party was already committed to the defense of national honor, preparedness, and Americanism. By 1916, wrote William Leuchtenburg, "imperialism and militarism had replaced the old liberal formulas of protest, and within a year the party was dead." Likewise, Wilsonian liberals, who with their leader had been "too proud to fight," soon enlisted en masse and turned their sneers on the "snobbish neutrality, colossal conceit, crooked thinking," and "dazed sensibilities" of those few liberals who still opposed United States entry into the war. What is more, the war was justified before the American people, as Hofstadter said, "in the Progressive rhetoric and on Progressive terms."[1]

When war clouds threatened again in the 1930's, the liberals were once more in the vanguard. With the outbreak of civil war in Spain, it was the liberals—John Dewey, I. F. Stone, Lewis Mumford, Max Lerner, Malcolm Cowley, and hundreds of others—who first abandoned isolationism and demanded an end to neutrality. Later, when war spread to the whole of Europe, it was those same liberals who earlier, with a most knowing air, had applauded Senator Nye's investigation of the munitions traffic with its sensational revelations of the huge profits made by "the merchants of death" who now reversed themselves and called loudly for war. Archibald MacLeish, whose sarcastic account of the cynical machinations of the munition dealers in *Fortune* (March, 1934) won praise from the *New Republic* as an impassioned plea for peace, turned about in 1940 and excoriated fellow intellectuals for their failure to defend either themselves or the world by which they lived. Similarly, the *New Republic*, which had viciously denounced armament makers as "buzzards" and "hucksters of death" creating wars to sell guns, also had a change of heart and demanded an immediate declaration of war by the United States. As in 1917 it was the liberal leader President Wilson who guided the nation into war, so in the thirties President Roosevelt led the way. While ex-President Hoover spoke out resolutely against war, Roosevelt brought the country ever closer to conflict: in 1937 proposing a "quarantine" of aggressors; in 1939 persuading Congress to repeal the arms embargo; in 1940 giving Britain fifty overage destroyers in exchange for overseas bases; in 1941 gaining Lend-Lease for the Allies, ordering the U.S. Navy to "shoot-on-sight," and then finally, after the debacle at Pearl Harbor, obtaining war.[2]

Strangely enough, American business in these years stood at the forefront of the peace movement. Although it was standard left-wing doctrine and almost a settled folk-belief of the American people in the thirties that wars were fomented by business, public-opinion polls taken in 1939 showed business executives to be more opposed to war than the general public. While President Roosevelt's "moral embargo" against aggressors met with chilly reception from the oil companies of the United States, which insisted on "business as usual," most of the business community accepted its validity. *Business Week* conceded that the embargo represented the desires of the American people, and the *Wall Street Journal* concluded that such a high price was not too much to ask for war immunity. Business response to the President's provocative "quarantine speech" was likewise strongly anti-war. The *Magazine of Wall Street* pretty well summed it up by saying, "It would take more than the Orient appears to offer us in economic advantages to induce the United States to risk war." Even when prospects of a German victory appeared imminent in the spring of 1940 and there was a pronounced swing away from isolationism, *Nation's Business*—a diehard isolationist journal claiming to speak for 700,000 members of the U.S. Chamber of Commerce—fought the Lend-Lease Bill tooth and nail.

But, if business arrived at the same sentiments of isolationism which many other Americans felt at this time, it was for different reasons. The difference was, as Roland

Stromberg pointed out, that while for a good many Americans the issue was a moral one, businessmen generally looked upon war as an economic proposition and calculated the risks and gains of war as a commercial transaction. The existing economic order tended to favor peace because "The intricate organization of modern economic life, the huge investments, the international investments of capital, the desire of large enterprises for market stability—all these made the disruptions of war more and more to be feared. Modern business functioned as a part of an intricate, world-wide economic organization into which war was apt to throw a damaging monkey wrench."[3]

Rather paradoxically, in view of its anti-war sentiments, American business in the twenties had favored rearmament and encouraged "defense" spending. In 1929, the President could declare that the United States had the largest military budget of any nation in the world. By 1930 expenditures of the government on strictly military activities were 197 percent greater than in 1917 at the beginning of World War I. Nor did the depression curtail military spending under the business administration of Herbert Hoover. In the first year of depression $2,800,000,000 was spent for military purposes while millions of needy Americans went hungry. As the economic disaster deepened, the federal government in 1933 was still paying out 119 percent of its total budgetary receipts on the war system. There seems little doubt, moreover, that business interests were behind heavy military spending. In 1929 and 1930, for example, a Senate investigation revealed that an "expert" on naval matters had been hired by three large American shipbuilding concerns to wreck the Geneva Disarmament Conference in 1927. Again, in 1934, the Senate Munitions Investigating Committee, under the leadership of Senator Nye, disclosed that munitions interests through the use of propaganda, bribes, and lobbying had played an important role in the ever-mounting expenditures for defense. In short, the old contention that "business breeds war" appeared justified to the extent that business, though stopping short of war, nevertheless promoted war by its hankering for the easy subsidized profits of military preparedness.[4]

Along with their fear of economic disruption, businessmen (and especially industrialists) favored staying out of war because they were afraid of wartime regimentation by an administration they regarded as unfriendly. To many the war scare seemed a sinister plot hatched by politicians to destroy free enterprise. "There is only one small group with a hope of profit in war," *Iron Age* contended in 1939. "And that is the vociferous group that looks to war as the golden opportunity to do away with the profit system and the Constitution at one fell swoop." Others worried about who would be the wartime President and how he would employ his tremendous executive powers. The president of the American Iron and Steel Institute claimed that if war came, "as certain as night follows the day, while we were fighting to crush dictatorship abroad, we would be extending one at home." According to Stromberg, the pages of business and industrial journals were filled with horrific predictions of the dreadful dictatorship war would bring.[5]

Business fears for the profit system, however, proved groundless. What business called "the totalitarian plan of nationalizing industry, conscripting the wealth and labor of all, and suppressing the normal incentives of management and industry in favor of the authority and control of government officials" did not materialize. When President Roosevelt chose the leading men of industry for his Defense Advisory Commission and began to organize national defense on a cooperative rather than a coercive basis, the great bugaboo of dictatorship was laid to rest. In fact, as Stromberg put it, "once businessmen were at the helm of the defense commission, their attitude toward government control underwent a remarkable change. It was not long before a good portion of business was demanding more centralization. The suspicion is aroused that business had never been afraid of state control as such, but only of the people who might be wielding that control."

After Pearl Harbor, the New Deal was quickly dismantled. Some major agencies of the depression years were disbanded even before the Japanese attack. The Civilian Conservation Corps was the first to go, because boys of eighteen were urgently needed by the armed forces. The Works Progress Administration was also given an "honorable discharge" by President Roosevelt. With full employment in booming war industries, there was no present need for work relief. Housing, public health, recreational facilities, maternity care, day nurseries for the children of working mothers, loans and advice for small farmers, camps for migratory workers, crop control were all either abandoned for want of appropriations or carried on in a timid and ineffectual fashion in order to escape the attention of conservative hatchetmen. For businessmen, now back in the saddle, had begun to complain bitterly about continuing large non-defense spending, contending that "national defense and the New Deal will not mix."

High on the casualty list were a great many New Dealers or plain liberals who lost their government posts when their peacetime agencies were killed or crippled after 1941. Some resigned in protest, others were forced to resign, were transferred to unimportant positions, or were suddenly dismissed. Most important wartime agencies were turned over to conservatives—often conservative Republicans—or to "practical" men borrowed from business. While not exactly a counterrevolutionary purge, there was no doubt the New Dealers were losing out, and a new crowd was preparing to take over. "What has happened in Washington since Pearl Harbor," said Malcolm Cowley, writing for the *New Republic* in 1943, "is the defeat of a whole class of people who went to work for the government, not in the expectation of becoming rich or powerful—though some of them learned to love power—and not in the hope of building up estates that would provide safe incomes for their children, but simply because they wanted to have fruitful careers and get things done." With the coming of war, the liberals who had hoped to be the architects and engineers of the better American future found themselves powerless, as in 1917 their expectations submerged in the national enterprise of war.[6]

Once again the businessman came out on top. Just as the first World War had created huge profits for industry, so World War II greatly enhanced the wealth and power of American business. Between 1940 and the end of war, nearly 200 billion dollars of war contracts were given to private enterprise. No less than two-thirds of this went to the top one hundred corporations—in fact, almost one-third went to the first ten. General Motors alone received $13,813,000,000 in prime contracts, not to mention its share of the nearly $2,000,000,000 spent by the government for research and development. War-built production facilities increased the nation's peacetime manufacturing plant by better than 60 percent, and roughly two-thirds of this twenty-six-billion-dollar plant expansion was provided by American taxpayers under tax terms that were extremely favorable to industry. If there was irony in the fact that "by means of a war it strenuously resisted, administered by a man it regarded as its inveterate enemy, American business gained new profits and prestige," the greater irony was that by means of a war it loyally supported and led by a man whom it trusted, American liberalism marched to defeat.[7]

II

No liberal worthy of the name thought of the better American future in terms of war. The liberal dream was of a world at peace, in the words of President Roosevelt, "a world founded on freedom of speech, freedom of worship, freedom from want, and freedom from fear." Liberals supported the President because they believed he wanted to achieve a new moral order for America and for the world. In their dislike of war, American liberals were as one, but they were less unanimous in agreeing upon the exact point at which America should resort to arms.

For those who supported war, civilization was at stake. Hating war, they were able to overcome their dislike of brutality and their aversion to force only by the conviction that America could not keep her soul if she stood idly by and watched the world rot. While not unforgetful of the "great betrayal of 1919," they rejected the notion so popular in the twenties that "war settles nothing." On the contrary, they argued that war settled what it was intended to settle. It settled who was to have charge of the immediate future, whether the world was to be run by dictators and militarists or by free men and their duly elected leaders. Although they realistically conceded that the war-won opportunity might be thrown away or illicitly diverted, the moral of the story, contended Herbert Agar, was "not that all wars are useless, but that peace is a struggle as exigent as war."[8]

Defense of national freedom and resistance to armed aggression might be sufficient cause for going to war, but it was not, in the opinion of more skeptical liberals, a sufficient answer to the question, what would follow victory? They recalled Wilson's wartime dictum: "Force, Force to the utmost, Force without stint or limit . . . the righteous and triumphant Force which shall make Right the law of the world, and cast every selfish dominion down in the dust . . ." and they reminded fledgling crusaders for democracy that Force did not cast down selfishness and was used only to make the dominion of might more secure. "And even the Germans," said one, driving the point home, "after we had traveled three thousand miles and spent thirty billions to introduce them to our American democracy, were openly critical of the way we did it."

To Lewis Mumford's ardent cry that the overwhelming

duty of the moment was "Prepare for battle!" Robert Hutchins calmly replied that America was not ready for war. Speaking not in a military sense, he meant that this country was morally and intellectually unprepared to carry out the holy mission to which the President called them: "A missionary, even a missionary to the cannibals, must have clear and defensible convictions. And if his plan is to eat some of the cannibals in order to persuade the others to espouse the true faith, his convictions must be very clear and very defensible indeed. It is surely not too much to ask of such a missionary that his own life and works reflect the virtues which he seeks to compel others to adopt. If we stay out of war, we may perhaps some day understand and practice freedom of speech, freedom of worship, freedom from want, and freedom from fear. We may even be able to comprehend and support justice, democracy, the moral order, and the supremacy of human rights. Today we have barely begun to grasp the meaning of the words." If Americans did not understand and believe in what they were defending, concluded Hutchins, they might still win, but the victory would be as fruitless as the last.[9]

But it was not only the futility of war that distressed some liberals; there was also a fear that democracy, in seeking to resist totalitarianism by arms, must itself become totalitarian. This was the view of W. H. Chamberlin, who asserted that war was a shortcut to fascism. "There has been one object lesson in this connection that should not be forgotten. When did America most resemble a fascist state? . . . It was when we were engaged in our crusade to make the world safe for democracy." As he pointed out in 1940, the ugly combination of profiteering and intellectual repression so characteristic of America during the first World War was once again raising its head. It was perhaps accidental but highly significant that the same issue of the *New York Times* that published President Butler's warning to all Columbia professors to accept his views or get out also published on its financial page the following note:

"A long war would be bullish for securities; and traders now apparently expect just such a state of affairs." Likewise, the bumbling activities of the Dies Committee, which had been authorized by Congress in 1938 to investigate all un-American groups, suggested that the country might be on the edge of another Red hunt. Although the Committee lost considerable credence when it implied that Shirley Temple was a subversive, it was not deterred from its scalp-hunting expeditions against New Dealers. Certainly such witch-hunting would have been unthinkable in the early days of the New Deal, when the scapegoat had been the "economic royalist," but there were clear indications of change in the political atmosphere of wartime Washington. As Malcolm Cowley remarked, "When a dollar-a-year man tells you late at night that maybe Hitler had the right idea—'But get me straight, we've got to lick him first'—and when an army officer says, 'We'll have to kick out all those long-hairs and set up a business government. Just wait till the boys get home'—at such moments you reflect unhappily that the United States Government is a vast machine that could be used for other purposes besides national defense and furthering the common welfare."[10]

Experience had shown, said Alan Valentine, president of the University of Rochester, that war and the American Bill of Rights were mutually contradictory. "It follows [then] that men who wish to think freely must strive to maintain a peaceful, secure society, for without it their influence wanes. It follows too that intellectuals should oppose the emotionalism which submerges rational thinking. The price that intellectuals pay in times of war is so high that the support of war is rarely, if ever, in their interests. No matter who wins, they are the losers." And the worst of it, concurred Oswald Garrison Villard, publisher and long-time editor of the *Nation*, was that all that civilization had painfully achieved must be sent into cold storage until war was over. "It leads our statesmen to believe that they fulfill their duty to their country and to humanity if they just see to it that we have armaments enough to satisfy the generals. It relieves them of any sense that they must find a way out of this human wilderness. . . . It deprives them of a compelling urge to build a new state of society. . . . It enables them to repeat the banal idiocy that there is now no time to think about anything else except destroying Hitler." Whether Hitler won or lost the war, Villard believed the average American must resign himself to the United States becoming a militaristic state.[11]

If nationalism was essentially capitalism's alternative to social revolution, as D. W. Brogan, a well-known British student of American affairs, maintained, then there were grounds for viewing with suspicion every increase in military preparedness as a fascist defense for capitalist civilization. The Roosevelt administration had already established for itself the record of making the most extensive preparations for war ever made by a peacetime government in the United States. And as the popular news analyst Elmer Davis commented in 1938, if the Industrial Mobilization Plan worked out by the War and Navy departments were put into force, "it would be ridiculous to pretend that we were fighting for democracy; for this is Fascism in spirit, if not in form and structure." Not only would this plan make war our biggest industry and our greatest public-works project, but it would make America's industrial leaders "preferred stockholders in the nation at war." As things turned out, his predictions proved quite accurate. The regimentation planned for wartime, however innocently initiated, drifted as in the last war toward a wartime dictatorship of big business. Not only did big business get the lion's share of war orders and profits, but as a result of placing most of the prime contracts in the hands of a few giant corporations, economic concentration in the postwar era was substantially higher and hence the power of big business greater than before the war.

Davis's conclusion that "this war dictatorship would be turned into a plutocratic class dictatorship which could hardly be thrown off by peaceful means" seemed far-fetched at the time, but later events appeared to justify his concern. As Eliot Janeway confirmed in his study of economic mobilization in World War II, along with a large armament industry, "the momentum of victory left behind it an unprecedented problem of Governmental organization—the Department of Defense. In the structure of big government, it is the Department of Defense which sets the limits of foreign policy and determines the course of the economy, not least by setting the tax rate." These wartime developments coupled with the postwar menace of Soviet imperialism furnished the ingredients as well as the provocation for maintaining a permanent warfare state. It was this conjunction of an immense military establishment and a large arms industry that led to President Eisenhower's warning to the American people on January 17, 1961, of the danger to their liberties and democratic processes by the "acquisition of unwarranted influence, whether sought or unsought, by the military-industrial complex. The potential for the disastrous rise of misplaced power," said the outgoing President, "exists and will persist."[12]

III

War revealed both the strengths and weaknesses of liberalism. The same lofty idealism that inspired the liberal to join in the universal fight against the powers of evil and destruction blinded him to the great risk to democracy at home; and the incurable optimism which enabled him to perceive the hopeful possibilities of intelligence as a means of social action led him to underestimate the disruptive influence of economic and class interests in the social struggle.

In the struggle for dominion between the conservative businessman and the liberal politician which began after 1929, the issue was not collectivism—for, as Tugwell observed, that was already an established fact—but rather what was to be the future character of the emerging collectivism. "Was it to be something like fascism's corporative state, frankly owned and operated by business; or would it be a collectivized state with industry and finance subordinated to a culture planned for and wanted by the people?" Except for the practical question of who was to be in control, no one—surely not the big businessman—quarreled with the liberal's insistence on the necessity of avoiding drift into chaos and the corresponding necessity of an intelligent direction of social change. But when it came to the crucial matter of how that control was to be established and maintained, the big businessman and the liberal reformer, in theory at least, parted company. More pessimistic in outlook, the businessman tended to rely upon coercion and force as the means of social control, while the liberal built his hopes on intelligence as an alternative method of directing social change and, by so doing, betrayed a constitutional weakness in the liberal approach to politics. Committed to the use of intelligence, the liberal not only overlooked the extent to which force, rather than intelligence, was built into the procedures of the existing social system—normally as economic and legal coercion, in times of crisis as overt violence—but he also failed to realize the lengths, licit or illicit, to which the dominant economic class would go in its struggle to keep and extend the gains it had amassed at the expense of genuine social order, liberty, and democracy. Further, by falsely assuming—as many liberals did—that the method of intelligence already ruled, the liberal was totally unprepared for the capture of the collectivist apparatus of the New Deal by the dominant economic interests and its wartime conversion into a powerful and profitable instrument of violence and social control.[13]

Ironically, it was the fascination of the New Dealers with the methods of wartime collectivism that made the takeover so easy. As William Leuchtenburg has shown, the lesson the first World War had taught—that the federal government could organize the nation's resources in a planned economy—was not forgotten; and when the depression came, the liberals turned almost instinctively to what Rexford Tugwell called the "great experiment in control of production, control of price, and control of consumption" as a design for recovery. While the liberal remembered the war as a time when intellectuals had exercised unprecedented power over the economy and the feasibility of a planned society had been brilliantly demonstrated, it was hardly the "war socialism" he thought it to be. Although intellectuals did wield some power, important agencies such as the War Industries Board had, after all, been run chiefly by business executives. "If they [businessmen] learned anything from the war," wrote Leuchtenburg, "it was not the virtues of [democratic] collectivism, but . . . how to achieve massive government intervention without making any permanent alteration in the power of corporations." Had the New Deal liberals been perhaps less idealistic and more critical, they might also have perceived that "the immediate consequence of the war was not a New Jerusalem of the planners but the Whiggery of Herbert Hoover as Secretary of Commerce."[14]

If the misreading of the war experience seemed to corroborate Reinhold Niebuhr's criticism of liberalism as being too optimistic in its interpretation of human nature and society, there was no doubt that with the approach of war the liberal faced a real dilemma. On the one hand, he stood the risk of sacrificing democratic institutions to a system which incarnated war as the ultimate good; on the other, he could hardly refuse to defend democracy because it would cease to be democracy if he defended it. To say then as Lewis Mumford did that the liberal, continually hoping for the best, was unprepared to face the worst, was not quite fair. For unlike the practical-minded businessman who did not act as if justice mattered, as if truth mattered, as if right mattered, as if humanity as a whole were any concern of his—the liberal by creed was intensely dedicated to truth, right, justice, and humanity. Like every sane person, he knew it was "a greater thing to build a city than bombard it, to plough a field than to trample it, to serve mankind than to conquer it." He was aware, too, of how insecurely we had been living, "how grudging, poor, mean, careless has been what we call civilization." And yet, knowing this, once the armies got loose, he was ready to fight for all that was to him valuable in civilization.

His gravest mistake—and that of the Progressives before him—was his failure to apprehend the devastating impact of war on democratic values and to take appropriate measures to protect those values. For he should have realized that war, once started, would sweep everything before it, seize all loyalties, and subjugate all intelligence. Infatuated by the analogue between war and depression, he had naïvely adopted, with few alterations, a collectivist system designed for the exercise of maximum force and autocratic power. Imputing superior intelligence and moral purpose to the New Deal, he embarked upon a program of economic nationalism using the authoritarian machinery of forcible regimentation. Though carried out in the name of democracy, with democratic intent and more often than not with democratic consequences, the New Deal was, in method, usually more coercive than persuasive. The overly centralized administrative system, thoughtlessly borrowed from the past, was essentially statist and provided no democratic safeguards strong enough to check a drift toward fascism. The truth of the matter was, in their concern to get results, the New Dealers abandoned democracy for totalitarianism.

Yet, the failure of liberalism was, in the end, the failure of American society. The hot crisis the New Dealers were called upon to handle had been mounting toward the boiling point for decades and was the cumulative product of years of error, selfishness, irresponsibility, and stupidity on the part of the American people. For it was they, not the liberals, who first abandoned democracy. Throughout our history the great peaceful adventure of democracy has never been able to excite the imagination of the American people as has war. For every thousand people who shuddered at the horrors of the battlefield, only a handful felt the horror of the slum. For the thousands who cheered the efficient machinery of war, only a few recognized the wasteful bedlam of peace.

The irony of the American dream, as the *New Republic* pointed out in 1914 and again in 1939, is that "War is the one activity that men really plan for passionately on a national scale, the only organization that is thoroughly conceived. Men prepare themselves for campaigns they may never wage, but for peace, even when they meet the most acute social crisis, they will not prepare themselves. They set their armies on a hair-trigger of preparation. They leave

The Price of Prosperity.

Culver Pictures, Inc.

their diplomacy archaic. . . . They turn men into military automatons, stamp upon every personal feeling for what they call national defense; they are too timid to discipline business. They spend years learning to make war; they do not learn to govern themselves. They ask men to die for their country; they think it a stupid strain to give time to living for it." Americans were never ready to spend on the enterprises of peace what they gladly spent on the devastations of war, but, loyal to long-standing tradition, they devoutly denied that the brain that invented the gun, organized armies, and conceived superb engines of destruction could understand the first principles governing the production and use of wealth or create a civilization free from hunger, fear, and war.[15]

After all, the crisis America faced in the thirties had not been a crisis of poverty, but a crisis of abundance. As the famed British economist John Maynard Keynes pointed out, it was not the harshness and niggardliness of nature which oppressed us, "but our own incompetence and wrongheadedness which hinder us from making use of the bountifulness of inventive science and cause us to be overwhelmed by its generous fruits."[16] Because it has always been ideologically impossible for any American government—except under war conditions—to plan or to organize on a scale necessary to meet the needs of the nation, the American people had to wait ten bitter years for war to end the depression. And although war provided a means of escape from immediate economic problems, in retribution it exacted a terrible cost, throwing away the wealth and treasure of generations to come in an orgy of profits and tragic waste, drenching earth and sea with the blood of millions of young Americans, and seriously—perhaps fatally—compromising the future of democracy.

NOTES

Prologue: The Businessman and the Politician

1 *Nation's Business*, XIV (July, 1926), 120; XIII (Nov., 1925), 52; *Literary Digest*, Dec. 11, 1926, p. 20.

2 H. L. Mencken, "The Last Round," Oct. 4, 1920, reprinted in *A Carnival of Buncombe* (New York: Vintage, 1960), p. 28.

3 *American Industries*, XXVI (Dec., 1925), 40; *Nation's Business*, XIII (Nov., 1925), 54.

4 Cleona Lewis, *America's Stake in International Investments* (Washington: Brookings Institution, 1938), p. 352.

5 Quoted in *Literary Digest*, Dec. 5, 1925, pp. 5–7.

6 E. S. Martin, "Shall Business Run the World?" *Harper's*, CL (Feb., 1925), 379, 381, and *Life* as quoted in James Warren Prothro, *Dollar Decade: Business Ideas in the 1920's* (Baton Rouge: Louisiana State University Press, 1954), pp. 94–5. I am heavily indebted to Mr. Prothro for the businessman's view of the politician and politics.

7 George E. Roberts, "Things to Tell Your Men: X—Price, The Basis of Industry," *Nation's Business*, XIII (Jan., 1925), 54; "The Nation's Business Through Editorial Eyes,"

American Industries, XXV (May, 1925), 21; cited in Prothro, *Dollar Decade* pp. 94–5.

8 *Nation's Business*, XVIII (Feb., 1930), 223; *ibid.*, IX (Feb., 1921), 12; *American Industries*, XXV (Oct., 1924), 7; Prothro, *Dollar Decade*, pp. 30–2.

9 Charles N. Fay, *Business in Politics: Suggestions for Leaders in American Business* (Cambridge: Cosmos Press, 1926), p. 18; Prothro, *Dollar Decade* pp. 147–8, 189–92, 197–200.

10 "What Young America Is Thinking: Why Youth Scoffs at Politics," *World's Work*, LIV (Aug., 1927), 446; *Independent*, Sept. 18, 1926, p. 313; *Nation*, CXVIII (Feb., 1927), 220; *Literary Digest*, July 14, 1923, p. 64.

11 Quoted in *Literary Digest*, Nov. 16, 1929, p. 65; *Proceedings*, N.A.M. (1924), 112.

12 Quoted in Prothro, *Dollar Decade*, p. 138.

13 *Proceedings*, N.A.M. (1920), p. 240.

14 Warren G. Harding, "Business Sense in Government," *Nation's Business*, VIII (Nov., 1920), 13–4; Coolidge quoted in William Allen White, *A Puritan in Babylon: The*

Story of Calvin Coolidge (New York: Macmillan, 1938), p. 253.

15 Quoted in Arthur Schlesinger, Jr., *The Crisis of the Old Order* (Boston: Houghton Mifflin, 1957), p. 61.

16 *Nation's Business*, XIII (May, 1930), 29; Herbert Hoover, *The New Day: Campaign Speeches of Herbert Hoover, 1928* (Stanford: Stanford Univ. Press, 1928), pp. 12–6; *Nation*, July 31, 1929, p. 112; *New Republic*, Dec. 11, 1929, p. 56.

17 Hoover, *New Day*, p. 214.

18 Coolidge quoted in Irving Bernstein, *The Lean Years* (Boston: Houghton Mifflin, 1960), p. 254; also see pp. 247–63.

19 *Report and Recommendations of the California State Unemployment Commission* (Sacramento: State Printing Office, 1932), pp. 145–6.

20 W. S. Myers and W. H. Newton, eds., *The State Papers and Other Public Writings of Herbert Hoover* (Garden City, N.Y.: Doubleday, Doran, 1934), I, 470, 496; *New Yorker*, Feb. 27, 1932, p. 10.

21 Louise V. Armstrong, *We Too Are the People* (Boston: Little, Brown, 1938), p. 10.

22 *Washington Star*, July 29, 1932, quoted in Bernstein, *Lean Years*, p. 454.

23 Alfred Kazin, *On Native Grounds* (New York: Harcourt, Brace & World, 1942), pp. 363–4; Bernstein, *Lean Years*, p. 294.

24 John Kenneth Galbraith, *The Great Crash, 1929* (Boston: Houghton Mifflin, 1961), p. 183; Ferdinand Pecora, *Wall Street Under Oath* (New York: Simon & Schuster, 1939), p. 283; N. R. Danielson, "From Insull to Injury," *Atlantic*, CLI

(April, 1933), 497–508.

25 Mellon quoted in Frederick Lewis Allen, *Since Yesterday* (New York: Bantam, 1961), p. 57; *Proceedings, N.A.M.* (1930), pp. 12–5; Prothro, *Dollar Decade*, p. 221.

26 "Vanished Prestige of Our Business Leaders, *Christian Century*, XLIX (June, 1931), 693–4; "Can Capitalism Be Trusted?" *ibid.*, 1301–3; O. G. Villard, "Failure of Big Business," *Nation*, May 25, 1932, p. 586; "Business on the Defensive," *ibid.*, May 13, 1931, p. 520; "Businessmen Are Bewildered," *American Mercury*, XXXIII (Sept., 1934), 69–76; John Moody, "Eclipse of the Superman," *Commonweal*, Aug. 10, 1932, p. 366; J. George Frederick, "Babbitt Cracks," *Scribner's*, XC (July, 1931), 46–9.

27 *New York Times*, Aug. 31, 1930, II, 1:1; May 10, 1931, III, 1:3; Oct. 4, 1931, II, 7:6; Sept. 18, 1931, 40:1; Jan. 17, 1933, 10:2; Apr. 14, 1933, 32:2; Oct. 21, 1933, 20:4.

28 H. Hart, "Changing Opinions About Business Prosperity: A Consensus of Magazine Opinion in the United States, 1929–32," *American Journal of Sociology*, XXXVIII (Mar., 1933), 686–7; F. R. Fairchild, "Government Saves Us From Depression," *Yale Review*, XXI (June, 1932), 661; Hoover, *State Papers*, I, 137, 184; *Business Week*, May 17, 1933, p. 3; W. M. Kiplinger, "Why Businessmen Fear Washington," *Scribner's*, XLVI (Oct., 1934), 207; Thurman Arnold, "The Crash—and What It Meant," in Isabel Leighton, ed., *The Aspirin Age* (New York: Simon & Schuster, 1949), pp. 223–4.

Chapter One: Back to Normalcy

1 William Allen White, *The Autobiography of William Allen White* (New York: Macmillan, 1946), p. 496; *Bulletin of the U.S. Bureau of*

Labor Statistics, CCCLVII (May, 1924), 466; George Soule, *Prosperity Decade* (New York: Rinehart, 1947), p. 188.

2 Frank Cobb, "The Press and Public Opinion," *New Republic,* Dec. 31, 1919, p. 144; the best account is Robert K. Murray, *Red Scare, A Study of National Hysteria, 1919–1920* (New York: McGraw-Hill, 1964).

3 Meno Lovenstein, *American Opinion of Soviet Russia* (Washington: American Council on Public Affairs, 1941), pp. 9–16, 33, 50. See also *Bolshevik Propaganda,* Hearings before a Sub-committee of the Committee on the Judiciary (Washington: Govt. Printing Office, 1919).

4 *New York Times,* May 2, 1920, pp. 1–2; Murray, *Red Scare,* pp. 239–62; Zechariah Chafee, Jr., Felix Frankfurter, Roscoe Pound, *et al., Report Upon the Illegal Practices of the United States Department of Justice* (Washington: National Popular Govt. League, 1920), pp. 1–8.

5 George E. Mowry, "The First World War and American Democracy," in J. D. Clarkson & T. C. Cochran, eds., *War As a Social Institution* (New York: Columbia Univ. Press, 1941), p. 177.

6 *Hearings on the Ku Klux Klan,* House Rules Committee, 67 Cong., 1 sess. (1921); New York *American,* Sept. 13–22, 1921; *Literary Digest,* Aug. 27, 1921, pp. 12–3; Robert L. Duffus, "Ku Klux Klan in the Middle West," *World's Work,* XLVI (July, 1923), 30–40; R. A. Patton, "Ku Klux Reign of Terror," *Current History,* XXVIII (April, 1928), 51–5.

7 Amy Jacques Garvey, ed., *The Philosophy and Opinions of Marcus Garvey* (New York: Universal Publg. House, 1923), pp. 11, 18, 36; Gunnar Myrdal, *An American Dilemma* (New York: Harper, 1944), p. 749; W. E. Burghardt DuBois, *Black Reconstruction in America* (New York: Harcourt, Brace, 1935), p. 703.

8 Walter Lippmann, *Men of Destiny* (New York: Macmillan, 1927), p. 28.

9 *The World's Most Famous Court Trial: Tennessee Evolution Case,* A complete stenographic report (Cincinnati: National Book Co., 1925), pp. 74–5, 77, 299, 338; J. W. Krutch, "Darrow vs. Bryan," *Nation,* July 29, 1925, pp. 136–7; H. L. Mencken, editorial, *American Mercury,* Oct., 1925, pp. 158–60; "A Country Trick—and a City Blunder," *Outlook,* Jan. 26, 1927, p. 108; "Tennessee vs. Civilization," *New Republic,* July 22, 1925, p. 221; Lippmann, *Men of Destiny,* p. 30.

10 White, *Autobiography,* p. 597; Alvin Johnson, "Why Will They Vote for Harding?" *New Republic,* July 28, 1920, p. 255.

11 Samuel Hopkins Adams, *Incredible Era: The Life and Times of Warren Gamaliel Harding* (Boston: Houghton Mifflin, 1939), p. 188; Lippmann, *Men of Destiny,* p. 107; Mencken, "The Last Round," Oct. 4, 1920, *Carnival of Buncombe,* pp. 25–6.

12 "Harding: Turning Back the Hands of Time," *Nation,* June 19, 1920, p. 816; *New Republic,* July 28, 1920, pp. 254–6; "The McKinley Qualities of Warren G. Harding," *Literary Digest,* Mar. 20, 1920, p. 55; F. M. Davenport, "Conservative America in Convention Assembled," *Outlook,* June 23, 1920, p. 375; Warren G. Harding, "Less Government in Business and More Business in Government," *World's Work,* XLI (Nov., 1920), 25–7.

13 "Eugene V. Debs, A 'Presidential Impossibility,' " *Literary Digest,* May 22, 1920, p. 53; Wilson in a speech of Sept. 5, 1919, quoted in Joseph P. Tumulty, *Woodrow Wilson as I Know Him* (Garden City:

Doubleday, Page, 1922), p. 505.

14 Harry Elmer Barnes, "Drool Method in History," *American Mercury*, I (Dec., 1924), 31–8; *Outlook*, May 26, 1920, p. 143; *Literary Digest*, Oct. 23, 1920, pp. 57–8; "European Impressions of Debs as a Presidential Candidate," *Current Opinion*, LXIX (July, 1920), 24–6; Ray Ginger, *Eugene V. Debs: A*

Biography (New York: Collier, 1962), pp. 424–5.

15 Herbert Croly, "The Eclipse of Progressivism," *New Republic*, Oct. 27, 1920, p. 210.

16 Will Hays quoted by Mark Sullivan, "One Year of President Harding," *World's Work*, XLIII (Nov., 1921), 27.

Chapter Two: Dollar Democracy

1 Calvin Coolidge, "Enemies of the Republic: Are the 'Reds' Stalking Our College Women?" *Delineator*, XCVII (June, 1921), 4–5, 66–7; White, *Puritan in Babylon*, p. 166.

2 Lippmann, *Men of Destiny*, pp. 12–3; White, *Puritan in Babylon*, pp. 278–88, 351.

3 *Proceedings*, N.A.M. (1920), 11, 112; "Meeting on Open Shop," *ibid.* (1923); *Nation's Business*, XI (Oct., 1923), 26; *Literary Digest*, Jan. 2, 1923, pp. 18–9; "Who Is Behind the Open Shop Campaign?" *New Republic*, Jan. 26, 1921, pp. 259–62.

4 Savel Zimand, *The Open Shop Drive* (New York: Bureau of Industrial Research, 1921), p. 6, *et seq.*; *New York Times*, April 19, 1921, 9:2, 16:3; A. G. Taylor, *Labor Policies of the National Association of Manufacturers* (Urbana: Univ. of Illinois Press, 1928), p. 163.

5 "The 'Law' and Labor," *New Republic*, Jan. 26, 1921, pp. 245–8; William H. Leiserson, *Right and Wrong in Labor Relations* (Berkeley: Univ. of Calif. Press, 1938), pp. 24–7; *American Steel Foundries v. Tri-City Central Trades Council*, 257 U.S. 184, 209 (1921).

6 Bernstein, *Lean Years*, pp. 190–243.

7 Leo Wolman, *Ebb and Flow in*

Trade Unionism (New York: Nat'l. Bureau of Economic Research, 1936), *passim*; H. L. Mencken, *Prejudices: Fifth Series* (New York: Knopf, 1926), p. 274.

8 "Report of Earnings of Bituminous Mine Workers" (Oct. 3, 1923), *Annals of the American Academy*, CXI (Jan., 1924), 5–6; "Living Conditions Among Coal Mine Workers of the United States," *ibid.*, 12–23; also *passim* 1–344; "Are Miners People?" *New Republic*, July 4, 1923, p. 139.

9 "A Rockefeller Hits Labor Abuses," *Literary Digest*, Nov. 11, 1922, pp. 9–10; "The Worker's Right to a Living Wage," *ibid.*, p. 7; *Daily News* quoted in Bernstein, *Lean Years*, pp. 130–1.

10 Soule, *Prosperity Decade*, pp. 77, 99, 124, 229–51; *Literary Digest*, Dec. 24, 1921, p. 10; Arthur Capper, *The Agricultural Bloc* (New York: Harcourt, Brace, 1922), p. 9 *et seq.*

11 *New Republic*, June 18, 1924, pp. 88–90; *New York Times*, July 6, 1924, p. 1.

12 Croly, "Eclipse of Progressivism," pp. 210–6; Kenneth C. MacKay, *The Progressive Movement of 1924* (New York: Columbia Univ. Press, 1947), p. 21; *World's Work*, XLIII (Dec., 1921), 164; *Baltimore Sun* quoted in Theodore Saloutos & John Hicks, *Agricultural Discontent in the Mid-*

dle West 1900–1939 (Madison: Univ. of Wisconsin Press, 1951), pp. 367, 562.

13   "A Business Administration," Nation, Feb. 27, 1924, p. 220; Allen, Only Yesterday, p. 109; Bruce Bliven, "Ohio Gang," New Republic, May 7–June 4, 1924, pp. 276–7, 305–8, 334–6, 9–11, 40–2; W. E. Dodd, "Political Corruption and the Public 50 Years Ago and Today," ibid., June 11, 1924, pp. 63–4.

14   Calvin Coolidge, The Price of Freedom, Speeches and Addresses by Calvin Coolidge (New York: Scribner's, 1924), pp. 334, 346; White, Puritan in Babylon, p. 396; Nation's Business, XIII (June, 1925), 15; MacKay, Progressive Movement, pp. 162–74.

15   Hugh Keenleyside, "The American Political Revolution of 1924," Current History, XXI (Mar., 1925), 833–40; Lippmann, Men of Destiny, pp. 23–5.

16   Robert L. Duffus, "Mr. Coolidge's Utopia," New Republic, May 7, 1924, p. 288; Coolidge, Price of Freedom, pp. 236–8.

17   Julius H. Barnes, The Genius of American Business (Garden City: Doubleday, Page, 1924), pp. 4–7; "Business Declares Its Principles," Nation's Business, IX (June, 1921), 48–50. For an elaboration of the business viewpoint see Prothro, Dollar Decade, pp. 79–95, 157–74.

18   Maurice Leven, et al., America's Capacity to Consume (Washington: Brookings Institution, 1934), pp. 93–6, 147–238; Simon Kuznets, National Income and Its Composition, 1919–1938 (New York: Nat'l. Bureau of Economic Research, 1941), I, 216–7.

19   Bernstein, Lean Years, pp. 144–89; "American Workingman," Fortune, IV (Aug., 1931), 54, 131; Kuznets, National Income, 332–3, 352–3.

20   R. H. Tawney, "The Churches and Social Ethics," New Republic, May 21, 1924, pp. 332–3; George Soule, "Why Isn't the Worker Satisfied?" Survey, Sept. 15, 1924, p. 635; John A. Fitch, The Causes of Industrial Unrest (New York: Harper, 1924).

Chapter Three: Collapse of the Old Order

1   Harry Jerome, Mechanization in Industry (New York: Nat'l. Bureau of Economic Research, 1934), passim; Historical Statistics of the United States (Washington: Bureau of the Census, 1949), pp. 71–2; Bernstein, Lean Years, pp. 53–4; John Moody, "The New Era in Wall Street," Atlantic, CXLII (Aug., 1928), 255–62.

2   Steffens to Jo Davidson, Feb. 18, 1929, Letters of Lincoln Steffens (New York: Harcourt, Brace, 1938), II, 830; Lippmann, Men of Destiny, p. 26; Thomas Nixon Carver, The Present Economic Revolution in the United States (Boston: Little, Brown, 1926), pp. 239–40.

3   A. A. Berle, Jr., "A High Road for Business," Scribner's, CXLIII (June, 1933), 325; Walter Lippmann, "A Reckoning," Yale Review, XXI (June, 1932), 659.

4   Thorstein Veblen, The Engineers and the Price System (1921) reprinted in The Portable Veblen (New York: Viking, 1960), p. 440.

5   G. Burck & C. E. Silberman, "What Caused the Great Depression," Fortune, LI (Feb., 1955), 96–7, 206; Edwin G. Nourse, et al., The Distribution of Income in Relation to

Economic Progress (Washington: Brookings Institution, 1936), I, 3–13, 415–29; II, 93–6; IV, 1–46, 142–54; Paul H. Douglas, *Real Wages in the United States, 1890–1926* (Boston: Houghton Mifflin, 1930), p. 391; Kuznets, *National Income*, pp. 332–3, 352–3.

6   *New Republic*, July 6, 1932, p. 193; Elmer Davis, "Can Business Manage Itself?" *Harper's*, CLXII (Mar., 1931), 387; John Dewey, "The Collapse of a Romance," *New Republic*, April 27, 1932, p. 293; Stuart Chase, *A New Deal* (New York: Macmillan, 1932), pp. 22–3.

7   Herbert Hoover, *American Individualism* (Garden City: Doubleday, Page, 1922), pp. 8–9, 19, 55; *Challenge to Liberty* (New York: Scribner's, 1934), pp. 145, 203–4.

8   This was a conservative picture, for it must be remembered that the influence of any one of these large companies extended beyond the assets under its direct control. Adolf A. Berle, Jr., & Gardiner C. Means, *The Modern Corporation and Private Property* (New York: Macmillan, 1932), pp. 18–46; *Literary Digest*, Sept. 6, 1930, p. 7; Burck & Silberman, "What Caused the Great Depression," p. 206.

9   Hoover, *American Individualism*, p. 56; Walter Lippmann, "The Peculiar Weakness of Mr. Hoover," *Harper's*, CLXI (June, 1930), 1–7; Allan Nevins, "President Hoover's Record," *Current History*, XXXVI (July, 1932), 385–94; *Cong. Record*, 71 Cong. 3 sess., 74: 407–8; Hoover, *State Papers*, I, 470, 496; William E. Leuchtenburg, *The Perils of Prosperity 1914–32* (Chicago: Univ. of Chicago Press, 1958), p. 253; H. G. Warren, *Herbert Hoover and the Great Depression* (New York: Oxford Univ. Press, 1959), *passim*.

10   Hoover, *American Individualism*,

pp. 24–5, 70; *Challenge to Liberty*, pp. 7, 57–9, 61, 70, 139; *The Memoirs of Herbert Hoover* (London: Hollis & Carter, 1953), I, 447–8.

11   Hoover, *Challenge to Liberty*, pp. 76–103; Lewis Mumford, *Technics and Civilization* (New York: Harcourt, Brace, 1934), pp. 395, 420; John Dewey, *Liberalism and Social Action* (New York: Putnam's, 1935, Capricorn edition, 1963), pp. 31–9; Rexford G. Tugwell, *The Battle for Democracy* (New York: Columbia Univ. Press, 1935), pp. 3–16, 193–207; "The Principle of Planning and the Institution of Laissez-Faire," *American Economic Review*, supplement, Mar., 1932, pp. 75–92; *The Industrial Discipline and the Governmental Arts* (New York: Columbia Univ. Press, 1933), p. 19.

12   George Soule, *A Planned Society* (New York: Macmillan, 1932), pp. 91, 187, 203, 310; Charles A. Beard, "A 'Five-Year Plan' for America," *Forum*, LXXXVI (July, 1931), 1–11; Paul H. Douglas, *Controlling Depressions* (New York: Norton, 1935), p. 84.

13   Walter Lippmann, *The Good Society* (Boston: Little, Brown, 1937), pp. x, 375. See also Albert Jay Nock, *Our Enemy the State* (New York: Morrow, 1935).

14   George R. Leighton, "And If the Revolution Comes . . . ?" *Harper's*, CLXIV (Mar., 1932), 466–7; *Literary Digest*, Aug. 13, 1932, pp. 16–7; *Nation*, May 13, 1931, p. 520; George Soule, "Are We Going to Have a Revolution?" *Harper's*, CLXV (Aug., 1932), 277.

15   Thurman W. Arnold, *The Symbols of Government* (New Haven: Yale Univ. Press, Harbinger edition, 1962), p. 106; Veblen, *Engineers and the Price System, Portable Veblen*, p. 445; *Harper's*, CLXIV (Mar., 1932), 466–9, 471–4; Davis, "Can

Business Manage Itself?" p. 387.

16 Franklin D. Roosevelt, *The Public Papers and Addresses of Franklin D. Roosevelt*, Samuel I. Rosenman, ed. (New York: Random House, 1938–50), III, 6, 9, 436.

17 For Rightist criticisms of the New Deal see *Documents*, American Liberty League, Washington, D.C., 1934; the best study is George Wolfskill, *The Revolt of the Conservatives* (Boston: Houghton Mifflin, 1962). For the Socialist view see Norman Thomas, *After the New Deal What?* (New York: Macmillan, 1936); for the Communist appraisal see the *Daily Worker*, 1933–35.

18 Robert L. Heilbroner, *The Making of Economic Society* (Englewood Cliffs, N.J.: Prentice-Hall, 1962), pp. 163–8; Frances Perkins, *The Roosevelt I Knew* (New York: Viking, 1946), p. 330; Roosevelt, *Public Papers*, V, 535.

19 Tugwell, *Battle for Democracy*,

p. 266; Heinz Eulau, "Neither Ideology nor Utopia: The New Deal in Retrospect," *Antioch Review*, XIX (Winter, 1959–60), 523–37; Mario Einaudi, *The Roosevelt Revolution* (New York: Harcourt, Brace, 1959), p. 179.

20 Under Section 7 (a) of the National Industrial Recovery Act (1933). When that Act was invalidated by the Supreme Court, Congress in 1935 passed the Wagner Act reasserting the right of collective bargaining.

21 Alexander Hamilton, *Report on Manufactures* (1791); Eugene O. Golob, *The "Isms"* (New York: Harper, 1954), pp. 143–4.

22 Gardiner C. Means, *The Corporate Revolution in America* (New York: Crowell-Collier, 1962), pp. 37–8; Heilbroner, *Making of Economic Society*, pp. 163–8; Arnold, "The Crash," p. 224.

Chapter Four: The Materialistic Faith

1 Irvin G. Wylie, *The Self-Made Man in America* (New Brunswick; N.J.: Rutgers Univ. Press, 1954), pp. 168–70; A. J. Stone, "The Dawn of a New Science," *American Mercury*, Aug., 1928, p. 446.

2 Calvin Coolidge, "The Press Under a Free Government," address before the American Society of Newspaper Editors, Washington, Jan. 17, 1925, *Foundations of the Republic, Speeches and Addresses by Calvin Coolidge* (New York: Scribner's, 1926), p. 188; Thorstein Veblen, *The Higher Learning in America* (New York: Huebsch, 1918; Sagamore, 1957), pp. 149–50.

3 Coolidge, *Foundations of the Republic*, p. 320; Neil M. Clark, "Putting Religion to the Test," *American*,

CIX (June, 1930), 50–51; Allen, *Only Yesterday*, pp. 125–6.

4 Schlesinger, *Crisis of the Old Order*, p. 71; Bruce Barton, *The Man Nobody Knows* (Indianapolis: Bobbs-Merrill, 1924), introd. & pp. 104, 126, 162, 165, 180; Thorstein Veblen, *Absentee Ownership and Business Enterprise in Recent Times* (1923), *Portable Veblen*, p. 501.

5 Edmund Wilson, "Mr. and Mrs. X," *The American Earthquake* (Garden City, N.Y.: Doubleday, 1964), p. 436.

6 James Truslow Adams, *Our Business Civilization* (New York: Boni, 1929), pp. 9–31; Sinclair Lewis, *Babbitt* (New York: Harcourt Brace, 1922), pp. 182–4.

7 Wilson, *American Earthquake*,

p. 434; Sinclair Lewis, *Main Street* (New York: Grosset & Dunlap, 1922), p. 267; Ralph Borsodi, *This Ugly Civilization* (New York: Harper, 1929), p. 16.

8 Henry Ford, *My Life and Work* (London: Heinemann, 1922), pp. 2, 105–7, 274; "Machinery, The New Messiah," *Forum*, LXXIX (Mar., 1928), 363–4; Glenn Frank, "Shall We Scrap Our Machines and Go Back to the Spinning-Wheel?" *Magazine of Business*, LII (Oct., 1927), 412.

9 Lewis Mumford, *Technics and Civilization*, pp. 266, 412; Barnes, *Genius of American Business*, p. 14; Elmer Rice, *The Adding Machine* (1923), in *Seven Plays* (New York: Viking, 1950), p. 107.

10 Ezra Pound, "Where Is American Culture?" *Nation*, April 18, 1928, p. 443; Irving Babbitt, *Democracy and Leadership* (Boston: Houghton Mifflin, 1924), pp. 240–3.

11 Letter to Van Wyck Brooks, May 22, 1927, Daniel Cory, ed., *The Letters of George Santayana* (New York: Scribner's, 1955), pp. 225–6; George Santayana, "Americanism," in *The Idler and His Works* (New York: Braziller, 1957), p. 36; James C. Ballowe, "The Last Puritan and the Failure of American Culture," *American Quarterly*, XVIII (Summer, 1966), 123–35.

12 Kazin, *On Native Grounds*, p. 363; Lewis Mumford, "The Need for Concrete Goals," *Common Sense*, Oct., 1933, reprinted in *Challenge to the New Deal* (New York: Falcon, 1932), p. 225.

13 Theodore Dreiser, "Flies and Locusts," *Common Sense*, Dec., 1933, *Challenge to the New Deal*, p. 57; Malcolm Cowley, "1930's Age of Faith," *New York Times Book Review*, Dec. 13, 1964, p. 5; Granville Hicks, *Where We Came Out* (New York: Viking, 1954), p. 33; Wilson quoted in Hicks, p. 33; Lewis Corey, *The Decline of American Capitalism* (New York: Covici-Friede, 1934), p. 547; Daniel Aaron, *Writers on the Left* (New York: Harcourt, Brace & World, 1961), p. 367. Aaron offers the most intelligent and open-minded account of Communism and American intellectuals in the 1930's.

14 John Maynard Keynes, "Soviet Russia," *New Republic*, Oct. 28–Nov. 11, 1925, pp. 246–8, 301–3.

15 Theodore Draper, *The Roots of American Communism* (New York: Viking, 1957), pp. 28, 293–300. For samples of proletarian literature see Harvey Swados, *The American Writer and the Great Depression* (Indianapolis: Bobbs-Merrill, 1966) and Louis Filler, *The Anxious Years* (New York: Capricorn, 1964).

Chapter Five: Liberalism and Democracy

1 H. L. Mencken, "To Him That Hath," *Smart Set*, May, 1920, pp. 33–4; Lewis, *Babbitt*, pp. 187–8; "Dare to Be a Babbitt," *Nation's Business*, XIII (June, 1925), 40.

2 John Dewey, "The Post-War Mind," *New Republic*, Dec. 7, 1918, p. 157.

3 Floyd Dell, *Intellectual Vagabondage* (New York: Doran, 1926), p. 260; Vernon Louis Parrington, *Main Currents in American Thought* (New York: Harcourt, Brace, 1927–1930), III, 368–9; Glenn Frank, "The Balance Sheet of Civilization," *Century*, CIX (Jan., 1925), 426–7;

Lincoln Steffens, "Bankrupt Liberalism," *New Republic*, Feb. 17, 1932, pp. 15–6.

4 Roosevelt, *Public Papers*, I, xiii; II, 5; Richard Hofstadter, *The Age of Reform* (New York: Vintage, 1955), p. 326; Herbert Croly, *The Promise of American Life* (New York: Capricorn, 1964), pp. 451–3; Henry A. Wallace, *Democracy Reborn* (New York: Reynal & Hitchcock, 1944), p. 73.

5 H. L. Mencken, *A Mencken Chrestomathy* (New York: Knopf, 1949), p. 623.

6 U.S. Army *Training Manual*, No. 200–25 (Washington: Gov't. Printing Office, 1928), p. 91; John E. Edgerton, "Annual Address of the President," *Proceedings*, N.A.M. (1929), 23; *ibid.* (1925), 10; *Nation's Business*, XII (July, 1924), 36, 38; *ibid.*, XV (Dec., 1927), 62; *Proceedings*, N.A.M. (1923), 289; Prothro, *Dollar Decade*, pp. 204–5.

7 Charles A. Beard, "Democracy Holds Its Ground," *Harper's*, CLVII (Nov., 1928), 680; Edmund Wilson, "Mencken's Democratic Man," *New Republic*, Dec. 15, 1926, pp. 110–1; G. K. Chesterton, "Persecuting the Common Man," *American Mercury*, XXXVII (Jan., 1936), 71.

8 Felix Frankfurter, "Democracy and the Expert," *Atlantic*, CXLVI (Nov., 1930), 650; Archibald MacLeish, *The Irresponsibles, A Declaration* (New York: Duell, Sloan & Pearce, 1940), pp. 15–6; William F. Borah, "Democracy Has Not Failed," *Fortnightly Review*, CXXX (Aug., 1928), 161.

9 Evans, "Klan's Fight for Americanism," p. 42; "Where Are the Pre-War Radicals?" *Survey*, Feb. 1, 1926, pp. 556–66; Lincoln Steffens, *The Autobiography of Lincoln Steffens* (New York: Harcourt,

Brace, 1931), p. 802; *Moses in Red* (Philadelphia: Dorrance, 1926), pp. 10–11; Granville Hicks, "Lincoln Steffens: He Covered the Future," *Commentary*, XIII (Feb., 1952), pp. 147–55; Aaron, *Writers on the Left*, pp. 126–30.

10 William Phillips, "What Happened in the 30's," *Commentary*, XXXIV (Sept., 1962), 204–6; Howard Zinn, "Emancipation from Dogma," *Nation*, April 4, 1966, p. 385.

11 *Daily Worker*, Mar. 5, 1933; *New Masses*, VIII (April, 1933), 3–13; Aaron, *Writers on the Left*, p. 156; also see *Writers Take Sides* (New York: League of American Writers, 1938) for a collection of statements by American writers on the Spanish Civil War. Of the 418 writers who gave their views, 410 strongly favored the Loyalists, 7 took no positive stand, and only one author, Gertrude Atherton, sided with Franco. The list included many prominent writers such as Ernest Hemingway, Thornton Wilder, Edgar Lee Masters, Fanny Hurst, Maxwell Anderson, John Steinbeck, etc.

12 John Dewey, "Imperative Need: A New Radical Party," *Common Sense*, Sept., 1933, *Challenge to the New Deal*, pp. 269–73; *Nation*, Dec. 14, 1932, p. 585; John Dewey, "Impressions of Soviet Russia," *New Republic*, Nov. 28, p. 41.

13 Keynes, "Soviet Russia," p. 246; Irving Howe and Lewis Coser, *The American Communist Party* (New York: Praeger, 1962), pp. 300–1; "Trotsky Appeal," *Literary Digest*, Mar. 20, 1937, p. 13; Hicks, *Where We Came Out*, pp. 70–9; Richard Crosman, ed., *The God That Failed* (New York: Harper, 1949), pp. 115–62, 196–228; Draper, *Roots of American Communism*, pp. 300–2; Lewis Corey, "Marxism Reconsidered," *Nation*, Feb. 17–Mar. 2,

1940, pp. 245–8; 272–5, 305–7.
14 From *transition* (Paris, 1928), pp.

100–1, reprinted in Aaron, *Writers on the Left,* p. 140.

Chapter Six: The Modern Ethic

1 Henry F. May, *The End of American Innocence* (New York: Knopf, 1959), pp. 219–332; *Nation*, Sept. 4, 1913, p. 205; John Flynn, "American Revolution: 1933," *Scribner's,* LXLIV (July, 1933), p. 2.

2 Henry L. Mencken, "The Flapper," *Smart Set,* XLV (1915), 1–2; cf. Bruce Bliven, "Flapper Jane," *New Republic,* Sept. 9, 1925, pp. 65–7.

3 Fitzgerald quoted in Kazin, *On Native Grounds,* p. 193; John Dos Passos, *1919* (New York: Harcourt, Brace, 1932), p. 200; Ezra Pound, "Hugh Selwyn Mauberley," *Personae* (New York: New Directions, 1926), p. 191.

4 Lewis, *Main Street,* p. 265; Randolph Bourne, "Twilight of Idols," *The Seven Arts,* II (Oct., 1917), 700–2.

5 Sigmund Freud, *The Standard Edition of the Complete Psychological Works of Sigmund Freud* (London: Hogarth, 1953), IX, 193–204; XI, 223.

6 Harold Stearns, "The Intellectual Life," *Civilization in the United States* (New York: Harcourt, Brace, 1922), pp. 147–8.

7 Sigmund Freud, *Civilization and Its Discontents* (London: Hogarth, 1963), p. 23.

8 Viola Paradise, "The Sex Simplex," *Forum,* LXXIV (July, 1925), 108–11; David Seabury, "The Bogey of Sex," *Century,* CXIV (Sept., 1927), 528–31; *New York Times,* Oct. 2, 1925, p. 22; Aug. 7, 1925, p. 4; July 28, 1924, p. 1.

9 George Jean Nathan, "The New View of Sex," *American Mercury,* XI (April, 1926), 492–4.

10 George Jean Nathan, "Psycho-Osteopathy," *American Mercury,* XII (July, 1927), 369; "Confessions of an Ex-psychoanalyst," *New Republic,* Mar. 24, 1926, p. 139; Harvey O'Higgins, *The American Mind in Action* (New York: Harper, 1924).

11 Grace Adams, "The Rise and Fall of Psychology," *Atlantic,* CLIII (Jan., 1934), 84–6; Stephen Leacock, "Manual of the New Mentality," *Harper's,* CXLVIII (Mar., 1924), 471–80; G. K. Chesterton, "The Game of Psychoanalysis," *Century,* CVI (May, 1923), 34–43; Aldous Huxley, "Our Contemporary Hocus-Pocus," *Forum,* LXXIII (Mar., 1925), 313–20.

12 C. E. M. Joad, "Psychology in Retreat," *New Statesman and Nation,* IX (1935), 956; Adams, "Rise and Fall of Psychology," p. 92.

13 F. Scott Fitzgerald, *The Crack-Up* (New York: New Directions, 1945), pp. 13–22, 69–74 (originally written in 1931 and 1936); Walter Lippmann, *A Preface to Morals* (New York: Macmillan, 1929), p. 17.

14 Dell, *Intellectual Vagabondage,* pp. 235–61; Freud, *Works,* XIV, 385, 287.

15 Frederick J. Hoffman, *The Twenties: American Writing in the Postwar Decade* (New York: Viking, 1949), p. 272.

16 William Pepperell Montague, "The Promethean Challenge to Religion," *New Republic,* Aug. 6, 1924, p. 295; Herbert Croly, "Re-

generation," *ibid.*, June 9, 1920, pp. 40–7; Kirtley F. Mather, "The Scientist Bends the Knee," *ibid.*, Sept. 9, 1925, p. 73; Alfred North Whitehead, *Process and Reality* (New York: Macmillan, 1929), p. vi; Whitehead, *Science and the Modern World* (New York: Macmillan, 1925), p. 298.

17 Lippmann, *Preface to Morals*, pp. 125–7; Whitehead, *Science and the Modern World*, p. 166.

18 C. E. Ayres, *Science, the False Messiah* (Indianapolis: Bobbs-Merrill, 1927); Karl Menninger, "Pseudo-Analysis: Perils of Freudian Verbalism," *Outlook*, July 9, 1930, pp. 363–5; W. Beran Wolfe, "The Twilight of Psychoanalysis," *American Mercury*, XXXV (Aug., 1935), 385–94. For the effect of Freud on American writers see Frederick J. Hoffman, *Freudianism and the Literary Mind* (Baton Rouge, La.: Louisiana State Univ. Press, 1957).

19 Harry Emerson Fosdick, "Are Religious People Fooling Themselves?" *Harper's*, CLXI (June, 1930), 59–70; A. Clutton-Brock, "Evil and the New Faith," *Atlantic*, CXXXI (Mar., 1923), 298–308. For a thorough study of liberal theology and social reform in this period see Donald B. Meyer, *The Protestant Search for Political Realism, 1919–1941* (Berkeley: Univ. of California Press, 1960).

20 Reinhold Niebuhr, *Moral Man and Immoral Society* (New York: Scribner's, 1932), *passim.*

21 Allen, *Only Yesterday*, p. 242.

Epilogue: War and the American Dream

1 Hofstadter, *Age of Reform*, pp. 272–5; H. C. Styrett, "The Business Press and American Neutrality, 1914–17," *Mississippi Valley Historical Review*, XXXII (Sept., 1945), 215–30; William E. Leuchtenburg, "Progressivism and Imperialism: The Progressive Movement and American Foreign Policy, 1898–1916," *ibid.*, XXXIX (Dec., 1952), 496; Randolph Bourne, "The War and the Intellectuals," *The Seven Arts*, II (June, 1917), 133–46.

2 John Dewey, "Aid for the Spanish Government," *Christian Century*, Mar. 3, 1937, pp. 14–24; I. F. Stone, "1937 Is Not 1914; Case Against Isolation," *Nation*, Nov. 6, 1937, pp. 495–7; Lewis Mumford, "Good Will Must Act," *Fight*, VI (Feb., 1939), 22–3, 26; Max Lerner, "Behind Hull's Embargo," *Nation*, May 28, 1938, pp. 607–10; Malcolm Cow-ley, "Abyssinia and Spain," *New Republic*, Feb., 16, 1938, pp. 50–1; Archibald MacLeish, "Arms and the Men," *Fortune*, Mar., 1934, pp. 53–7, 113–4, 116–7, 118, 120, 125–6; and "The Irresponsibles," *Nation*, May 18, 1940, pp. 618–23; "Hucksters of Death," *New Republic*, Mar. 7, 1934, pp. 88–9; "What Are We Waiting For: Declare War on the Axis," *ibid.*, Nov. 10, 1941, pp. 603–4.

3 For the business attitude toward war, I have relied heavily upon Roland N. Stromberg, "American Business and the Approach of War, 1935–1941," *Journal of Economic History*, XIII (Winter, 1953), 58–78. *Business Week*, Nov. 11, 1939, editorial; *ibid.*, Aug. 31, 1935, p. 32; *Wall Street Journal*, Oct. 31, Nov. 8, 1935; *Magazine of Wall Street*, Oct. 10, 1936, p. 750; *Nation's Business*,

Mar. & April, 1941, editorials; cited by Stromberg, "American Business and the Approach of War," pp. 63, 65–6, 67, 73–4, 61.

4   Merle Curti, *Peace or War* (New York; Norton, 1936), pp. 263–8.

5   *Iron Age*, June 1, 1939, p. 48; Stromberg, "American Business and the Approach of War," pp. 69, 74–5.

6   Stromberg, "American Business and the Approach of War," p. 75; Malcolm Cowley, "The End of the New Deal," *New Republic*, May 31, 1943, p. 731.

7   79th Cong., 2nd sess., Senate Document 206, *Economic Concentration and World War II* (Washington: Gov't. Printing Office, 1946), pp. 27, 29, 31, 37, 39, 51; Stromberg, "American Business and the Approach of War," p. 78.

8   Herbert Agar, "The War Is Worth Fighting!" *American Mercury*, LI (Dec., 1940), 404; Lewis Mumford, "Corruption of Liberalism," *New Republic*, April 29, 1940, pp. 568–73.

9   Rexford G. Tugwell, "Frightened Liberals," *New Republic*, April 26, 1939, pp. 328–9; H. Coggins, "Planning for a Better War," *Forum*, CII (Aug., 1939), 81; Mumford, "Corruption of Liberalism," p. 573; Robert Hutchins, "America and the War," a radio address given over a coast-to-coast network of the National Broadcasting Co. on Jan. 23, 1941.

10   W. H. Chamberlin, "War—Shortcut to Fascism," *American Mercury*, LI (Dec., 1940), 392, *Times* quoted, 395; Cowley, "End of the New Deal," p. 732.

11   Alan Valentine, "Intellectuals on Trial," convocation address, reprinted in *Vital Speeches*, Nov. 15, 1939, p. 78; O. G. Villard, "Death of Our Humanity," *Christian Century*, Nov. 19, 1941, p. 1441.

12   Denis W. Brogan, "Capitalism and War," *Harper's*, CLXXIII (July, 1963), 147; Elmer Davis, "We Lose the Next War," *ibid.*, CLXXVI (Mar., 1938), 345–6; Eliot Janeway, *The Struggle for Survival* (New Haven: Yale Univ. Press, 1951), p. 361; Eisenhower's speech reported in *New York Times*, Jan. 18, 1961, 22:4.

13   Tugwell, "The New Deal," p. 425.

14   Rexford G. Tugwell, "America's War-Time Socialism," *Nation*, April 6, 1927, p. 365; William E. Leuchtenburg, "The New Deal and the Analogue of War," *Change and Continuity in Twentieth-Century America*, John Braeman, *et al.*, eds. (New York: Harper, 1966), pp. 91, 106, 129.

15   "Force and Ideas," *New Republic*, Sept. 20, 1939, pp. 172–3.

16   John Maynard Keynes, "The World's Economic Outlook," *Atlantic*, CXLIX (May, 1932), 525.